Managing Explosive Corporate Growth

Managing Explosive Corporate Growth

Steven M. Bragg

John Wiley & Sons, Inc.

New York • Chichester • Weinheim • Brisbane • Singapore • Toronto

This book is printed on acid-free paper. ∞

Published simultaneously in Canada.

Library of Congress Cataloging-in-Publication Data:

Bragg, Steven M.
Managing explosive corporate growth / by Steven M. Bragg
p. cm.
Includes bibliographical references and index.
ISBN 0-471-29689-9 (cloth : alk. paper)
1. Controllership. 2. Managerial accounting. 3. Just-in-time systems—Accounting. I. Title.
HF5657.4.B72 1998
658—dc21 98-27427

Printed in the United States of America.

10 9 8 7 6 5 4 3 2 1

To Andrea and Victoria, who challenged my powers of concentration while writing this book.

About the Author

Steven M. Bragg, CPA, CMA, CIA, CDP, CSP, CPM, CPIM, is the controller of Intertech Plastics. He has been the Chief Operating Officer of Isolation Technologies and a consulting manager at Ernst & Young. He received a master's degree in finance from Bentley College and an MBA from Babson College. He has also written *Just-in-time Accounting*, *Advanced Accounting Systems*, and *Outsourcing*, and has coauthored *Controllership* and *The Controller's Function*.

Acknowledgments

A special note of thanks for my managing editor, John DeRemigis, who provided so much assistance in getting this project under way and seeing to it that it never strayed from its course. Also, special thanks to Paul Lego for supplying several examples used in the text.

Preface

Managing Explosive Corporate Growth addresses the problems that a company faces when explosive growth occurs. When sales suddenly skyrocket, company management has great difficulty in meeting demand while also hiring hundreds (if not thousands!) of new employees, designing a plethora of new products, spreading sales into new regions, designing distribution systems to handle larger shipments, and ensuring proper management of computer systems. Management must also grow fast enough to handle the ever-increasing demands of more employees, more orders, and more customers. This sudden rush of problems may make management wish it never embarked on corporate growth. However, if a rapidly growing company can successfully avoid a multitude of potential disasters it can become a large and profitable organization.

Managing Explosive Corporate Growth is designed for the company manager or owner who faces an explosive growth situation. It addresses the many problems that can arise in all main functional areas, such as manufacturing, distribution, sales, engineering, accounting, and computer services. This book systematically describes the methods that management must use to surmount these problems. In this book are separate chapters for each functional area. Each chapter highlights key tasks that management must focus on, as well as detail key areas that management must avoid, to ensure explosive growth.

In addition, this book describes key strategic factors that will point an explosive growth company in the direction of success with a particular emphasis on the key concept of pacing, which is necessary to ensure a moderately manageable rate of growth. This book also describes a method for budgeting in a growth situation, which varies significantly from a typical budgeting process, and pays particular attention to cash management, since this can be a prime determinant to a company's ability to grow. There is also a section describing the control systems needed to ensure that management retains a sufficient level of control to keep profits and growth rates in hand. There are discussions of the concerns of company owners, whose ownership shares, risk of loss, and potential for new-found wealth are all greatly impacted by growth. Finally, this book describes the advantages and disadvantages of using outsourcing and partnerships to enhance a company's ability to grow, and how these options reduce a company's funding requirements. All of these issues are crucial to a company going through the pangs of explosive growth, and all are addressed in this book.

If you are a manager or owner and need advice on how to navigate the storm-wracked seas of explosive growth, this is the book for you.

STEVEN M. BRAGG

Englewood, Colorado
June 1998

Contents

Chapter 1

Introduction

Explosive growth can send a company spiraling up to the giddy heights of the *Fortune* 500 or send it plummeting into bankruptcy. It is extremely difficult to predict when this growth period will commence or how long it will last. Due to its unpredictability, it can cause wrenching changes within a company, including changes to new systems, the hiring of thousands of new employees, and continuing strains on company finances. Explosive growth is so difficult to manage that even some of the world's best companies have trouble handling it. For example, Boeing has recently been flooded with orders as the worldwide market for new airliners has grown. Accordingly, it hired 19,500 employees in 1996 through 1997 to double its production schedule. However, for a variety of reasons, Boeing had to shut down its 747 and 737 production lines for a short time so that workers could catch up on out-of-sequence work while waiting for back-ordered parts to arrive. That delayed deliveries to several airlines, and forced Boeing to pay an estimated $300 million in penalties to customers. And this is one of the world's best-managed companies! How can anyone manage through such a difficult process? Read on.

This book gives a company manager or owner the advice needed to steer a company through a period of explosive growth with the minimum amount of damage. When a company finds itself with rapidly expanding sales, it is very difficult to balance the demands of all functional areas and still provide quality products or services to customers in a timely manner. In addition, the owners of the business face difficult choices in how to finance the expansion—do they give up some ownership by going elsewhere for equity, or do they increase the company's financial risk by adding layers of debt? This book gives detailed advice in all main operational areas to assist the reader in focusing on the key tasks that will help to accelerate growth profitably while avoiding a number of situations that can lead to a drop in the rate of growth or even bankruptcy.

The book is divided into two main sections. The first section addresses fundamental explosive growth topics. These include the primary underlying factors that can drive a company toward success or failure, which are noted in Chapter 2. Several techniques to use when trying to budget through a period of explosive growth are covered in Chapter 3. In addition, an explosive growth company will soon perish without proper control over cash, so this issue is discussed in detail in Chapter 4 and at various points in succeeding chapters. Many controls are needed to ensure that a company is staying on the correct growth track at minimal cost, and these controls are explained in Chapter 5.

Proper management of the growth situation is especially difficult, and therefore Chapter 6 reviews such issues as the proper extent of delegation and the need to bring in managers from outside the company. Besides managers, there are also owners to consider, so Chapter 7 covers such ownership issues as when to have an initial public offering, when to stay private and rely on debt financing, and the risks of doing one or the other. A strong alternative to keeping all functional areas in-house is to outsource all areas not critical to the company's strategic direction. This topic is addressed in Chapter 8, including reasons why (and why not) to do it, the benefits and risks of outsourcing, and ways to maintain control over the suppliers who take over outsourced functions. A variation on outsourcing is to use partnerships with other companies, as covered in Chapter 9, which also notes the reasons for using partnerships instead of outsourcing and the costs and management issues associated with doing so.

The second section of the book addresses explosive growth issues that are specific to each functional area of the company. Each chapter begins with the identification of key areas that must be addressed for the function to successfully support the company's high rate of growth while noting those tasks that require minimal continuing support. Each chapter then discusses a key area in detail, along with the measurements, reports, and controls needed to maintain a proper level of management control. These chapters are as follows:

- Chapter 10—Accounting
- Chapter 11—Auditing
- Chapter 12—Computer Services
- Chapter 13—Customer Service
- Chapter 14—Distribution
- Chapter 15—Engineering
- Chapter 16—Finance
- Chapter 17—Human Resources
- Chapter 18—Manufacturing
- Chapter 19—Materials Management
- Chapter 20—Sales and Marketing

Appendix A includes suggested readings for the reader who wants to explore some aspects of explosive growth in greater detail. The readings focus on specific explosive growth case studies.

In short, this book is designed to give the reader a thorough understanding of how to make a company succeed in all areas when it embarks upon explosive growth. Alternatively, if the reader is only interested in a small portion of company operations, then the book is sufficiently segmented to allow for a rapid perusal of the needed topic without having to scan the entire book to find the necessary information. In either case, for a general overview or for detailed information, this book is for anyone who needs to learn about managing explosive growth.

Chapter 2

Success or Failure

INTRODUCTION

Mr. Cedric Jones has just invented a revolutionary new engine that is sure to replace every automobile engine now on the market. He has patented the engine and has only to create a company and expand it to the point where he supplies the new engine to every car manufacturer on Earth—a few million engines per year. How can Mr. Jones go from no company to the largest engine producer in the world? How does he manage explosive growth?

This chapter presents an overview of the key challenges faced by anyone, such as Mr. Jones, who is faced with a chance to grow a company at explosive speed, but who has no idea of how to do it. The chapter covers the key elements of success, some of the many ways in which a company's growth path can be sharply curtailed, and the strategy of explosive growth.

THE ELEMENTS OF SUCCESS

A company has a minimal chance of succeeding in an explosive growth environment if it does not focus on a few key areas. If it remains weak in even one of these areas, it may begin on the explosive growth path, but it is very unlikely to stay there. The key points, which center on the quality of employees, cash flow tracking, planning, and attention to processes, are as follows:

- *Attend to hiring and retention.* The foundation of any company, much less one that is growing, is the staff. They possess the knowledge to operate the company correctly, improve operations, and convince customers to come back for more business. Good employees are hard to find and keep, so a key determinant of success is a company's ability to find new ones as well as retain those it has. This major issue is addressed at length in Chapter 17.
- *Avoid investing cash by using outsourcing and partnerships.* A company will be faced with the prospect of large investments, usually for manufacturing, materials management, and distribution. Most growing companies have little cash, so management must take a hard look at handing over some or all of these functions to other companies, depending on the circumstances. See Chapters 8 and 9 for more information about this approach.

- *Budget for success.* A focused budget is crucial for growth. As noted in Chapter 3, a company must focus its budgeting primarily on targeted growth areas, allowing management to home in on those growth areas that are not meeting their targets. Without budgeting, management has no basis of comparison to see if the company is performing well. It is also useful to supplement budgetary information with a daily management report that lists key operating statistics, so that management does not have to wait for the monthly report to see if there were problems four weeks before. Several kinds of budget models that are most appropriate for high-growth situations are noted in Chapter 3.
- *Focus on working capital.* Cash is the fuel that keeps a company running. One of the repositories in which it lies is working capital, especially accounts receivable and inventory. Management can free up a large amount of cash from working capital by implementing a variety of just-in-time methods that squeeze inventory out of the system. There are other techniques for reducing accounts receivable, as well. These issues are addressed in Chapters 10, 14, 18, and 19.
- *Implement tight control systems.* It is easy for management to lose control over a company if it is stretched to its limits to deliver products or services to customers. Although this is the correct direction in which to focus the company, there must be a strong underlying control system to ensure that spending remains within tightly controlled boundaries. This control keeps management from being surprised when a company meets its revenue goal but shows a loss. These issues are discussed in Chapters 5 and 11.
- *Obtain strong management at the highest levels.* As noted in Chapter 6, a company has no chance of success if it does not obtain the finest possible managers to run it. These must be people who have been through an explosive growth situation before and who recognize the associated pitfalls. Because there are three primary ways to grow a company (see The Strategy of Explosive Growth section), it may be necessary to hire different kinds of managers, depending on the types of experience they have had with each growth strategy. Chapter 6 covers this topic in detail.
- *Respond to the customer.* The customer is the best judge of the company's ability to sell a quality product or service. If the customer complains and the company does not listen, then it will continue to churn out more of the same, resulting in even more customer dissatisfaction. Only happy customers help a company grow through referrals and add-on sales. See the next point.
- *Track complaints.* When a company is growing rapidly, it rarely has enough time to do a thorough job of ensuring that its interfaces with customers are perfect. If they are really poor, customers are quite willing to tell the company. It is important to gather this incoming complaint information into a database and make it available for common access, so that the company can

respond quickly to complaints and ensure that they do not happen again. This concept is enlarged upon in Chapter13.

These points show that the keys to success for a growing company fall into just a few main categories. First is attracting and retaining qualified employees, without whom a company cannot begin to function. Next is the planning and budgeting needed to direct those employees. After that comes continuing attention to anything that can impact cash flows, so that there is enough cash to fund further growth. Finally, the company must have feedback systems to see how it is doing, the best of which involve the customer. These are the ingredients of success, but it is also useful to know where growth companies have had trouble, so that these areas can be avoided. The following section discusses these traps.

THE ELEMENTS OF FAILURE

There are more instances of failure than of success when a company is on the treacherous path of explosive growth. One need look no further than the newspapers and Securities and Exchange Commission (SEC) filings to obtain a long list of problems that companies have encountered. Here is a short, but representative, list of companies that were growing but fell upon hard times:

- *Oxford Health Care.* This company grew at prodigious speed, but forgot to verify that its computer systems were sufficient to handle the massive influx of new members and physicians. They were not. The company suddenly found itself with millions of dollars of invoices that were never sent to customers and millions more of payments to suppliers (e.g., doctors) who were never paid. As a result, the company's founder retired, while the company still seeks to install an operable computer system.
- *Safety First.* This company expanded well beyond the boundaries of its core competency areas by increasing its product line to 650 products. The company found itself unable to compete with more knowledgeable competitors in many of the markets in which it now found itself, and it had to take large inventory write-downs on the way to a major reduction of its product mix.
- *Union Pacific.* This railroad company had great difficulty digesting large mergers with Southern Pacific in 1996 and Chicago & North Western in 1995, which resulted in many shipping delays, angry customers, threats by union leaders over alleged safety violations, and customers defecting to competitors.
- *USA Detergents Inc.* This regional company tried to expand nationally from a solid base in the Northeastern United States, but it ran into distribution problems because it had not done an adequate job of expanding its manufacturing and warehousing facilities into the new territories.

The foregoing companies only had a few problems each. Things can be worse. The 10K filing for NAI Technologies listed *all* of these problems: a drop-off in orders, technical difficulties, cost overruns on new products, problems consolidating facilities, the refusal of key people to relocate, and poor inventory controls. This experience could not have been pleasant for anyone involved.

These problems are not isolated; in fact, they were all gleaned from the business press in a *two-day* period! Just how common these problems are is highlighted by a November 1997 *Forbes Magazine* study, showing that 58 percent of the companies on its 200 Best Small Companies list end up having some kind of problem that drops them off the list. Thus, most of explosive growth companies do not meet their growth goals. What are the most common causes of failure?

There are many ways to fall into the traps described in this section. The following list is representative of issues to watch out for, although a company owner should always keep in mind that new ways to sink a company are being found every day:

- *Customized engineering*. The engineering function must be efficient, or else it cannot issue a steady stream of new products. When it is not efficient, it is common to see each product engineered from scratch, rather than trying to use existing part designs for portions of the new products. This issue is covered in Chapter 15.
- *False reporting*. Continued success fuels a higher stock price, which makes owners happy. If the owners of the company happen to include those who do the financial reporting, there is a temptation to stretch accounting methods to report higher-than-actual sales and profits. Although these problems nearly always come to light over time, they can have a massive impact on a company when the truth is finally reported, for there is typically a massive employee exodus, leaving no one to push for continued growth. This issue is discussed in Chapter 11.
- *Heavy investments in the wrong areas*. One of the most common problems for a growing company is to identify the areas in which it must invest its scarce funds. If it puts them in the wrong place, the company can run out of cash and promptly find itself out of business. For example, a company may invest in a new production facility, a warehouse, or a distribution scheme that calls for lots of inventory, when it could have avoided the investment by outsourcing production or modifying the production method to a just-in-time system that avoids a significant investment in inventory. This issue is noted in Chapters 8, 9, 18, and 19.
- *Lagging computer services*. A rapidly growing company can easily outstrip the capabilities of its computer systems, resulting in system crashes or slow downs that impact the performance of all company operations that depend on the computer systems. This issue is noted in Chapters 11 and 12.

- *Poor cash management.* A growing company can find itself out of business in one day if it does not keep adequate track of its cash flows. Ignoring this issue may result in an empty bank account at the precise moment when payroll is due. See Chapter 4 for more information about this problem.
- *Poor controls.* When company growth explodes there is a flood of new business. The management team usually focuses all of its attention on processing orders, to the exclusion of all other responsibilities. This is a major failing, for management is ignoring the key processes that run the company, such as the processing of accounts payable, ordering materials for production, and payroll. Any or all of these (and other) areas not only *may* cause trouble, they probably *will,* because no one has the time to verify that they are operating properly. This issue is discussed in Chapters 5 and 11.
- *Weak managers.* Any manager who cannot meet a deadline, shifts blame elsewhere, or who is not willing to act as a team with the other managers cripples any business flowing through the area for which he or she is responsible. The key characteristics of a top-flight manager are noted in Chapter 6.

The most important of all these failings is the last one, weak management. If a company has an experienced group of top managers who have previously managed growing companies, they know what areas are critical, which can be ignored, and which to hand over to another company through an outsourcing agreement. This group will also be capable of taking a long-term view of the business, resulting in advance planning to deal with computer problems, manufacturing systems, and the like that might otherwise sink a company without such a strong team at the helm.

THE STRATEGY OF EXPLOSIVE GROWTH

This book is entirely concerned with detailed actions that a company must concern itself with in order to stay on the explosive growth path. And yet, it seems incomplete not to at least mention the means by which a company first thrusts itself into an explosive growth trajectory. This section gives a brief overview of the three primary methods for doing so.

An explosive growth company almost never gets that way by accident. It takes a great deal of preplanning by management to bring it into that position. That preplanning can take three paths, which are as follows:

- *Grow by acquisition.* Company management can assemble several teams of acquisition experts, each of which scours the world, looking for other companies to buy. A carefully organized second team then moves in behind the acquisition team and integrates each new subsidiary's operations with those of the parent company. If investors think that the company is adding value through this process of acquisition and integration, they will bid up its stock price; it can then swap this expensive stock for more companies, which feeds the growth cycle. A good example of growth by acquisition is represented by Wayne Huizenga, who used it to build Waste Management, Blockbuster Video, and AutoNation into giant companies in a very short time.

- *Grow by adding products.* Company management can reorganize and team together the entire company, but especially the marketing and engineering functions, so that they create a steady stream of new products. This type of company assumes that its products will eventually fade away, so it must constantly derive new ones. Of the three growth strategies, this one causes the most internal disruption, because the entire company must figure out how to develop, produce, and sell new products at an extraordinarily fast clip. A common solution to this problem is create small spin-off companies that build each product. A good example of this practice is the 3M Company, which plans to derive one-third of each year's sales from new products.
- *Grow by adding territories.* Company management can focus very tightly on selling the same product, but in more places and with greater market penetration. The classic example of this is Coca-Cola. It has one primary product, Coke, that it attempts to sell in every corner of the globe. And wherever it already sells it, it tries to sell more. This strategy only works with a branded product, however. Otherwise, the product will eventually reach the end of its product life cycle and wither away, no matter how many locations in which it is sold.

These three strategies have one common element: Management has a specific plan for growth and shapes the company to match that growth plan. A company that grows by acquisition must have an experienced set of acquisition teams, whereas one that grows by adding products is organized around the development, production, and marketing of those products. A company that grows by adding territories needs a strong sales, marketing, and distribution staff to open up new regions. Thus, it is evident that explosive growth occurs by design, not by accident.

SUMMARY

An explosive growth company has the unique chance to vastly increase its sales and market share while generating a great deal of wealth for its owners. However, any organization embarking on the growth path must avoid the many hazards that can bring down a company, perhaps wiping out the majority of an owner's equity and even resulting in the liquidation of the company. Consequently, it is of the greatest importance for the owner of a business that faces such prospects to be aware of the key pitfalls to avoid.

This chapter noted the key areas needed for a company to succeed, as well as those areas in which a lack of attention could be fatal. However, each key area was noted only briefly. For a more complete understanding of how to deal with explosive growth, the reader must delve into the remainder of this book, which describes in detail the topics in this chapter and many other issues.

Chapter 3

Budgeting

INTRODUCTION

The budget is a core document for any growing company. This chapter describes why it is very important in a growth situation, not only as a control but also as a planning document. The chapter also discusses how to use a budget for transition and multioption budgeting, neither of which is commonly used outside a rapid growth environment. In addition, it describes how to add on to the standard budget to derive working capital and personnel budgets, both of which are critical to a growth company, so that it can plan for new funding and personnel needs. Finally, the chapter covers how to use the budget for motivational purposes and under what circumstances it is safe to ignore the budget. This chapter does not purport to cover all aspects of standard budgeting, just those facets that vary for a rapidly expanding company.

PURPOSE OF THE BUDGET IN AN EXPLOSIVE GROWTH COMPANY

The typical company spends a minimum of four months constructing a budget for the next year, with some companies exceeding half a year for this task. For an explosive growth company, why bother with a budget at all if the company is going to grow at a rate that will rapidly outpace the budgeting process?

An explosive growth company usually does not grow uncontrollably like a wildfire; on the contrary, company management carefully planned for the growth, either through geographic expansion of sales, the rapid addition of new products, or through corporate acquisitions. If this much planning goes into the growth process, then management can certainly use a budget to track progress against it. For example, if a company plans new product introductions every other month, then the budget should reflect increases in expenses at set intervals to support those introductions. As long as growth increases in a controlled and deliberate manner, then management can use a budget to see if actual revenues and expenses are close to expectations.

Another reason for using a budget is that the chief financial officer (CFO) needs it to determine the timing for acquiring new equity and debt to support company operations. The budget shows planned increases in financing needed to support working capital. The CFO uses the amounts and timing of funding needs in the budget to work in advance on obtaining new funding. New equity requires an especially long time to procure, and the CFO needs the budget to get some sense of the time available before the company runs out of cash.

Finally, the budget for a growing company does not just cover monetary issues. It can also translate corporate growth into a need for more personnel, by function and skill level. The human resources staff needs this personnel plan to determine when it should recruit new people into the organization. Without a plan, the organization would find itself constantly playing catch-up, scrambling to hire people at the last moment. Preplanning with the budget helps the human resources staff hire people in an orderly manner.

In short, a growing company still needs a budget, not only to help it compare its preset growth plan to reality, but also to determine funding and personnel needs. Growth is never going to exactly match the expectations of the budget, which will throw off its predictive value for funding and personnel needs, but it still gives management some idea of what is going on, which would not be the case if the budget did not exist.

TRANSITION BUDGETING

The best way to budget for an explosive growth company is to use transition budgeting. This method assumes that a small number of underlying activities from the previous year will not change significantly and can be given roughly the same budget and then ignored. In addition, other activities require a more extensive budgeting effort. These activities usually relate to the assumed addition of new business units in the upcoming budget year. Each business unit receives its own budget, which is layered on top of the budget for underlying activities from the previous year. This section describes how to conduct transition budgeting.

A company going through explosive growth usually does so in accordance with a very strict growth plan. This plan typically involves growth either by adding new products, sales territories, or subsidiaries. For example, a health club chain may want to grow by an additional $12 million for the upcoming year, and plans to do so by acquiring 12 health clubs, each with sales of $1 million. If so, management can easily arrive at a standard acquisition cost for a typical health club, as well as any associated operating costs. It then creates a business unit budget for each health club. The budget should include the acquisition cost, the expected transition cost for each acquisition (e.g., legal, accounting, and related costs that go along with any purchase), and the expected operating costs in a business unit budget. It then adds all 12 of these business unit budgets to the underlying budget from the previous year to determine the new budget for the upcoming year. The main factor is timing—when will management buy the 12 health clubs? It can simply purchase one per month to establish a steady transition rate throughout the year, or it can cluster them in case it contemplates a bulk purchase of clubs from a single owner. In either case, the resulting budget gives management a good idea of the revenues, expenses, and cash flows to be expected as the company works through its annual transition process of adding health clubs.

This style of budgeting is shown in Exhibit 3.1, which has four parts. The first section lists the budget for continuing business from the previous year. The second section lists the average cost to purchase and operate a single business unit. The third section lists the number of business units (i.e., health clubs) to be purchased in each month of the first quarter of the budgeting period, as well as the extended cost of all such transactions for each of those months. The final section combines the first and third sections into a cumulative summary budget. The advantage of this layout is that if all four budget sections are linked on a spreadsheet, it then becomes an easy matter to simply change the month in which a business unit is acquired (as shown in the third part) for the financial impact of the change to ripple through the entire budget. This type of budget is driven by the amount and timing of the addition of business units, so it is structured to make this type of change very easy.

This transition budgeting approach works just as well for adding sales territories, for the costs associated with adding them are quite similar, and also makes it easy to set them up as business units. For example, the typical costs of selling in a new territory include adding sales and support staff, facilities, finished goods inventories, and a marketing campaign. Although the geographical size and number of prospective customers in each territory will vary these costs, such factors are readily estimated in advance. The transition budgeting approach also works for new product development, because the size and related costs of a product development team are easily estimated, along with product-launching costs. Thus, for all forms of deliberate corporate expansion, it is quite possible to use transition budgeting to rapidly determine the budget for the upcoming year.

Transition budgeting can also be used for business units that are in decline. This type of budgeting is especially useful for budgeting a large number of product lines, for these will eventually suffer some decline in sales over time, unless the company acts continually to refresh product lines by such means as renewed marketing or new product features. When used in this way, the budget must be separated into business units for each product family so that many business units sum into a total budget for the year. It is then an easy matter to budget for reduced sales for various business units while assuming more sales for others, which is naturally the case when a company has many products. An example of this type of budgeting is shown in Exhibit 3.2. This method is equally applicable to any kind of business unit for which revenues can be readily identified, such as a subsidiary, in the case of a company that grows by acquisition, or for sales territories, for a company that grows by geographic expansion. In the example in Exhibit 3.2, the key factor is the budgeted sales change. Multiplying the budgeted sales change by the previous year's sales, gross margin, and variable cost figures yields a revised profit figure for each business unit that can be readily summarized for inclusion in the general budget.

Exhibit 3.1 Transition Budgeting

Section 1: Summary of budgeted costs for existing business units

Expense Type	*Month 1*	*Month 2*	*Month 3*
Production expense	$50,000,000	$50,000,000	$50,000,000
Sales expense	$6,000,000	$6,000,000	$6,000,000
Administration expense	$3,000,000	$3,000,000	$3,000,000
Engineering expense	$3,500,000	$3,500,000	$3,500,000
Interest expense	$1,000,000	$1,000,000	$1,000,000
Capital expenditures	$158,000	$325,000	$72,000

Section 2: Average cost to acquire and operate a business unit

Expense Type	*Cost per Business Unit ($)*
Production expense	2,500,000
Sales expense	300,000
Administration expense	150,000
Engineering expense	175,000
Interest expense	50,000
Capital expenditures	1,000,000

Section 3: Number and cost of business units to be acquired

Expense Type	*Month 1*	*Month 2*	*Month 3*
No. business units added	2	4	2
Production expense	$5,000,000	$10,000,000	$5,000,000
Sales expense	$600,000	$1,200,000	$600,000
Administration expense	$300,000	$600,000	$300,000
Engineering expense	$350,000	$700,000	$350,000
Interest expense	$100,000	$200,000	$100,000
Capital expenditures	$2,000,000	$4,000,000	$2,000,000

Section 4: Summary budget, including costs of old and new business units

Expense Type	*Month 1*	*Month 2*	*Month 3*
Production expense	$55,000,000	$65,000,000	$70,000,000
Sales expense	$6,600,000	$7,800,000	$8,400,000
Administration expense	$3,300,000	$3,900,000	$4,200,000
Engineering expense	$3,850,000	$4,550,000	$4,900,000
Interest expense	$1,100,000	$1,300,000	$1,400,000
Capital expenditures	$2,158,000	$6,483,000	$8,555,000

Exhibit 3.2 Transition Budgeting for Existing Business Units

Description	*Business Unit No. 1*	*Business Unit No. 2*	*Business Unit No. 3*	*Total*
Prior year sales	$2,000,000	$18,000,000	$33,000,000	$53,000,000
Prior year gross margin	30%	28%	25%	26%
Prior year fixed costs	$180,000	$425,000	$3,418,000	$4,023,000
Prior year variable costs	18%	20%	19%	19%
Budgeted sales change	**–11%**	**1%**	**–3%**	**–2%**
Budget year sales	$1,780,000	$18,180,000	$32,010,000	$51,970,000
Budget year margin	$534,000	$5,090,400	$8,002,500	$13,626,900
Budget year fixed costs	$180,000	$425,000	$3,418,000	$4,023,000
Budget year variable costs	$320,400	$3,636,000	$6,081,900	$10,038,300
Budget year profit	$33,600	$1,029,400	–$1,497,400	–$434,400

In short, transition budgeting accounts for a rapid increase in the number of business units, which is a common occurrence in a growing company. It can also be used to track the continuing performance of existing business units, which fluctuates over time. It is the premier budgeting technique for any company that has a clear plan for expansion.

MULTIOPTION BUDGETING

Not all companies grow by a clear method of expansion, which was the underlying assumption in the previous section on transition budgeting. Some companies grow by entering entirely new markets where they have no readily predictable expectation of growth. This is a particular problem for companies in the forefront of entirely new industries, for example, the cloning of animals, where no one knows what the revenues or cost structure of the industry will be. Similarly, any company expanding into a completely untested market will have the same problem; this issue arose when the Eastern Bloc countries opened their doors to sales from capitalist countries. This type of environment is not suitable for transition budgeting, for there is no predictability to incorporate into the budget model. Here multioption budgeting is the most useful.

Multioption budgeting is similar to a high-stakes poker game in which each player adds just enough chips to the pile to keep his or her hand in the game. It assumes that the players (i.e., the competitors) do not know the most likely outcome of changes in the marketplace, and so they invest just enough in the most probable outcomes to assure themselves of a continuing seat at the poker table as the situation resolves itself. Each player should also factor the risk of each investment into the poker game, so that it is relatively painless to back out of the game if the player no longer wishes to continue. For example, the price of gold has declined for a number of years. How would a company use multioption budgeting to cover its bets on the future outcome of gold prices? It might assume that there is only a modest probability that gold prices will go up, but just in case, it wants to place a small bet on higher prices. One way is to purchase another gold mine. However, doing so can be very expensive, so perhaps the company can keep its hand in play by just purchasing an option to buy a gold mine. This is the minimum bet to place on the option of high growth and also represents a minimal investment, so the company will not suffer markedly if it lets the purchase option expire. However, the company may assign a large probability to a continued decline in gold prices. If so, the best bet is to spend money on cost reduction efforts. Since there is no downside to lowering costs, management can authorize a significant expenditure on cost reduction equipment; it accordingly places a large bet on this option. In short, multioption budgeting involves placing bets on a number of possible outcomes, so that a company has the option to proceed along multiple paths.

This budgeting method may sound like it is only conducted in smoke-filled rooms where nothing is ever committed to paper, but there are some standard techniques for rationalizing the process. They are as follows:

- *Concentrate on probable outcomes.* Any market can proceed in an infinite number of directions, but someone using multioption budgeting would never complete the budget if it included every possible option. Instead, the management team should determine the most probable outcomes and just concentrate the budgeting effort on them.
- *Merge options.* Some options have many common elements and can therefore be treated as just one option. By doing so, management can concentrate on a limited number of market variations.
- *Determine key indicators.* A company must know the direction in which a market is trending so it can alter its mix of resources in the right direction. To do this, the company must develop a small number of indicators. For example, a consumer electronics company should track the market share for digital video disc (DVD) compact players to see if it should sell DVD players. If the market share rises, it should bet heavily on this technology.
- *Always include guaranteed payoffs in mix of bets.* If a chief executive officer (CEO) does nothing but place large bets on high-risk options, the CEO will eventually lose on all current bets and (rightfully) be ousted by the board of directors. A more balanced approach that shows some return on bets is one that includes a few no-risk bets. These are usually cost reduction efforts in existing businesses. Since cost reduction is totally within the control of the company, it is an easy bet to make.
- *Periodically review for new options.* New options arise as a market changes. Management should include these options in the budget by holding formal reviews that cover developing market trends.

Thus, one can use a procedure to concentrate the attention of management on just a few probable options. A procedure can also periodically force the management team to address new options as well as review its mix of bets for the overall level of risk.

Multioption budgeting varies significantly from transition budgeting, because it is based on probable *outcomes*, whereas transition budgeting is based on *actions*. For example, a company that is growing based on a predetermined rollout of new locations will use transition budgeting, because it already knows the cost to complete each rollout; the company only needs to know the timing of the expenditures, which a transition budget gives it. A multioption budget, however, is designed for situations where there is more than one possible outcome. To use the previous example, the same company might use it if there were a problem with the local government not approving the erection of a new building. Consequently, these budgeting models are used for different situations; either transition budgeting for a highly predictable expansion or multioption budgeting for uncertain situations.

Another difference between transition and multioption budgeting is that transition budgeting is based on a highly automated financial model and only requires a few changes to shift business unit expenses into other time periods or to alter the assumed expenses for each business unit being rolled out. However, a multioption budget is difficult to shoehorn into a standard budget model because there are so many layers of uncertainty. For example, a decision to open a new sales territory may be driven by government regulations for transferring money out of the country and the extent to which that money can be transferred. Even if a company could not repatriate all of its funds, it might still be able to invest the money in local production facilities, except that there may be further government restrictions on the percentage of local ownership required for foreign-owned companies. This scenario may vary for every country in which a company wants to create a new sales territory, with more possible variations based on government regulations. The multioption budget must address each option in this scenario, which can result in a staggeringly complex budget. Thus, multioption budgeting requires a great many customized modifications to the budget model, as well as far more analysis time than is required for transition budgeting.

In summary, multioption budgeting is useful for situations with multiple outcomes and large degrees of uncertainty, where a company wants to spread its risk over numerous outcomes. It is a difficult budgeting process to quantify, involving large amounts of detailed analysis work to thread a path through the maze of possible results. Despite this difficulty, it can be a powerful tool for placing a company squarely in the best possible strategic position in a growth environment.

WORKING CAPITAL BUDGETING

The CFO needs accurate information on when the company will run out of money so that he or she has sufficient time to line up more cash, either through debt or equity offerings. The only source of this information is the budget. Some companies try to use a cash forecast for this purpose, but it is usually only accurate for a one-month period. Because the cash forecast does not usually include projected sales from such activities as new product introductions or corporate acquisitions, it tends to be especially inaccurate in a rapid growth situation. Thus, an accurate budget is the only source of cash flow forecasts for the CFO beyond the one-month projection of the cash forecast.

The typical budget contains nothing more than estimated revenues, costs, and profits or losses by month. For it to be usable by the CFO for cash forecasting purposes, it must also include a working capital budget. This budget, as shown in Exhibit 3.3, takes the profit and loss information from the regular budget, along with cash flow timing information, to derive the amount of excess cash or cash shortfall for each budgeting period. It should also be combined with the capital budget to ensure that all possible cash flows are accounted for.

The working capital forecast shown in Exhibit 3.3 is for a startup company that does the bulk of its business during the Christmas season, but which builds the same amount of product throughout the year. The first line of the example shows projected revenues for each quarter. The second line assumes a significant delay in collecting accounts receivable, so the company will not collect cash from first quarter sales until the second quarter, and so on. The next line shows continuing expenses for each quarter. Since there is a shorter delay in paying for these accounts payable, the fourth line shows a more rapid drawdown of cash for the previous quarter's expenses. The fifth line indicates that the company is producing the same amount of inventory for the first three quarters, while the sixth line notes that the company must pay for the inventory immediately, while retaining most of it for the final quarter of the year. The final two lines summarize the net

Exhibit 3.3 The Working Capital Forecast

Description	*Timing*	*Quarter 1*	*Quarter 2*	*Quarter 3*	*Quarter 4*
Revenues		$50,000	$75,000	$100,000	$6,670,000
Collection delay	90 days	—	$50,000	$75,000	$100,000
Sales, general, and administrative expenses		–$350,000	–$400,000	–$500,000	–$600,000
Payment delay	75 days	—	–$375,000	–$450,000	–$550,000
Inventory added		$2,290,000	$2,290,000	$2,290,000	—
Sales delay	In Q4	-$2,290,000	–$2,290,000	–$2,290,000	—
Net change in working capital		–$2,290,000	–$2,615,000	–$2,665,000	–$450,000
Cumulative change in working capital		–$2,290,000	–$4,905,000	–$7,570,000	–$8,020,000

changes in cash flow. The reason for the extremely large negative cash balance at the end of the year is that cash receipts from the prime year-end selling season do not arrive until the first quarter of the next year. Also, since this is assumed to be a startup company, there is no carry-forward of cash receipts from the previous year. In this extreme example where there is an excessive amount of working capital needed to fund operations, the budget is critical for the CFO's planning for additional debt and equity.

The capital budget can be more important than the working capital budget if a company is growing through acquisitions or a rapid ramp-up in production of existing products. In either case, a company will probably make massive expenditures to acquire companies or equipment, purchases that may vastly exceed the company's normal working capital requirements. If so, the CFO must combine the two budgets to gain a true understanding of the timing and amount of cash flows.

Cash flow timing is one of the key elements of the working capital budget. It assumes that cash will be received in payment of accounts receivable on a specific date following invoicing, while accounts payable will likewise be paid on a specific date following receipt of supplier invoices. These numbers are crucial to the accuracy of the working capital forecast, but unfortunately, they tend to be inaccurate. For example, if a single very large invoice is not paid on time by a customer, projected cash receipts are thrown off. Also, if the company pays a large supplier invoice early to take advantage of a discount, this cash outflow alters the expected cash balance. Although the numbers tend to work out as expected on an average basis, large transactions can skew the results.

Another problem with the working capital forecast is that any variation in adding business units drastically alters the resulting cash flows. The most obvious example is delaying or accelerating an acquisition, which usually involves millions of dollars. This problem also occurs for a new sales territory, because the expenses for advertising as well as staging finished goods inventory in the territory are significant. Likewise, delaying or accelerating a product launch has a cash flow impact based on factors similar to those for a new sales territory. In short, any change in the timing of business activities has a major impact on the timing of cash flows that the CFO relies on to procure funding.

Although it is clear that the working capital budget and associated capital expenditures budget used by the CFO can be quite inaccurate, it is important to remember that the CFO drives this budget, not the reverse. For example, if the CFO determines that the company is running out of cash and he or she cannot procure enough new financing in the short term to fund any more activities, this person can put a halt to any events that will drain cash until the new financing is in place. Thus, the CFO can use the budget to determine when new activities have been planned in the near term, and work with the rest of the top management team to either halt them or change their timing to track more closely with the availability of cash.

If the timing of very large transactions, such as acquisitions, is highly variable, or if working capital needs are very difficult to predict, the CFO usually avoids all attempts at prediction and simply acquires all funding needed for the year at the beginning of the year, thereby avoiding any attempt to line up funding only as needed. Although this method can be expensive, it also means that the acquisition of funding does not play a role in a company's growth rate during the year.

The working capital budget can be easily constructed from a standard revenue and expense budget, although its accuracy is highly dependent on several assumptions. If these assumptions are inaccurate, the budget will not yield acceptable results. However, the CFO can at least use the information on these budgets to alter the timing of major transactions so that they match the company's available cash flow.

PERSONNEL BUDGETING

The human resources staff can add a section to the budget giving a good idea of the number of additional staff it must hire, as well as when to hire. For example, a transition budget, as described in the Transition Budgeting section, includes all of the expenses for each block of additional business. There is no reason why this transition budget cannot include the number of additional staff required, by position, in order to add a discrete business unit. For example, if a company determines that adding a sales territory requires five external salespeople, three internal sales support staff, one sales manager, one billings person, two collections employees, and part of an assistant controller, then this same personnel configuration can be applied for the addition of several sales territories, as is shown in Exhibit 3.4. In the case of the assistant controller, which is listed as part of a person per territory, the human resources staff can work with the controller to determine if this person should be hired early, when there is not sufficient need for the position, or later on, when the existing assistant controllers are overworked by the added underlying staff.

Exhibit 3.4 Personnel Budgeting for Extra Sales Territories

Employee Type	*Quantity per Territory*	*Quarter 1 (Add 3 Territories)*	*Quarter 2 (Add 2 Territories)*	*Quarter 3 (Add 4 Territories)*	*Quarter 4 (Add 2 Territories)*
External sales	5	15	10	20	10
Sales support	3	9	6	12	6
Sales manager	1	3	2	4	2
Billings clerk	1	3	2	4	2
Collections clerk	2	6	4	8	4
Asst. controller	.2	.6	.4	.8	.4

The partial manager listed in the example contains a span of control assumption, which the human resources staff should build into its personnel budget. In the example, it is assumed that an assistant controller is needed to manage 15 accounting personnel, hence the 20 percent of an assistant controller listed in the Quantity per Territory column alongside the three accounting personnel. The same concept applies to the sales manager in the example, for which there is a proportion of one sales manager for every eight sales staff. One can go further and note smaller percentages for higher-level positions, although these tend to be more discretionary, since there is not a direct span of control linkage with the underlying staff. In short, by including span of control percentages in the personnel budget, the human resources staff can predict how many managers to hire for supervising the staff.

The example in this section assumes that the same number of people are needed for an additional unit of business. This is rarely such an easy assumption. Instead, there may be variations in expected sales or transaction volume to cause a considerable shift in the number of anticipated personnel. For example, the acquisition of a multibillion dollar company requires far more staff to assimilate than the acquisition of one with only a few million in revenues. The best way to get around this problem is to budget personnel based on anticipated transaction volumes. This prediction method is better than sales volume, because the amount of sales volume may be contained in a very small number of shipments, invoices, or cash receipts, which gives the human resources staff a false impression of the number of new employees needed to handle the volume. By using this approach, we can alter Exhibit 3.4 so that it lists a specific number of transactions per employee and the number of transactions expected for each added business unit, thereby yielding a much more accurate estimate of required head count. The revised example is shown in Exhibit 3.5 for a one-quarter period. This approach also focuses attention on the company's ability to process a large number of transactions per employee; by improving this number, a company can reduce the number of staff it must add for new operations. Thus, predicting future head count based on trans-

Exhibit 3.5 Personnel Budgeting Based on Anticipated Transaction Volumes

Employee Type	*Total Transactions in Quarter*	*Transactions per Person*	*Span of Control*	*Number of Employees Needed*
External sales	1,500	300	—	5
Sales support	1,800	600	—	3
Sales manager	—	—	8	1
Billings clerk	900	900	—	1
Collections clerk	900	450	—	2
Asst. controller	—	—	15	.2

action volumes is more accurate and leads to more efficiencies than using a standard head count per business unit.

In summary, the human resources staff should add a section to the budget that predicts the need for additional staff, based on such factors as additional sales volume, new territories, or acquisitions. The personnel budget can also be driven by the predicted number of transactions, which focuses attention on the efficiency of transactions.

BUDGETING AND MOTIVATIONAL SYSTEMS

An explosive growth company typically does not have a large amount of money available to pay its best employees, even though it must have them to assist in growing the company. A very common solution is to grant them stock options or some similar contrivance, such as pseudostock. These financial devices are designed to spur employees into taking actions to raise the stock price, thereby enriching not only the owners but the employees as well. This section builds a case for a modified motivational system that continues to use stock price increases for some employees, but which also calls attention to the growth process itself.

There are several problems with stock options. One is that a stock's price is bid up and down by investors in a sometimes seemingly irrational manner. For example, numerous studies have proved that a general change in the stock market, either up or down, causes a similar change in a company's stock price, even if it has done nothing to deserve the change. Likewise, employee stock options change in value along with the stock price, even if they have taken no action to cause the change. Another problem is that many employees who are granted options can see no direct link between their actions and changes in the stock price. For example, an assistant controller cannot appreciably alter a company's profitability, which has the greatest impact on the stock price. A third case is that employees may do a superb job of improving their company, only to see its stock price fall due to extraneous industry matters that they could not possibly alter; the best recent example is that, as the price of gold drops, so too does the stock price of all gold mining companies, many of which are extremely well run. Clearly, motivating employees solely with stock options is a flawed approach due to the number of uncontrollable reasons why a company's stock price can change and the perceived impact of employee actions on its price.

Is there a more meaningful way to involve many company employees in the continuing success of the company, especially in such a way that the involvement will change their behavior in the company's favor? Because the primary determinant of growth for most companies is the continual transition of the organization from the assimilation of one business unit to another, and because many people are involved in these transitions, this basis for motivation is better. For example, an engineering team can earn a bonus based on the profitability of the products they develop (a system used by Microsoft), which is something over which they have total control. This system can also impact the timing of new product introduction, because the engineering team wants to see it on the market as soon as possible so that they can start receiving bonuses. For another example, the sales staff can receive a commission override if they sell products into a new territory, thereby giving them a major incentive to open up the new region. In addition, an acquisitions team can receive bonuses based on the speed with which they can integrate an acquired company into the parent company's operations (as measured by, for example, the point at which the new subsidiary's sales begin to trend upward following the purchase). All of these bonus systems are targeted at spurring the bulk of the employees in a growing company to work together to make rapid and profitable transitions to grow the company at a predetermined pace.

However, the concept of matching bonuses to specific transitions does not work for the top management team. This group is in charge of coordinating a number of transitions but takes no part in the detailed implementation of each one, and so it should not share in the results of the teams that complete them. Instead, it is more appropriate for top management to use the old compensation system of stock options, since they are more concerned with the overall results of the corporation, as is the stock market, which rewards good result with a higher stock price, which increases the value of the stock options.

WHEN TO IGNORE THE BUDGET

The board of directors usually approves a company's annual budget. Very few managers want to go against the dictates of the board by ignoring the budget. However, to ignore the budget may be the only way to grasp new market opportunities on short notice, which is a common occurrence in a growth situation. How, then, to ignore the budget without causing problems with the board of directors?

The board approves the amount of money in the budget, not the timing of when the money is spent (as long as it is within the usual one-year period covered by the budget). The manager who wishes to ignore the budget can use this point as an appropriate means to delay or accelerate projects within the budget period without getting into difficulties with the board. The exact timing of projects and their related expenses is very difficult to determine in a fast growth situation, so this ploy is common for a manager to use. However, any significant timing changes must be communicated to the CFO at once, because this person is relying on the budget information to determine when additional funding is required to support the business.

It is also useful to cluster expenses into a few general categories in the budget, rather than subdivide them into a large number of expense line items. This method gives a manager enough leeway to shift budgeted expenditures within an expense category without running afoul of the intent of the budget. For example, a large part of the administrative budget can be listed as Miscellaneous General and Administrative for a large sum, rather than being subdivided into categories for Office Forms, Office Supplies, Office Utilities, and Office Repairs. This division gives the manager a great deal of leeway to shift expenditures to the areas that need it, rather than the areas that were authorized. A smaller number of expense accounts gives management enough slack to purchase what they need without spending money that the budget does not allow them to spend.

The board should grant limited approval to a few company officers to approve changes to the budget, within a specific dollar limit, thus allowing management to alter the budget within reason in order to react to an opportunity that will not wait until the next regularly scheduled board meeting. If this delegation makes the board uncomfortable, it can either reduce the amount of money that the officers are allowed to spend, have more frequent board meetings, or arrange for frequent votes by telephone. Any of these arrangements keep managers from trying to circumvent the budget by making it easy to authorize changes.

Managers in growth situations are constantly confronted with special situations requiring spending not authorized by the budget. It is better to alter the budget and the budget authorization process to accommodate the managers than it is to retain a rigidly enforced budget, which forces managers to act underhandedly to attain their goals. These modifications include allowing changes to the timing of expenditures; clustering expense categories into fewer, larger ones; and arranging for easier and more rapid approvals of budget changes.

SUMMARY

This chapter explained the need for budgeting in an explosive growth situation, especially in regard to several subsections of the budget, working capital, and personnel planning. Without some forecasting method derived from the budget, the human resources staff would have no way of telling when to hire people, nor what kind to hire. In addition, the CFO needs the working capital budget in order to predict when additional funds are needed to support continuing operations. This chapter also covered transition and multioption budgeting, which are useful techniques for determining future revenues and expenses based on a variety of possible actions or outcomes. Finally, the chapter addressed the uses of a budget for constructing motivational systems, as well as when the circumstances are appropriate for ignoring the budget. Taken together, this chapter gives the reader a good idea of the special budgeting situations to consider in an explosive growth company.

Chapter 4

Cash Management

INTRODUCTION

One of the key factors for any growing company is the conservation of cash. A company cannot fund new facilities, staff increases, acquisitions, or any other activities without the conservation of cash. No matter how well funded, every explosive growth company eventually butts up against the seemingly intractable problem of not having enough cash.

This chapter discusses the relationship between cash and growth and then describes the key components of changes in cash, which include product or service margins, working capital, and capital purchases. It finishes with a review of other means of conserving cash. This chapter presents an overview of a company's need for cash, where it is used in a corporation, and how to extract it for use in fueling additional growth.

THE RELATIONSHIP BETWEEN CASH AND GROWTH

From the cash management perspective, three main factors drive a company's ability to grow: product margins, working capital needs, and capital acquisitions. This section discusses why these three areas are so important for growth.

If two companies with equal growth prospects attempt to grow at a rapid rate, all other points being equal, the company with the higher net margins will grow at the faster rate, because the company with higher margins generates more cash, which it can then use to pay for more facilities, staff, equipment, and inventory to support additional sales. A good example is the chip manufacturer Intel, which regularly attains gross margins as high as 70 percent, which gives it the money to fund all kinds of new revenue-producing activities. A company with low margins, however, has much less cash available for these expansions. Although it can use equity offerings and additional debt to fund expansion, the owners of the low-margin organization will rapidly conclude that the effort is not worthwhile, because the company's leverage becomes very high and its ownership interest very low as a result of the cash needs of the expansion. Thus, maintaining a high profit percentage is critical if an expanding company wants to continue that growth.

The issue of profit margins is of just as much concern after a company has been growing for some time. The reason is that, as it grows, other competitors jump into the market with competing products, which usually results in a dramatic drop in prices and a corresponding drop in profits, which, in turn, results in less cash to fund further growth. If a company wants to continue growing, it can avoid this problem by constantly upgrading or replacing its products, so that they continue to demand premium prices, resulting in more profits and therefore enough cash for an additional round of growth. Thus, a company must keep watch over its product margins if it desires to stay on the growth path.

As a company grows, more and more of its cash is invested in working capital. Its two primary components that suck up cash are accounts receivable and inventory, while accounts payable provides cash through what is essentially an interest-free loan from suppliers. If not managed properly, a growing company can find its growth sharply curtailed because it is paying suppliers too quickly, loading up on extra inventory that it does not need, or failing to collect accounts receivable on time. Much of the difficulty in the inventory area is also due to a lack of effective materials management and production systems (see Chapters 18 and 19). Thus, a company may find that it has no money left to fund expansion if, through lack of management or systems, it is investing too much in its working capital.

The amount of cash a company invests in capital goods has a direct impact on its rate of growth. For example, if a company invests all of its available cash in a new computer system from which new efficiencies will not be realized for at least a year, it has essentially frozen its rate of growth until it can replenish its cash horde, which may have to wait until the benefits from the new system are realized. Without that cash, it cannot fund new acquisitions (unless it uses stock), enter new sales territories, or create new products. Consequently, buying capital assets is a major issue that requires in-depth analysis by the chief financial officer (CFO) to ensure that only the bare minimum of the most productive assets are purchased.

The three factors noted in this section have a major impact on the rate of company growth and lend credence to the saying, "it takes money to make money." However, there are a few ways to avoid these cash constraints. They are as follows:

- *Create a virtual corporation.* It is now possible to design a product, have someone else build it, another party deliver it, and have a third party collect the accounts receivable. This means that there is very little cash that a company needs to worry about, because working capital and capital equipment needs are minimal. A good example of this is Amazon Books, which takes book orders electronically over the Internet. It forwards its orders to a local Ingram book warehouse (which owns the books) and receives cash from the bank that took the up-front credit card payments. Thus, Amazon has no investment in accounts receivable or inventory. Although there are other operating costs, this arrangement still allows Amazon to grow with fewer concerns about cash flows.

- *Use multiple rounds of equity financing.* It is common for a company to initially issue stock at a relatively low price per share in its first equity offering. The company then uses the resulting cash to fund further growth, at which point it issues more stock; the stock valuation is frequently higher in these later rounds, because the company has (presumably) used its earlier cash windfalls from stock offerings to increase the company's profits. This means that a company can obtain large sums of cash outside of the traditional cash management areas previously noted in this section. However, this approach also dilutes the owner's equity in the company.

The main cash-related areas that impact growth are profit margins, working capital, and capital purchases. If a company keeps a tight watch on these areas, it may obtain enough cash available to launch itself on a rapid growth path and to stay there.

CASH MANAGEMENT AND WORKING CAPITAL

Working capital is one of the great untapped sources of cash. A few companies, such as General Electric, have figured out how to strip enormous amounts of cash from this area, but the vast majority of companies still squander an excessive portion of their cash reserves to maintain their working capital. This section discusses the sources and uses of cash in the working capital area, as well as the concept of zero working capital, which is cash flow heaven.

The first significant working capital area is accounts payable. This area is a source of cash, because suppliers are essentially lending the company money for the period before their invoices are due. It is clearly in the interests of a company to extend the period before it pays, thereby extending the term of its supplier "loans." However, extending them beyond a reasonable period will bring on the wrath of suppliers, who are, in turn, trying to keep their accounts receivable down. They can impose draconian credit terms, such as cash on delivery or even cash in advance, if a company abuses its credit terms too far. Nonetheless, there are some methods for extending payment terms. They are as follows:

- *Extend payments a reasonable amount.* Paying a few days late is not a major problem for most suppliers, and may even be customary in some industries. There is no way to rigorously derive the appropriate number of days by which a company can drag out its payments, but the accounts payable staff can probably determine the correct interval through experimentation—keep extending the payment interval until there is significant feedback from suppliers. It is also possible to vary this by supplier, because some enforce collections more tightly than others.

- *Ignore jawboning for early payment.* Some suppliers call key managers with whom they have close, long-standing relationships, and wheedle early payments for selected invoices (usually big ones). Paying early can seriously impact a company's cash flow. However, it is difficult to turn down such requests from managers, so it is helpful if the chief executive officer (CEO) promulgates and backs up a strict policy of only paying supplier invoices when due. If a manager has a problem with this, the accounting staff can then direct him or her to the CEO.
- *Negotiate longer payment terms.* The easiest way to extend terms is to ask for it. This approach will not work with many suppliers, simply because the company does not do enough business with them to justify such a concession. This negotiation is especially difficult for a growing company that starts quite small, but it may become a viable option once the continued rate of growth gives it some serious purchasing power.
- *Use controlled disbursements.* As noted in Chapter 16, a company can arrange to have its checks issued from a bank location that is as far away from the recipient as possible. It takes longer for checks to clear, which gives the company an extra day or two in which to use the supplier's money. This approach is very commendable, for the supplier is generally quite satisfied upon receipt of the check and does not realize that the underlying cash is not yet available.

A combination of all of these methods allows a company to extend its effective payment terms, thereby creating an interest-free loan for the company.

On the other side of the balance sheet from accounts payable lies accounts receivable. Many companies can successfully mine this area for a significant amount of cash. A company normally has an excessive investment in this area for three reasons. One is that it is selling on easy credit, which results in lots of accounts receivable that are difficult to collect; this problem is common for an explosive growth company that is trying to extend sales to anyone in an effort to keep up its rate of growth. Another reason is poor collection work. This task requires a good, well-motivated collections staff that is highly trained in extracting payments from customers. Investing in a quality collections staff is one of the best investments that a company can make. Finally, the most difficult invoices to collect are those that are being protested by the customer because the information on the invoices is wrong. This may include an incorrect address (in which case the customer never received it), incorrect pricing, or missing purchase order information. Only by following up on these problems and issuing corrected invoices can a company hope to collect the overdue amounts. In short, excessive accounts receivable are caused by loose credit policies, poor collections work, and error-laden invoices.

Although these problems present a formidable challenge to anyone wanting to reduce the amount of accounts receivable, there are several proven methods for reducing the amount outstanding. They are as follows:

- *Automate collection record keeping.* One of the largest problems for a collection person is the proportion of time not spent talking to overdue accounts. There is typically a great deal of note taking to track the history of each account; the collections person frequently scribbles this information onto the accounts receivable aging report, and copies it to a new aging report whenever a new one is run. This takes away from the time that could be better spent on collection calls. A better approach is to add a notes field to the accounts receivable database, in which the collections person can keep notes on a specific invoice. The accounts receivable aging report can then print these notes alongside the collections data, which eliminates all time spent by the collections person in manually transferring this information to the new report.
- *Change the timing of commission payments.* The sales staff is usually paid commissions at the time of sale, rather than when cash is received. By shifting commission payments to this later period, the sales staff becomes an enthusiastic group of supplemental collectors. They are frequently better than the in-house collections staff, because they have good connections with customer personnel, and can even go to customer locations to pick up payments.
- *Stratify collections.* Many collections staffs make the mistake of giving equal attention to their largest and smallest collection problems. When focusing on reducing the total amount of working capital, however, it is much more important to collect the largest accounts receivable. To do so, a collections person can split, or stratify, the overdue accounts and focus attention on the largest items much earlier than the smaller collection problems. This results in more customer contacts for the largest invoices and more rapid resolution of any payment problems.
- *Tighten credit.* Although it may impact reported revenue growth, it is frequently worthwhile to review customer credit records more carefully and alter their credit if necessary. This procedure may even involve eliminating the credit of some customers; if so, the company should contact them, perhaps in person, to discuss the situation and to suggest that they continue on a cash-on-delivery basis until the customer's financial position improves. There is no need to aggravate customers who may later become prime sales targets.

The final major working capital area is inventory. Inventory is the most intractable store of cash, because it takes a great deal of effort on several projects to reduce the investment in this area. Inventory tends to balloon over time due to a simple lack of attention; no one weeds out obsolete parts, makes any attempt to return unused parts to suppliers, or makes an effort to reduce purchases to nothing more than the company's immediate production needs. This inattention is a reflection not only on the quality of a company's materials management staff, but also on its systems, for a missing material requirements planning system inevitably leads to overpurchases of parts, which then become permanent fixtures of the warehouse. The only good reason for having a large inventory is if a company provides lots of service work and needs to have replacement parts available in case of a sudden repair need by a customer. Otherwise, the inventory represents a company's mine tailings—the detritus from years of production that no one knows how to eliminate.

There are several methods for reducing inventory. These take a considerable effort to complete, so it is necessary for a company to temporarily add staff to clear out inventory. Some of the following recommendations do not result in the realization of much cash in exchange for eliminating inventory, so management has a poor trade-off; spend more for extra staff to get rid of inventory for which it gets no return. A reasonable conclusion is to simply send much of the inventory to the local trash heap rather than to pay for the extra staff. Once that has been done, the following options are still available for squeezing cash out of inventory:

- *Install a material requirements planning (MRP) system.* A warehouse continues to have an inflow of excess parts unless the materials management staff can curtail it by only purchasing the exact quantities needed for current production. This method prevents any excess parts from being sent to the warehouse, where they will languish. However, purchasing the exact amount needed requires several inputs that most companies are not used to generating. The engineering staff must create an accurate bill of materials for every product to be produced, and the purchasing staff must use this in combination with a highly accurate production schedule to determine the total quantities needed and the dates on which parts must arrive. This system also requires an MRP software package to make the necessary calculations. If a company can install such a system, it will completely stop any further influx of parts into the warehouse.
- *Install just-in-time (JIT) manufacturing techniques.* As noted in Chapter 18, a number of JIT techniques reduce the amount of inventory in the production process. These techniques focus on minimizing the amount of inventory stored between production workstations, and include such methods as reduced setup times, and creating manufacturing cells and subplants.
- *Return parts to suppliers.* It is very time consuming to negotiate with suppliers to return parts. Nonetheless, a company will find that it has some very expensive parts that it cannot afford to throw away and that are worth the effort to return. As previously noted, less expensive items are not worth the effort, and should be thrown out if there is no other use for them.

An odd circumstance that sometimes arises in a heavily leveraged company is when top management decides not to shrink inventory and accounts receivable, because it needs these assets as a borrowing base on which it can then borrow money. This reason for maintaining excess assets is not logical, because a prudent financial institution rarely lends money at a rate that matches the amount of the borrowing base; on the contrary, it typically lends based on 80 percent of the accounts receivable and only 50 percent of the inventory. Thus, it is clearly better to liquidate the accounts receivable and inventory at face value and use this money to reduce debt than it is to keep it on hand in exchange for a lesser amount of debt. If the management team still insists on leaving the accounts receivable and inventory alone, a prudent person may suspect that these two accounts are being artificially inflated in order to qualify for additional debt; if so, it is time to leave the company. In short, maintaining a large borrowing base is not a valid excuse for avoiding a reduction of the investment in accounts receivable and inventory.

The best way for company management to determine if the organization is doing a good job of keeping its working capital investment low is to compare its performance in this area to that of other companies in the same industry. For truly world-class performance measures, it can look outside the industry as well. Three key performance measures track a company's ability to conserve working capital, one for each of the three primary working capital accounts. They are as follows:

1. *Days of accounts payable*. This measurement shows the average time that a company takes to pay its bills. A long payment term indicates a good ability to hold off on payments, but is counteracted by the less measurable irritation of suppliers at this kind of treatment. To calculate it, divide the total amount of purchases in the year by 365, and then divide this amount into the average accounts payable amount for the year. The measure can be heavily skewed if the company takes advantage of a large proportion of discount deals for early payment. Consequently, it is necessary to first strip these early discount payments out of the measurement before arriving at an accurate result. Good performance in this area is any payment period that exceeds standard payment terms.
2. *Days of accounts receivable*. This measurement reveals the ability of a company to obtain timely payment on invoices due from its customers; this measure is both a function of its credit policies and its collection abilities. To calculate it, divide the average accounts receivable total by the annual amount of sales on credit and multiply it by 365. It is difficult to note a standard days of accounts receivable, for collection terms vary dramatically by industry. However, as long as the number of days outstanding is no more than 25 percent greater than the standard number of days allowed for payment, this figure can be considered good performance, while anything matching or below standard collection terms is excellent.
3. *Inventory turnover*. This measurement reveals the number of times that a company's stocks of inventory are used in a typical year. To calculate it, di-

vide the inventory into the annual cost of goods sold. A poor turnover figure in almost any industry is under three, with some manufacturers recording turnover of more than 100. Moderate performance is 10 turns per year. These numbers can vary dramatically by industry.

The ultimate in cash flow management is when the amount of cash invested in working capital is zero or negative. It takes a great deal of effort to reach this state, but it is possible through a combination of the tactics noted in this section. When a company has taken all of these steps, it is possible that the cash it has invested in accounts receivable and inventory is offset (or more) by the amount it owes suppliers through accounts payable. This means that the company has invested no cash at all in working capital, which is a superior achievement in the world of cash management.

Zero working capital is a much easier accomplishment if a company is located in a service industry, because such a company has minimal inventory (if any), thereby eliminating one of the largest working capital investments faced by a production company. It then becomes a much simpler matter to offset accounts payable against accounts receivable to achieve a state of zero working capital.

CASH MANAGEMENT AND CAPITAL PURCHASES

A company can bring all of its attention to shrinking its working capital investment and still make a mistake on a capital purchase that can seriously impact its cash position. Some companies have an alarming habit of spending millions of dollars on capital expenditures that are not subjected to the critical review that more and more companies are bringing to their working capital. This section discusses how to create systems that require an adequate amount of review prior to making large capital expenditures.

It is a rare company that does not require a string of management approvals for asset purchases, because so much money is involved. A growing company cannot afford to have many unauthorized asset purchases, for this may result in incorrect purchases that are not only unnecessary, but which also represent a considerable drain on cash. One way to avoid this is to require management approval for extremely small asset purchases. For example, a company can define an asset as any item costing $1,000 or more and require a manager sign-off on the purchase order for any item of this amount or more. In addition, the approval of a higher-level manager can be required for a very low amount, such as $5,000, and so on. Although it is irritating for all involved to run paperwork through the management team in order to secure approvals, it also ensures that only those assets that are really needed are purchased.

If an asset is especially expensive, it is not sufficient merely to obtain management approvals on a purchase order. A company should also have a capital budgeting form that must be completed and reviewed in detail before purchase authorization is given. This form should contain some or all of the following features:

- *Alternatives.* There may be alternatives to purchasing an asset, such as refurbishing existing equipment to last a few more years, or buying a cluster of smaller-capacity machines that, in total, equal the capacity of the large machine. The form should include space for a discussion of these alternatives.
- *Expected returns.* The form should contain an estimate of cash inflows and outflows caused by the asset, including the initial cash expenditure plus any estimated subsequent payments, such as maintenance, spread over at least a five-year period. These expenses should then be offset by any expected revenues during the same time period. The form should net the cash inflow and outflows for each year and then use the company's cost of capital as the appropriate discount rate to determine the net present value (NPV) of these cash flows. A positive NPV justifies purchasing the asset.
- *Risks.* The form should include room for a discussion of risks, including such factors as the potential early obsolescence of the equipment (a common problem for high technology equipment), the uncertainty of potential incoming cash flows, and the risk that the company may shift out of the line of business that uses this equipment.

The problem with a capital budgeting form is that it can be enhanced to show any asset purchase in a favorable light. This occurrence is common, because the person filling out the form is usually the one who wants to purchase the asset. Accordingly, it is very useful to assign an analyst to review and provide commentary on the reality of the information shown in a capital proposal. If the asset in question is exceptionally expensive, the person doing the analysis may be a very high-ranking person in the organization. For example, the CFO of Coors Brewing Company personally reviews the company's largest capital purchasing proposals and has succeeded in saving millions of dollars by doing so. An alternative is to schedule capital proposal review meetings, in which the person proposing a purchase is grilled by a panel of top managers regarding the details of the purchase. As long as there is a detailed review of every large purchasing proposal, it does not matter what form the review takes.

Part of the process of purchasing assets should include a comparison of how the asset purchase helps the company achieve its strategic plan. In too many companies, cash is wasted on assets that do not assist the plan, thereby leaving so little cash on hand that the company cannot afford to purchase those assets that *do* assist it in fulfilling the plan. Thus, part of the review process should be a careful examination of how an asset purchase will help a company achieve its goals.

Once a company has gone through this review process and purchased an asset, it should conduct an audit of actual results some time later. The purpose of this audit is to see if the assumptions used in the original proposal were accurate. If not, management must change its assumptions for future purchases until they agree with the company's history of results. It may be many months before this review can be conducted, because one must wait until a new asset has been fully integrated into the company. If it is a complex piece of equipment, it may take a long time to install and test before anyone can tell if it functions as expected. A common result of this review is that management finds that the person who wrote the original proposal exaggerated the expected benefits in order to ensure the purchase of the asset. This issue is difficult to prove, but simply publicizing the fact that there will be a subsequent, rigorous review of asset purchases may keep these people from making wild estimates in their purchase justifications. It also gives management some idea of which people can be relied upon to create accurate cost justifications, which may result in more favorable purchasing decisions for those people. In short, a subsequent audit to see if projected benefits actually occurred as a result of an asset purchase will reveal any incorrect assumptions made, which can be incorporated into future asset purchase proposals to make them more accurate.

Although this section has focused attention on the *purchase* of assets, it is also necessary to determine when to *eliminate* them. By waiting too long to sell off assets, a company may lose a large part of its investment to obsolescence. It may also continue to pay interest on debt that could otherwise have been retired if the company had realized a significant amount on the sale of the asset. The main method for avoiding these problems is to closely track the utilization of all assets. The simplest approach is to walk through the company's facilities with other managers and discuss the need to continue using each asset. This approach usually results in the sale of a few odd pieces of machinery that have long since fallen into disuse and have been tucked away in a corner. But this does not normally free up much cash, because the equipment is frequently old or broken. A better approach is to set up a tracking system for calculating the amount that the company uses its equipment. If a machine's usage (or warehouse, etc.) drops below a predetermined amount, the management should either look into increasing its utilization or selling it off. For example, a truck rental company will find that some of its vehicles are continuously rented, while others sit idle most of the time. Being trucks, they will depreciate fairly rapidly, so it behooves the company to track utilization and promptly liquidate any trucks that are not being used enough to generate an adequate return on their investment. Thus, promptly selling off underutilized assets improves a company's cash position.

OTHER METHODS FOR CONSERVING CASH

Most of this chapter has been concerned with removing cash from the balance sheet, because a company may have millions of dollars stored in this area that can be released to fuel further growth. However, some companies have managed the cash out of their balance sheets and are now looking for other ways to improve their cash flow. The next place to look for improvements is the income statement.

This section covers the primary areas on the income statement where a company can lose large amounts of cash. The list of areas is not comprehensive, for there are a multitude of expense areas, depending on the type of industry. Accordingly, the following list only includes those areas that are likely to soak up large amounts of cash for a wide variety of companies in most industries. A thorough review of each of these points typically reveals at least a few possibilities for reducing the outflow of cash. They are as follows:

- *Budget comparisons.* The budget for a growing company can be very inaccurate, because growth outstrips all expected expenditures. However, as noted in Chapter 3, there are ways to construct a budget that at least give the user a fair understanding of the general amount of expenses to be expected. Consequently, it is a worthwhile exercise to compare actual year-to-date and monthly costs to the corresponding budgeted amounts to look for unusually large expenses. This exercise is particularly useful for year-to-date comparisons, because it becomes obvious if a manager has used up all budgeted funds when there is still lots of time left in the year; such cases require immediate management review to determine if it is necessary to supplement the budget or to cut back on expenses for the remainder of the year.
- *Custom sales.* A company may think that it is earning large profits on custom work, but it must be sure to factor in all expenses related to it. Nearly all types of custom work require additional expenses from many parts of the company. For example, product packaging, delivery, and installation costs are higher, as well as warranty costs for special repairs afterwards. In addition, a company may have to stock special parts in case the custom projects require servicing. Also, the up-front sales work required to sell such a product is considerable, typically involving multiple sales calls, revisions and approvals of drawings, and late changes that interfere with the design and production processes. A company should constantly review all of the costs of custom sales work to see if the expected gross margins are actually being realized.
- *Gross margins.* A company usually offers a mix of products and services for sale. Of them, some have margins that were once good, but, for any number of reasons, have now declined to an unacceptable level. It takes a periodic review of all margins to spot these problems. Management must then decide to either upgrade the product or service, reprice it, or eliminate it. Any decision will improve the remaining margins, leading to better cash flow.
- *Insurance.* An insurance agent is compensated based on a percentage of the insurance sold to a company, so the more insurance sold, the better. Some of this insurance is not necessary. A company should bring in a risk management expert to review its insurance policies to determine if the amount of coverage offered is excessive or overlapping. In either case, there may be

grounds for a reduction in the insurance expense. This review should center on the largest insurance items, so that the company can realize the largest possible savings. As part of this review, the risk manager may also be able to recommend operational changes that will convince an insurance company that the company is at minimal risk of loss, possibly resulting in a reduced insurance premium.

- *Marketing costs.* A growing company must frequently expend a large amount to create a name for itself or its products. It does this through such marketing techniques as advertisements, special events, trade shows, and promotions. This marketing is frequently an excellent use of a company's money, because it eventually pays off in brand recognition that may be worth millions. However, it is still important to ensure that the marketing staff only spends money that has been previously approved, because marketing costs can be singularly expensive. With some television ad spots selling for a million or more dollars per minute, it is critical to ensure that all such transactions have been properly authorized. If not, the company just lost a large amount of cash.
- *Occupancy costs.* A growing company can put on airs and spend too much money to build its own grandiose headquarters. This expenditure is a massive drain on cash and is rarely justified beyond inflating the management team's collective ego. In contrast, a software development company uses doors laid across packing crates as its desks, and uses valet parking so that it can stuff as many cars as possible into a tiny parking lot. Although a bit extreme, this company illustrates the extent to which it can go to conserve cash.
- *Overstaffing.* Although most growing companies have a constant shortage of employees (see Chapter 17), it is also possible to have pockets of inefficiency where there are too many employees. This condition can be caused by inefficient systems that require too much work to process transactions, or simple empire building by a manager. It is possible to spot these problems by comparing best practice measurements from other organizations to the company's internal measurements. This comparison highlights the problem areas in which it is possible to reduce head count.
- *Overtime.* It is very common for a growing company to pay large amounts of overtime to its production staff in order to ship products on time. The problem with this approach is that the overtime premium may take a large bite out of gross margins, which in turn reduces the company's store of cash. It is cheaper to start additional shifts and bring in more employees than it is to continue to pay large overtime premiums.
- *Sales expenses by customer.* The 80/20 rule applies to customers; 20 percent of a company's customers demand 80 percent of the company's sales effort. This condition is acceptable as long as these customers purchase large volumes of high-margin products. If not, they are wasting valuable sales resources, because the company is probably not making any money on sales to them,

once sales costs are included. This problem can be especially large if the sales force must make numerous extended trips to certain customers; it is not difficult to access salesperson expense reports to determine the cost of visiting each customer, and to then subtract these costs from sales to those customers. A company can then eliminate unprofitable customers, leaving extra time for the sales staff to look elsewhere for more profitable customers.

- *Travel and entertainment expenses.* This area is easy to abuse, especially in a growing company where there may not be sufficient controls. The easiest way to reduce these costs is to skim through the highest-cost categories in expense reports, looking for excessive items such as first-class air fares, high-end car rentals, or rooms at fancy hotels. Such a search requires minimal effort, but it must be done continually to keep offenses from reoccurring.

The foregoing tips require a good deal of analysis to determine where there are valid cash savings, so it is necessary to employ a team of financial analysts and cost accountants to ensure that a company gives proper attention to these areas of potential savings.

SUMMARY

This chapter explained why cash is such a vital ingredient for a growing company, not only as a means to start it, but also to fund each incremental increase in growth. It is especially important to focus on the highest-margin products when a company is expanding at an extremely rapid rate, because existing margins must cover expansion costs to the greatest extent possible; conversely, it is difficult to grow at a high sustained rate if the company has low margins, without resorting to debt or equity infusions.

There are several main cash repositories in a company, mostly in the area known as working capital. A company can invest inordinate amounts of money in accounts receivable and inventory, while not maximizing its use of accounts payable; this chapter covered the techniques a company can use to improve the situation enough to achieve zero working capital. The other main cash repository is capital assets; the chapter noted several ways to ensure that a company invests the absolute minimum in this area. Finally, it covered a number of methods for preserving cash by reducing expenses, focusing on what are traditionally the largest expense line items in the income statement, such as payroll, insurance, and occupancy costs.

Chapter 5

Control Systems

INTRODUCTION

When a company is growing at a ferocious pace, it is very difficult for the management team to keep track of operations, and especially to pinpoint any key areas that are causing trouble. When growth is rapid, a small control problem can rapidly inflate into a full-blown crisis that threatens deliveries, profits, cash flow, and the stock price. Accordingly, management must install control systems over the key areas in which the company cannot fail if it is to achieve its growth goals. This chapter describes the key factors that determine where a company should concentrate its attention when designing these control systems and the specific controls needed for three types of growth strategies.

This chapter pays particular attention to operational controls. It does not cover financial controls, which are addressed in Chapter 11.

KEY FACTORS FOR DETERMINING CONTROL POINTS

Any good auditor will point out that there are more controls available than grains of sand on a beach. If a company were to implement all of them, it could retain perfect control over every possible activity. Unfortunately, this would also require so many extra transaction steps and supporting staff that a company could not begin to adequately service its customers, resulting in its rapid dissolution. Instead, management must arrive at a midway point where it installs a sufficient number of controls over the most critical issues to ensure that problems will not reach an advanced state without being detected, while avoiding having so many controls that they interfere with corporate growth. This section describes where those key controls should be located.

Control points in a high-growth environment must center on two key factors. Either they must spot problems that can keep a company from growing, or they must locate trouble in key areas that are central to company growth. These two types of controls are very different. Examples of areas where a lack of controls can stop growth are cash flow tracking and computer services. It is absolutely mandatory that a company have sufficient cash to fuel its operations, as well as computer systems to process transactions, so there must be adequate control over these areas to ensure that they will not fail. These controls are noted in the next section.

The other type of control is over key areas that are central to company growth. These controls vary dramatically, depending on the type of growth strategy that a company follows. For example, a company that grows by territorial expansion must keep a close watch over the capacity of its sales and distribution systems to ensure that they are capable of keeping up with the planned growth rate. A company growing by adding products, however, needs to keep close track of its product release schedule to ensure that a sufficient number of products are sent to market to meet the company's growth target. Finally, a growth strategy based on acquisitions focuses on the pace of the acquisitions, as well as the company's capacity to integrate each acquisition and to obtain funding for it. Consequently, the types of controls needed vary greatly by the type of growth strategy that a company follows. Later sections of this chapter cover a complete set of controls for each of these growth strategies.

None of the controls noted in these examples have anything to do with accounting issues, which is the type of control most people think of when they consider control points, because financial controls are necessary in any environment, but they are not of overriding importance in a high-growth environment. For example, a company will not fail if it issues invoices a few days late (which requires a financial control), but it will run into serious difficulties if it cannot maintain a roll-out schedule for moving its distribution and sales functions into new territories (which requires other types of controls). Accordingly, this chapter focuses on only the controls that directly impact growth and ignores financial controls. For a discussion of financial controls, see Chapter 11.

In summary, the most important controls that an explosive growth company can implement are those that touch upon areas having a direct impact on company growth. In addition, the internal audit staff can focus on a variety of more typical financial control points.

CONTROLS ON FACTORS THAT CAN STOP GROWTH

Although most of this chapter covers control points on growth areas, there are also a few spots in a company where inaction or mismanagement can stop growth. This section addresses those areas. See Chapter 11 for an additional discussion of this topic.

The computer services area supports most of the transaction processing of a modern corporation. This setup allows a company to complete transactions quickly and with little error, but it also exposes the company to a major problem—if the computer systems go down, so too does the company's ability to conduct business. Consequently, the following control points are useful for ensuring that a company can quickly recover from a system failure and continue with its rapid rate of growth.

- *Data backups.* The internal audit team should regularly test for the presence of data backup systems that are updated and properly stored. This can include disk mirroring at an off-site location or tape backup storage with a periodic transfer to an off-site storage facility. Without this, a company does not have the means to recover from a crash of its primary storage medium, resulting in complete chaos while the company tries to manually reconstruct its records.
- *Disaster recovery planning.* The internal audit team should review the company's disaster recovery plan, which should include a periodic test of the system. This plan addresses a company's ability to recover from the complete destruction of its data-processing facility. The plan normally includes a provision for the transfer of data processing to a reserve location, along with all data backups, along with the staff to run it, within a specific time period. Without this plan, a company probably cannot recover from a major disaster without months of system recovery work that may bankrupt the company.
- *System conversion testing.* A key computer system can be shut down if a company switches to it without adequate testing of various kinds. The internal audit team should review the ability of a new system to process transactions by running dummy transactions through it and should also conduct stress testing to see if the system is able to handle the demands of many users at the same time. Without this testing, a company may find that it has switched to a new system that repeatedly fails, leaving the company completely unable to conduct business.
- *Uninterruptible power supply (UPS).* One of the most common causes of system downtime is when the power fails. This problem is easily remedied for smaller systems by means of a battery backup and for bigger installations with an in-house electrical generating facility. Without it, a company's systems are inoperable until the power company can restore service.

In short, the key controls over computer services center on keeping key systems from failing.

Another factor that can stop growth is regulatory. A company may find that there is either existing or upcoming legislation that so dramatically increases its costs that it can no longer compete. A good example of this is the series of restrictions in California that progressively requires car manufacturers to reduce their engine emissions over time. Another is the smokestack scrubber legislation that requires factory owners to install expensive equipment that reduces the emissions from their smokestacks. A company must be aware of the full ramifications of this kind of legislation, so it is wise to employ a law firm that can review pertinent laws on an ongoing basis and warn the company of any issues that may impact its expansion plans.

A final area that can stop growth—and quite abruptly—is cash, or a lack thereof. Cash flow is something that is quite predictable, unless management has no control over its spending habits. The best control is to maintain a cash forecast (see Chapter 16) that tracks the timing of all key cash inflows and outflows. The finance staff can supplement this forecast with a listing of all debt that has not yet been drawn upon, which gives management a better idea of the amount of cash really available for use. This forecast can be made even more accurate by constantly tracking its predicted results against actual results and modifying the forecast to account for these variances. When reviewed constantly by the top management team, steps can be taken well in advance of any forecasted difficulties to ensure that additional debt or equity is in place to keep growth from being stalled by a lack of cash.

CONTROLS ON TERRITORIAL GROWTH

Some companies grow by finding new territories in which to sell their products and new uses for them in old territories that will increase market penetration. Examples of companies that grow by these means are the eternal competitors, Pepsi and Coca-Cola. They both enter into licensing deals with local bottlers in new territories, gaining royalty revenues in exchange for letting the bottlers sell their soft drink formulas. Both companies then work on greater market penetration by building a brand image in the new territories, resulting in increasing sales per capita as acceptance of the product grows. Any retail chain grows by the same means; it develops a storefront concept, polishes it in a few locations to make sure that it works, and then quickly rolls out hundreds of stores over wide swathes of territory. The best example of this is Wal-Mart, which grew from a local Arkansas retailer to the world's largest in just a few decades. It is now carrying the concept overseas. This expansion strategy is the most common, because the concept is simple—get the sales concept down pat, and then duplicate it all over the world. This section describes how to establish controls over this type of growth strategy.

The system used by a company that grows based on territorial expansion is to determine the target revenue figure for the year, estimate the sales for each new territory, and devise a territorial expansion plan to achieve the required sales. This system usually involves adding to existing production capacity, creating distribution systems in the new territory, and managing a sales and marketing campaign. Unlike a strategy for growing through a series of new product introductions, this approach does not assume that there will be a significant number of new products, so the key areas of emphasis do not include engineering. Once a company has made these estimates, it creates a schedule of milestone dates that must be met if the company is to expand sales on schedule and meet its revenue targets.

Before a company can create effective controls over its territorial expansion plans, it must first develop a set of baseline expectations for performance, which are noted in the following bullet points. Without them, it is impossible to determine if a control point is signaling poor or good performance. The baseline measures are as follows:

- *Complaints database*. When a company grows through territorial expansion, it is common to have glitches in new territories that lead to customer dissatisfaction, such as poor sales support, faulty delivery, or bad servicing. These are correctable, but management must first know that there is a problem in order to do so. The best way to get rapid feedback from new territories is to use a complaints database (see Chapter 13) that directs problems straight to top management with a minimum of delay. This information then forms the basis for corrective action to eliminate the chance of lost sales through customer dissatisfaction.
- *Distribution capacity.* If a company is distributing to many points in its new territories from a small number of production or distribution facilities, it must have a solid distribution system in place prior to initiating sales in a new territory. This may be as simple as using overnight mail delivery from a central distribution point, but it may require a sophisticated regional warehouse with satellite tracking of inbound and outbound delivery trucks, as well as computerized stock replenishment linkages between all retail and distribution locations. The exact level of distribution capacity is most easily determined by reviewing a company's optimal distribution configurations in older territories.
- *Pacing schedule*. If a company wants to grow at a steady rate through territorial expansion, then it must follow a pacing schedule, that is, a list of milestone dates for each territory, noting when production capacity will be added to support the new sales, when distribution systems will be in place, and when the sales and marketing campaign will begin for each territory. As noted later in this section, the pacing schedule is the primary tool for controlling the speed of territorial expansion.
- *Production capacity*. A key factor in rapid territorial growth is the speed at which a company can bring new production capacity on-line to service the revenue volume. Production capacity can be a simple addition of equipment within an existing facility, or it may require the construction of a whole new facility in or near each new territory. In the case of a restaurant chain, the production facility is each restaurant, so the number of eateries is the key factor in the success of a company's expansion. Because production capacity is also an expensive proposition, any discussion of it should also include planning for the funding needed to create this capacity.
- *Revenue trend line by quarter*. This type of expansion is heavily driven by the ability of the sales force to penetrate the new territory as rapidly as possible. Consequently, there must be a system in place that not only contains a budgeted level of sales by customer and product for each customer, but which also compares this information to actual results on a trend line. This information should be reviewed at least quarterly to see if corrective action is necessary, but reviews may occur far more frequently during the first few weeks

and months of a territorial expansion, to ensure that revenues are in the expected range.

- *Sales capacity.* Any territorial expansion requires an estimate of the number of sales staff needed to bring sales up to expected levels. This staffing is usually a mix of internal and external sales staff, as well as a group of managers to supervise them. It requires detailed analysis to derive the correct number of sales staff, usually including a breakdown of the desired first-year revenues by product category, and then factoring in the number of sales staff required for each type of product (and its volume) based on the company's first-year sales history in older territories. Only by making this analysis can a company determine a reasonable estimate of the correct number of sales staff needed to generate the planned revenue volume in each new territory.
- *Support capacity.* A large number of support staff are needed for any territorial expansion, including employees for both inbound and outbound call centers, product service employees, and a variety of administrative staff covering materials management and accounting. A company can derive the required number of these personnel by extrapolating its current head count in these areas in older territories to new ones, varying the number based on planned revenue volume.

Once these baseline measurements are installed, management can create controls that use them as a comparison to see how the company is performing.

The first control is weekly monitoring of the pacing schedule. The monitoring is conducted by the sales and marketing staffs, with frequent support from the production and distribution staffs for issues involving shortcomings in the capacity of those areas. The purpose of this group is to examine the milestone dates for each territorial expansion to see if the scheduled roll-out will be completed on time. A roll-out is not usually achieved without problems, because there inevitably is trouble adding production capacity, hiring qualified sales staff, and building new distribution points and retail outlets. This group uses the pacing schedule to spot these problems as they develop and adjusts the plan or adds resources as needed to ensure that the targeted revenue level is reached. As part of its control function, this group uses the following baseline measures: the pacing schedule, the revenue trend line, and customer complaints. The revenue trend line and complaints database are only useful once a territory has been launched, but this information is still good, because this control group's responsibility does not end when a territory has been set up; it continues until each territory's revenues have matched expectations. In short, the primary control point for territorial expansion is a group that frequently reviews a pacing schedule and adjusts company resources as needed to meet that schedule.

The second control is a periodic review of the capacity needed to support the pacing schedule. This review normally coincides with the weekly review of the schedule, and may precede it so that capacity information is available for the pacing meeting. The review should include capacity at all key points in the territorial expansion: production, distribution, and sales. This review should include a comparison of sales figures to the existing capacity so that the capacity review team can recommend changes to the number of staff or facilities to either bring these needs in line with existing sales (especially if the company has no intention of increasing sales further) or to help fuel further growth. For example, if territory sales are stalled at $10 million and are likely to remain there, the capacity review may reveal that there are too many salespeople for this volume, and the reviewers may recommend a selective reduction of the sales staff. Alternatively, the capacity review team may find that the existing sales staff is already so overworked that it cannot possibly add more sales and therefore recommends an increase in the number of sales staff. The capacity review team represents a key control over the number of assets and employees that a company commits to its territorial expansions.

Earlier in this section, it was noted that this type of expansion can be accomplished through either territorial growth or deeper penetration of existing markets. The section then described controls over just territorial growth, ignoring expansion by means of greater market penetration, because territorial expansion is the more difficult of the two, involving more functional areas and requiring more controls. If a company is more concerned with greater penetration of its existing markets, it does so primarily by means of altering its marketing and sales efforts, which require less control. The primary control point in this situation is to set up a target market share or revenue number and monitor expenditures to alter product positioning or sales efforts to attain that target. This comparison gives management a good correlation between the incremental cost of extra sales and marketing efforts and the resulting revenues.

CONTROLS ON PRODUCT GROWTH

Some companies grow by creating hordes of new products each year, flooding the market with so many purchase opportunities that their sales are bound to increase, even as their older products are gradually discontinued. Examples of companies following this strategy are Rubbermaid, Emerson Electric, and 3M. They churn out new products in hopes of maintaining high margins, for they know that competing products will soon appear. By rapidly upstaging the competition with new offerings, they can stay one step ahead of the competition and offer higher-margin products before anyone else has anything on the market to drive down margins. This section discusses the controls that management should put in place to ensure that it has adequate knowledge of a company's continuing ability to create new products in a timely and cost-effective manner.

A company that grows through new products does so by concentrating on expanding specific product families. For example, Emerson Electric focuses on electronic goods, whereas 3M creates new products based on adhesives, and Rubbermaid (as the name implies) designs common household and industrial goods based on rubber or plastic compounds. The advantage behind developing new products in specific target areas is that the company is already equipped to handle them. For example, the Emerson Electric design staff is composed of electrical engineers who are quite capable of designing a new radio, but who would have no idea how to create a rubber spatula, as the Rubbermaid engineers can. This focused expertise extends into all parts of the business. For example, Rubbermaid has factories that are designed to churn out the same general types of products year after year and to sell them to the same distributors and retail outlets—they are not designed to produce, distribute, or sell the adhesive-products made by 3M. Thus, a product-focused company keeps itself strictly within self-imposed constraints related to the types of products it is best able to design, produce, distribute, and sell.

The system used by a company that grows by creating new products is to create a plan for introducing a specific number of products per year that add up to an estimated revenue target. The design teams then work with the marketing staff in sorting through a variety of new-product ideas or old-product enhancements to create a list of the best prospects. The design teams then combine with the materials management, production, and marketing staffs to review this short list with a focus on any problems that may get in the way of creating each product and bringing it to market. Examples of problems are additional research required to make products perform within desired specifications (e.g., a battery for a portable computer that will keep it operating for a week is still in the realm of science fiction), component parts that are in short supply, or needed production equipment that must be specially designed. If a product concept passes this quick review, it is entered into a queue of many potential products that move in regimented order through the design, procurement, and production phases, until they are delivered to a sales force that is sufficiently informed in advance to successfully push the product into the marketplace. This process is not one that occurs entirely within one year, however. From the time even a simple product is first approved to the time it reaches the market may require two or three years of intensive work. Also, some potential products do not make their way to the market, for any number of reasons—unforeseen design problems, pricing that the market will not bear, or changes in the market that have bypassed the product are common examples. Accordingly, the product queue should be extra long in anticipation of some product fallout during the design and production process.

Rapid product development is the most difficult of the three expansion strategies outlined in this chapter, and consequently is the one in which the most problems can occur. Therefore, management must pay particular attention to implementing and reviewing the appropriate number of controls. Before creating controls, however, one must first have in place a baseline set of expected performance figures against which to set the controls. Otherwise, a manager would have no idea if the results reported from a control point were good or bad. Accordingly, the following baseline standards should be in place before management creates any controls:

- *Design time.* In a company where new products must be introduced on time, it is critical that the engineering staff release new product designs on time. It is easy to measure this design time, because the dates on which all drawings and accompanying information are signed off on by the receiving functions (materials management and production) are the dates that should match the design completion dates on the pacing schedule.
- *Engineering capacity.* A common problem for a growing company is to load too many design projects onto an engineering staff that is not growing fast enough to accommodate all the projects. A common result is that the engineering staff allocates only a little of its time to each design project, resulting in no projects being completed on time. This problem can be avoided by closely monitoring the workload of each design team and only giving each one a very small number of projects, with all other work held in reserve. This system gets projects completed more quickly. It is also easier to gauge the number of projects for which there is no assigned design team and determine if there is a need for additional engineering assistance.
- *Line extension or new product family (yes/no).* It is vastly easier to introduce a new product to the sales force if it is something they can easily integrate into their sales patterns (i.e., sales calls, presentations, contacts). For example, adding a new mop to the product line of a janitorial supplies salesperson is far easier than getting the same salesperson to sell office supplies, because the salesperson can easily sell the mop to the same customers, whereas he or she would have to create a whole new set of sales contacts to sell the office supplies. This baseline measurement is critical.
- *Pacing schedule.* If a company wants to attain explosive growth through a consistent roll-out of new products, it must have a pacing schedule, which is a list of product introduction dates for a year (though a multiyear schedule is even more common, due to the time it takes to create a product), showing the series of milestone dates that each product must meet if it is to enter the market on time and meet its sales goals for the year. Key dates on the pacing schedule for each product include the scheduled design release date, pilot production approval date, beginning of production date, and official product launch date.
- *Percentage of designs held in reserve.* The problem with relying on a steady stream of new products to fuel revenue growth is that some of the products never reach the market, or do so late, thereby negatively impacting the revenue figures. This situation may occur because a product fails or is delayed because its research costs were too expensive, the design took too long, or the pilot production test revealed many production issues needing resolution. This set of problems is standard for even the best-run companies, so it is entirely

natural for a company to not always meet its product release dates. A good way to avoid this problem is to hold in reserve a small number of product designs that can be inserted into the pacing schedule as other designs drop out. These reserve product designs are usually kept in the design stage; this is where a company has yet to make a major investment in production facilities, so management can "park" a product design for a few months without incurring significant additional expenses, while waiting for a hole in the product introduction schedule in which to place one of the designs being held in reserve. The number of reserved designs can be held at a steady percentage of the total, which is a figure that can only be derived based on a company's experience with product dropout rates.

- *Pilot production time.* After the designing process, the other area where a product release can be significantly delayed is in pilot production, where the company creates a miniature production process to see if it can create the product in bulk, and to find any problems that must be fixed before switching to full-time production. It is common for the more technologically advanced products to have problems in this area, since creating a problem once in the laboratory under the eye of a Ph.D. is different from having a staff of comparatively less well-trained production staff assemble the same product on an ongoing basis. Consequently, management must be sure to set a date for the expected completion of pilot testing.
- *Research costs.* The research work on a new product can grossly exceed expectations. Because the nature of research is such that it is very difficult to estimate in advance the cost of creating a new product, management may find that, after years of work and millions of dollars of research costs, it now has a product design that cannot possibly command enough sales to return the research cost. Consequently, management should constantly review the ongoing cost of research needed for a new product to see if the expenditure (as well as the estimate of future costs before research is completed) can be recouped. If not, the research must be stopped. There is no clear dollar cutoff figure beyond which research cannot proceed, for the work may be usable for other spin-off products as well, making the work worth an additional cost. Instead, this decision is a management judgment call.
- *Revenue trend line by quarter.* Once a new product reaches the market, the company must still watch it carefully to see if it warrants continued sales effort, or if it is clearly failing and should be dropped to make way for more favorable prospects. In a company that grows based on hordes of new products, there is rarely time to reposition a product in the market and try again; instead, the product is unceremoniously dumped. This information is normally summarized quarterly and tracked on a trend line, although some companies may review sales weekly or even daily for an expensive new product launch, in case it can make quick marketing adjustments to help the early growth rate.

Once this baseline information is in place, management is in a position to install controls that use the baselines as a starting point to determine if there are problems needing correction. It is apparent from the baseline figures noted in this section that a company growing through new product introductions must keep an especially close eye on the timing of introductions, because any slow-down in this rate has a serious impact on the company's ability to grow revenues at the planned rate. The cost of ensuring that the pacing schedule is met tends to be secondary to making the scheduled release dates.

The primary control over the product introduction process is a weekly review of the pacing schedule. The review team should include a representative from each of the functional areas involved in the product introduction process. The primary task of this review group is to see if each of the products on the schedule is meeting its milestone dates, of which the primary ones are the scheduled design release date and the pilot production completion date. If products will not make their scheduled dates, which is a common occurrence, the review team must reschedule other product releases or perhaps bring in product designs that have been held in reserve, in order to ensure that the company's revenue goals are met for the year. This review process includes many of the previously noted baseline measures, such as the pacing schedule, engineering capacity, pilot production time, and design time. The weekly review of the pacing schedule is by far the most important control in a company that grows based on the development of many new products.

The second control is over the initial list of products to be developed. The group responsible for this control is somewhat smaller than the group that reviews the pacing schedule, because it only requires people who can render an opinion about the salability of a prospective design and the ability of the company to design it. These criteria reduce the group to representatives from marketing and engineering, with some input from production if the group is contemplating a design that falls outside of the current product families and which the company therefore has no experience in producing. This group sorts through the proposals for new product designs and selects the most likely ones for inclusion on the pacing schedule. This group must also meet later on, usually with senior management, to review the development costs of these products and to eliminate those whose costs are exceeding any possible returns that the company may later make on sales. This group must also review the number of product designs held in reserve to see if there are enough on hand to fill in the inevitable holes in the pacing schedule that will arise as other designs are abandoned or delayed. In short, this group is in charge of periodically adding products to or deleting them from the pacing schedule.

The final control is over products once they have been released for sale. The members of the group that exercise this control are from sales and marketing, with some input from the engineering staff, as needed. The purpose of this control is to frequently review the sales of new products to see if there are problems that can be rectified, perhaps by using different pricing, sales channels, or other incentives. The review tends to be intensive during the first few months of a product's release, and less so after that period. The engineering staff is only called in to assist in this review if the group thinks that a product design change may be necessary to increase sales. In short, this control covers the period subsequent to product release.

Of the previously noted measurements, the only one without a directly linked control point is the one entitled "Line extension or new product family (yes/no)." This one is more an indicator of the likely success of a product than of any control that management can exercise over it. For example, if a company creates a new camp stove that fits into its existing lineup of camping equipment, there is a good probability that both initial and continuing sales will be acceptable, simply because the sales force can easily integrate it into its sales pitch to existing customers. However, if the product is not one that the sales staff can sell so easily, it is a strong indicator that initial sales will be poor, although continuing sales may be quite good if management is willing to pour sufficient resources into creating new marketing campaigns and sales channels to move the product. The product introduction process probably will not initially result in success if a company introduces a new product family.

CONTROLS ON ACQUISITION GROWTH

Some companies grow by acquisition, snapping up dozens of companies per year. Examples of such organizations are Corporate Express (office supplies), Blockbuster Video (movie videos), and AutoNation (car dealerships). They promise investors greater efficiencies, usually through combined purchasing power; if investors buy the company's story, they bid up its stock price to very high levels. The company then uses its stock to buy other companies, and continues to do so until the stock price drops. When it does, the company can continue to acquire companies by using cash flow or adding debt, but the preferred form of funding is equity. This section discusses the controls that a management team should install to ensure that it is aware of any problems in its growth strategy.

The basic system used by an acquisition-minded company is to first develop a growth plan for the upcoming year, which typically means that management sets a targeted revenue figure that it wishes to attain by buying other companies and thereby adding their revenues to that of the acquiring company. This measure may be supplemented by targeted additions to profits or earnings per share, but revenue growth is the usual underlying goal. Management then creates a list of potential acquisition candidates and determines, based on their current sales, how many must be acquired in order to achieve the revenue target. It then sets up an acquisitions assembly line, whereby companies are acquired steadily throughout the year. For example, a company decides that it must buy 25 companies, so it sets up a schedule that spaces the purchases at intervals of roughly two weeks. In reality, the acquisitions are "lumpy," for the companies being acquired do not necessarily cooperate by being bought on the exact dates listed in the plan. Also, some companies are much larger than others, so may require more time to purchase. In addition, it is impossible to plan for exactly who is being purchased in any given time period, because some companies resist being bought, forcing the acquirer to try some other target company further down its list. This is the general method for acquiring a string of companies.

In order to devise a control system for this acquisition process, it is first necessary to create a baseline of expectations. Without it, there is no way for management to determine if the measurements used in its control system are revealing good or bad performance. This baseline should include all of the following information:

- *Pacing schedule.* In order to achieve its growth goals, a company must have a set in stone acquisition schedule that lists the number of acquisitions planned for the year, by date. Although it is difficult for a company to acquire companies on the exact dates listed in this pacing schedule, it should be possible to meet the schedule on a year-to-date basis. For example, if a company wishes to increase its sales through acquisitions by one billion dollars during the current year, top management would consider the acquisition plan to have been met if the company had acquired companies with revenues of $250 million as of the end of the first quarter, irrespective of the exact timing of when those purchases were made within the quarter.
- *Time to acquire.* Although this time will vary by company, the acquisition team can budget a specific amount of time to contact a target company, investigate it, make a bid, and negotiate the sale agreement. Time to acquire is a reasonably standard amount of time when averaged over a large number of acquisitions, so the baseline can include a mid-range acquisition time interval. The interval should also include an allowance for time spent on fruitless acquisition studies and offers; this time varies by industry.
- *Time to transition.* The transition team that follows behind the acquisition group is in charge of reorganizing the acquired company, setting up reporting systems, and making any other alterations to create economies of scale. The time needed to transition varies by the size of each company and the system problems found by the transition team. Nonetheless, it is possible to estimate an average transition time when averaging over a large number of acquisitions.
- *Cost to acquire.* A company can create a broad range of estimated acquisition costs, using estimated low and high purchase prices that are typically based on multiples of the estimated cash flows of acquisition targets. If a company has already set a high-end price limit on its purchases, it can back away from any excessively expensive acquisitions, rather than being sucked into a price

war with another company over the purchase. This budget should be grouped into a pool that is sufficient for all planned purchases over the course of the year. The chief financial officer (CFO) uses this information to plan for acquiring enough cash or stock to fund all planned purchases.

- *Cost to transition.* This crucial baseline figure is composed of widely differing costs, such as the personnel on the acquisition team, system conversion costs, and write-offs found subsequent to the purchase. Because these costs can vary wildly from one acquisition to another, it is best to create two sets of budget costs: one for the personnel costs of the integration team, which tend to be very consistent, and a second set for unexpected costs, such as write-offs for inventory or accounts receivable. The second budget should be drawn upon as unusual expenses arise. By splitting the budget, a company can establish a reasonable degree of predictability in its transition costs.

Once the baseline information is in place for the pace of acquisitions, as well as the cost and timing of acquisitions and transactions, management has enough information to set up controls over its acquisition process.

The first key control is a weekly review of acquisition pacing, which means that the management team must review the dates by which acquisitions have been completed as compared to the budget. The key elements of pacing are the time needed to complete acquisitions *and* transitions. It is not sufficient have a white-hot group of acquisition hot shots if the transition teams following them cannot integrate the acquired companies at the same pace. If the teams responsible for these activities are completing their tasks too slowly, management must either add more experienced personnel to the teams to speed up their work, hope that the teams will improve their efficiency as they gain experience, or add more acquisition or transition teams. It may require more than one of these actions to ensure that management attains its acquisition goal.

The second control is over the cost of acquisitions. The management team should have a pool of funds available to cover purchase prices and after-the-fact write-offs related to purchases. This usually large amount of money can be spent all too quickly on large acquisitions; it requires close attention to ensure that the company has enough funding available toward the end of the year for it to complete any remaining acquisitions. An example of this pooled budget is shown in Exhibit 5.1. It notes the decline in the pool of money, due to draw-downs needed to complete various acquisitions. It compares this decline to the remaining amount of revenues yet to be acquired (which can be substituted for some other measure, depending on company acquisition goals), and gives a percentage comparison of the two. If the percentage of cash left in the pool drops significantly below the percentage of revenues still to be acquired, management knows that it must either complete the remaining purchases for lower prices or increase the size of the pool with more funds.

Exhibit 5.1 shows that, as of the end of the second quarter, the company has been very efficient in acquiring more revenues for prices that are less than ex-

Exhibit 5.1 Acquisitions Budget

Time Period (end of)	*Pool of Funds for Acquisitions ($)*	*Percentage of Pool Remaining*	*Targeted Revenues to Acquire ($)*	*Percentage of Remaining Revenues to Acquire*
Quarter 1	50,000,000	100	250,000,000	100
Quarter 2	38,000,000	76	180,000,000	72
Quarter 3	27,000,000	54	147,500,000	59
Quarter 4				

pected, because the company has a larger percentage of its acquisition pool available than of the percentage of remaining revenues to acquire. The situation is reversed at the end of the third quarter, where the company has paid more than expected to acquire additional companies. Also, going into the fourth quarter, the company has only completed about half of its planned acquisitions, so it is in considerable danger of missing its year-end revenue goal. Please note that, for clarity, this example gives the simplest possible measure for determining the success of an acquisition—revenue growth. In reality, a company would review the impact of an acquisition on earnings per share, as well as many other factors, such as tax loss carry-forwards, patents, and potential synergies.

The management team should also set up a budget for the acquisition teams. The acquisition team is most easily handled as a separate department. The primary factor in this budget is the payroll, followed by travel and entertainment costs, because it funds the acquisition and transition teams that are constantly in the field to acquire and merge organizations into the parent company. This budget is easily controllable and can be treated like any other department by comparing budgeted expenses to actual ones and following up on variances. Of the two budgets, the pooled one for buying companies is by far the more variable as well as the larger, so it is the one to which management should turn the bulk of its attention.

This section noted that the two primary controls over a company that is growing by acquisition are to closely monitor the pace at which organizations are being purchased, while simultaneously reviewing the costs of buying them, given general high–low purchase price guidelines. These controls give management good control over the timing and cost of its acquisition strategy.

SUMMARY

This chapter covered the control systems needed to ensure that a company grows as planned. It did not cover the standard financial controls that the internal and external auditors are concerned about (see Chapter 11). Instead, it only covered those controls that can tell management if there are problems with its growth plans, including controls over growth by territorial expansion, adding products, and corporate acquisitions. The discussion of controls for each growth strategy focused heavily on the need for up-front planning, because it is difficult to control something if there is no baseline criterion against which to measure it. In addition, the chapter addressed controls over any issues that can stop a company's growth, such as computer system failures, declining cash flows, or regulatory concerns. A company can pick only those controls from this list that specifically apply to its growth strategy and use them to verify that it is progressing at the expected rate of growth.

Chapter 6

Management Issues

INTRODUCTION

Although a company may have invented a hot new product or procured a vast amount of funding, this means nothing unless it has a good management team. A good management team is the single most important factor for a company that wants to sustain a high rate of growth, because good managers know how to create an organization that focuses on continuing that growth.

This chapter discusses the key factors for managing an explosive growth company, including the ability to plan for and lead a continual process of transition, which is noted in the next section. The chapter also covers key issues for the top and middle management teams, plus changes in the span of control and whether to tightly centralize decision making. Also, the chapter notes how management can use various communication channels to spread information through a company and how to include the organization in the planning and budgeting processes. This chapter gives the reader a good overview of the key management issues faced by an explosive growth company.

TRANSITION MANAGEMENT

The single most important feature that separates an explosive growth company from a typical company is its ability to manage transitions. If the management team cannot run an ongoing transition process, then explosive growth will remain a wish, not a reality. This section discusses the importance of having a constant transition process and what the management team can do to ensure that it happens.

It is possible for a company to experience explosive growth if it providentially invents the next great new product. However, that splendid rate of growth will soon wither if the company cannot put itself into a constant transition mode, whereby it brings a continuous stream of new products to market in an orderly and predictable flow. For example, several companies, such as 3M and Emerson Electric, have company policies of deriving roughly one-third of all revenues with new products that did not exist the year before. They do this by creating carefully designed systems that force new products through their product development cycles and into the marketplace, along with new advertising campaigns and distribution systems. Other companies, such as Banc One and Corporate Express, grow primarily by acquisition and have clear-cut strategies for acquiring a specific number of companies each year; this strategy includes a system for sending acquisition and integration teams into the acquired companies to ensure that they convert over to the parent company's systems within a specific time period. Thus, continual explosive growth that goes on for years is largely caused by well thought out, standardized systems for adding new products, sales regions, or subsidiaries to a company on an ongoing basis.

It is up to the management team to not only create the continual transition process, but also to manage its pacing so that it occurs at a speed that does not overwhelm the company. For example, a company that is rolling out a large number of retail stores may find that its biggest constraint is finding good store managers in the new sales regions, so management must tailor the growth rate to the number of new store managers that it believes it can find each year. If the management team pushes for a growth rate that is too fast, the company will become mired in an overwhelming amount of change, resulting in very little being done. To increase the pace of change, the management team must look for the bottlenecks in the transition process and add resources to eliminate them. These bottlenecks are usually people. For example, a company may only be able to acquire four companies per year because it only has one corporate transition team, and it takes three months for the team to complete the transition for each acquired company. Consequently, management must create additional transition teams if it wants to accelerate the pace of growth. Thus, the management team is largely responsible for continued explosive growth because it must drive the speed of transition.

What kind of managers can drive a fast rate of transition? Managers who have already done it elsewhere. It is dangerous for a company owner to rely on the existing management team if it has not been through the expansion drill of continual planned transitions. By using inexperienced managers, the company owner may be foregoing a chance at tremendous corporate growth and greatly enhanced wealth. The characteristics of the top management team are described in the next section.

In short, the top management team must be able to install a process of continual transition in order to continue a company's high rate of growth.

MANAGEMENT AT THE EXECUTIVE LEVEL

This section covers the most important qualifications of the top management team, as well as any problems that a growing company faces in the executive suite. Specifically, it deals with job descriptions and related issues for each of the chief positions (e.g., chief executive officer [CEO], chief operating officer [COO], and chief financial officer [CFO]), as well as between them, and how to resolve these problems.

The CEO must have the vision to steer a company through the shoals of competition at very high speed, which requires an excellent knowledge of business strategy. Preferably, this person should already have experience in running a fast-paced company, because the company owner may not want to take the chance of having an inexperienced person take the corporate reins at a time of fast growth, when any mistake can bring ruin. Also, it helps if the CEO is a skilled negotiator with outstanding people skills, because one of the ways to grow fast is by acquisition, which requires strong negotiation skills, at least until the company grows to the point where acquisitions work can be taken over by a specialized team. Also, superb people skills are needed to juggle the personalities of the management team to yield the best possible outcome. The CEO position is no place for an introvert. In short, the CEO of a successful explosive growth company is an extrovert with strong strategic planning and negotiation skills who has experience in running a fast-growing operation.

The COO must have superb organizational skills. This person is responsible for the smooth operation of a company that may be adding acquisitions or introducing new products every few weeks, and which must do so in a seamless manner that does not disrupt the organization. This person needs a good overall knowledge of how each functional area of the company works, as well as actual or at least theoretical knowledge of how it can be made to work better. Also, because the company is expanding so fast, this person must be able to delegate large chunks of work to subordinates, who may require motivation and training to fulfill their jobs. Consequently, the COO must have a strong operational understanding of many functional areas, as well as the ability to rapidly raise a crop of lower-level managers into positions of authority, which requires nurturing and training.

The CFO must have a strong finance background; accounting knowledge is absolutely secondary to a gift for understanding cash flows and securing funding. This points more toward a Wall Street background than one from the Big Six. The CFO must have strong experience in cash forecasting, in order to properly predict when more funds will be needed, as well as experience with obtaining debt and equity financing. Finally, the CFO should at least know the theory of accelerating cash flows through such means as lock boxes and cash concentration accounts, although this responsibility can safely be handed off to a treasurer. Accounting issues are always important, but they are not as critical to the survival of an explosive growth company as cash flow concerns. Thus, the CFO must have strong financial experience, as opposed to accounting experience.

The foregoing job descriptions make it clear that the company owner needs top managers who have experience in rapidly growing a company. Frequently, the existing team does not have the experience to put the company on the explosive growth path. The owner may need to replace some or all of them to gain the requisite level of experience. If so, the owner will probably have to look outside the company for this kind of talent. Very few people have successfully navigated a company through an explosive growth situation, and they are in high demand because of this skill. Consequently, the company owner must be willing to pay for the requisite executive experience in order to have some assurance of shifting a company onto the high-growth path.

One of the biggest problems in a growing company can be the CEO. This person may have started the company or been with it since it was a small organization. In either case, the CEO is used to making all key decisions and does not realize that, for a growing company, this makes the CEO the key decision bottleneck in the company. As a company continues to grow, the CEO may act as a brake because of this bottleneck problem, either resulting in the slowing of growth or the replacement of the CEO. To avoid this problem, the board of directors should encourage the CEO to seek training and advice, either through consultants or executive education programs, regarding how to delegate authority further down the chain of command.

A key problem that can arise between the members of the executive suite is when there are obvious imbalances in the amount of effort, experience, and skill among the CEO, COO, and CFO. If, comparatively speaking, one member of the team is not pulling his or her weight, the remaining members of the team may try to force out that person. This problem is common in a high-growth environment, where there are great strains on the top management team due to the rapid rate of transition. When this happens, the odd man out is usually let go. However, this person may be highly qualified at a lower level. Few people will allow themselves to be demoted, but it may be possible to create a small spin-off company that this person can run. Thus, by reducing the size of the task, the top management team can keep those top managers who are no longer qualified to run the company, but who can still contribute by managing a small portion of it. Also, running a subsidiary company is not considered so demeaning as a straight demotion or firing, and the subject person may even find the work environment more acceptable.

In short, the top management team is the foundation upon which to build the organization of an explosive growth company, but building the team may require a transition to a new executive team with more expertise than the current one, as well as continual assistance from consultants or training programs to keep the top management team on the correct growth path.

MANAGEMENT AT THE MIDDLE LEVEL

Unlike the top management ranks, it is possible to maintain some existing middle managers, even if they do not have sufficient experience in high-growth situations, because most of these people manage day-to-day operations that do not change rapidly. However, a small number of functions in an explosive growth situation require excellent middle managers. This section describes when a company can safely leave its middle managers alone and when it must bring in top-level replacements.

The skill level for middle managers is highly dependent on a company's type of growth strategy. For example, if the company relies on growth through new product introductions, it must have top-flight engineering management to oversee the development of an orderly flow of new products. If growth is by expansion into new sales territories, it must have superb sales management, as well as a strong manager to set up distribution systems in the new territories. Finally, if growth is through acquisitions, then the company must have an excellent team of acquisition conversion managers whose skills focus on human resources, accounting systems, and computer systems. Thus, the growth strategy drives the need for improvement in specific mid-level management areas.

The growth strategy drives the determination of skill levels by management position. To arrive at specific job requirements by position, the human resources staff must work with the top management team to determine what kinds of skills are needed to support its growth plans. The human resources staff then compares the skills on its hiring plan to those of each manager to decide if it is necessary to upgrade a position, or if it is safe to keep the current manager.

It is very important to decide which middle management positions truly need a skills upgrade, because more skilled managers are more expensive. It is justifiable if a company proves its need for a more skilled manager by linking the need through a hiring plan to the strategic plan. However, if a company's growth strategy allows for some weakness in certain positions, then the existing managers should certainly be left where they are. For example, if a company is growing by acquisition, there is no great need to upgrade the controller position in an acquired company, because that position is not critical to the growth of the subsidiary. If anything, the acquiring company may eliminate the position by consolidating the controller's work into the headquarters accounting department.

In summary, there is only a selective need for an upgraded middle management team in an explosive growth situation, because only a few positions are critical to increasing the rate of growth, with the type of position varying based on the growth strategy.

SPAN OF CONTROL

Management theories over the last few decades have espoused a wider span of control; that is, more employees reporting to each manager. This is not necessarily the case in an explosive growth situation, but it is frequently the result of growing without enough qualified personnel.

The theory behind a wider span of control is that by giving its employees more latitude to make their own decisions, there is less need for a company to hire large numbers of managers to control everyone's activities. There are a few industries where this system is possible, resulting in spans of control of 30 or more people reporting to one supervisor. However, in many situations it is not possible to force decision making down to the lowest levels of a corporation, resulting in the traditional span of control, which is usually approximately seven people reporting to one supervisor. How does this ratio vary for an explosive growth company?

The span of control varies for a growing company, depending on the strategy it uses to grow. The following points illustrate the issue:

- *Growth by acquisition.* If a company grows primarily by buying other companies, it does not require any changes to the existing span of control. For example, a company may purchase another company and save money by shifting its accounting and human resources staffs to the corporate headquarters. This shift does nothing to the local span of control, because the other functions are still there, with the same management.
- *Growth by new product development.* If a company grows by rapidly adding to the number of products it sells, it needs a tightly integrated set of engineering teams and a closely managed effort to procure parts, assemble them into completed products, and deliver them to the customer. This level of tight integration calls for a very narrow span of control, with lots of managers. Without them to monitor and adjust all phases of product development and production, a company will not be able to maintain a rapid rate of growth.
- *Growth by territorial expansion.* If a company grows by expanding the number of sales territories, it must keep the span of control quite small, although it can widen it somewhat over time. Because the company is adding newly hired personnel who usually only have the briefest training in what they do, it is important to have adequate supervision to give them guidance. As the level of staff experience improves over time, management can selectively increase the span of control. Thus, the span of control depends on the experience of the staff.

These examples show that there is some variability in the span of control for a growing company, depending on the method of growth. The human resources staff should incorporate the span of control into its hiring plans to determine the appropriate number of managers to hire. However, the realities of hiring scarce personnel may result in a wide span of control, whether a company wants it or not, because it cannot bring in enough qualified managers.

CENTRALIZATION OF DECISION MAKING

If a management group has no experience with taking a company through a high-growth situation, it will probably be a very nervous group, because it does not know how to handle the flood of incoming orders or the monstrous amount of overtime being worked by the materials management, production, and distribution staffs in order to complete all orders and get them to customers. When an inexperienced management team finds itself in this position, it tends to centralize all major decisions, because this gives it tighter control over a situation that it does not know how to handle. This section discusses the opposing impacts of centralizing and loosening management's level of decision making in a fast-growth environment.

When a management team centralizes decision making, it makes itself the primary bottleneck for all activity. For example, if a high-growth company finds that its production line requires an extra drill press to ensure that products are completed on time, this decision must wait for the next executive committee meeting for management approval. Similarly, the decision to purchase an additional computer for the engineering staff must also wait for the same committee meeting. The management group will be flooded with decisions of this magnitude, under which it will become buried, not giving it time to address more strategic decisions or to even figure out which issues are tactical and which are strategic. When this situation happens, a company rapidly loses its focus on fast growth and collapses into its old, plodding ways. The management team may even heave a collective sigh of relief and congratulate itself on having survived a scary surge of growth. What really happened was that the management team's unwillingness to shift some decision making down into the organization crippled its ability to grow, but management will never know how far the company could have gone, because it immediately stepped off the growth track.

Now review the same examples, but assume that the management team has pushed some management authority down into the employee ranks. The production and engineering supervisors are both given authority to spend up to $5,000 without prior approval, which means that the production line will gain a new drill press with little time delay, while an engineer can buy a new computer at lunch time and have it operational by the end of the day. The management team has lost a small amount of control over its cash flow, but not enough to have a serious impact on the company. At the same time, it has eliminated many minor decisions that clogged its strategic view of the company and interfered with its key management purpose, which is overseeing the continual transitions (see the Transition Management section) that feed corporate growth. Pushing decisions down into the organization helps management focus on only those issues that deserve its attention.

Although it is very useful to distribute decision making down into the lower levels of a company, this cannot be done overnight. Employees are not used to the extra responsibility, nor do they know how to use it. Furthermore, they will be nervous when using it, and so will consult with management before making any decisions. This does nothing to reduce the work thrust upon the management team. To bypass this problem, management must gradually roll out the concept of decentralized decision making through the organization, with lots of hand holding. Once employees see that management supports their decisions, the process becomes much easier. However, it can take months for the concept to penetrate through layers of employee uncertainty and distrust, so decentralizing decision making is a concept that the management team cannot expect to implement overnight.

COMMUNICATION CHANNELS

If a company chooses to decentralize decision making by handing off much of it to employees, as noted in the previous section, the people who are going to make decisions must have enough information to do so. This section discusses how to use various communication channels to force information down into the organization.

Giving decision-making power to employees will only work if the employees have enough information to make the correct decisions. For example, if an employee is empowered to purchase anything needed to keep operations running, it is helpful for the employee to know how much money is in the budget before buying it. If an employee wants to extend credit to a new customer, it is useful to know that customer's credit record. Finally, if an employee wants to purchase a cheaper part for a product, it is helpful to know what the design tolerances should be for that part. These types of information are not commonly disseminated to employees, so management must make these kinds of decisions. By shifting information to the employees, such as (to use the examples) budget data, credit information, and engineering specifications, management finds that decentralized decision making results in much better decisions.

The common concern for management is that it does not want to distribute high-level, "secret" information to the staff, because this information will find its way into the hands of competitors. This reasoning is used as an excuse for not giving quite a bit of lower-level information to employees. Management must realize, however, that overall corporate strategy is *not* the information that employees need to make the vast majority of their decisions. To use the previous examples, employees simply need access to low-level information to make most operational decisions; they need credit reports, department-level budgets, and part specifications. If management thinks that this information must remain secret, it is time for some group paranoia discussions. Management does not necessarily have to reveal high-level strategic information to all employees, because most of them neither need to know about it or even care to; they simply need access to the specific information that allows them to make informed decisions in a decentralized decision-making environment.

Transferring information to employees is not a single communications project, but rather many small projects, because no company contains all of its information in one database, where everyone can easily access it. On the contrary, it is clustered in untidy heaps throughout a company, sometimes in digital format and sometimes on paper. If management truly wants to force decision making down into the employee ranks, it must alter the communications channels so that supporting information reaches the people who are expected to make decisions. Sending supporting information to employees may require a major restructuring of a company's information systems, so that it is no longer clustered in those untidy heaps; this approach assumes that the company must "push" information to the person making the decision. An easier approach to implement is one where the company assumes that managers can pull the information from its present location, which requires no restructuring of the current stores of information at all. To use the same examples, an employee must know how much money is in the budget before buying something. To give this person the correct budget information, management can go through the painful process of passing out the budget to everyone in the company and explaining it, or simply installing it on a company network, so that it is available to anyone who wants to access it. If employees have questions about budget numbers, they can ask the budgeting analyst in the accounting department. Alternatively, if an employee needs to find credit information for a new customer, management can simply give the employee a one-page procedure for calling a credit service and requesting the information. Likewise, it is not necessary to push engineering specifications onto employees by giving them dozens of volumes of parts specifications, all of which must be constantly updated. The information can just be kept in a central location for easy access, where it can also be easily updated.

Management may go to great lengths to make new information accessible to employees, and then find that decisions are still not being made or are not being made correctly, probably because employees are not using the information available to them. There are a number of reasons for this situation. One is that new employees are not given training in how to find information. Another is that old-timer employees are used to doing things the old way and have no interest in making decisions or finding the information to support those decisions. Finally, the information may be more difficult to reach than management believes, resulting in employees ignoring communication channels to find or receive information. A key ongoing task for management, then, is to constantly review the flow of information through the organization to verify that it is being used. This task is not easy, because employees may not want to admit that the communications system does not work. One way to find problems is to issue a generic survey that does not identify the person filling it out, which makes employees feel more free to give vent to any concerns. Another is to have the internal audit staff investigate the usage of some information sources; for example, the number of credit report requests received by the credit reporting agency. Armed with this information, management can continually monitor and improve communication channels throughout the company, so that employees have access to sufficient information to make quality decisions.

PLANNING AND BUDGETING

The previous sections of this chapter advocate that a company decentralize a large part of its decision making and distribute more information to help people make those decisions. This change also means that the people who are now in the best position to make informed decisions about projected expenses, which is a large part of the budgeting process, are the employees who routinely use budgeting information every day. Although this does not mean that top management can post a blank budget form on a company's intranet and expect employees to fill in the blanks, it does mean that managers should consult with their subordinates before completing their portions of the budget. This policy is not because management has any particular need to "empower" employees (one of the more overused and suspect words in the business vocabulary), but rather because the employees are the ones who are now routinely using budget information and who know if projected budget numbers are accurate. Soliciting employee input results in a better budget.

Although employee input is useful for expense line items in the budget, it has no place in devising strategy. The reason is that, in an explosive growth environment, there is no time to solicit employee opinions regarding the direction in which the company is proceeding. When key strategic decisions must be made every week, there is no place for a town hall type meeting with employees, especially when there may be thousands of them. Instead, top management must make decisions regarding strategy, while employees provide input in some areas of the budget that, in turn, is designed to support the strategy.

In short, employees can help to create budgets at the operational level, because they have the most knowledge of operations if management is giving them enough decision-making authority, but strategy still resides with management.

MEASURING THE CORPORATION

How does the management team measure a company's performance? It can divide measurements into two categories: those that cover key daily operational information and those that measure the company's transition performance.

As is noted in Chapter 12, an explosive growth company should install an executive information system (EIS) that gives management ready access to all key information variables. The EIS has links to many key company databases, and extracts just the key information that management needs to determine the financial and operational health of the organization, such as sales backlogs, overdue accounts receivable, and bank balances. The EIS then compiles this information into a single database for easy access and review by management. A number of measures that can be included in an EIS are noted in the chapters in the second part of this book that cover specific functional areas. The EIS is the primary source of measurement results for management.

In addition to the EIS, management needs to know how well it is performing in its key area, transition management. If a company cannot continually add to its list of new products, sales territories, or acquired companies, then it ceases to grow. The following list of measurements is useful for determining management's ability to continually transition a company into more growth opportunities:

- *Average time from design initiation to product introduction.* Management must drive the pace at which new products are introduced to the marketplace. You may think that the timing of a new product introduction depends solely on technology, but it is really management driven, because technology problems can usually be sidestepped in favor of older components or processes that result in a less nifty new product, but one that at least reaches the market when expected. Management can calculate this measurement by subtracting the production introduction date from the date when a product first entered the design stage.
- *Number of products launched per period.* Management must launch a preset number of products if it is to maintain growth through new product sales. If so, it is very simple to add up the number of new products added each period. However, this total can be confused by additions of product options.
- *Time to absorb acquisitions.* The most important measurement when growing through acquisitions is the time needed to absorb each new subsidiary, because an acquired company is not of much use, and may be bleeding off cash, if it is left in a state of turmoil. There is a variety of subjective ways to measure this; however, an easy quantitative approach is to determine the time from the date of acquisition to the date when the acquired company's sales growth rate turns positive. This figure may be subject to some skewing for seasonality or by the receipt of a very large order, but it is a good indicator of acquisition absorption. A more qualitative measure is when the acquired company implements a new organizational structure, although this restructuring may hide a great deal of organizational turbulence.
- *Volume of sales acquired per year.* Management must acquire a specific number of companies if it is growing through acquisitions and wants to reach a specific consolidated sales goal. If so, it is an easy matter to derive the target sales figure for the end of the reporting period and then subtract out the sales volume already acquired, thereby leaving the amount still to be gained through acquisitions in the current period.

In short, management needs an EIS to tell it how well the company is performing in all operational areas, while it must also track a set of measurements that reveal its performance in driving the company through a variety of transitions that are critical to its growth rate.

SUMMARY

This chapter covered several key areas for managers in an explosive growth environment. The most crucial issue is transition management, which is an orderly approach for continuing fast growth. Next is the need for highly qualified managers in the top management positions, as well as selected mid-level positions where the growth effort is focused. The type of growth may also have an impact on a company's span of control, although this does not necessarily vary due to the rate of growth. The chapter also covered how excessive centralization of management decision making acts as a bottleneck on further growth. Management can help to eliminate bottlenecks by disseminating volumes of the most important operating information to the organization, which can use it to make many decisions without further review by management. This information must also be used by the explosive growth organization for planning and budgeting, which tends to be more diffused than in a traditional organization. Finally, the chapter covered a set of measurements for tracking the effectiveness of a management team's transition efforts. Taken together, the sections of this chapter give the reader a clear understanding of the key issues faced by the management team of an explosive growth company.

Chapter 7

Ownership Issues

INTRODUCTION

Ultimately, it is the company owner who chooses to start a company on the explosive growth path. And this is a choice, for the owner can decide to avoid growth and keep a company small. Several reasons are noted in this chapter for avoiding the explosive growth path, many of which are quite reasonable for an owner. However, there are a number of good reasons for embarking on the growth path; these are also noted in this chapter. If the owner elects to go for growth, the chapter notes several key decisions that the owner must make. This chapter, then, addresses the key owner issues for an explosive growth company.

THE RISKS OF OWNERSHIP

Embarking on an explosive growth path presents a number of problems for the owner. Many times, the issues are so great that the owner backs down from the growth opportunity in favor of a lesser amount of growth, or just the status quo. In other cases, the owner goes ahead with the expansion, only to find far less pleasure in the enlarged corporation because of the attendant problems. Accordingly, an owner should review the following issues that are likely to arise in a growth situation and decide in advance if the opportunity is worth overcoming these challenges. The risks to the owner of rapid growth are as follows:

- *Less ownership.* A rapidly growing company requires a large amount of working capital. This money may come from increased borrowings or better management of working capital. However, there may come a time when the owner has no choice but to add equity to the company. If the owner has no capital available, it may be necessary to solicit equity contributions from other people, who then share ownership of the company. The owner may potentially lose control of the company.
- *Loss of business relationships.* An owner may have long-standing relationships with other businesses that cannot continue as the company grows, because the other businesses are too small to support the company. This experience can be wrenching when the owner has relationships with people in

those businesses that may go back one or more decades. For example, a company may have to drop its law firm, accounting firm, bank, and insurance agent in favor of larger companies with more expertise.

- *Loss of community support.* An owner who has supported the community for years may find that the realities of having a growing business include such factors as moving facilities away from the community or firing long-term employees who are no longer needed at the company. Such actions may turn community opinion against the company, and therefore against its owner.
- *Loss of family atmosphere.* Many owners treat their employees like extended members of their own families, which may include special gatherings, gifts, and other perks. When the owner installs a professional management team that is tightly focused on growth, this family atmosphere will probably come to an abrupt end. This change may also lead to the departure of some long-term employees who are not used to the new, more businesslike environment.
- *Loss of family positions.* An owner frequently has family members working in the company. When the owner transfers the company to a professional management team, however, they are likely to demote these people into less responsible positions so that highly qualified personnel can be brought in to help the company's growth plan. The family members may leave in frustration, and they will complain to the owner. The owner must be willing to deal with this issue, which can be especially difficult if other family members exert additional influence because they also own stock in the company.
- *Loss of friends in the company.* A common occurrence is for a newly hired management team to review the capabilities of the existing staff and to replace or demote a number of long-time employees who do not have the expertise to help the company grow. These people may be friends of the owner, possibly for many years, and may blame the owner for their loss of jobs or status.
- *Loss of leadership position.* The company owner is also commonly the founder and has been its leader since its inception. Opting for an explosive growth strategy, however, frequently includes bringing in professional management, resulting in the owner stepping aside from the traditional leadership role. Although this is not always the case, the owner should consider in advance what it will be like to occupy a secondary role in daily management activities, and possibly no role at all.
- *Loss of owner perquisites.* Many owners treat their companies like personal banks that hand out largesse to themselves and their families, including loans to family members, family air travel, and exorbitant levels of pay. An owner may find that some of this largesse must be curtailed, partially because working capital needs may reduce the amount of available cash, and partially because it grates upon the professional management team that is now running the company.

- *Less sense of control.* Even if an owner deliberately sets up a number of control points that allow him or her to maintain control over company operations, it does not feel the same when day-to-day control passes over to a professional manager. Some owners cannot let go of the feeling that they are missing out on key operational decisions, and they end up second-guessing manager decisions and driving managers out. This problem particularly affects micromanager types who cannot content themselves with an occasional review of the strategic plan and monthly financial reports.
- *More leverage.* If a growing company needs to add working capital to support its rate of growth, a standard source of cash is debt. For a growing company, it is not uncommon to have debt that exceeds the amount of equity by several times. This much debt is a major problem if the company finds that it does not have enough cash flow to pay the interest on the debt, resulting in action by the lender to repossess and liquidate assets. If matters reach this stage, the owner may find that the company very suddenly faces complete liquidation.

In short, there are many reasons why an owner does not want to take a company through the turmoil of explosive growth. The reasons mostly fall into two categories. One is financial risk; the owner may lose the entire organization if it becomes highly leveraged or requires so much extra capital that the owner is pushed out. The second, and frequently more important area, is social; the owner may lose status within the organization, or lose contacts with family members, the community, or friends within the company who feel betrayed by the changes that have occurred. These are the principal reasons why owners have second thoughts about launching their companies on the explosive growth path.

THE BENEFITS OF OWNING AN EXPLOSIVE GROWTH COMPANY

There are several major advantages to owning an explosive growth company, and an owner should balance them against the risks noted in the previous section. In brief, the advantages are power and wealth. This section describes the benefits in more detail.

The primary ownership benefit is a potentially vast increase in personal wealth. If managed properly, the profits of an explosive growth company can grow at the same rate as revenues, or even exceed it. The problem for the owner is that, as long as a company is in its high growth mode, it will suck up so much cash that the owner cannot extract any cash. Instead, the owner finds that the value of his or her shares goes up a great deal but that there is no way to realize any benefit from this increase without selling some of the shares, either through a private placement or a public offering. Thus, the owner is in the difficult position of not being able to use newfound wealth that may stretch into the hundreds of millions of dollars, without selling all or some of the company. When faced with this much money, a fair proportion of owners find the trade-off to be easy, and sell out. Others want to hold on in hopes of even further gains, so they retain their ownership interests for a longer period without any immediate prospect of added personal cash flow. Some owners take a part-way approach by selling portions of the business as it grows, thereby realizing some gain while still retaining an ownership interest. Thus, rapid growth creates wealth, but cashing in frequently involves selling part or all of the company.

Cashing in on the company's growth may involve an initial public offering (IPO). If the owner decides to take this route, as opposed to a private stock placement, it requires a significant amount of company resources to complete all of the attendant regulatory requirements, which can even interfere with the rate of growth. This issue is addressed more fully in Chapter 16.

Along with great wealth comes power. The owner of an explosive growth company has great power in the community, for several reasons. One is that the company becomes a large employer, and therefore has considerable control over the lives of much of the community. It also means that there may be a number of local firms that depend on the company, either directly or indirectly, for a portion of their revenue. In addition, the owner has great influence over the company's contributions to the community. These may take the form of grants to local civic activities, or they may be a donation of employee time to local activities. Owners have also been known to use their wealth as springboards into regional or national politics. Consequently, the prospect of considerable power is a strong motivator for a company owner.

In short, an owner can possibly be placed in a position of great wealth and power as a result of successfully forcing a company through a period of explosive growth. However, an owner should always compare these benefits to the problems that go along with growth. The road to success is littered with the carcasses of companies that did not reach their goals, resulting in the total loss of their owners' investments.

THE OWNER'S PRIMARY DECISIONS

Once an owner decides to change company strategy in favor of fast growth, there are several key decisions to make, which are outlined in this section. These are all high-level decisions, for it is assumed that the management team that the owner brings in will handle all lower-level details. These decisions focus on bringing the right people in to run the organization, determining the level of risk that the owner is comfortable with, and determining the amount of control that the owner must have in order to feel that the company is being directed down the path that the owner wants.

The first decision the owner must make is the level of financial risk that is acceptable. This decision even comes before the decision to bring in professional managers, for the level of risk drives the speed of growth, which determines the types of managers the owner should hire. For example, a modest amount of budgeting work will reveal that, to rapidly grow a company, the owner needs money to fund increased working capital requirements. If the owner is not willing to relinquish control by accepting equity from elsewhere, then this money must come from debt. If the owner is only willing to accept the risk of a certain debt/equity ratio, then he or she must calculate the growth that can be generated with that amount of debt, and then make the remaining decisions based on that maximum level of growth. This issue is critical, for an owner may hire a superstar manager to push for astronomical growth, but then decide to severely restrict the sources of new debt and equity because of financial risk, thereby immediately curtailing the means to grow; this situation usually results in the loss of the manager, who becomes frustrated with these restrictions.

In addition to the financial risk issue is the problem of giving up a stake in the company in exchange for more equity. This alternative to debt is safe, because there is no obligation to repay and no formal interest payment. However, the owner must decide in advance if it is acceptable to sell some of the company and possibly give up majority control. If not, then the only option is to increase the financial risk by acquiring more debt, as previously discussed. Thus, the issues of giving up a stake in the company and acquiring additional debt are inextricably intertwined.

Once the owner has determined the tolerable amount of financial risk and loss of control over equity, it is time to hire a management team. Chapter 6 describes the characteristics of the ideal managers for a growth situation, which is a major consideration for the owner. However, the owner must also pick someone with whom he or she is comfortable in having a long-standing relationship. This is very important, for the manager may perform with uncertainty if it appears as though the owner's support is weak, and the owner will second-guess the manager and otherwise interfere in company affairs if there is not a sufficient degree of trust by the owner. In addition, the manager should have a good track record for preserving assets. An owner does not want someone who treats the company as a large gamble that can be thrown at new opportunities with no regard for the risk of loss; the owner must feel that each manager will treat the company as his or her own company, which reduces the chance of irresponsible behavior. These elements, as well as the characteristics noted in Chapter 6, are key factors for the owner to consider when hiring the top management team.

Once the management team is in place, the owner should become deeply involved at the strategic level, especially when the company is just starting out on the growth path and is probably adopting several new approaches to achieve that growth. It is very appropriate for the owner to become involved in strategy, especially early on, because the new managers may have been recruited from outside the industry and do not have sufficient industry knowledge, whereas the owner has enough special knowledge to be of valuable assistance in determining the right strategy. In addition, the owner can tie his or her previous financial risk decisions to the appropriate strategy direction. For example, if a high degree of leverage as well as loss of equity control is not acceptable, then the strategic plan should probably exclude any mention of growth through acquisitions, because this requires payment in cash or stock. Thus, the owner should become involved in the strategic direction of the company, especially at the beginning of the growth phase.

Once the company begins to use its new strategy to grow, the owner should not do several things. These include micromanaging the new top management team, who will find themselves buried with enough work without having to respond to all of the owner demands. In addition, the owner should not second-guess the management team, unless the issue is one that may result in major problems. Otherwise, the management team will not feel that it is allowed to control company direction; employees may also feel that managers have no power, so they may find it acceptable to go around the management group and take their problems straight to the owner. Finally, the owner should not single-handedly alter the strategy and require the management team to immediately shift the company into the new direction. Doing so just makes the managers feel like hired lackeys who have no real control over operations or direction and will probably result in the eventual departure of the managers. Because these issues interfere with the proper running of the company by management, the owner should avoid them.

However, the owner may feel that these constraints do not allow any activity in company operations at all, which can be quite frustrating for someone who probably ran the company for years. Not to worry! There are several perfectly acceptable company activities for the owner to engage in that do not interfere with management. They are as follows:

- *Audit committee.* This committee is composed of board members, who determine the schedule of the internal audit function; it also hires and receives the final report of the company's external auditors. This committee exerts considerable control over the company's key controls over assets and can mitigate the risk of loss by that means.
- *Board of directors.* The owner normally occupies at least one board seat, with other family members sometimes occupying additional seats. This group usually approves major decisions, such as the annual budget or any large capital expenditures or corporate acquisitions, thereby exerting considerable influence over company direction. It can also hire and fire the chief executive officer (CEO).
- *Executive compensation and search committees.* The owner can be on the committee of board members that determines pay for each member of top management, as well as the committee that searches for new top managers to fill vacant positions. Both committees exert a powerful influence over corporate direction.
- *Strategic planning committee.* The top management team typically forms a strategic planning committee to create and maintain a strategic plan. The owner

can become a permanent member of this group. It is especially important for the owner to become involved when the company *changes* its strategic direction, because then the owner is at most risk of losing some portion of his or her investment in the company, if the new strategic direction fails.

In short, the owner should determine the degree of acceptable financial and ownership risk and then hire a management team and work with it to create a strategic direction. The owner should subsequently avoid active interference in management affairs, but can still control the direction of the company through various high-level committees and the board of directors.

SUMMARY

This chapter dealt with the problems, opportunities, and key decisions faced by the owner of an explosive growth company. Key among the problem areas are the vastly increased risks of a growth situation. The owner stands a good chance of at least losing some ownership interest in the company, and may lose the entire company if it botches its expansion plans. Also, it may be difficult for the owner to leave the collegial atmosphere of a small company, getting rid of long-term employees, in favor of a larger, more professionally run organization. Against these risks are the exceptional benefits of much greater wealth, and the opportunity to own an organization that can have a significant impact on the community, either through increased employment or by civic contributions or activities. In order to launch a company onto a growth path, the owner must make a few key decisions. These include selecting the appropriate management team, the appropriate degree of leverage (and therefore the amount of growth), and also the means by which the owner wishes to maintain control over the organization. Only by correctly making these decisions can a company owner set his or her company on the path to explosive growth.

Chapter 8

Outsourcing

INTRODUCTION

One of the best ways to add capacity during explosive growth is to outsource functions to suppliers who already have the excess capacity to assist the company. Simply stated, outsourcing involves handing over a company's operations to a supplier, who uses either the company's or its own facilities and staff to run the function. This is an effective way to rapidly acquire a distribution network and manufacturing capacity, as well as a broad range of administrative activities. This chapter describes the advantages and disadvantages of using outsourcing, as well as the specifics of how to find, set up, and maintain outsourcing relationships in the key areas of distribution, production, and sales. A final section covers the outsourcing of other functional areas. This chapter gives the reader a broad overview of the major outsourcing issues and how to enter into outsourcing arrangements in key areas.

ADVANTAGES

A growing company is well advised to look at the advantages of outsourcing at the beginning of its growth path, for bringing in a strong outsourcing supplier can strongly complement a company's own strengths while eliminating its weaknesses. Outsourcing has the following points to recommend it:

- *Avoids major investments.* As is pointed out repeatedly throughout this book, an explosive growth company has little cash available, because it is constantly investing every penny in more growth-related activities. It can use outsourcing in such capital intensive areas as distribution and production to avoid investing in its own equipment and facilities in these areas, which can strip millions of dollars out of a growing company's capital budget.
- *Better management.* An explosive growth company typically is scrambling to attract top managerial talent to run all of its functions. It is rarely possible to bring in the best managers for all areas, because they are very expensive to obtain, as well as because candidates' perceived level of risk in going to the company is probably quite high (since many explosive growth companies fail). By outsourcing major functions, a company can reduce its need for top man-

agement talent in all areas, although it must still have capable people in-house who can manage supplier activities.

- *Enhances credibility.* An explosive growth company can enhance its image with its customers if it can bring in a strong partner to run some of its functional areas. For example, a customer that sees UPS or FedEx running a growing company's distribution system will have no concerns about that company's ability to deliver products. Similarly, having a large Japanese computer manufacturer produce all of a company's computers under a private label deal will settle any customer concerns about product quality.
- *Focuses on core functions.* A growing company usually starts with a small area of core competency, such as engineering. As it grows, it must acquire new skills in order to produce, distribute, and sell its products over an ever-wider area. If the company does not have these additional skills, it will not prosper. Instead, it can hand over these weaker functions to suppliers, and turn back to a tight focus on its core competency, which it can continue to strengthen, giving it a competitive advantage.
- *Handles overflow.* A growing company may want to keep all of its functional areas in-house, and may have the management to adequately run them. However, because it is growing so fast, there will be times when the workload exceeds the company's ability to handle it. In these cases, a company can call in a supplier to take on the extra work. A common example of this is an inbound call center that takes customer calls on behalf of a company when the company's own call center is overwhelmed with calls.
- *Improves performance.* A supplier sells its services in the outsourcing arena because it can do a better job of managing a function than can its customers, especially in highly specialized areas, such as computer services or equipment maintenance, where the supplier has a large corps of experts on staff who are well-trained in solving any problem a company may have.
- *New skills.* A growing company may find that the skill set of its employees in a specific area is not adequate to bring that area up to a new standard of performance. This problem is particularly common in the computer services area, where the in-house staff is trained to support existing systems, not to replace them with better hardware and software that can run circles around the older systems. In such cases, management can bring in a supplier to install new systems while the existing staff maintains the old ones, and then the supplier trains the old staff in how to use the replacement systems.

Clearly, there are decided advantages to using outsourcing in an explosive growth environment. It reduces a company's cash requirements, introduces new managerial and technical skills, allows the company to handle overflow situations, and lets it concentrate on a few core areas of competency. However, these advantages must be balanced against the downside of outsourcing before making a decision; these disadvantages are covered in the next section.

DISADVANTAGES

Before handing over a large part of a company's operations to a supplier, it is useful to peruse the disadvantages noted in this section. If the advantages outweigh these concerns, then go ahead with the outsourcing. The disadvantages of outsourcing are as follows:

- *High cost.* Despite what suppliers may say in their promotional materials, it is unlikely that they can lower a company's costs in any functional area, unless the company is replacing a remarkably inefficient function. The reason for the higher cost is that the supplier must add a profit margin as well as sales and marketing costs to its fees; these are costs that an internal department does not include in its cost structure. In other respects, the internal staff should be able to complete tasks with at least the same efficiency as the supplier's staff, because it has a better knowledge of how the company operates. The only case where a supplier can truly charge lower prices is when it can take advantage of economies of scale. For example, a supplier can run a company's software on a portion of a mainframe computer located in a large computer processing facility that administers to the needs of many client companies; this setup is cheaper than having the supplier administer a large number of smaller, separate computer facilities at each client site. With this exception, there is usually no cost advantage to using a supplier for outsourcing.
- *Losses during transition.* There is a great deal of employee turmoil when a company switches a function over to a supplier, because some of the staff will be let go and then hired by the supplier. These employees have no idea of how the supplier manages its staff, and may expect pay cuts, fewer benefits, more travel, and longer hours. Even if this is not the case, there will be rumors and false expectations. When this happens, key employees may leave for positions that they perceive to be safer. This reduces the number of knowledgeable and skilled employees that the supplier may have been relying on to assist in running the company's functions, which reduces the supplier's effectiveness in taking over the function.
- *Supplier does not meet expectations.* Despite the best possible efforts at screening candidates, a company may still find that it has selected a supplier that is inadequate for any number of reasons—management conflicts, poor service, or continual contractual disagreements are common problems. When this happens, it can be both costly and time consuming to break free from the supplier. The time and cost involved may have a profound impact on a company's ability to continue to expand.
- *Supplier's situation changes.* A supplier may perform its functions for the company very well, but the supplier's management may decide that it will now get out of the outsourcing business, perhaps due to profitability problems or because the supplier has been acquired by a company that has no

interest in outsourcing. Whatever the reason, this leaves a company in an exposed position, because it has little time to either bring the function back in house or find a new supplier and transition the work over to it.

In short, the disadvantages of using outsourcing include the possible loss of personnel during the transition to the supplier, high transaction and fixed costs, and problems with the supplier that result in inferior service. If there is a significant chance that any of these issues will arise, management may need to reconsider any decision to enter into an outsourcing agreement with a supplier.

OUTSOURCING DISTRIBUTION

A growing company can use outsourcing to enhance its capabilities in many parts of the distribution function. Examples of areas that can be outsourced are logistics management, freight hauling, freight brokering, and audits of freight billings. By using logistics management, a company essentially hands over the entire function to a supplier, whereas the other areas involve subsets of the distribution function. This section briefly covers the advantages and disadvantages of using outsourcing in the distribution area, as well as a few major contractual issues, controls, and measurements.

The main factor favoring outsourcing of distribution is eliminating any investment in equipment and facilities. By using someone else's tractors, trailers, and warehouses, a growing company can avoid any significant investment in this area. Also, by using freight brokers or logistics management services, a company can avoid a significant quantity of logistics paperwork that would otherwise require a major amount of clerical and management attention. Offsetting these factors is a lack of responsiveness by freight haulers in comparison to an in-house fleet—they cannot deliver products on the exact schedule that a company is used to when it has its own fleet, so the company must change its deliveries to match the schedules of its haulers. However, the advantages of outsourcing clearly outweigh the loss of convenience.

There are several contractual issues to be aware of when dealing with distribution suppliers. One is that when obtaining space in a supplier-owned warehouse, it is not normally a good idea to obtain long-term storage commitments, even at very low rates. Especially if the company is rapidly growing, it may find that its distribution strategies may change so suddenly that it no longer needs the space, but must still pay for the long-term commitment. It is also important to negotiate a cost per mile for full and partial loads when entering into a long-term agreement with a freight hauler. Otherwise, the supplier will attempt to charge special rates for every freight haul, resulting in a mix of fees that are likely to be higher than a straight cost-per-mile charge would have been. Also, because there is a risk of damage to inventory at warehouses and during shipment, it is important to require insurance coverage by all distribution suppliers, so that the company can be reimbursed for any damage. The company should also require a specific reimbursement percentage for freight auditors, so that there is no issue regarding their compensation for negotiating reductions in freight billings on behalf of the company. Finally, the company must have a break-out clause in any contract with any of the suppliers noted in this section; if the supplier cannot perform at a predefined level, the company must have the option to terminate the relationship with no penalty clauses. These are some of the more important contract clauses to consider when entering into outsourcing agreements with distribution suppliers.

It is not sufficient to bring in suppliers and then let them run a portion of the company with no management control. The key control over any of these suppliers is to have a qualified team inside the company that is responsible for the operations of the suppliers. This group should be headed by an experienced distribution manager. The team should monitor the flow of materials and finished products, the performance of each supplier, and compare the prices charged by suppliers to the contractual rates. The team should also conduct periodic reviews of supplier facilities, where applicable, such as for fire suppression systems at supplier warehouses to ensure that there is a minimal risk of damage to company-owned goods. Also, the team should negotiate for reimbursement for any company products that were damaged while under the control of a supplier. Only by retaining an in-house distribution team can a company exercise proper control over its distribution suppliers.

A company can use a wide array of measurements to determine the performance of its distribution suppliers. For freight auditors, the best one is the cost per dollar collected, because it tells the company how much it is losing in audit charges in order to obtain reimbursements on freight billings. This measurement can be supplemented by tracking the total reimbursement obtained per $1,000 of freight billings reviewed, because this figure reveals the ability of the freight auditor to extract the largest possible refund from freight companies. For a freight hauler, the primary measurement is the rate charged per mile for full loads and partial loads; however, this measurement must be supplemented by an additional review of supplier performance and picking up and delivering loads in a timely manner, as well as its record for damage to shipments. Finally, the primary measurement for a warehouse is the price it charges per square foot of storage space occupied. A warehouse frequently adds a number of small additional fees; it is best to aggregate them all into a single monthly cost and divide this figure by the amount of storage space used to derive the measure. These are the most common and effective measures used for tracking the performance of distribution suppliers.

Outsourcing the distribution area is an option well worth the effort, because it allows a company to avoid a large investment in facilities and equipment. However, it is important to exercise sufficient control over distribution suppliers to ensure that they are supporting other company operations, and that they are doing so in a cost-effective manner.

OUTSOURCING PRODUCTION

This section describes the advantages and disadvantages of outsourcing production, key contractual issues to consider, and the controls and measures needed to ensure that the supplier is properly supporting company operations.

A company can either outsource all of its production to a supplier, do so just for some key components (as most car manufacturers do), or have them just complete the final assembly at various distribution points. All these options are increasingly common, and depend largely on the availability of quality suppliers who are capable of producing to a company's exacting specifications.

The advantage of using a supplier for production is that a growing company can avoid the sometimes massive expense of building production facilities (especially in the case of electronic chip fabrication facilities, which can cost over $1 billion each). For a growing company, this factor is crucial. Another factor is that having a supplier gives a company immediate extra capacity to build more products, although a company must realize that the supplier has other customers who also want a piece of that capacity for their needs. In addition, the best suppliers can produce at astronomically high quality levels that a company cannot hope to match without years of effort. A significant offsetting problem is that a supplier may charge high per-unit rates, but a company must balance this against the fixed costs that must no longer be incurred because the company needs no production facility. Also, a supplier may engage in illegal business practices, such as using child labor, that may have a negative publicity impact on the company. Finally, there may be no qualified suppliers available to meet a company's needs. Thus, only if a company can find a top-quality supplier with excess capacity, are there strong reasons in favor of outsourcing the production function to it.

When entering into a contract with a production supplier, a company should work on reducing the required minimum purchase amount per year that the supplier will want, because this gives the company some protection in case its sales falter (hopefully not an issue for an explosive growth company). Also, the company must pay attention to up-front fees that the supplier charges to cover the cost of tooling changes and molds; it may be possible to spread these costs over an extended time period, thereby allowing the company to conserve some cash. Finally, there must be a clause that allows the company to unilaterally terminate the agreement if the supplier cannot produce contracted quantities on time or at predefined quality levels; otherwise, a company will have a function that gives suboptimal results. These are the minimum contractual issues to consider when dealing with a production supplier.

It is very important to impose tight controls on a production supplier, because it is creating products that are labeled as a company's own, and customers will perceive any problems as being the company's fault. This control begins with a top-level production manager who is assisted by a strong staff of process engineers. These employees must constantly review supplier operations for quality and process issues that may impact the resulting products. Without this constant review, there is a strong chance that a supplier will falter in matching company objectives. Another way to impose a minimal level of control is to require a supplier to earn the International Organization for Standardization (ISO) 9001 certification, which ensures that a company is following a consistent set of procedures in its manufacturing and other processes. Because production is such a key area, a company must retain an experienced internal staff that can oversee supplier operations.

A company can use many measurements to see if its production supplier is performing at expected levels. A key determination is whether a supplier is shipping products on the expected date, which can be measured by comparing the shipping log to promise dates to derive a percentage of shipments that go out on time. It is also important to determine the number of manufacturing problems that are leading to customer returns. One approach is to measure the percentage of products that are returned; although some returns may be caused by engineering problems, another possible cause is incorrect manufacturing procedures. Finally, a company must know if a supplier has such a large backlog from its other customers that it cannot meet the company's production needs. The appropriate measure here is to track the size of the supplier's production backlog in terms of days or weeks to see if it conflicts with company needs. Although by no means all of the necessary measurements, these measures give a company a rough grasp of a production supplier's ability to produce quality goods on time.

On the whole, outsourcing production is a major opportunity for a growing company, because it can avoid a major investment. However, success is predicated on finding a quality supplier with sufficient capacity to meet a company's production needs.

OUTSOURCING SALES AND MARKETING

Many elements within the sales function can be outsourced. A growing company has especially good reasons for doing so. This section addresses the sales areas to outsource, the advantages and disadvantages of doing so, and a variety of associated contractual, control, and measurement issues.

Within sales and marketing, a company can outsource its public relations, advertising, direct mail, telemarketing, and direct sales. Separate industries are quite capable of servicing each of these areas most professionally. For example, a company can hire a specialist in public relations, which probably has better media contacts than the company and only pays it when there are specific public relations tasks to handle. Similarly, a company can hand off its advertising work to an agency that can create advertising copy and place it with the appropriate media. This brings a variety of creative expertise to a company that its in-house staff may not have. In addition, a direct mail supplier can handle all of a company's direct mail work, from reproducing mail to issuing mailings, much more efficiently than it could do itself. Finally, a company can use outside sales representatives who work on a commission-only basis to sell its products in areas that it otherwise could not afford to address. This situation also keeps a company's fixed costs low, because an outside salesperson receives no fee unless there is a sale. In short, a growing company can quickly build its brand image with the help of outside marketing suppliers and rapidly expand sales with the help of outside salespeople.

Several disadvantages go along with using an outside supplier for sales or marketing. One is the cost. These suppliers are specialists who provide a quality product, and they expect to be well paid for quality work. Also, outside salespeople have no company loyalty, so they may sell competing products during the same sales call. In addition, these salespeople require large commission percentages to offset the base salaries that they would receive if they were employees; extremely high commissions can have a major impact on margins. In short, the primary disadvantages of outsourcing sales and marketing are the cost and the lack of loyalty by sales personnel.

There are several contractual issues to consider when outsourcing sales functions. One is avoiding retainer payments. These are commonly charged by public relations and advertising companies. A growing company has little cash to spare for such up-front payments, so the contract should either eliminate or reduce the size of such payments. Also, the commission rate paid to outside salespeople is an obvious source of contention—too high and the sales staff loves the company but it makes no money, while a low commission generates no sales activity. This decision is a judgment call based on customary commission rates in the industry. Another contractual issue is the return of mailing lists from direct mail suppliers. Although rarely a problem, a company wants to be sure that its proprietary list of customers and prospects does not end up in the hands of a competitor. Also, salespeople may want exclusive territories. This arrangement is acceptable if they have the sales organization to support it, but a company must protect itself with a termination clause if it feels that it can achieve a higher sales level by stripping away a territory and awarding it to someone else. These are some of the key contractual issues a company faces when it outsources sales and marketing.

There are a variety of ways to control the sales function. One is to have a senior sales and marketing manager in-house who tracks supplier activity, approves advertising and public relations campaigns, meets with and reviews the performance of the sales staff, and reviews customer complaints related to sales. This person may be supported by a staff if the sales function is large enough. Other controls include reviewing the amount and type of sales by salesperson and reviewing supplier reports. The crucial control is having an in-house staff on hand to watch over supplier activities.

Part of the control function is measuring supplier performance and acting on any measurement results that are not acceptable. For direct mail, a good measure is determining the revenue gained per dollar of mailing costs, which shows a company's return on investment in this area. A good measure for an outside salesperson is the revenue per person or territory and the commission percentage paid. It is also useful to track the bad debt percentage on accounts receivable for each salesperson, because this reveals if a salesperson is selling to subpar customers. Finally, one should track the revenue gained per dollar of telemarketing expense, which shows a company's return on the outbound call activity. These measures are among the most common ways to track the performance of sales and marketing suppliers.

OUTSOURCING OTHER FUNCTIONAL AREAS

The prior sections of this chapter touched upon the special issues surrounding the three main functional areas that an explosive growth company should most strongly consider outsourcing: distribution, production, and sales. However, every company function can be outsourced, so it is worthwhile to explore the advantages and disadvantages of doing so in other areas. This section scans through the other functional areas of a typical company, describing the tasks that are most frequently outsourced, as well as some of the advantages and disadvantages of doing so. Janitorial and administrative outsourcing are not covered, because these are so commonly outsourced that there seems little point in describing them here.

Some portions of the accounting function can be outsourced. For example, Arthur Andersen has a contract services division that will take over an entire accounting staff. Or, a company can go partway by outsourcing just a few areas. For example, Ceridian and ADP can handle all payroll services, while RHI Management Resources and Arthur Andersen are happy to provide a contract controller or chief financial officer (CFO) to run the department. Any of the Big Six accounting firms are also available for reviewing and finalizing a company's monthly financial statements and accompanying notes. The advantage of using these services is that a company may want to eliminate an area that it is not doing a good job of managing, or because the area is so technically complex that it is easy to make a mistake (especially payroll taxes or financial statements). However, outsourcing these services typically raises a company's costs, not lowers them. Consequently, a company must balance the extra expertise of a supplier against the higher cost.

Internal auditing is a service that most external auditing firms are increasingly selling. They provide considerable expertise, because auditing is their business and they have the added advantage of the option to swap out different people based on the nature of each assignment, thereby closely matching skills to audits. They also only charge for services while they are conducting an audit, as opposed to an internal staff that must be paid no matter what they are doing. In addition, an auditing firm frequently has many offices, so it can assign local auditors to nearby company locations, which avoids the expense of sending a company's internal audit team to each one. However, external audit firms do not have the inside expertise needed to complete some audits, and they also have a large proportion of junior auditors who are not especially experienced. In addition, external auditors charge very high hourly rates. Finally, some companies use the internal audit function as a training ground for managers, because it gives a good overview of many company areas; by eliminating the function, a company loses its training facility. In short, a company must consider the many pros and cons of outsourcing its internal audit staff before shifting it to a supplier.

In the customer service area, it is becoming increasingly common to outsource inbound call handling. This outsource involves a call center that answers questions for customers, gives them the status of orders, or relays information to other parts of the company. The advantage of this outsourcing is that the suppliers of inbound call centers are experts at rapidly constructing and staffing large call centers on short notice; they are also very good at attracting, training, and retaining the multitudes of people needed to staff these centers. Most companies do not want to deal with the considerable management issues that accompany building and maintaining a call center, so they are willing to pay the higher fees that go along with having someone else manage this function for them.

Computer services are receiving the most attention in outsourcing, because the costs and attendant profits that go with an outsourcing contract are very large. Either the entire function can be outsourced, or just a few pieces. Areas subject to outsourcing are data center management, application development, network management, hardware servicing, and telephony support. There are several advantages to taking this route. One is that the supplier charges a variable rate per transaction, rather than a large fixed fee (although there is usually a minimum payment per period, so there is still a fixed fee); this method reduces a company's break-even point by reducing its fixed expenses. Another reason is that many companies do not have the technical expertise to manage or enhance their own systems, so they must call upon specialist suppliers to do so. Opposing these factors is the high cost of using a supplier, as well as the considerable amount of supplier management needed to ensure that a company receives a sufficient level of service at a respectable price. Finally, the terms of these outsourcing agreements can last up to 10 years; during that time, it is common for a company to fall out with its suppliers, so maintaining a high level of cordial relations for a long period can present a challenge. Although there are clearly some factors mitigating against the use of suppliers in computer services, it is becoming increasingly common for companies of all sizes to employ suppliers in at least a few areas.

The engineering function is not commonly outsourced, because many companies want this strategic function to be kept in-house. However, a number of companies are finding that they have only an infrequent need for certain types of engineering skills, so they can rely on suppliers to fulfill these needs, rather than hiring additional staff. Engineering suppliers are also useful when a company has a short-term overflow of projects for which it does not wish to hire extra staff. Finally, some companies only consider a small segment of the engineering function to be a core competency, and accordingly only staff that area; for example, a company may only be concerned about the electronic innards of a product, and it farms out the product design work to another company, as well as the engineering for building redesigns or production equipment layouts. Balanced against these benefits are the high hourly costs charged by suppliers. However, for most companies, it is cost effective to at least occasionally call upon the services of an engineering supplier.

Human resources frequently contains a few areas that are handled by a supplier. One is benefits administration. Many suppliers handle corporate life and medical insurance programs, as well as 401k and other pension plans. By grouping these programs together with those of many other companies, these suppliers can offer services that cost far less than what a company would incur if it were to do so internally. Recruiting firms can also fulfill a company's hiring needs, although the fees they charge can safely be described as outrageous. By moving some or all of these functions to suppliers, a company can reduce its human resources staff to a group of paper handlers and senior staff who deal with administering programs and planning for corporate personnel needs.

SUMMARY

This chapter presented a brief overview of the reasons why a growing company should consider outsourcing, as well as offsetting problems to be aware of before making such a decision. Elements of every corporate function can be outsourced. Not all of them are a good idea for an explosive growth company, but there are usually good reasons for bringing in suppliers to service at least a few areas. Foremost among the reasons in favor are that it allows a company to avoid a large investment in facilities and equipment while allowing it to focus on a small core group of key activities. These favorable points must be offset against the risks of a supplier performing poorly and of high costs. The chapter then touched upon a number of areas that a growing company will find to be especially tempting targets for outsourcing, due to the cost and amount of management time they require: distribution, production, and sales. The chapter then concluded with a very brief summarization of outsourcing opportunities in nearly every other functional area. Outsourcing is a prime alternative for a growing company looking for ways to expand more easily.

Chapter 9

Partnerships

INTRODUCTION

The concept of a partnership between companies has existed for many years and was refined by the Japanese, who formed *keiretsu*—groups of companies so closely intertwined that they could almost be considered a single entity. This type of linkage has become more common in the United States as companies have reduced the number of their suppliers. When a company finds that it depends on a small number of suppliers, it is inevitably necessary for it to draw closer to those suppliers, since its ability to deliver products and services is closely linked to their ability to deliver parts and services to the company. This situation leads to a number of advantages for all business partners, which is the primary focus of this chapter.

The chapter contains many brief discussions on the multitude of advantages to be derived from forming partnerships, followed by a brief description of the level of ethics required to make a partnership work and the general steps needed to form effective partnerships. The chapter concludes with a set of measurements useful for determining the success of a partnership. The intent of this chapter is to give the reader an overview of the many benefits of using partnerships, especially in an explosive growth environment.

IMPACT ON INTERCOMPANY RELATIONS

A typical company is used to having confrontational relations with its suppliers. This tradition stretches back many years, and includes dickering over every last cent of product cost, providing the customer with the minimum amount under the terms of the contract, late deliveries, long and detailed purchase contracts, and frequent lawsuits to settle any perceived failures in those contracts. This environment requires many purchasing agents to track supplier activities; lawyers to write up, review, and bicker about contracts; and legions of receiving personnel and accounting staff to ensure that the correct products have been received and that the company pays for only the exact amounts received. This section notes the drastic changes that can occur in these areas when a company switches to a long-term partnership.

A common step in a partnership is for companies on either or both sides to send employees to their counterparts' locations on a permanent basis. For example, Dell Computer maintains personnel at the Boeing offices in Seattle, not only to take orders for more computers, but also to receive comments from Boeing personnel about ways to improve its computers. By having someone who is empowered to handle most transactions on-site at all times, it is much easier for company personnel to communicate with their counterparts.

It is also less necessary for a company to use purchasing and sales staff to communicate product or service orders to each other, because they have dedicated on-site staff who can perform these functions. This staffing tends to reduce the level of confrontation (something for which many purchasing personnel are known). It also reduces the number of people through whom orders must flow, which favorably impacts several issues. One is time; because there are fewer people who handle transactions, they can be completed more rapidly. Another is errors; if fewer people touch a transaction, that is fewer people who can introduce errors, resulting in better deliveries to the customer.

All of this enhanced communication will only work if both parties are willing to accept and act on feedback from their counterparts. For example, in a nonpartnership situation, any problems can easily be blamed on the other company, even if the problems are internal. Once there is a partnership, however, the two organizations must work together to root out and eliminate problems. In this environment, one can no longer impose a blanket accusation on the other company to hide one's own flaws. If either member of a partnership is still in the habit of blaming the other company, the perennially blamed company will probably become frustrated and exit the relationship quickly.

Enhanced communications should include having each partner create a report card on the activities of the other partner (as described in the Measurements section). This evaluation gives each partner a periodic view of its performance in the eyes of its partner. If each partner is not willing to accept this information, especially if the results are poor, there will be no basis for working together to resolve the issues. Thus, judging each other's performance and working together to improve it is part of the partnership experience.

In summary, intercompany relations are greatly improved by placing employees at each other's locations, which can eliminate some sales and purchasing staff to streamline the flow of information. It is also important for both companies to report on the performance of their counterparts, and to take steps to improve any poor performance.

IMPACT ON CAPACITY

Capacity is a constant problem faced by growing companies, and it is the reason that is perhaps most appealing to them when contemplating a corporate partnership. A growing company can take advantage of the resources of its partners to provide customer services that would otherwise greatly exceed its capacity to do so. This section lists examples of capacity improvements in several areas.

It is common for companies to combine their efforts in research and development. If, for example, a growing company has invented a new miracle drug, but does not possess the resources to produce it in more than minute quantities, it can form a partnership with a large pharmaceuticals firm that has the production capabilities readily at hand to deliver large quantities of the drug to the market. The two companies then share the profits from the expanded sales.

Companies can also combine forces to cross-sell each other's products in their respective markets. Each company may have a specially tuned ability to sell to a specific group of customers, perhaps through catalog sales, retail outlets, or good customer contacts that cannot be duplicated by the other company without a great deal of work, so it is reasonable to sell in each other's markets in exchange for a share of the profits. This arrangement allows both companies to realize more sales volume without any additional investment in sales expenses.

Membership organizations can team with other companies to provide the services of those companies to their members. The membership organization is either paid by the other companies for this service, or takes a percentage of any payments made by members to the other companies. Thus, the members receive more services, the membership organization receives more money, and the other organizations gain access to a desirable target group.

In these examples, it becomes clear that a growing company can greatly increase its actual capacity in such widely diverse areas as production and sales by sharing its resources with those of its partners.

IMPACT ON COSTS

In a traditional product design environment, a company focuses attention on those costs it can manage internally. It shops around for the best prices on components made by its suppliers, and goes no further than picking the best price resulting from this procedure. This section describes a way to use the partnership concept to reduce these costs even further.

A major advantage when using a partner is that the company allows the partner to participate in the product design process, allowing the partner to look at the total product design and recommend changes that will allow it to supply a cheaper or more appropriate part. This is in contrast to the traditional method of simply telling a supplier what is needed, how many are required, and when to deliver them. By giving a supplier input into the design process, a new source of information about designing for lower costs is introduced. For example, an electric motor manufacturer may review a product design and realize that a slight change to the product will allow it to supply a less powerful (and cheaper) motor that delivers the same result listed in the product specifications. Because the company's design team does not have the same level of expertise in electric motors, it would never have come up with the same design change.

This joint development of new products is especially powerful when supplemented by target costing. This approach explores the range of product prices currently on the market and sets a target price before design work begins. Then the design team uses the target price to subtract out a target margin, thereby deriving a target cost. By dividing the total target cost into subsidiary target costs for product components, the team can work together to assemble a product that meets the company's requirements. Because partners have the best knowledge of those parts they supply, they not only understand why the company needs to reach a specific price level, but also why they must create a part that fits the target cost. Consequently, the partner is more likely to be of help in creating parts that meet the company's costing needs.

Besides the product development process, a company can also reduce the cost of incoming parts by sending engineering teams into partner facilities to assist them in reducing costs. This work usually centers on inventory reductions, shrinking machine setup times, altering the work flow into machine cells and subplants, and reviewing overhead for excessive costs. If this review works, the partner can take some of the savings as profit while still reducing part prices to the company, thereby reducing its costs, too.

In summary, product costs tend to decline when a company includes partners in the new product design process, since they have a better understanding of the costs and performance characteristics of the parts they supply. A company can also send its staff to partner locations to work on saving costs, in exchange for a share of the resulting savings.

IMPACT ON KNOWLEDGE

A growing company does not normally have a complete set of the finest minds in the country running each of its functional areas, unless it is astoundingly well financed, thereby allowing it to buy the necessary talent. Instead, it relies on a few highly paid and very knowledgeable people in key areas, for this is all it can afford. However, it is possible to expand upon this knowledge base through a partnership, since the best minds in both companies can swap information on designs, processes, procedures, and other techniques that help a company to run better. By trading these best practices among themselves, a group of partners can gain a significant competitive advantage in the marketplace.

One of the best examples of knowledge sharing is the Chrysler Corporation, which has constructed a billion dollar automobile design center in which it brings together many of its closest parts suppliers to assist it in the design of new automobiles. The company is now well known for its advanced design concepts and high profitability.

Partnerships are especially important for a growing company that probably only has a very small core of highly knowledgeable people. Because these people can only attend to small parts of the company, the large number of remaining areas would benefit greatly from any expertise they can gain from a partner. Thus, partnerships can have a very large impact on the knowledge base of a growing company.

IMPACT ON FINANCIAL RISK

Some business projects require so much funding that it is far too risky for one company to invest billions of dollars in them and run the risk of failing because the projects do not become profitable. This problem is especially common for a small company, because its definition of a large investment may be only a few hundred thousand dollars. In these cases, it is wise to form a partnership with one or more companies, each of which contributes to the project. The partners determine how any profits will be split, and each will take a loss up to the amount of its investment in the event of project failure. This major advantage of partnerships will become increasingly common as high technology solutions require enormous investments. A good example of a partnership designed to reduce financial risk is the large number of partnerships now being formed or already in place to build competing satellite networks designed to transmit calls from telephones anywhere on the planet. Because the risk on these projects is high, due to the possibility of satellite launch failures and competition from the competing satellite networks, the best option has been to create a consortium of investors, each of which share in the eventual profits.

One of the problems for a growing company is that its resources are very limited and must be devoted to a single product or concept. If that product or concept fails, the company goes out of business. However, if it has technological expertise (possibly resulting in a valuable patent), the company has a good chance of forming a partnership with a richer company, in which the partner puts in the money while the company contributes nothing but its knowledge. Consequently, if the venture fails, the growing company will have only lost its investment in the research that led to the patent, which may leave the company with enough money to try again with a different concept.

IMPACT ON PLANNING

A company's planning process can change dramatically if it includes its partners in the process. This section discusses how partners can become involved in planning.

It is common for an explosive growth company to construct new facilities very frequently to keep up with the demands of its growing revenue base. If so, it should confer with its partners to see if they should cluster their facilities near those of the company, thereby shortening lines of communication and travel. It is useful to discuss the specific timing of such additions, as well as their configurations and precise locations, in case partners need to construct physical linkages between their buildings and the company's.

Another reason for including a partner in the planning process is to ensure that the company plans for the correct amount of inputs from the partner that the partner can actually supply. For example, a computer board assembly operation may budget for work in the upcoming year that includes an extra one million random access memory (RAM) chips. If it does not give this information to its partner, who makes RAM chips, the company may not know until it has already ramped up its assembly lines that there is a shortage of RAM chips, and that it is impossible to obtain so many in the upcoming year, no matter what the source may be. This example shows a good use of the partner's knowledge to derive a more accurate plan.

In addition to giving information on available input quantities, partners can also give excellent advice on input costs. They may have a better knowledge of upcoming price changes on underlying commodities that will alter the input costs paid by the company. This change may have a bearing on profit margins, which in turn has an impact on funding needs, which is a constant source of concern for a growing company.

In summary, it is common practice to include one's partners in the annual planning process. Doing so gives a company extra information about its inputs that may have an impact on its production plans and is also useful for giving a partner due warning regarding the need to construct additional facilities to service company needs.

IMPACT ON DESIGN TIME

As noted earlier in the section on the impact of partnerships on costs, a company frequently invites its partners into the product design process, which has a positive impact on product costs. As discussed in this section, this participation also has a very positive impact on design times.

The product design process is vastly hampered by the number of design iterations, as a design team completes initial drawings, sends them to suppliers, makes corrections based on their comments, and then reissues the designs for another round of critiques. It is possible to avoid many of these iterations by including partners on the design teams. By reviewing product designs early in the design process, partners can suggest changes to the overall design to eliminate many of the issues that would not normally have been discovered until months later, when the partners would normally have received information about part specifications. Thus, by putting partners in the front of the design process, a company can greatly shrink its overall design time.

This process can be enhanced by installing an electronic distribution system (or something less sophisticated, such as overnight mail) for delivering a complete set of product specifications to partners, along with any design updates. Many companies are unhappy about doing this, because it gives competitors the chance to intercept and copy secret information. However, because it also gives partners a chance to see and review designs on a continual basis, it also causes a sharp reduction in design time that outweighs the chance of losing valuable information to the competition.

One problem that engineering managers must be aware of is that including partners in the design process can add many extra people to the design team and raises lots of design questions early in the process, which seems to result in a large and unwieldy design group that initially does not seem to finish much design work. This situation requires a very experienced team leader to manage the group, one with the people skills to resolve any issues between the representatives of multiple organizations. Also, it is useful to split each design team into smaller groups who work on component parts of the overall design, with regular meetings to verify that all components fit into the overall design. This approach effectively reduces the size of the design team, making it easier to manage. The enlarged design team, including members from partners, is a much more challenging management task than the traditional design team, but there are ways to resolve the situation.

ETHICAL CONCERNS

Many companies say that they want to enter into partnerships, but then behave poorly to their newfound partners, which may take several forms, and which normally results in the rapid dissolution of the partnerships. This section discusses the ethics of dealing with partners.

Many companies are so used to the confrontational style of traditional dealings with suppliers that they have a hard time adjusting to the demands of a partnership, and accordingly treat partners in the same old manner. For example, a partner may work closely with a company to develop a new component that will be a major part of the company's newest product. When completed, the company then takes the new part design and shops it around among all possible suppliers for the lowest bid, rather than automatically giving the business to the partner who designed the part. It is a safe bet that this partner will not unnecessarily waste its time designing parts for this company in the future. One of the major American automobile manufacturers used to be well known for this practice. Exclusive dealing is part of the underlying reason for entering into a partnership agreement, and a company must abide by this rule.

Another common ethical problem is harassing a partner for all types of concessions on the grounds that there has not been a formal contract between the two parties. This thinking is confrontational, whereby negotiations continue until the moment when signatures are inked on the contract. In contrast, a partnership situation assumes that both parties share information about their costs and profit margins, which gives them a basis for arriving at a mutually agreed-upon sharing of expenses and revenues, so that both parties benefit from the arrangement. Clubbing one's partner into submission in order to grasp all benefits does not help to build a lifelong partnership.

Yet another common failing is to believe that a partner will do anything for a company, just because it is a close partner. This expectation usually takes the form of requiring the partner to devote all of its resources to company business. However, any partner cannot afford to tie its existence to just one company, and so a company must reasonably expect to command a fair percentage of a partner's staff, funding, or production capacity.

Sharing knowledge is another concern. A company that does not understand partnering may believe that partners are required to send crucial information to the company, but that this information stream does not work in reverse. A partner opens its facility to a company's quality engineers, shows the company its cost structure, and sends employees to work at the company, while the company promptly closes itself off from the partner and uses all this additional information to acquire an advantage over it. On the contrary, it is customary to take such actions as allowing partner engineers into the company's facilities to suggest improvements, including partner staff on design teams, and making the company's production schedule available to the partner. Only by trading key information can a partnership work effectively.

The previous points are not merely high ground ethical standards that a company may observe or not at its whim. There is also a very concrete reason for observing a strong sense of ethics in partnership dealings. When a company searches for qualified partners, it will quickly find that there are very few viable candidates. Most possibilities are ones with major flaws, such as inadequate capacity, poor management, a bad service record, or financial problems. There are very few star partners in the market, and the company should consider itself lucky to land one of the good ones. Any problems that a company engenders by a lack of ethical dealings with a partner will very likely result in the prompt termination of the partnership by the other entity, who probably has so many other suitors that it is easier to shift its allegiance to a different company than to continue under the difficult conditions imposed by the company. A company can still find partners, but they will not be of as high a standard, and consequently will not help the company as much as a top tier partner. In short, deal fairly or lose your partners.

ESTABLISHING PARTNERSHIPS

A company should not simply approach its largest supplier with an offer to link functions in a partnership agreement, nor should it join forces with any other company to fund a risky venture, just because the other company has large stores of cash. Instead, it should go through a series of steps to determine if another company is a good match for a partnership. This section describes those steps, on the assumption that the partner is a supplier.

The first step in selecting a small core group of partners is to shrink the ocean of current suppliers down to a manageable pond. Otherwise, a company will spend months if not years sorting through the list of potential candidates to find a few really qualified partners. Doing so would require an inordinately large staff. Also, a partnership requires lots of staff time to maintain, and having too many partners requires too many staff. Thus, shrinking the supplier base is the first partnering step.

Cutting back on the number of suppliers can be accomplished in several ways. One is a simple review of the supplier database. It is very likely that the same supplier is listed under several addresses, perhaps because there are multiple "ship to" or "bill to" locations. If so, these addresses can be consolidated on the master list of suppliers for the purposes of shrinking the list (although they can remain as separate addresses on the supplier database, because there may be valid reasons for the multiple addresses). This task is difficult if a company is growing by acquisition, for it may find that, when it combines the supplier databases of all its acquired companies, it has a remarkable number of duplicate suppliers. The reason is that if a company is acquiring within a single industry, most companies use the same suppliers. Another way to shrink the database is to compare the company's records of suppliers for the past year to the total database; anyone not having made a delivery is assumed to be inactive and is dropped from the list. Thus, shrinking the supplier database is the first task.

The next step is to combine suppliers. The best approach is to sort the purchase order database for the last year by commodity code, so that an analyst can see the range of companies from which the company orders similar parts. It is then possible to combine purchases of the same types of items and buy them all from one company. There may be a few items that a single supplier cannot deliver; if so, the company can either encourage that supplier to stock the item on the promise of guaranteed orders, or line up a small number of secondary suppliers to handle the miscellaneous parts.

The third step is to set up a rating system for the suppliers to see who is adequately servicing the company. The easiest measurement is to subtract the actual receipt date of a shipment from the date requested on the company's purchase order, which reveals if a supplier is shipping on time. A continued history of poor deliveries, especially with no evidence of improvement, can eliminate even more suppliers from consideration. This measurement system can be expanded to include the quality and quantity of goods delivered as well as other, more ephemeral information, such as the difficulty the company has in dealing with a supplier. When taken together, these measurements make it obvious that some suppliers must be dropped.

The company is now in a position to set up closer partnership arrangements. This process is generally slow and should be tried with a few suppliers to start with, so that the company can work on ironing out any problems with the partnership concept and get used to the idea of working closely with employees of other companies. As the company becomes more used to the concept, it can spread the arrangement to more of its suppliers. It is then possible to create tight lines of communication, for example, with electronic data interchange links and video conferencing, to bring the organizations as close together as possible.

Even after partnerships are in place, a company should continue to raise its expectations of what it expects from its new partners to keep the group of partners as lean and competitive as possible and allow them to prosper in the face of other partnership groups that are doing the same thing. However, an inevitable outcome of constantly "raising the bar" is that some partners will not be able to keep up. If so, a company should give the partner a grace period in which to improve its standards. If improvement does not happen, the company should certainly look elsewhere for a replacement partner.

Another problem with establishing partnerships is that they will not all be of the same quality. A few will have sterling reputations, bolstered by fine performance. Others will not have the same standards and may never rise to that level. Although a company may want to substitute new partners for these poor performers, it is very likely that, for the service provided, the current partners are the best of a mediocre lot. If so, a company has no choice but to work with what it has and endeavor to convince its low-end partners to upgrade their performance. This is a particular concern for explosive growth companies that start very small, because the best potential partners will ignore them due to their small size. Although the situation changes as these companies grow and their size makes them more attractive partner candidates, it may still be some time before they form a nucleus of top-notch partners.

MEASUREMENTS

Once a partnership has been formed, a company must have some way of determining that the relationship is bearing fruit. This section outlines several measurements that are useful in making this determination.

Many advantages of using partnerships have been listed in this chapter, but it is difficult to measure their results; for example, how does one measure the increase in knowledge resulting from a partnership? Fortunately, a few measures are available that quantify some benefits of using partnerships. They are as follows:

- *Design time reduction.* A company can create a trend line of the time required to develop new product designs. Although this time period varies dramatically based on the level of complexity of each design, a reduction in design time caused by the involvement of partners should be discernible over a large number of projects.

- *Number of suppliers.* As a company switches to close partnership arrangements with its closest suppliers, it will find that it concentrates much more of its business with them, because it is easier to do business with partners who have close links to the company. It should be easy to plot the number of suppliers on a trend line that lists the total number of suppliers.
- *Partner report card.* A company can create a report card that describes the product delivery information for each of its partners. This report card can vary by company, depending on the emphasis that an organization wants to place on such factors as the percentage of parts sent to rework, the accuracy of delivery times, and the accuracy of quantities delivered. For example, the report card can create a high score of 10 for any shipment that is delivered within a one-hour receiving window and can reduce the score to 0 for a delivery outside of a two-day window; it can summarize this score for all deliveries during a month to reveal a composite score for deliveries. Combining this score with similar scores for other criteria gives a partner a good idea of its performance for the company.
- *Proportion of transactions conducted electronically.* A company usually switches to a greater proportion of electronic transactions with its long-term partners, because it is cost-effective to pay for the setup expense while leaving the remaining suppliers on paper-based transactions. It is possible to measure this transaction shift by summarizing the total number of electronic transactions in a time period and dividing it by the total amount of transactions for the same period.

SUMMARY

In summary, a growing company is well advised to seek out partnerships with other companies. By doing so, it combines the company's own strengths with those of its partners, resulting in lower product costs, greater production capacity, less financial risk, a greater knowledge of best practices for enhanced operations, and quicker product design times. Partnerships allow a growing company to enhance its ability to meet demanding revenue targets during its critical growth period. The chapter also covered some key ethical issues regarding dealings with partners and how to set up a partnering process and measure the results of this program.

Chapter 10

Accounting

INTRODUCTION

The accounting function performs many vital functions for the typical company. However, only a small subset of these functions are critical for an explosive growth company. Other tasks must still be performed, but only those noted at the top of Exhibit 10.1 must be completed as promptly and flawlessly as possible.

The key tasks noted in Exhibit 10.1 relate to cash flows and product costing. Cash flow is critical because an explosive growth company must receive cash in payment for services performed or products shipped as rapidly as possible. Product costing is of great importance because a growing company is typically churning out many products for which it may not be aware of the profits. If it sells many products for which margins are inadequate or even negative, then the company will quickly fail. These two areas, then, are of primary importance for the accounting function in a high-growth environment.

Other common accounting tasks, such as processing payroll, issuing financial statements, and calculating tax payments, must still be performed, but they do not require any additional attention when a company is in a growth mode.

The first section of this chapter includes several underlying principles that form the foundation for why some accounting tasks are more important than others in a growth situation. This discussion is followed by separate sections dealing with each of the key areas previously noted in Exhibit 10.1. The chapter concludes with a discussion of the controls, measurements, and reports needed to support the key accounting tasks.

UNDERLYING PRINCIPLES

This chapter discusses only a few selected tasks within the broad range of tasks that the typical accounting function performs. Why only this small number? Because there are just three underlying principles that the accounting function must follow to ensure success in an explosive growth environment. Those principles, which focus on maximizing cash flow and profits at the lowest possible cost, are as follows:

1. *Maximize cash flow at the minimum cost.* A successful accounting staff rapidly issues invoices to customers, collects cash from them as efficiently as

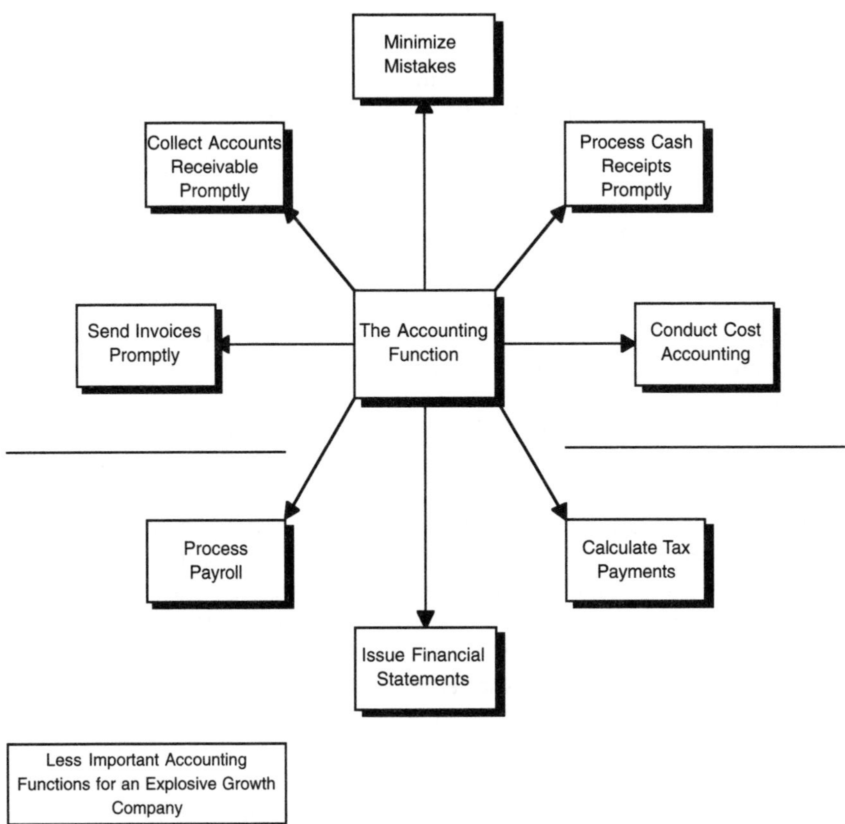

Exhibit 10.1 Explosive Growth Tasks for the Accounting Function

possible, and quickly applies the incoming cash to the correct accounts receivable, so that no time is wasted collecting cash that has already arrived. This activity contributes to reducing a company's need for debt or equity financing and gives it more cash to fuel additional growth.

2. *Minimize mistakes.* An efficient and effective accounting staff can bring cash into a company very rapidly by avoiding any mistakes that might delay the inflow of cash. These mistakes include issuing incorrect invoices for which customers will not pay, pouring effort into collections on small accounts receivable instead of large ones, and not immediately applying incoming cash to accounts receivable balances, which leads to many unnecessary collection calls.

3. *Only sell at a profit.* This principle seems obvious, but many companies do not have a clear understanding of the margins on each of the products or services they sell. This can be deadly for an explosive growth company that has little cash, for sales of a product with negative margins can eat up what little cash is available, leaving the company with no choice but liquidation.

In short, the successful accounting staff must focus on the speed of cash flows and the profitability of products. These underlying principles are the foundation for the following sections.

SEND INVOICES PROMPTLY

When one of the underlying principles for the accounting staff to follow is to maximize cash flow, it is apparent that a key concern is to issue invoices as soon as possible after a product has been shipped to a customer or a service has been rendered. There are a variety of ways to do this.

The accounting staff typically issues an invoice as soon as it receives notice of product shipment from shipping. Traditionally, this notice has arrived on some paper-based form. The problem with this approach is that the notice can be lost in transit or take a long time to reach the accounting person who is in charge of issuing invoices. With the advent of computer-based systems, it is now possible to have the shipping staff enter a shipment into the computer database, which can not only notify the accounting staff of each shipment with total reliability, but even create an invoice. This approach greatly increases the speed of invoicing.

A less technologically sophisticated approach is to have the shipping staff fax shipping notices to the accounting staff. This approach is useful when the shipping department is located a long way away from the accounting staff. However, although it nearly matches the speed of information transfer offered by a direct electronic connection, it is possible for a fax notification to be lost. Also, this approach does not allow the computer system to automatically prepare invoices. Thus, although faxing is faster than mailing shipping information to the accounting staff, it is still inferior to direct entry into a computer system.

It is also possible to get an invoice to a customer much more rapidly than by dropping it into the mail, which includes a transit time of several days before it reaches the customer. One approach is to encode the invoice into an electronic data interchange (EDI) format and send it electronically to the customer. This approach can be accomplished simply by retyping each invoice into a computer that is capable of EDI transmissions, but it introduces the danger of typographical errors from the retyping and of missing the entry of invoices entirely. A better method is to create an automated interface from the accounting system to an EDI transmission program that automatically encodes and transmits invoices to customers with no manual interference by anyone on the accounting staff. This approach avoids all risk of adding mistakes to invoices, as well as of human errors that might result in an invoice not being sent at all. Unfortunately, not that many companies are equipped to receive EDI transmissions, so a company may have to send some invoices by mail and others by EDI, which reduces the effectiveness of this method. Forcing customers to switch to EDI is not as easy as would be the case if they were suppliers, for suppliers will do it to keep their share of the company's business, whereas customers can simply go elsewhere to purchase products and services. Therefore, EDI transmissions can avoid the time wasted when an invoice is sent to a customer through the mail, although a company may not be able to do this with its entire customer base.

A less common approach is for a company to deliver a product or service directly to the customer and then hand over an invoice on the spot. This also avoids the transit time needed for an invoice to be sent to a customer through the mail. For this method to work, a company can preprint an invoice and give it to the delivery person to hand to the customer, or it can equip the delivery person with a computer and printer, so that the invoice can be created at the time of delivery. It is better to let the delivery person create the invoice, because this allows the delivery person to alter the amount of the invoice based on any problems found by the customer, such as the delivered quantity being different from the amount expected. By changing the invoice on the spot, the accounting staff avoids the problem of having to issue a credit to adjust invoices to the amount that the customer has agreed to pay, which can be a time-consuming process. Although the technique of altering invoices at the point of delivery to the customer sounds attractive, it will remain a niche alternative, because not that many companies deliver directly to their customers; normally, a third party does the shipping, and no one has yet come up with a method for having the third party do the invoicing.

COLLECT ACCOUNTS RECEIVABLE PROMPTLY

One of the key principles noted at the beginning of this chapter is to maximize cash flow at the minimum cost. For the collections staff, this means collecting the maximum amount of overdue accounts receivable at the minimum cost. This section discusses how to do that, including account stratification, cash discounts for early payment, collection problem resolution, use of a problem database, and the use of top-notch collections personnel.

An explosive growth company's accounting staff does not normally have enough time to collect all outstanding accounts receivable, because the company is growing so fast that the staff is burdened with many other tasks as well as collections. How, then, can it focus its energies most effectively on the principle of maximizing cash flow at the minimum cost? The answer is stratified collections. Under this method, the collections staff separates the accounts receivable into very large invoices and all other ones. The largest invoices are tagged for attention as soon as they become overdue, and those customers are called continually to ensure that the cash is collected as rapidly as possible. This routine brings in the most overdue cash with the least effort. The collections staff can wait until a specific number of days have passed before calling other customers about smaller invoice amounts; usually, by waiting the extra days, some of the cash will come in without any calls being made at all. The collections staff can then make a limited number of collection calls for these smaller invoices, and then turn them over to a collection agency. Larger invoices are almost never referred to a collections company, because this involves a large fee that seriously reduces cash flows. In short, stratified collections allows the collections staff to focus on the largest cash items, which maximizes the amount of incoming cash.

Some companies offer cash discounts for early payment. This policy gives customers an incentive to pay early, because the implicit interest rate on most discounts is quite high (if not, no one would pay early!). An explosive growth company is typically more concerned about accelerating cash flows than about the interest rate being given to customers, so this idea can be good. The only problem with offering discounts is that some customers abuse it by taking the discount and then paying late, thereby slowing down incoming cash flows while also cutting into the amount being paid. When this happens, the response of the collections staff can vary from a simple warning to reducing the amount of credit allowed or even switching a customer to a cash-on-delivery status. Thus, offering a discount to customers for early payment can accelerate the amount of incoming cash, although the accounting staff must watch for customers who violate the terms of the discount.

It is very important to determine why accounts receivable are late in being collected. Of course, credit may have been extended to customers who were incapable of paying in full by the due date (see Chapter 16 for a discussion of credit policy), but there are many other reasons for late payments. When properly researched, these other problems can be corrected so that future payments by the same customers will arrive much more quickly. The following list describes several of the more common problems uncovered during the collection process:

- *Damaged goods.* Products shipped to a customer may have been damaged by the shipper. This problem can be corrected by bringing it to the attention of the shipper, switching to a new shipper, or using better packaging to ship the product. The last option is the best, because it is completely under the control of the company.
- *Mailed to wrong address.* The invoice or product may have been sent to the wrong location. This error can be fixed by creating multiple fields in the accounting database for customer addresses, so that one is used for the ship-to address and another for the billing address. Also, any incorrect address information should be immediately changed in the customer database so that no other products or invoices go to the wrong address.
- *Missing information on the invoice.* Some customers do not pay if the information listed on the invoice is incomplete. The most common issue is a missing

customer purchase order number. This and other information can be identified by periodic audits of outgoing invoices, with follow-up action to ensure that the billing staff corrects the problem. Another approach is to make the customer purchase order field a required one in order to print a billing, although this can be circumvented by entering a false number in the field.

- *Returned goods.* A customer may have returned goods to the company for a variety of reasons, and the company then lost the paperwork and did not issue a credit for the sale. This is startlingly common. The receiving department tends to put the paperwork for returns at the bottom of its work pile, so return information is a long time in coming to the collections staff. The best way to avoid this problem is to issue a return authorization to each customer prior to allowing a product return. The authorization information can be immediately forwarded to the collections staff, so that it does not waste time on collection calls while the goods are in transit back to the company and the paperwork is being processed by the receiving staff.
- *Wrong items or quantities shipped.* A common problem is when the customer receives the wrong quantity or type of goods and pays for only the amount it wanted. The company first finds out about this when the collections staff notices that an invoice has only been partially paid. This problem must be corrected by the shipping department, which can use inspections, sign-offs, automated picking, and standardized container sizes to ensure that the correct quantities and part types are shipped.

Whenever any of the above problems are discovered, they should be entered into a problem database for management review, so that the root causes of the problems can be corrected. Doing so will greatly improve the ease of collection, since there will be far fewer late payments, which allows the collections staff to concentrate its efforts on a much smaller number of customers. In addition, much less cash will be tied up in accounts receivable, which is of great importance for a typical explosive growth company that is chronically short of cash.

The collections staff should be of the highest quality, for only an experienced person who is well organized and with excellent people skills will succeed in keeping the amount of overdue accounts receivable at a minimal level. An inexperienced person who is poorly motivated is worse than useless, for this person can muddle the record keeping for collection calls and confuse customers, resulting in an increase in the amount of overdue accounts receivable, rather than the reverse. If management is having a difficult time keeping a high level of staff quality in this position, it can pay for the services of a collections agency. This collections agency can be quite expensive, however, since it prefers to keep a large percentage of the money it collects, but this percentage can be reduced for long-term arrangements involving large amounts of accounts receivable. In short, the collections staff should be of the highest quality if an explosive growth company is to succeed in keeping its working capital needs related to accounts receivable at a minimum.

MINIMIZE MISTAKES

The accounting staff of an explosive growth company is always playing catch-up with the ever-increasing volume of transactions coming in the door. Even when hiring additional staff at a prodigious rate, it is still difficult to keep up with the work, because anyone who is newly hired requires additional work by the existing staff because of the need to train them as well as to correct their initial mistakes. How can a company avoid this problem?

It cannot be completely avoided, but the burden can be reduced if the accounting staff focuses on avoiding transaction mistakes. Any mistake in any area of accounting, such as cash, accounts receivable, or accounts payable, requires an inordinate amount of time to correct. By eliminating these errors, an accounting staff finds its work load to be much reduced. How does one eliminate errors? By first spotting the errors that are being made and then by devising techniques for making a transaction "bombproof," so that each mistake cannot happen again.

One error-prone area is cash. There are a variety of ways to spot mistakes, such as performing bank account reconciliations every month and by scheduling periodic internal audits that examine every step in the cash handling. Another way to spot errors is to ask the collections staff for comments on why some accounts receivable have not been collected; an occasional response is that the cash *was* collected, but was applied to the wrong account. Bombproofing the cash area centers on setting up cross-checks at each step of the process that includes cash receipt, application, and delivery to a bank. For example, when cash is received, it should be totaled; when it is applied to accounts receivable, it should be totaled again and compared to the first total to ensure that they match; when it goes to the bank, the amount deposited should, once again, match the previous totals. In addition, there will be problems in applying cash, because some cash will come in without an explanation. This cash should be forwarded to a senior clerk for resolution, rather than to a junior clerk who will puzzle over it and perhaps apply it to the wrong account. Thus, there are many ways to spot cash problems. Problems can be prevented by spotting them early through comparing totals at each step of the cash receipt process.

Mistakes in the accounts receivable area are most commonly found through the collections process, because customers will not pay an invoice if they think it is incorrect. It is more difficult to spot situations where the error was not sending an invoice *at all*. This problem is most easily found by comparing the shipping log to the invoice register to ensure that all items shipped were accompanied by an invoice. Both of these problem areas are major, since they both worsen a company's cash position. The best way to bombproof the lack of invoicing is to enter the shipping log into the same computer database used by the accounting system, so that the computer system can automatically compare shipments to invoices, and issue a report listing all shipments for which invoices were not generated.

It is more difficult to completely bombproof the information on an invoice, but a company can certainly reduce the quantity of errors. One problem is not including the customer's purchase order number on the invoice, which the customer frequently uses to verify that the order was authorized. The computer system can be modified so that an invoice is not printed unless there is a purchase order entered in the database. This type of automated data checking can be expanded to include any other fields in a typical invoice. Another problem is billing to the wrong address, but this error can be avoided by having the collections staff enter corrected addresses into the customer file as soon as they become aware of an address change. In short, there are several ways to detect problems with a company's accounts receivable, while automated data checking and inputs from the collections staff can reduce the number of initial and repeating errors that may occur.

Problems with accounts payable are just as important to an explosive growth company as accounts receivable, because they may entail double payments to suppliers or worsening relations due to no payments at all that lead to losing key suppliers. A double payment is most easily found by comparing the supplier invoice numbers that have been paid recently; any invoice number that appears on the list more than once has been paid more than once. It is more difficult to obtain information about missing payments to suppliers, because, by definition, there is no information about the missing payment in the company's computer system. The best way to obtain this information is to have all supplier account statements routed from the mailroom to either the internal audit staff or accounting management. These statements can then be perused for outstanding payments that are well overdue, and inquiries can be made to see why they were not paid. One way to avoid problems with nonpayment is to automatically pay any invoice that is so small that going through the work of verifying that the item or service was authorized is not cost effective. For example, any invoice under $50 can be automatically paid upon receipt. Another solution is to automatically link the purchase order file to the supplier invoice file and shipping log; the computer system can then match all three files (known as three-way matching) to ensure that every invoice has a matching authorization and receipt, and then automatically schedule a payment. This system avoids much error-prone manual labor that might otherwise result in an invoice not being paid. Another reason for lack of payment is that the company has lost the supplier's invoice. This problem can be rectified by switching to electronic invoices that are sent straight from the supplier to the company's computer system, thereby avoiding all of the usual spots where the paperwork might have been mislaid. All of these methods can be used to reduce the number of errors in the accounts payable area.

PROCESS CASH RECEIPTS PROMPTLY

The accounts receivable collections staff of an explosive growth company cannot waste its time in making calls to companies that have already sent in their payments, because this detracts from efforts to collect cash from customers who have not done so. This section discusses how to process cash receipts promptly in order to avoid this problem.

A properly run cash application function applies all cash received to the proper accounts receivable accounts and does so on the same day that the cash was received. This is easier said than done, because the cash application staff may have no idea of where to apply a cash payment that does not have an accompanying remittance advice that clearly states the customer's name and the invoice that is being paid. The cash sometimes is not even for payment of an account receivable; it can be for a warranty reimbursement, a sale of a fixed asset, a purchase by an employee, a customer deposit, or even the return of an overpayment on an account payable. Nonetheless, the bulk of all cash receipts *is* for payment of accounts receivable, and can be dealt with promptly and accurately by the cash application staff. When there is no immediate way to accurately apply cash, the problem can be entered into a holding account and then forwarded to a senior accountant who has extra experience in the area and who can more accurately apply the cash. This approach ensures that all cash is applied to some account (even if it is only a holding account) as soon as the cash is received, but runs the risk of having the holding account mushroom in size if it is not reviewed every day. The controller can avoid this problem by including the amount in the cash holding account in the company's daily management report. If the amount becomes too large, it will become very apparent to management.

CONDUCT COST ACCOUNTING

When a company is growing at a high rate of speed, it is critical to be sure of the margins earned on all products sold. Otherwise, a company may find that it has sold an astounding number of units of a new product at a price that has placed it in bankruptcy proceedings before management ever knew that it had a profitability problem. For example, if a company brings out a hot new product that replaces an older one that was its sales mainstay, it may find within just one sales cycle (presumably the 30 days for invoices to come due) that it earned so little on the new product that it cannot cover its overhead or increased working capital needs, and must go out of business—in one month. This problem is even worse if a company has many products and does not know which ones are causing the profitability problem. How does a company avoid this issue?

It is mandatory that a company involve the cost accounting staff in all aspects of the design of a new product, so that there is no question about the cost of the product before it is ever released. Because a product's costs are essentially locked in once it has been designed, the most appropriate time to determine the product's cost is when changes can still be made. This not only keeps a company from releasing a new product with an excessively low margin, but also allows it to set a price that will bring in the anticipated margin. Some naysayers may point out that the market determines a product's price, and that a company cannot raise prices much beyond this level without seriously eroding the sales level. However, an explosive growth company is frequently exploiting a new market where there are no competing products or services, so the company may have considerable discretion in setting prices. If so, having accurate costing information in advance allows a company to make the right decisions regarding initial product pricing, or if a product should be introduced to the market at all.

Product costs also change over time, so it is not sufficient to calculate a product's costs at its introduction and then assume that the cost will stay unchanged through its life. Instead, the cost accounting manager should schedule periodic reviews of product costs that can then be plotted on a time line (see the Measurements section) so that any cost changes are immediately obvious and can be acted upon. This time line can even include a targeted cost, because the more advanced companies are now including costing plans in their product design processes that budget for continual cost reductions. It is also useful to break down product costs into smaller subsets, such as for labor, materials, and overhead, so that problem areas can be more easily spotted. A company will have a better knowledge of its product costs if it periodically schedules a cost review of each product.

Whenever a cost accounting staff reviews a product's costs, it must look for more than the traditional costs of material and labor. There may also be some exceptionally high costs lurking in the overhead expenses. Here are some examples of these costs:

- *Cost of sales staff.* A company may think that it is making exceptional profits on custom products and services, because customers are paying extra for them; that is, until sales costs are factored into the overhead expense. Custom sales frequently require the sales staff to travel to the customer or at least to spend inordinate amounts of time with the customer. When these costs are added to overhead, there may be no remaining profit at all.
- *Obsolescence.* A product may be perishable, such as many food products, or it may quickly go out of style or be outdated, such as fashionable clothes or computer parts. In any of these cases, the obsolescence cost may drastically reduce profits.
- *Sales volume.* A company may purchase special equipment to create a truly unique product but not realize that low sales volume is keeping the product from ever recouping the cost of the special equipment.
- *Scrap.* It may take a large amount of materials scrap to produce a product, which frequently is not included in the product cost.
- *Shipping cost.* A company may sell a product at what it thinks is a profitable price, but absorb the cost of freight, which is very high because the product is bulky or is so expensive that it requires freight insurance.
- *Warranties.* A particularly dangerous cost to ignore is a product's warranty cost, because it can be very high if there are problems with the product's design that result in product failures. It is difficult to accurately estimate the

warranty cost when a product is still being designed, but the cost accountant can make estimates based on the warranty costs of similar products (if any).

Clearly, there are many factors to consider when deriving a product's total cost. The accounting staff can also include an activity-based costing analysis to more accurately assign overhead costs to a product. If this level of costing detail is used for all product cost analyses, an explosive growth company probably needs to hire additional cost accounting personnel, enough so that this part of the accounting staff may seem excessively overstaffed. However, when the price of not having cost accountants to review product costs is a drop in product profitability, company management finds that it is much cheaper to have a large cost accounting staff.

A final point is that many companies religiously obtain new cost accounting studies at regular intervals, but then do nothing to resolve any problems uncovered. To avoid this problem, company management must create a permanent team for each product family, composed of members of the accounting, engineering, and production functions, that reviews the results of ongoing costing studies and decides what must be done to improve product profitability. Without this multidisciplinary group, the results of costing studies will languish.

In short, cost accounting is a key area for the accounting staff of an explosive growth company, because it is dangerous to release a product to market without being sure of its profit margin in advance. This issue can be avoided by including a cost accountant on the product design team. The cost accountant must also review product costs over time to ensure that costs are not varying from expectations. This review should include a number of cost elements that fall outside of the traditional material and labor expenses. Whenever these costs are reevaluated, a team drawn from several functional areas should use them as the basis for product changes that will bring profitability back to expected levels, which allows the company to continue to grow.

MEASUREMENTS

A multitude of measurements are available for tracking the effectiveness of the accounting function in issuing invoices, collecting and processing cash, and costing new products. A selection of the better measurements are included in this section, along with several reports that address the same topics. Each measurement includes a brief discussion of why it is useful, any pitfalls to be aware of, and how it is measured. They are as follows:

- *Average time to issue invoices.* This measurement tells the user the length of the interval between the time a product ships and the customer is sent an invoice. The problem with it is that many accounting systems allow the user to alter the date shown on the invoice, so that it may be sent many days after shipment, although the printed date appears to be immediately following shipment. To calculate it, subtract the invoice date from the shipment date for the product being invoiced. It is useful to create a list of all invoices included in the measurement that have exceptionally long time periods between the shipment date and the invoice date; this list can be used by the controller to track down and correct problems with the invoice creation process.

- *Days of outstanding accounts receivable.* This measurement tells management if it is having difficulty collecting cash, which may be caused by an excessively loose credit policy or an inadequate or ineffective collections staff. However, the measure can be skewed if there are a few large accounts receivable that are old. To calculate it, divide the average accounts receivable by the annual amount of sales on credit, and multiply by 365.
- *Percentage of accounts receivable over xx days old.* This measurement identifies the percentage of accounts receivable that may never be collected, since the *xx* target number of days can be set to equal an amount beyond which collections are unlikely (which varies by industry). If the resulting percentage is high, a growing company should add staff to the collection effort to bring in more needed cash. To calculate it, print an aged accounts receivable report, and then summarize the accounts receivable exceeding the targeted date, and divide this amount by the total open accounts receivable.
- *Percentage of cash applied within same day of receipt.* This measurement is useful for determining how much of received cash is not immediately being applied to the list of open accounts receivable, which may lead to wasted energy in trying to collect cash that has already been received. To calculate it, divide the daily register of applied cash (generated by the computer as soon as cash has been applied) by the total amount of cash deposited for the day.
- *Percentage of products costed prior to release.* The cost accounting staff should be heavily involved in the calculation of product costs prior to the release of all new products. Anything less than involvement in 100 percent of all new products is not acceptable, because a single product that is miscosted can have losses significant enough to seriously impact total company profits. To calculate this measurement, have the cost accounting staff keep a log of all products for which it has calculated a cost. Then compare this log to the company's list of released products, and divide the number of uncosted products by the total number of released products.

The management of the accounting function will find that an exception report is most useful when attached to many of the above measurements. For example, the measurement for the average time to issue invoices should be accompanied by a list of any invoices that took an exceptionally long time to create. Similarly, any measurement of overdue accounts receivable should include a list of the largest and oldest outstanding items. Also, the measurement for the percentage of products costed prior to release should include a list of all products for which a costing was *not* completed. All of these accompanying exception reports allow management to focus on the key problems that are causing the measurements to be skewed in the wrong direction, without having to wade through the much larger amount of data that is correct and requires no action. Thus, the key accounting measurements should include exception reports that management can use to improve the measurements.

A costing trend chart is useful for determining which components of a product's costs are changing over time and which may require action by the engineering staff to bring costs back to budgeted levels. The primary components that are typically listed are direct labor, overhead, and materials, although these categories can be further subdivided. An example of this chart is shown in Exhibit 10.2. The chart shows measurements being taken only quarterly; this is sufficient, and even excessively frequent for some products, because product costs usually change only slowly.

Another useful report is one that tracks the percentage of overdue accounts receivable over time. This report is much more useful than one that only lists the total amount of overdue dollars, for that figure will rise as sales increase, as is the case for an explosive growth company, and may give management the false impression that the collections team is not doing its job. Showing the information on a percentage basis may show a declining percentage even while the total amount of overdue dollars increases, due to an increase in sales volume. An example of this chart is shown in Exhibit 10.3. The chart shows measurements being taken once a month, which is a sufficiently long interval for this measurement.

CONTROLS

The accounting function has more control points than any functional area, which is necessary due to its role in handling company transactions. Many of these controls

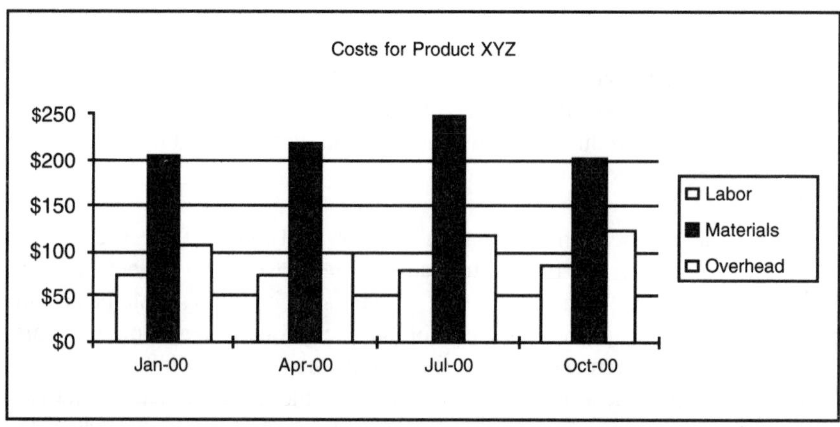

Exhibit 10.2 A Costing Trend Line

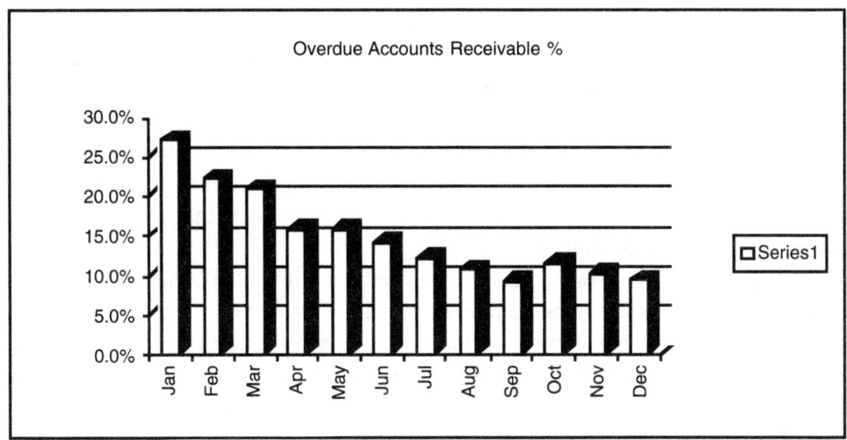

Exhibit 10.3 An Overdue Accounts Receivable Trend Line

are covered in detail in Chapter 5. This section only covers a subset of those controls, which are the ones needed for the oversight of the key functional areas pertaining to explosive growth, as seen earlier in Exhibit 10.1.

The internal audit staff can be used to provide spot-checks of various functions. This control is weak, because such a review will only spot problems after they have occurred, and will only be a random sample, so many potentially serious problems may not be found. Nonetheless, this is a valuable tool for the accounting manager who has minimal resources and cannot otherwise create effective controls over selected processes. Samples of internal audit tasks for an explosive growth environment are as follows:

- *Review cash applications.* An audit program can compare a selection of cash receipts to accounts receivable to ensure that cash was applied to the correct customer account. This procedure is typically done by comparing a remittance advice to the cash application register.
- *Review credit approvals.* An audit program can compare all sales credits in the sales journal to a log of approved credits. Any credits noted in the sales journal that have no matching authorization require further review. Also, another audit program can target the reasons for sales credits, which should be noted in the log of approved credits. Any continuing problem that results in a credit being issued should be brought to the attention of management for resolution.
- *Review missing invoices.* An audit program can compare shipments as noted in the shipping log to invoices. Any shipment for which there is no matching invoice indicates that there is a flaw in the invoice creation process and requires further (and immediate) action, because this problem has a major impact on cash flow.

- *Review speed of invoice creation.* An audit program can compare the date when a product was shipped to the date when the related invoice was created to see if there was an exceptionally long lag between the two events.

After an audit review, the internal auditing staff creates a report containing recommendations. The controller should review this report with care and implement the recommendations made by the auditors to ensure that proper controls are in place for the accounting function.

In addition to the work done by the internal auditing staff, the controller has several other controls to track. One is exercising control over the product costing process by ensuring that all new products have received a cost prior to release and regularly scheduled follow-up costings. A good way to ensure that every product is costed prior to release is to create a report with the cooperation of the marketing staff that lists all products scheduled for release, along with the calculated cost of each product. Also, it is possible to detect an incorrect product costing by comparing the calculated costs of products that are grouped into families. These products tend to have similar costs, so any costs that are substantially different from those of similar products should be reviewed again to verify that there are no costing mistakes.

Another control area to review is the bank reconciliation. The controller or an assistant should review and sign off on the bank reconciliation of every bank account and follow up with the preparer of the account if there are any problems. This reconciliation should even include those accounts with minimal ending balances or little activity, because there may be small numbers of very large transactions passing through these accounts that could drastically alter the company's cash position if recorded incorrectly.

The controller should also be very careful to ensure that the amount of cash received is fully applied to accounts receivable every day to keep all customer accounts current. To verify application accuracy, compare the sum of the cash application register to the amount of cash received for the same day, and track down any differences between the two amounts. Determining the reasons for differences, and correcting the underlying problems, is a key control over the accurate application of cash to accounts receivable.

Finally, the controller should verify that the total amount shipped for the previous day matches the amount invoiced. This verification is most easily done if the shipping log is automated, so that the computer system can automatically compare the shipping log to invoices produced. If the shipping log is not linked to the computer system, however, this task can be a laborious process of manually comparing shipments to invoices. It is critical to do this comparison, so that a company does not suffer from reduced incoming cash flow because of missing invoices.

All of the foregoing controls are designed to support the key tasks noted earlier in the Underlying Principles section, which center on the maximization of cash flows, the minimization of mistakes, and selling products at the highest possible profit.

SUMMARY

This chapter addressed a set of goals that are of primary importance to the accounting function of an explosive growth company: maximizing cash flows, minimizing mistakes, and ensuring that products and services are sold at a reasonable profit. To meet these goals, the chapter covered rapid invoicing techniques, accounts receivable collection methods, ways to reduce accounting errors, and methods for processing cash receipts as quickly as possible. In addition, the chapter covered cost accounting techniques that help a company to avoid selling products and services at less than acceptable profit margins. All of the foregoing items will assist the accounting function of an explosive growth company in meeting its goals.

The discussion of cash flows in this chapter is supplemented in Chapter 16, dealing with finance issues. Whereas this chapter covered how invoices are prepared, issued, and collected, Chapter 16 also covers policies for extending credit to customers, as well as using lock boxes, cash concentration accounts, and zero-balance accounts to accelerate and centralize the flow of incoming cash. The reader should review that chapter to gain a full understanding of incoming cash flows in an explosive growth company.

Chapter 11

Auditing

INTRODUCTION

When a company is working through an explosive growth situation, the last thing anyone thinks about is making sure that there is an internal audit staff. Instead, the management team focuses on bringing in sales, adding production capacity, acquiring new companies, or moving into new territories. When expanding so rapidly, though, a company frequently develops very large holes in its control systems that no one has the time to locate, much less fix. These holes can fester over time, resulting in missed billings to customers, missed or duplicate payments to suppliers, missing or misstated assets, or a host of other problems. When these issues come to light, the grow mode comes to an abrupt halt while management frantically scrambles to fix the problems. Consequently, it is best to place emphasis on the internal audit function at the *beginning* of the grow cycle, not the end, so that it can spot problems when they are still small.

A typical company has a small internal audit staff that is handed a program of internal audits to conduct, and then it leisurely plods through the program over the course of a year. In a growing environment, however, that program may change every week and expand as fast as the company, resulting in frantic changes to the audit schedule and extreme overworking of the internal audit staff. To avoid this situation, a growing company must retain a large audit staff to deal with the ever-changing problems that arise when a company adds product lines, subsidiaries, or new locations.

This chapter covers the major internal audit tasks that this function must complete on an ongoing basis, as shown in Exhibit 11.1. Unlike similar graphics in other chapters, this one does not show any tasks that the function can safely avoid. For the internal audit staff, all audit tasks are critical, because the penalty for dropping an audit review is missing a control problem that can later cause serious difficulties for the company. Each of the audit areas noted in Exhibit 11.1 are clarified in separate sections in the remainder of this chapter. Other sections deal with the measurements, reports, and controls that management can use to assure itself of the performance of this key area.

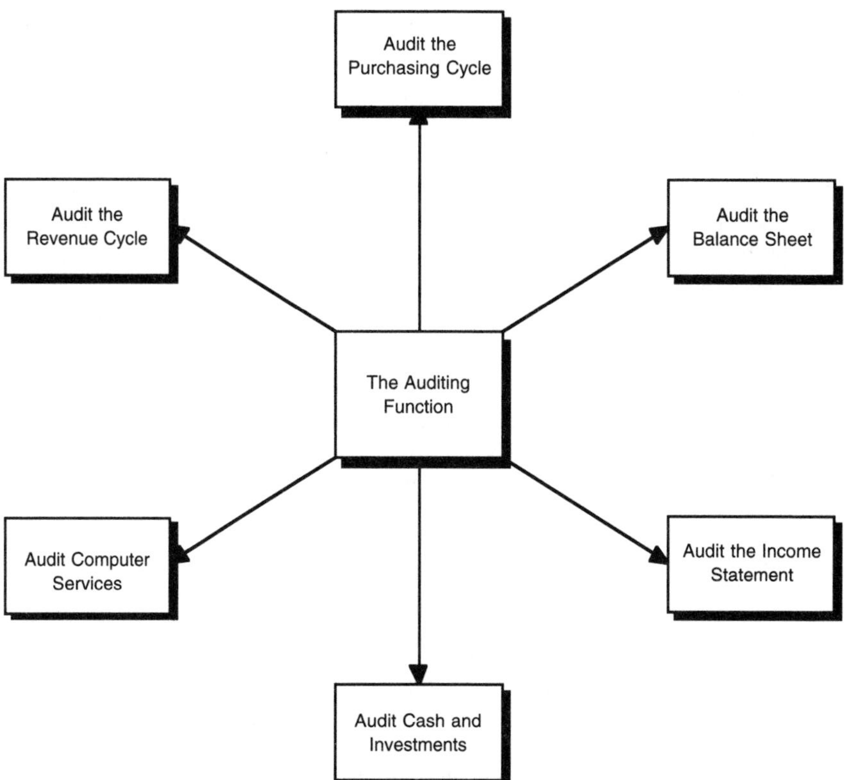

Exhibit 11.1 Explosive Growth Tasks for the Audit Function

UNDERLYING PRINCIPLES

The underlying principles that form the foundation for running an internal audit function are the same for any company, whether or not it is growing. However, these principles *must* be followed in a high-growth situation, for there is no room for error in an explosive-growth company; a systems failure can bring down a high-flying company, and the internal audit staff is management's watchdog that keeps this from happening.

Two of the underlying principles for the internal audit function are common—ensuring that assets are properly tracked and that systems handle transactions consistently. In the case of a high-growth company, however, it is also necessary to ensure that the computer systems supporting operations are not at risk of crashing and bringing down any operations with them. Consequently, there is a third principle in the following list for ensuring that computer systems do not stop company operations, one that is repeated in Chapter 12. The underlying principles for the internal audit function are as follows:

1. *Do not let systems stop operations.* It is critical that a growing company's operations not be halted by flaws in its computer systems. Unfortunately, this problem is common for expanding companies that must frequently upgrade their computer hardware and software. The internal audit staff can help by reviewing a number of common problem areas involving system backups, installations, and software development.
2. *Track assets.* A growing company has great difficulty in ensuring that all asset purchases and sales are authorized, and that all assets listed in the financial statements actually exist. The internal audit staff can recommend a number of ways to tighten control over assets.
3. *Ensure transaction processing consistency.* A growing company has a very hard time ensuring that all of its staff in all locations are capable of processing the same transactions in the same manner. If it cannot do this, then financial results will probably be skewed, due to incorrect or missing processing of crucial accounting information. The internal audit staff can review the consistency of transaction processing and recommend changes where necessary.

The remainder of this chapter expands upon these three principles with a number of specific suggestions.

AUDIT THE REVENUE CYCLE

If a company cannot bill its customers and collect money from them in a timely manner, it cannot generate the cash flow to grow. Consequently, the internal audit staff must review a number of key aspects of the revenue cycle to ensure that all transactions in this area are dealt with promptly and consistently. At a minimum, the audit staff should conduct the following audit steps:

- *Check invoice prices against price lists.* The billing staff may occasionally price a product incorrectly. If the amount is too low, the company will lose money; if the amount is too high, the customer will be angered and may take its business elsewhere. The audit staff can find this problem by comparing official price lists to a sample of issued invoices.
- *Confirm that credit approval is required to ship.* A company should never ship a product for which the finance staff has denied credit, because there are

low odds of collecting on the invoice. The audit staff can review this problem in two ways. One is to review a sample of shipped products to see if credit problems should have held up shipments. The better approach is to review old accounts receivable to see if collection problems were caused by an initial bypassing of the finance staff by the shipping department.

- *Review customer complaints.* If a company keeps a database of complaints, the audit staff should review it for complaints by customers related to billing issues and then follow up on these problems with the staff who are responsible for them.
- *Review timing of invoices.* If a company is too leisurely about issuing invoices, it will take that much longer for customers to pay the company. The audit staff can check this problem by comparing the shipment date according to the shipping log to the date on which the related invoice was prepared.
- *Trace incoming cash to accounts receivable balances.* Improperly matching incoming cash against the wrong accounts receivable balances creates considerable problems with customers, because collection calls targeted at amounts that have already been paid will meet with some resistance from the customer. The audit staff can review the issue by comparing a sample of incoming payments to where they were applied.
- *Trace difficult collections to bad billings.* Many times, the reason that a company cannot collect an account receivable is that it did not issue an accurate billing to the customer. The audit staff can look for this type of error by going over the old accounts receivable list with the collections staff to determine the reasons customers give for not paying.
- *Trace the speed of information from shipping to billing.* A company cannot issue an invoice to a customer if its billing staff has no information about the shipment. This situation may be due to a problem in sending information from the shipping area to the billing staff, and may be so bad that some information never reaches the billing staff at all, resulting in no invoices being issued. The audit staff can review this issue by comparing the shipment dates noted in the shipping log to the related invoice dates and by taking a sample of shipping paperwork as it arrives in the billing area to determine the transfer time based on the date of arrival.
- *Verify that billed products were shipped.* One of the most common problems for a company that is trying to meet aggressive revenue goals is to bill a customer at the end of a reporting period, even if the product has not yet been shipped. The audit staff can review this problem by comparing month-end invoices to the shipping log. Another possibility, if there is a job-costing system, is to see if the last date on which labor was charged to a job was later than the date on which it was invoiced, which is a clear sign of premature invoicing.

Besides reviewing the foregoing audit points, the audit staff can also recommend that several best practices be implemented, which will help to streamline operations in the revenue cycle. These recommendations can include giving the customer an invoice at the same time as delivery of the product, eliminating month-end customer statements, automating the collections tickler file, and sending invoices to customers using electronic data interchange. All of these methods can help to reduce the work required in the revenue cycle.

In short, the internal audit staff has a number of options for reviewing the operations of the revenue cycle, from issuing invoices to collecting and applying cash received in payment for those invoices. The audit staff can also recommend a number of improvements to enhance the efficiency and effectiveness of this transaction cycle.

AUDIT THE PURCHASING CYCLE

Purchasing is responsible for the majority of all expenses incurred by the typical company. Consequently, if it does a poor job of purchasing, the added costs will have a significant impact on a growing company's cash flow, and hence its ability to grow. The internal audit staff can follow a number of routines to give it a good idea of problems in the purchasing area. It can recommend changes to fix them, partially by altering purchasing procedures and partially by ensuring better transaction processing consistency. The internal audit routines are as follows:

- *Check complaints database for payment problems.* If a company maintains a database that stores all incoming complaints, the internal audit staff should review it to see if there are complaints from suppliers regarding such items as excessive amounts of returned goods for no reason, late payments, or unexplained discounts taken by the company. The audit staff should investigate these complaints to see if there are any operational issues worth correcting.
- *Compare actual receipt dates to required dates.* The purchasing staff may not be doing a good job of managing its suppliers if they are delivering products sooner than the company needs them. This results in earlier than necessary payments by the company, which may cause a cash flow imbalance. The audit staff can check for this problem by comparing the required dates on company purchase orders to the receipt dates listed on the company's receiving log.
- *Compare large purchases to market rates.* Many purchasing staffs do not have the time to compare the prices they are paying to market rates. For large purchases, this may result in very large and unnecessary overpayments. The audit staff can review the problem by conducting a limited comparison of company-paid prices to market rates for a sample of the largest purchases.
- *Ensure that discounts are taken.* The end of the purchasing cycle is paying the supplier. If the supplier offers a large discount for early payment and the

company does not take it, the purchasing system has failed to identify early-payment invoices and pay them within the required time frame. The audit staff can investigate this issue by identifying those suppliers who offer discount terms, and then scanning through the payments made to them to ensure that all discounts were taken.

- *Review supplier relations.* Some companies incur added expenses because purchasing personnel only buy from certain suppliers who give them gifts or kickbacks in return. Sometimes, the purchasing staff may even own the suppliers! This problem is difficult to trace, but the audit staff can start by reviewing the time interval over which each purchasing person has been responsible for buying a particular commodity. If the period appears to be excessively long, the audit staff can recommend that responsibility for commodities be swapped, thereby effectively ending any one person's control over purchasing from a particular supplier. The audit staff can also look at the time interval over which items have been purchased from a supplier and recommend a pricing review against the competition if the time interval appears to be excessively long. These methods will prevent some purchasing abuses from continuing, but may not prevent all such cases from occurring.
- *Trace purchase authorizations.* A growing company must have a solid purchase authorization system in place, or else it runs the risk of buying many items it does not need, resulting in a significant drop in anticipated cash flows. The audit staff can review this issue in two ways. One is to check for an authorization document or signature for every purchase. However, this does not normally apply to cost of goods sold items. The second method addresses this problem by verifying that the bill of materials for a production item requires the purchase of an item. The biggest problem in this area tends to be late changes to bills of material, forcing the purchasing staff to retract orders for previously ordered parts and replace them with orders for new parts, which inevitably results in some unneeded parts being left in the warehouse.
- *Verify payment packages to ensure that correct amounts are paid.* The end of the purchasing cycle is when the accounts payable staff compares the original purchase order to receiving documentation and the supplier's invoice (called *three-way matching*) and then pays the supplier based on this information. The audit staff can review these packages of payment information to ensure that the accounts payable staff is making the correct payments to suppliers.

As part of its review of the purchasing cycle, the audit staff can also recommend that several best practices be implemented. These can include using corporate purchasing cards to reduce the volume of purchasing paperwork, centralizing purchasing for commonly ordered parts with a single supplier, and paying suppliers directly from purchase orders, thereby ignoring supplier invoices. Other possibilities are automating expense report processing, reviewing expense report documentation only by random audit, and eliminating approvals for purchase requisitions. All of these best practices are designed to reduce the workload of anyone involved in the purchasing cycle, thereby reducing company personnel costs while processing purchases and payments more efficiently.

The internal audit routines shown in this section reveal that there are a number of ways for the audit staff to determine if there are problems in the purchasing area that are costing excessive amounts of money, which can cripple a growing company.

AUDIT THE BALANCE SHEET

The balance sheet can cause lots of problems for a growing company, because it is frequently misstated. The internal audit staff can review this area and make recommendations for improving its accuracy.

One of the key principles of this chapter is to properly track assets. This activity is particularly important for a growing company, because those assets are listed in the borrowing base against which a company borrows money from its lending institution. Consequently, the accuracy of the typical borrowing base elements, which are inventory, fixed assets, and accounts receivable, is especially important. The audit staff should review these areas to ascertain their accuracy with the following audit routines:

- *Accounts Receivable: Compare to detail.* The most common borrowing base of all is accounts receivable, because a lender can easily liquidate it in the event of a loan default. The lender will be most unhappy if the reported borrowing base is incorrect. The audit team can verify its accuracy by comparing the general ledger balance to supporting detail by examining a representative sample of invoices to ensure that products or services were actually delivered, and by sending confirmations to customers to ensure that no accounts receivable in the detailed listing are falsely recorded.
- *Fixed Assets: Compare to detail.* The borrowing base must be accurate or the lender will accuse the company of fraudulent reporting. To avoid this issue, the internal audit team should verify that the total fixed asset amount on the general ledger matches the detailed listing shown in a subsidiary ledger and should also conduct a fixed asset review to ensure that all of the assets actually exist.
- *Fixed Assets: Verify depreciation calculations.* The fixed asset borrowing base agreement usually requires the borrower to subtract depreciation from the recorded cost of all fixed assets; this means that the internal audit team must review depreciation calculations, especially for those assets with the largest cost, to ensure that calculations include the proper depreciation periods and rates.

- *Inventory: Audit inventory quantities and costs.* After accounts receivable, inventory is the second most common item in a borrowing base. Lenders rarely require an exact accounting of the inventory detail along with the monthly borrowing base certificate (which is commonly required for accounts receivable), but the inventory balance must still be accurate. The auditors can verify this by reviewing a representative sample of inventory items, especially the most costly ones, and the supporting costing detail.

The balance sheet is heavily reviewed when a company's external auditors conduct their year-end audit, because an external audit program assumes that if the balance sheet is correct, every other expense must, by default, have flowed through the income statement, thereby yielding a correct profit number for the year. Consequently, it is reasonable to have the internal audit staff review the other major accounts in the balance sheet besides those already noted, so that the company does not have to make large (and potentially embarrassing) adjustments as a result of the annual audit. Consequently, the audit staff should use the following routines to ensure the accuracy of additional balance sheet accounts:

- *Accrued sales taxes.* If a company incorrectly charges sales taxes to its customers, it is liable for the difference. There are two ways to review this area. One is to compare the computer system's tax tables to the official tax rates published by the local and state governments; the other is to review invoices to see if the correct taxes were calculated. Either method is effective, but reviewing the tax tables corrects the base cause of inaccurate taxes and therefore should be tried first.
- *Advances.* A company typically has a small number of advances outstanding to employees or owners. The audit staff should verify that these advances are in the process of being repaid, and that they have not been sitting on the books for an inordinately long time; if so, the auditors should recommend that each employee or owner be put on a formal repayment schedule to clear the advances off the books.
- *Other accruals.* Every company must accrue some expenses, such as property taxes or unpaid salaries, that were expensed during the year, but for which there is not yet any supplier invoice. The audit staff can verify the accuracy of some of these accruals, such as property taxes, simply by seeing what the actual expense was for the previous year. For more variable accruals, such as unpaid salaries, the audit staff can review any calculations made by the accounting staff to derive the accruals.
- *Prepayments.* Customers may make payments to a company that are advances on the future delivery of products or services. The auditors should verify that there is a regularly updated schedule that records the detailed amounts paid by each customer. If the prepayment dates are excessively old, the auditors

should look further to see if there are old accounts receivable against which the prepayments can be offset, thereby canceling the amount in the prepayment account.

The many audit routines that were recommended in this section indicate that there is a great deal of continuing work to be done in an explosive growth company to ensure that the balance sheet is accurate. When the internal auditing staff finds a problem, it should not only recommend how to correct it, but also highlight any procedural changes needed to ensure that the same errors do not happen again.

AUDIT THE INCOME STATEMENT

Many growing companies get into trouble because they use very aggressive financial reporting methods to recognize income and expenses. These methods appear to show unusually high revenue and profit gains, which bolsters a company's valuation in the short term. In the long term, however, these reporting methods cause problems that grow to such a size that they can no longer be hidden, resulting in sudden (and large) losses and an abrupt drop in the value of the company, frequently accompanied by the rapid departure of top management. The internal audit staff can help to avoid these problems by continually reviewing the two parts of the income statement where these problems can arise—revenue recognition and the cost of goods sold. Part of its recommendations in this area should always include changes to the transaction processing methodology, which ensures more consistency in how transactions are processed and therefore in how financial results are reported.

The single largest problem area on the income statement for a growing company is revenue. In order to show rapid growth, a company may resort to a variety of types of financial trickery to show large revenue gains. For example, pressure by top management at MiniScribe, the disk drive maker, resulted in fake shipments to customers, which led to a government probe of the operation and its eventual liquidation. The internal audit staff has a difficult chore in this area, for false revenue reporting may be caused by pressure from top management. If the audit team recommends changes in this area that are ignored, it may be wise to find employment with a different company. If, however, revenue is being recognized simply based on a particular person's opinion of how accounting rules are interpreted, the audit team may want to bring in an expert, perhaps a specialist from one of the Big Six accounting firms, who can render an opinion regarding the appropriate timing and amount of revenue to recognize. This problem is so extensive in growing companies that this area should be one of the first that an audit team investigates. To demonstrate the prevalence of the problem, here are more revenue recognition examples from a variety of industries:

- If a company completes a product for sale to a customer, but the customer does not yet want it, can it record the product as a sale even if it remains on company premises? Does the situation vary if the company built the product for delivery sooner than the customer specified in its purchase order?
- If a company sells a service contract to a customer, can it recognize all of the revenue at once, or recognize it gradually over the term of the service contract?
- If a company leases a product to a customer, should it recognize all lease revenue immediately, or only as it receives payments on the lease?
- If a company receives product back from a customer, how long can it wait before recording the credit?
- If a company acquires another company that observes a different method for recognizing revenue, should it alter the new subsidiary's methodology, or operate with multiple methods?

These points demonstrate that revenue recognition is a serious problem to address in nearly every environment. It may be useful for senior management to formally agree on a precise definition of revenue recognition, and then have the internal audit staff verify that it is being observed throughout the company.

After revenue recognition, the next largest problem area is the cost of goods sold, primarily because it is so difficult for many companies to track the inflow and outflow of materials (for those companies who do not build what they sell, this area is less of a problem). Even a small error in this area can lead to a large profit variance, because cost of goods sold comprises such a large proportion of a typical company's expenses. The following audit procedures are ones that the internal audit staff should carefully address to ensure that the cost of goods sold information is accurate:

- *Compare purchase order cost to paid cost.* It is an easy error for a company to be billed a higher price than expected for a product or service and for it to pay the higher rate without anyone noticing. The audit staff can locate this problem by comparing a sample of purchase orders to supplier invoices, noting the presence or absence of approvals by company managers for excessive billing amounts by suppliers.
- *Compare received quantity to paid quantity.* It is possible for a supplier to ship one quantity to a company and bill for another quantity, resulting in an incorrect cost of goods sold. The audit staff can locate this problem by comparing the quantities shown on the receiving log to the quantities listed on the supplier's invoice.
- *Look for duplicate payments.* It is easy to pay a supplier twice if an invoice is for a cost of goods sold, because many companies approve payment for cost of goods sold if there is a purchase order in the system, but, because of

primitive computer systems, there is no way to see if multiple invoices were paid on the same purchase order. The audit staff can locate this problem by matching a sample of supplier invoices to purchase orders.

- *Review inventory cutoff procedures.* It is very easy for a company to record the expense for a received product and not record the corresponding item in inventory, which creates a fake expense; the reverse is also possible when a company returns parts to a supplier without also entering a credit in the accounting system to offset the corresponding account payable. The audit staff can review this problem by comparing inventory receipts near the end of a reporting period to accounts payable entries.
- *Review freight payments.* It is possible that a company has no idea if it is double paying for freight invoices or not paying them at all, because many companies do not use manager sign-offs before paying freight bills, nor do they use any purchase orders. This is a real problem for large shipments, because no one knows that an expensive freight bill is coming, resulting in incorrect reporting of the cost of goods sold. The audit staff can locate this problem by comparing freight charges to the shipping log, looking for charges that do not match the company's record of shipments.

Third in importance behind revenue and cost of goods sold are all other company expenses. These can still have a number of problems, but they are smaller in size than the previous two categories and are also easier to control. The following points cover problem areas that the internal audit staff can review. These do not focus on specific expenses, but rather on methods for finding problems.

- *Compare payments to contracts.* Some large payments, such as building leases, are predetermined based on a long-term contract. Because there are frequently clauses in those contracts that change prices, the audit team should review the contracts to ensure that the accounting staff is altering its payments in the correct amounts and at the right times. The audit team may also recommend that the accounting staff create a formal schedule of expected changes to all contracts, so that it becomes an easy matter to review it each month and alter payments accordingly.
- *Review accruals.* Some very large expenses, such as period-end payroll, are made with accruals. Incorrect accrual calculations can have a significant impact on reported profits. The audit team can review the underlying calculations for each accrual and recommend changes to each calculation method, as needed.
- *Review credit card purchases.* With many companies now encouraging their employees to make purchases with corporate purchasing cards, it is necessary for the audit staff to make spot checks of the purchases made with these cards to ensure that they are appropriate.
- *Review expense consistency.* The audit staff can review the trend of expenses for each expense line item. A sudden increase or drop in expenses is a good

indicator that an expense may have been incorrectly added to or dropped from a general ledger account, which the audit staff can fix by recommending a tighter procedure for recording expenses.

- *Verify that people on the payroll are listed in the correct departments.* It is very common for a company to switch people between functional areas and forget to tell the payroll staff to switch those people to new departments in the payroll system, resulting in their costs being charged to the wrong areas. The audit staff can easily find this problem by reviewing head count lists with the manager of each functional area. This verification also tells the audit staff if there is an extra paycheck being cut for a fake employee or someone whom no one can account for, which may be a fraudulent transaction.

In addition to all of the previous points regarding audit steps for the income statement, the audit staff can also review the procedure that the accounting staff uses to create the income statement, because this procedure has a bearing on the results of the income statement. For example, the audit team can see if the accounting staff is accruing properly for any supplier invoices that have not yet been received, but for which the receiving log indicates that a product was received. Also, the financial statement closing sequence must follow a proper order, or else it may change the financial statement results. For example, if the overhead calculation is completed before the accounts payable module is closed, it is possible that extra accounts payable that are added at the last minute will not appear in the overhead pool for the reporting period, resulting in incorrect overhead allocations. Consequently, the internal audit team should include a review of closing procedures in its review of a company's financial statements.

AUDIT CASH AND INVESTMENTS

It seems that the primary concern of many auditors is the proper control of cash. This does not make sense in many industries, where there is little cash on hand to lose, with the bulk of all cash or investments being easily protected in banks by board-approved transfer authorizations. Nonetheless, there are still industries, such as retailing or gambling, where there is a significant amount of incoming cash that requires tight control. This section deals with the primary audit objectives for the control of incoming and outgoing cash, objectives for reviewing transfers, and the safety of investments, and concludes with a short list of best practices that the audit staff can recommend.

The internal audit staff can review several controls to see if there is a potential for loss. The controls are the following:

- *Compare cash register totals to cash counts.* It is possible that a cash register operator will steal cash from the register. To detect this problem, the audit team can compare the cash register transaction totals to the amount in the cash drawer to see if there are any differences.

- *Compare mail room control totals to deposit slips.* It is possible for incoming cash to be lost in transit from the time it arrives in the mail room to the time it is sent from accounting to the bank for deposit. To detect this problem, the audit staff can compare the amount of money the mail room staff received each day, according to its records, to the amount the accounting department recorded on its deposit slip for the same day.
- *Review bank reconciliations.* It is possible to cover up the loss of cash by altering the bank reconciliation. In particular, if someone is stealing money and is doing so in concert with the person who is preparing the bank reconciliation, it is an easy matter to charge off the loss to an expense account. To detect this problem, the audit staff can review the bank reconciliation to see if there are expenses recorded that are not shown on the bank statement, as well as outstanding checks that do not really exist.
- *Review timing of cash sent to bank.* It is possible for a company to lose cash if it stays within company premises for too long, because this gives people an opportunity to take it. To detect this problem, the audit staff can compare not only the amounts but also the dates on the mail room control totals to the deposit slips being sent to the bank. If the deposit slips are dated late, then there is a timing problem.
- *Review value of assets sold.* It is possible for an employee to sell an asset, pocket a portion of the cash received, and record the sale at a lesser amount. To detect this problem, the audit staff can have an outside appraiser value the asset sales to see if the recorded values are excessively below market rates. A continuing trend of low valuations may indicate a problem, at which point the audit staff should contact the entities to whom assets were sold to verify sales amounts according to their records.
- *Trace cash receipts to related accounts receivable.* It is possible that cash from a customer that is a payment for an account receivable will be sidetracked, so that the receivable is still incorrectly noted on the company's books. To detect this problem, the audit staff can compare the daily deposit slip to a summary of cash applied to look for incorrect cash applications.
- *Verify cash sales against inventory records.* It is possible for someone to sell a part from inventory and then pocket the customer's cash payment, rather than record it anywhere. Although it is a weak control, the audit team can compare reductions in inventory balances to recorded sales to see if there are any discrepancies. If there is a problem, the audit team can recommend involving two people in the sales process, which increases the amount of coordination needed to steal from the company, or even installing a video monitoring system.

The foregoing audit procedures allow a company to exercise proper control over its cash, which is also one of the underlying principles of this chapter, that of tracking assets.

It is also important to review the account agreements with all banks that a company uses. This review should include a comparison of banking fees charged for each account to market rates, and any compensating balance agreements on loans that may require a company to retain an excessive amount of cash in its checking accounts. This review is intended to spot any excessive costs charged by a bank and to recommend cheaper alternatives.

The primary risk in the cash and investments area is not any cash held within the company, which is usually minimal; instead, it is unauthorized transfers of large blocks of funds from a company's investment accounts. To keep a company from being on the unhappy list of those who have been the victim of large losses through illegal transfers, there are a few controls to implement. The first, and most important, is to require multiple authorizations to transfer money outside of any company accounts. This control can only be abrogated if more than one authorized person decides to form a conspiracy to withdraw the money, which is much less likely than when one person steals money. In case this control proves burdensome from an operational perspective, a company can require an authorization by just one person for the transfer of smaller amounts of money. There is also no risk of theft if a person is transferring funds between accounts that are held by the same company, so the authorization for this transaction can be just one person. Another control is for the financial institution being asked to transfer funds to call back a person at a higher level of responsibility within the company to confirm transfers made by other people; this is also a double authorization. A company can also set up strict paperwork tracking systems so that it can trace transfers after they have occurred; however, although this is an admirable objective, it does nothing to keep the funds from being stolen in the first place. In short, a company should require multiple authorizations to transfer large amounts of funds from investment accounts.

A company can also lose invested cash, not because of any problems with illegal transfers, but because of the riskiness of the investments. The audit team can uncover this problem by reviewing the risk and related returns on all investment vehicles that a company uses. A risky investment is one where there is a high risk of losing some or all of the invested cash; this can also apply to financial transactions that are not strictly investments, but which put the company at risk of incurring a significant loss, such as derivatives. The audit team must carefully review the investment prospectus or other information for all investments to determine the level of risk and bring any perceived problems to the attention of top management.

The internal audit staff can include several best practices for cash and investments in its audit recommendations. One is to use a lockbox system for collecting cash from customers. In this practice, cash goes straight to a bank for depositing, so that a company receives cash a day or two sooner than normal. Another approach is to use a zero-balance checking account. Under this system, cash stays in an interest-bearing account; the bank only withdraws enough cash each day to cover any checks that have been presented for payment. A third practice is to use cash concentration accounts, wherein cash may be received into as many accounts around the country as a company desires, but it is then automatically forwarded to a central account every day. This system earns a company money by centralizing all cash in one spot, where it can be placed in large investment vehicles that earn more interest than would many small investments. These best practices are all useful for the orderly marshaling and investment of a company's cash reserves.

AUDIT COMPUTER SERVICES

A crucial underlying principle for the internal audit function is to ensure that a growing company's computer systems do not stop operations. Although the role of the internal audit function is only to advise, it can look for computer system problems that may stop other normal business activities and then point out these problems to management. This section discusses the problems to look for that can bring down a computer system and thereby other company operations. The key review points to include in an internal audit of the computer services function are as follows:

- *Application audit.* A computer system may appear to be functioning properly, but may actually be causing such problems as missed billings to customers, missed payments to suppliers, or the incorrect recording of revenues and costs in the general ledger. Many of these problems may lurk unseen in the computer system for years, until they grow to a size where they become painfully obvious, causing considerable disruption. The internal audit staff can guard against this trouble by tracking test transactions through the computer system in a variety of ways to ensure that everything is being processed as expected. A typical test transaction is a customer order, including shipment of the product to the customer, billing, and receipt of cash. The transaction's characteristics can be modified in a number of ways (e.g., size of the order, length of the customer name, or date of the order) to verify that the system can handle all possible data variations. This type of testing is an effective means of ensuring that existing systems are operating properly.
- *Backup system audit.* A computer system can be brought down if the system fails with no backup system in place. The backup system should include a separate power supply to ensure that each file server remains operational if there is a power failure. There should also be, at a minimum, a daily backup of all databases, with off-site storage of the backups in case the main storage area is destroyed. Preferably, the system should also include disk mirroring,

whereby information is stored in two places at once, which further reduces the risk of lost data. There should also be an automatic fire suppression system installed around every file server. In addition, there should be a disaster recovery plan that includes regular testing of a procedure for rapidly shifting all major computer operations to a new location. An internal audit of computer backup systems should include these audit review points, at a minimum.

- *Developing systems audit.* New software may be incorrectly developed missing key features and rendering it useless. The internal audit staff can review the development documentation of new systems to spot these problem areas and bring them to the attention of the development team. In particular, the audit team should look for any missing controls that would allow someone to remove assets from the company without any warning or documentation from the computer system. Other problem areas are ones that might keep proper billings from taking place or purchases from being made. For the more technical areas, the internal audit staff should be supported by specialists who are more familiar with computer controls.
- *Systems installation audit.* It is very difficult to replace a computer system without causing disruption in company operations. The internal audit staff can review the system installation plan for a number of factors that can keep the disruption to a minimum. One such factor is a plan to operate the new system in a test mode with test data until management is sure that the new system works properly. Another factor is a plan to keep the old system operational for a designated period after the switch-over date in case the new system fails and the company needs to revert back to the old system. A final factor is the presence of a plan to properly train all users in how to operate the new system. Without all of these plans in place, there is a high risk of system failure. The internal audit staff should not only review the systems installation plan, but also come back to the installation project very regularly to ensure that the plan is being followed.

In short, the internal audit staff should review the computer services area to ensure that there are no disruptions that could cause a failure of operations elsewhere in the company. These reviews should include all computer system backups, existing and incoming software applications, and upcoming and current system installations. These reviews will warn the management of an explosive growth company of any potential issues that could abruptly terminate that growth.

MEASUREMENTS AND REPORTS

The internal audit function is one of the more difficult areas to measure, because it does not have clear-cut results. Instead, a company invests in an internal audit staff and gets in return a series of reports on a number of audits. To see if the internal audit staff is being managed efficiently and effectively, it is necessary to use a combination of several measures and reports, as well as some outside opinions. The following measurements center on the ability of the audit staff to stay within its budget while completing its scheduled audits. Other measures and reports give senior management some idea of the quality of the work performed. The measurements are as follows:

- *Budgeted costs versus actual costs.* The audit committee will work with the internal audit manager to create a budget for all internal audit costs for the upcoming year, which should include all related costs, such auditor payroll and travel costs. This budget can be sorted by expense, but may be more relevant if broken down by cost per audit, which the audit committee can then compare to actual costs as each audit is completed. To calculate the budget, store internal audit costs and budget figures in the general ledger using a unique set of account codes. Then extract this information with a report writer to compare the budgeted and actual costs for each account code for each reporting period.
- *Number of audits scheduled versus completed.* The audit committee usually works with the internal audit manager to devise a schedule of audits for the upcoming year or quarter. It reflects well on the manager if the entire schedule is completed on time. To calculate it, compare the number of audit reports presented to the audit committee during the measurement period to the amount expected. However, the internal audit manager may shrink the scope of some audits in order to ensure that they are completed on time, which results in a good measurement but a poor audit.
- *Number of recommendations made.* Some audits are completed mechanically by employees who do not have a sufficient knowledge of the systems they are reviewing to recommend improvements; if so, they should be replaced by more competent personnel or receive additional training. One can find evidence of this problem by reviewing the number of recommendations made following an audit. If there are very few, there may be a problem with auditor expertise. To calculate it, simply summarize the recommendations listed in the audit report. However, there could be no audit points because the system under review is so well designed and managed that there are no problems to correct. Also, the number of recommendations can be inflated by adding any recommendations from the previous audit report that were not acted upon.
- *Savings suggested versus cost of the examination.* Although it is not the only focus of an audit, it is useful for the audit team to come up with recommended improvements to save money. This is a reasonable way to justify the cost of the audit. To calculate it, summarize the projected savings from audit recommendations and divide this amount by the total labor and other costs of the audit. However, when auditors know they are being judged with this mea-

surement, they tend to inflate the estimated savings to be realized from their recommendations. Consequently, it is best to either have a third-party verification of the estimated savings, or at least require the auditors to provide calculations that support their estimated savings figures.

In addition to the foregoing quantitative measurements, there are several qualitative reports that are very useful for determining the success of an internal audit department. These reports are written by the audit staff or by others who review its work. They are as follows:

- *Activity reports.* The audit managers should issue periodic activity reports regarding the status of all internal audits under their supervision. Management can review the content and timing of these reports and compare them over time to see if the audit managers have sufficient management skill. However, a good report writer can mask a great deal of management incompetence, so this source of information must be supplemented by other measurements and reports.
- *Audit reports.* Audit reports issued by the internal audit teams tell a great deal about the teams. If there are few recommendations, or if the recommendations are copied from the previous review of the same area, it indicates lack of skill or that little time was spent on the audit. If the auditee objects violently to the report, it may also mean that the audit results were not reviewed with the auditee, which indicates a lack of communication skill. One may also discern the writing skill level of whomever prepared the report. A careful review of audit reports reveals a great deal of circumstantial information about the quality of the audit staff.
- *Quality reports.* Company management can bring in outside experts, such as the company's external auditors, to conduct periodic reviews of the internal audit staff's workpapers and audit reports. Outside experts can tell if sufficient attention is being given to audits, if the skill level of the staff is sufficient, and if the resulting audit reports are based on sufficient evidential matter. Their quality reports should go to the audit committee for review. The only problem with this approach is that external auditors are now becoming more interested in the business of providing internal audit services to their clients, therefore they have a vested interest in showing a company's internal audit staff to be inadequate so that they can replace it.

In short, no individual measurements or reports can tell a manager precisely how the audit function is performing, but a combination of many of the measurements and reports shown in this section can give management a good idea of its operations.

CONTROLS

Exercising control over the function that reviews the controls of the rest of the company is a surprisingly easy task. It involves arranging the number and order of audits to be conducted in a given time period, creating budgets and work programs for the audits, and then comparing actual expenses to those budgeted, while also reviewing the results of the audits. The first step in this chain is the most important, that of determining which areas of the company are most in need of an audit. The audit committee, which is a subset of the board of directors, is responsible for making this decision, but does not normally have enough in-depth knowledge of the company to determine the exact types of audits to be conducted. Accordingly, it is customary for the audit committee to take the advice of the audit manager, as well as the chief financial officer (CFO) or controller, regarding areas that have some financial risk and should therefore be reviewed. Many of the previous sections of this chapter provide guidance on which portions of each functional area should be reviewed.

The middle steps, those of creating budgets and work programs for the audits, involve the mid-level managers of the internal audit staff. The easiest control here is to use previous budgets and work programs from similar audits as a guideline for upcoming work. However, this option is not viable for an explosive growth company for two reasons. One is that since the company is growing so fast, there may not have been a previous audit, because the area under review had not previously existed. The second reason is that a prior audit program may be missing key audit tasks that will still be missed if the program is simply duplicated for a follow-on audit. Consequently, it is best to only use information from previous audits as a general guideline for designing new ones; it is more important to use a careful review of each subject area and prior experience when designing audit programs and budgets.

The final control over the internal audit function is the review of audit results. One review is the comparison of budgeted to actual costs (mostly comprised of hours charged by auditors), which is adequately managed by a detailed review session involving the manager of the function and the audit supervisor. However, the primary control here is not the budget but the audit report and its repercussions. The audit manager must review every audit report (as well as the underlying workpapers, if necessary) to see what problems were found and what recommendations were made. This information not only tells the manager a great deal about the ability of each audit team, but also forms the foundation for further audit work, either in the form of new audits of areas that have not yet been reviewed, or of areas that have problems and require a follow-up audit to ensure that they have been corrected. In addition, it is necessary to determine the opinions of those people who have been audited. If they are unhappy with the audit report, it is very possible that the audit team did a poor job of reviewing its findings with them, which reveals a communications problem that the internal audit manager must deal with. Finally, management can bring in an external audit firm occasionally to conduct an independent review of internal audits to see what could be improved. In short, the results of every audit must be carefully reviewed by the internal audit manager for clues to further control problems and issues with the audit teams.

In summary, the internal audit function is best controlled at the beginning and end of the audit process; by determining at the beginning the types of audits to be conducted, and by reviewing the results at the end, with information not only in the workpapers and audit reports, but also from the auditees and an independent quality assurance firm. A combination of these steps gives management good control over the internal audit function.

SUMMARY

This chapter covered the key areas that the internal audit staff must address in an explosive growth environment. The key areas, unfortunately, are *all* areas, because a growing company has considerable difficulty maintaining consistent control over its operations due to the addition of many new managers and staff, probably extending into geographical areas where they are not under the direct control of corporate headquarters. The impact of such rapid growth can lead to several crucial problems. One is that the computer systems running the company can collapse for a variety of reasons, resulting in the stoppage of all transactions throughout the company. Another is that assets can easily disappear, resulting in large losses. Finally, it is very common for a company to have inconsistent treatment of transactions, which leads to inconsistent financial results. All of these problems are serious.

This chapter addressed these serious problems by recommending a variety of audit objectives in such areas as the revenue cycle, purchasing cycle, balance sheet, and income statement, with the intent of pointing out the most likely areas of failure. By coordinating audits in these areas, a company can protect against serious losses or failures as a company grows. However, the key points of risk vary by company, so management must be ever vigilant and follow up on any rumors of potential trouble with an immediate internal audit that can verify or deny the rumors. Only through such constant attention to a company's systems will it survive its growing years.

Chapter 12

Computer Services

INTRODUCTION

The computer services function provides many of the most important systems that an explosive growth company needs. Without these systems, which support many crucial areas such as accounting, warehousing, production, and purchasing, it would be impossible for a company not only to grow, but to exist. How does a manager determine what parts of this functional area require enhancement and what can be safely ignored when a company is growing at an extraordinary rate? The key areas requiring attention are shown in Exhibit 12.1, which also shows those items that can be given less support. Computer services also support other areas, such as hardware and network maintenance, a help desk, and disaster planning, which must be given the resources needed to maintain them, but which do not require enhanced support.

This chapter discusses each of the items highlighted in Exhibit 12.1, including the reasons for and against the need to either increase or reduce the level of support for each item. In addition, the next section discusses a set of underlying principles essential to understanding why certain tasks are more important in an explosive growth environment than others. The chapter finishes with sections that discuss system upgradeability and the controls, management issues, and measurements needed to support the computer services function.

UNDERLYING PRINCIPLES

A multitude of topics in the computer services area have some bearing on explosive growth, but only a few are crucial to supporting the explosive growth track. If management gives resources to the wrong areas, the computer services function will find itself slowing down the company rather than supporting it. The following four principles form the basis for understanding why some topics are more important than others and are useful for understanding many of the later sections of this chapter. The principles are as follows:

1. *Rapid access to key information.* It is critical for managers of an explosive growth company to know the status of all key operational indicators every day. Because even waiting a few days to find out about crucial information

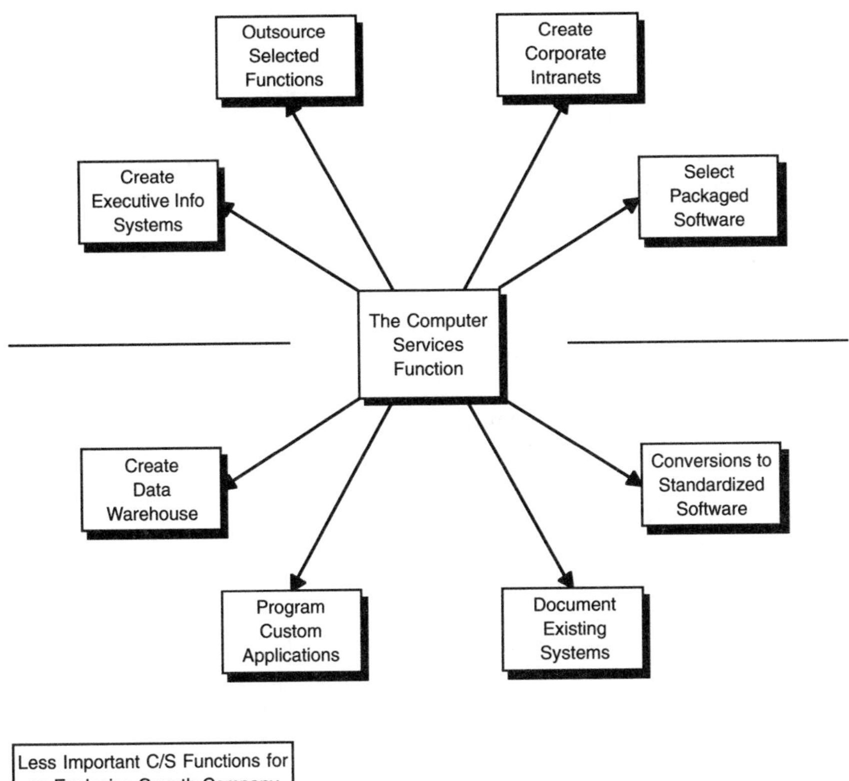

Exhibit 12.1 Explosive Growth Tasks for the Computer Services Function

can lead to a loss of market share or excessive expenses, the computer services staff must focus its efforts on supplying this information as quickly and accurately as possible.

2. *Minimum number of system conversions.* The rapid distribution of information, as noted in the first principle, can be impacted by having too many system conversions. During a conversion, it is possible that key information is not passed along to management with its accustomed speed, meaning that management will not have a clear picture of company operations during some phases of a system conversion. In addition, conversions are extraordinarily expensive, both in terms of expenses and the use of management time to

complete the conversion; neither of these resources is available in great quantities in an explosive growth company. In short, the number of conversions to new systems must be kept to an absolute minimum.

3. *Rapid roll-out of new systems*. When a company decides to create a new computer system, the focus should be on completing the new system as rapidly as possible in order to give management access to new information, as well as to give the company new transaction-processing capabilities. This emphasis on speed should preclude any significant amount of customized programming on new systems, because the programming and debugging process uses valuable amounts of time. When installing new systems, speed is of paramount importance.
4. *Support operations*. A company's computer systems must not keep it from performing its basic tasks of providing products or services to customers. As the company grows at high speed, systems will probably fail to keep pace, so a key role for the computer services staff is to monitor the impact of this growth on existing systems, predict when new systems will be needed to support that growth, and seamlessly provide those systems when the predicted conversion time arrives. These do not have to be the most advanced or even the most perfectly suited (i.e., customized) systems—they must simply be available on time, and they must meet the bulk of the company's needs.

The foregoing principles are the basis for the topcs discussed later in this chapter. The following sections on executive information systems and data warehousing are founded upon the principle of rapid access to key information, while outsourcing is justified by the principles of not letting systems stop operations and of having the minimum number of system conversions. In addition, the customization section evolves from the principle of the rapid roll-out of new systems. Also, the intranet section is based on giving rapid information access to the largest possible number of employees. Finally, the system upgradeability section covers the principle of having a minimal number of conversions.

THE EXECUTIVE INFORMATION SYSTEM

In an explosive growth situation, it is necessary to keep constant track of key indicators of a company's performance. These indicators are not necessarily financial. They may cover the sales backlog or production overtime, which may require rapid action to fix if the indicators take a turn for the worse. This information cannot wait until the next financial statement is released, because that is only released once a month, and problems may arise in the interim that can seriously impact employees, customers, processes, and profits. Instead, the information must be available to senior management every day. Although the information can be manually gathered, usually by the accounting staff, and presented to management every day, a different approach is to develop an executive information system (EIS) that senior management can tap into at any time.

An EIS is a database that periodically pulls in information from other company databases and presents it in a format for analytical use by management. At its most elementary level, the information can be manually collected and input into the EIS database, although this approach is very primitive. A better method is for the EIS to have automated links to other databases that extract information from them at set intervals and store it in the EIS database. Data collection, however, is only one piece of the complete EIS system. The other part, and the one that managers need the most, is data presentation. This presentation can be a graphical view of key information, possibly showing trends in performance measures, or it may be a numeric comparison of performance measurements as compared to a goal. The EIS system must present information quickly and easily, because managers do not have the time or inclination to write their own queries to extract information—they want to press a button and have information leap onto the screen in the format they need. By having rapid polling of databases throughout the company and an easy-to-understand presentation of the resulting information, management can rapidly respond to changing conditions in the company.

One problem that arises as soon as management decides to install an EIS is whether to purchase one or create one. A custom-designed EIS has the advantage of giving management the exact information it needs in the precise format desired, but it takes time to program and debug. Purchasing a packaged solution has the advantage of putting an EIS in place much quicker (although it still can take months to install—there are many program interfaces to write!), and for an explosive growth company, time is of the essence. Thus, for an explosive growth company, purchasing an EIS is clearly a better decision than creating one in-house.

A key problem for an EIS in an explosive growth company is keeping it linked to all of the new databases being created as a company creates new locations, buys other companies, and creates new products and methods of distribution. It is entirely possible for a manager who is relying on an EIS to not know about key information, because it has not been added to the database. This situation is dangerous, for a manager may rely too much on an EIS, assuming that it contains all pertinent information. The manager may not even consider that the EIS is not linked to additional information that may yield a very different view of the company's business position. For example, a company may consider day-to-day sales by store location to be a key indicator. If initial sales are poor, then the company may have a policy of immediately shutting down retail locations, having found from previous history that such locations do not experience a sufficient gain in sales to later turn a profit. What if this information is not available through the EIS? In this situation, a company may inadvertently keep stores open that are bleeding cash. The best way to avoid this problem is to schedule continual reviews of the EIS by the company's internal audit team that examine the completeness of information offered through the system. Only continual audits are acceptable, because an explosive growth company may require changes to its EIS every month, if not every week. In short, constant vigilance is necessary to ensure that the information provided to management through an EIS is complete.

Another EIS issue is the volume of information supplied through it to management. Managers in an explosive growth company have no free time in which to peruse vast amounts of information. They must handle a myriad of operational details every day and can only devote a quick glance to the information being presented to them through the EIS, no matter how important it may be. Accordingly, the EIS information must only be for the bare minimum of the most essential statistics. All other data may either be accessed through a second and more detailed layer of information in the EIS database, or management can simply assign a staff person to personally investigate any problems spotlighted by the key statistics noted by the EIS. Either approach allows management to grasp the essentials of company operations in a few moments without forcing them to wade through excessive reams of detail to find it.

A final EIS problem is that its links to underlying (and outlying) databases must be changed every time a company upgrades to new databases. This happens whenever a company must move to new computer systems to meet the demands of transactional growth or new information needs. For example, a personal computer(PC)-based accounting system may only be able to handle inventory for a single location, so when a company acquires additional warehouses, it must purchase a new software package in order to track multiple locations. The problem also arises if a company has so many computer users accessing its database that the system has unacceptably long response times. In either case, the company must build new links between the new databases and the EIS, so that management can continue to receive timely information. The easiest solution to this problem is to initially purchase software systems that have plenty of capacity for growth, thereby allowing a company to avoid system changes for long time periods. If this is not possible, a company should at least factor this into its purchases of new systems, so that new systems do not require replacement, which allows links to the EIS to be maintained for long periods of time. An EIS is less effective if the underlying databases from which information is being taken are constantly being replaced.

In summary, it is critically important for the computer services function to set up an EIS, preferably bought from a supplier, that presents management with key information that is linked to the company's various databases to give up-to-the-minute information. The EIS should be frequently reviewed by the company's internal auditors to ensure that the information given is both accurate and complete.

DATA WAREHOUSING

Many companies are creating data warehouses. These are not large warehouses with forklifts puttering about, but instead are very large databases that pull in information from outlying databases and store it in one place, where it can be mined by a number of functional areas to help them run the company. Is this necessary for an explosive growth company? Probably not. A data warehouse requires a team of database administrators to manage, as well as programmers to update. This team tends to slow down a company's expansion of its computer systems to new functions and locations, because they want to carefully refine the definition of each data element to be used. Because of the staff requirements, it can also be expensive to maintain a data warehouse. Because two of the primary driving forces of an explosive growth company are speed and growth at the lowest possible cost, a data warehouse is not helpful.

An EIS is a leaner version of a data warehouse and provides the bulk of a data warehouse's functionality to a company without as much investment in time or money. If a company uses this alternative, which was described in the previous section, it can avoid the expense of maintaining a data administration staff and a central repository of many data elements. An extreme version of this alternative is to use an EIS with nothing more than manually transferred information from outlying databases, perhaps by fax, into a simple management report that is maintained and distributed by someone at corporate headquarters. Although this EIS would be very weak, it illustrates the range of effort that a company can expend in order to collect and disseminate key information.

OUTSOURCING

Many companies have outsourced all or part of their computer services functions. Outsourcing is particularly appropriate for a company experiencing explosive growth, for any of the reasons noted in the following list:

- *Less capital needed.* Switching a company's computer systems over to a supplier entails selling off the equipment, either to the supplier or to an equipment broker, which frees up capital for other purposes, which is of particular concern to an explosive growth company. In addition, all hardware and software upgrades from that point on are paid for by the supplier, so the company no longer has to worry about the need for capital to fund future computer system expansions.
- *Less management needed.* A fully staffed computer services function that handles all possible tasks, including the help desk, network maintenance, programming, and hardware maintenance, requires a large staff and a large group of qualified managers. However, the top management of any explosive growth company will find that gaining top-performing managers is one of its hardest tasks, so removing some of these functions will relieve it of the need to bring in so many managers.
- *Less in-house technical expertise needed.* As was the case for finding qualified managers, so too is the case for technical staff to maintain a company's

computer services. They are hard to find and retain, plus their skills tend to decline over time. Management can avoid the entire issue by outsourcing tasks in which there are staffing weaknesses.

- *No upgradeability concerns.* One of the most management-intensive tasks is upgrading to new hardware and software. A company can avoid this problem by handing over its transaction processing to a supplier, who will be in charge of this task. However, it may not be possible to hand over the management of more specialized software, such as that used by the engineering or production departments, so this advantage tends to be centered on only the accounting function.
- *Switch from fixed to variable costs.* It is important for all companies, not just those experiencing explosive growth, to keep their fixed costs as low as possible, so that profits can be achieved even at low revenue levels. This is made possible through outsourcing, because the supplier takes on the fixed cost of computer equipment as well as staff, while only charging the company a fee per transaction processed. However, this variable cost tends to be much higher than a company's internal variable cost. Also, there is normally a minimum price per month to be paid to the supplier, irrespective of the level of transactions actually processed. In reality, then, there is still a fixed cost, but it is lower than would be the case without outsourcing.

CUSTOMIZED VERSUS PACKAGED SOFTWARE

Every growing company must deal with the problem of either purchasing a software package that probably does not contain all the features it wants or of spending the extra time and money to create its own software. The underlying principles noted in the second section of this chapter give some guidance regarding the appropriate direction to follow.

One of the underlying principles for computer services in an explosive growth company is that systems should not be allowed to stop operations. However, this can happen if a company decides to create its own software. The reason is that customized software can take a very long time to create and debug, whereas packaged software takes no time to create and is generally much easier to install, which means that it is available to assist a company's operations much sooner than a customized package would be. Packaged software is allowable under another of the aforementioned principles, that of always having a rapid roll-out of new systems in order to put information in the hands of management as rapidly as possible. Thus, based on the principles of not interfering with ongoing operations, as well as of rolling out new systems as rapidly as possible, the computer services function should purchase software packages rather than create its own software.

Several additional reasons for using packaged software are noted in the following list. In general, packaged software allows less management involvement and a smaller programming staff, while also reducing a company's time and monetary investment.

- *Less management required.* The management of any programming initiative is intensive and takes valuable time away from other critical functions that may have more strategic importance. Packaged software, on the other hand, only requires intensive management assistance when it is being selected and installed. After that, there is little demand on management for continuing attention.
- *No technology concerns.* When a company selects a reputable supplier of packaged software, it does not have to worry about keeping its software technologically up to date, because this is now the problem of the software supplier. If the company had elected to create its own software, it would have problems with retraining its programming staff to give them the latest skills, or may even have to replace them with better-trained personnel.
- *Use upgrades instead of customization.* If a company is an active participant in a user group that directs software upgrade requests at its packaged software supplier, it can eventually receive upgrades to its software for the features it needs, rather than having to program changes into the package, thus reducing the need for in-house programming staff and managers.
- *Cut costs.* A software package has a large up-front cost and ongoing maintenance fees, typically in the range of 10 to 15 percent of the purchase price, but this pales in comparison to the total cost to design, program, and debug a matching system with an in-house programming staff that must also be kept for ongoing management.
- *Cut total time to bring a new system on-line.* One of the key factors for an explosive growth company is time. It is usually operating within a tight marketing window, and its sales will fall off rapidly if it cannot upgrade its functionality in all respects to match its sales growth. Therefore, a software package, which can be installed immediately, is a much better alternative than the painfully slow programming process needed to create a new software application.

Despite the many reasons previously noted for purchasing a software package, there are still several instances when it is appropriate for a company to develop its own software. One case is when there are no software packages available to perform the functions that the computer services staff needs. This application is usually for a relatively minor niche, because packaged software has been developed for most major applications. If the computer services staff claims that it cannot locate an appropriate software package for a major application, such an application probably does exist, but the staff thinks it has a special requirement that the packaged software cannot handle. In such a case, management should investigate the need for the special software function prior to giving approval to a custom programming project. It is very possible that the extra requirement is not necessary, and that, once dropped, the application can be handled by an existing package. A common ploy by a programming staff (who want the programming work) is to develop a set of software requirements so specialized that no software package can possibly meet them. However, if management adopts the mindset that no software package is perfect, and that probably no more than 80 percent of all requirements will be matched by any package, then it can still find off-the-shelf software to approximately meet its needs. In short, customization is still appropriate in an explosive growth company, but usually only for minor niche applications for which no one has bothered to develop a software package.

Another instance when it is appropriate for a company to develop its own software is when doing so creates a competitive advantage. This situation generally arises when a company is operating on the leading edge of a new application, and packaged software has not yet been developed to handle its requirements. Although this advantage may very well be worth the time and money needed to create the software, management must consider how long the company will probably have a strategic advantage once the software has been developed. If the advantage is only for a short time, the effort may not be worthwhile. Thus, creating custom software is an acceptable option for an explosive growth company if it generates a long-term competitive advantage.

It is also necessary to have some ongoing customization work in order to create custom reports from a software package. Custom reports are not only an option but very nearly mandatory, because a company should go to great lengths to ensure that the store of information located in the packaged software is mined for all possible information that the company may need. Software packages never provide all of the various combinations of data that employees need to more perfectly conduct their jobs, so customization is quite allowable for writing new reports.

A final area in which customization is allowable is in the improvement of inputs to a software package. Most packages assume that all incoming data is manually punched into a computer terminal. However, there are more efficient ways to do this now, and a company should certainly use customization to achieve this goal. For example, incoming electronic commerce transactions can be loaded directly into a software package if there is an interface in place that converts the incoming transactions into the format used by the packaged software. By creating this interface with custom programming, a company can eliminate the labor and input errors that go with manual data entry. Thus, creating more efficient modes of input to a software package is an excellent use of customized programming.

For a real-life example of what happens when an explosive growth company elects to create its own software rather than purchase an existing package from a supplier, consider the case of Oxford Health Plans. This six-year-old company had grown to have revenues of $3 billion, 1.9 million enrollees, and 1996 earnings of $100 million, which certainly qualifies it as an explosive growth company. It lost $3.4 billion in market value in one day when it revealed a $78 million quarterly loss due to glitches in its software, which was developed in-house. The system had not billed millions in premiums to its members and had not paid accounts payable worth millions to doctors participating in the plan. The primary mistake the company made was in trying to create its own software when packaged software was already available that was extensively tested and would have given the company adequate performance in this noncritical aspect of the company's operations.

CORPORATE INTRANETS

An intranet is a file server that contains information that can be accessed and (sometimes) modified by anyone who is linked to the server. It is exceptionally useful for an explosive growth company, because it allows key information to be brought out in the open for anyone in the company to review. Here are several examples of intranets, which contain reasons why they are so useful:

- *Complaints intranet.* Also known as the complaints database, this is the central repository of customer complaints—who made the complaints, what was done to resolve the underlying problems, and a series of dates noting when key resolution issues were completed. This database is tremendously useful for management, because anyone can access the information on this intranet to see if new problems are arising or what is being done to fix old ones. Quickly finding a new problem through an intranet and fixing it immediately is much better than not discovering a problem until it has become fully developed and has caused a series of additional problems. For example, a car manufacturer can use this information to look for possible problems in newly released car designs; fixing them immediately with a small product recall is better than waiting a year and recalling hundreds of thousands of cars. Having access from many people allows all of them to offer suggested solutions, which can be entered directly into the database. For more information on the complaints database, see Chapter 13.
- *EIS intranet.* The EIS can be put on an intranet, so that many employees can review the status of operations. This is quicker than having only a few managers access the information and then pass portions of it along to a few additional personnel. By giving this information to everyone, the chances are much better that someone will think of a meaningful solution for problems that are highlighted by the information.
- *New product design intranet.* This intranet is a compilation of all product requirements, designs, and project status on new products. This information can be used by a variety of functional areas that are traditionally involved in product design. The advantage of having this intranet, rather than using the traditional process, is that a product is usually designed sequentially, where one function does not see the design until the previous group is finished with

it, whereas an intranet allows all groups to look at the design and spot problems at any point in the design process.

- *Policies and procedures intranet.* It is the job of the controller to constantly update all policy and procedure manuals, which can be quite a chore for companies with thousands of policy and procedure manuals that are spread over dozens of company locations. It is much easier to simply post updates on an intranet and allow employees to download the information they need whenever they have a question that can be answered by the electronic policy and procedure manual. This feature eliminates all of the paper-based updates that the controller's staff previously performed.
- *Production plan intranet.* This intranet contains the most recently updated production schedule. It is of great use to many people, both inside and outside of a company. For example, customers may want to access the intranet to see when their orders are scheduled for completion. Or, they may call a salesperson, who can also access it to see when the order is to be completed. The purchasing staff can review it to see when they must have materials available for each production job. Many people can use this intranet to conduct their jobs more easily.
- *Sales intranet.* This intranet contains information about actual sales by territory, and can also include information from salespeople about sales prospects. This information is of great use to both the sales personnel and the sales manager, for the personnel can use it to determine who has been buying product in their areas, and then target sales calls at those companies. The sales manager can use the information entered by the salespeople (which can take the place of weekly sales reports) to compile sales forecasts by region.

All of the foregoing intranets share a common feature—they allow many people to access, and in some cases, to update information about a topic. This setup is vastly better than the traditional approach of having all information channeled to top management, which then doles out small portions of it to employees for resolution. By handing out all of the information to everyone, a company taps into the full knowledge and productive potential of the entire staff. This is especially important for an explosive growth company, because it can use the power of intranets to resolve or avoid problems that might otherwise take it off the path of high growth.

CONVERT SUBSIDIARIES TO STANDARD COMPUTER SYSTEMS

It is common for a growing company to purchase other companies in order to expand its product line, bring in qualified staff, or simply to add revenues. Whatever the reason, the computer services group is frequently asked to convert the computer systems of each new subsidiary to that of the parent company. Several reasons for this approach are as follows:

- *Lower per-user fees from the software supplier.* When a company has only a few users for each of the software packages its uses, the software suppliers charge a higher cost per user license than is the case when many users are forced to use just one package. It is therefore cost-effective to have everyone use the same package, which reduces the licensed user cost per person.
- *Fewer computer personnel needed.* When there are many systems to maintain, it takes more people to watch over them, and also more people at each location, because the systems are scattered throughout the company locations. By consolidating all hardware and software in one location and having users access it by phone lines, a company can concentrate the majority of its computer services staff in that location, allowing it to cut back on the total number of staff needed to service it.
- *Fewer technical skills needed.* When there are many systems, the computer services staff needs a very broad skill set to maintain the different kinds of hardware and software. By consolidating systems, much of this technical skill is no longer needed.
- *Easier consolidation of information.* It is always easier for the central accounting staff to consolidate information from subsidiaries when they are all operating on the same system, because they all use the same chart of accounts and store information in the same database. This is much less expensive and time consuming than manually extracting information from the system of each subsidiary and consolidating it by hand.

With so many good reasons for having the computer services staff work on the standardization of computer systems across all subsidiaries, why would anyone not want to do so, especially because it supports the principle of giving management rapid access to key information? Because it violates all of the other principles. Forcing all subsidiaries onto the same computer system requires the function to be perpetually bogged down in system conversions, which runs a strong chance of stopping the operations of some subsidiaries during the conversion. In addition, the company can probably gain all of the management information it needs through an EIS, rather than going through the pain of a systems conversion, while the cost of doing the conversion is much higher in the short term than just leaving the multitude of systems alone. In addition, common systems require common methods of doing business, which may not work if subsidiaries have different (and necessary) operating procedures; the common computer system goal may require a subsidiary to fit the square peg of its procedures into the round hole of the common system. In short, there are just as many reasons to avoid system consolidations as there are reasons in favor.

Given the pros and cons of consolidated systems, which way should an explosive growth company go? The deciding factor here is the amount of resources needed to carry out system conversions. If a computer services staff is concentrating its effort on consolidating systems, then there is no way for it to release enough resources to perform many other tasks, even though they may be critically important to company growth. Also, a system conversion is a very absorbing task for management, which must put a disproportionate amount of its time into the conversion and little time into supporting the company's growth. In short, due to its inordinate impact on resources, it is best to avoid consolidating computer systems of subsidiaries in the middle of a corporate growth spurt.

DOCUMENTING EXISTING SYSTEMS

One of the chief roles of a typical computer services function is to adequately document the programming used to create existing computer systems. This documentation is certainly necessary for a company that has designed and programmed its own computer software, because it is very difficult to alter program code unless the programmer making the change has sufficient documentation on hand to determine what will happen when any code is changed. For example, a change to an apparently minor block of code may bring down an entire system. However, as noted earlier in the Customized versus Packaged Software section, an explosive growth company should purchase packaged software instead of creating its own, because doing so keeps the company from spending large amounts of time and money on a programming project that may not even be strategically important to the company. Purchasing the software significantly alters the need for documentation, because a packaged application should already have documentation that is created by the supplier. Inadequate documentation should be a factor (though by no means the key one) in making the decision to purchase the software. Thus, with the bulk of the documentation work already completed by the supplier, the computer services function is reduced to the lesser task of documenting any programming needed to create or alter inputs to or outputs from the packaged software, which is a minor task when compared to the documentation needed for fully customized software.

SYSTEM UPGRADEABILITY

System upgradeability is a major concern for the computer services manager. It refers to the ability of a computer system to expand in size to serve greater corporate needs, without having to make expensive and time-consuming changes to application programs, operating systems, or hardware. If a system is very upgradeable, then a company can go from one employee and a thousand dollars in sales to a multibillion dollar enterprise with thousands of employees all over the world; this follows the underlying principle, noted at the beginning of this chapter, of having the minimum number of system conversions. Unfortunately, such a system does not exist. What, then, is the computer services manager to do?

The answer to the upgradeability problem can be broken into four areas, each of which has a different solution. The areas are hardware, data, operating system software, and application software. These are the four primary components of any computer system. Each upgrade area is described in the following list, along with possible solutions.

- *Hardware.* The computer hardware suppliers are coming out of an era when the hardware they provided was not open—a company could not move software from it to the hardware platform of a different company. This meant that a company was locked into the upgrade path provided by that supplier, unless it wanted to ditch all of its computer systems and start from scratch with the hardware (and related software) of a different supplier. Luckily, times have changed. Some hardware platforms are now more open, allowing companies to transfer their software among different hardware platforms. This situation allows a company to easily upgrade to more powerful hardware to deal with the greater transaction processing requirements of an explosive growth path. At this time, the best upgrade option is to start with PC-based hardware that is founded on Intel chips. Some suppliers, such as Compaq, are now using the Intel chip for everything from a PC to the equivalent of a mainframe computer, so this allows a company to use the same hardware architecture through its entire growth path.
- *Data.* The transfer of a company's underlying data to a new application program may require that it be converted to a different format. For a smaller company, this conversion is sometimes done manually by rekeying all of the company's information into the new system. This approach is fraught with danger, for it is slow, time consuming, and very error prone. The better approach when upgrading is to bring in professional assistance to automatically convert the old data to the new format required by the new software. This approach can complete the conversion of data very rapidly, usually in a few minutes or hours (depending on the size of the database), and makes the upgrade much easier.
- *Operating system software.* Ever since the start of the computer era, there have been many operating systems, one or more for each of the many hardware platforms. Because application software was typically written to run on only one operating system (with the notable exception of Oracle software), a company was forced to first pick the application software it wanted, and then work backwards to purchase the operating system and hardware on which the application software could run. Then, once the company outgrew the application software, it had to find new software that could run on the old hardware and operating system. This situation has changed somewhat as the num-

ber of operating systems has shrunk along with the reduction in the number of computer hardware suppliers. In particular, the Windows NT operating system has been rapidly improved by the Microsoft Corporation to the point where it runs on anything from a PC to one of the mainframe-sized computers produced by Compaq. As application software suppliers have realized that there is finally a hardware and operating system platform that operates along the entire range of computers, they have scrambled to modify their software to run on Windows NT. Thus, using Windows NT now allows a company to use the same operating system software, no matter how big the computer system.

- *Application software*. As noted in the previous point on operating systems, application software was tied to specific operating systems and hardware platforms for years. This has changed with the advent of Intel-based computers and the Windows NT operating system, which allow for easy upgradeability for transaction processing requirements of any size. For a company looking into purchasing application software of any kind, this means that a key requirement for the software is that it must run on Windows NT and the Intel platform. If it does, a company can keep from upgrading the application software to something else for far longer than would otherwise be the case. Of course, many low-end application software packages are not robust enough to handle thousands of users or millions of transactions, so an upgrade to new software must eventually occur. However, the number of upgrades can be drastically reduced by only using software that runs on Intel hardware and the Windows NT operating system.

Is the problem of upgradeability worth the time and effort suggested by the previous bullet points? Is it really necessary to obtain the correct computing hardware, operating system, and application programs at the start of a company's growth period? Yes and yes are the answers, for there are several reasons, as noted in the following list, for trying to keep the number of upgrades to new systems to an absolute minimum. They are as follows:

- *Requires new EIS links*. The EIS provides key operating information to management, and does so by extracting key information from the various corporate databases. If a system is upgraded, the linkage between it and the EIS no longer functions, which means that management cannot see the information that was formerly provided by that system, so the company will be operating with a blind spot until a new linkage is created to the new system.
- *Interrupts operations*. Even if there is a seamless conversion from an old system to a new one (a rare occurrence indeed!), there is still much training required so that the personnel who use the system are conversant in its operation. This training period is lengthy and includes the time subsequent to training

when the staff unavoidably makes mistakes in using the software and requires extra time to fix their mistakes. This time interval is critical to an explosive growth company, for it could have used that time to further the company's growth objectives.

- *Requires lots of cash.* An upgrade to a major new system almost always requires assistance by consultants who have special skills in system conversions. These consultants can charge in excess of $300 per hour, and if there is a large team of them, which is necessary if the software being installed is especially complex and involves multiple functions or locations, the expense can easily run well into the millions of dollars. For the typical cash-strapped explosive growth company, this expense should be incurred as infrequently as possible.

It is clear from the foregoing points that system upgrades should be avoided whenever possible, so paying attention up front to the type of hardware platform and operating system used is certainly worth the effort.

Despite previous advice for how to avoid system upgrades, it is also clear that a company must occasionally go through them. This may be due to a change in the business that requires new software, the inability of the current system to deal with vastly increased transaction volume, or a variety of other reasons. If so, an explosive growth company should obtain a very "heavy weight" system to replace the old one, which means that the hardware should be capable of handling greatly increased transaction volumes, while the software should not be lacking in any of the key features needed to run the business. This may mean that the company must purchase an enterprise software solution. This software package handles all corporate transactions, ranging from human resources to manufacturing and order fulfillment, and does so seamlessly. These packages are sold by such companies as SAP, Oracle, and PeopleSoft, and are very expensive, with price tags in the $20 million range for the software and installation being quite typical. Most explosive growth companies do not have this kind of cash, but if they are well funded by investors or have access to large amounts of debt, installing an enterprise software solution is a good approach for putting a system in place that will more than adequately serve all corporate needs for many years to come.

One alternative to engaging in guesses at the future of computing platforms is to outsource a company's primary transaction processing functions, which shifts the upgradeability burden onto the supplier. By doing so, management can turn its attention to other matters that can proactively expand the business. A supplier is typically able to upgrade systems more easily than a company, for the simple reason that the supplier already has a hefty computer system on which to process the company's transactions. The supplier can afford to do this because it is trying to achieve economies of scale by clustering the transaction processing requirements of many companies on a cluster of mainframe-level computers in a single data center. This strategy has been key for such well-known outsourcing suppliers as Electronic Data Systems and Andersen Consulting. The only point a company should be aware of is the size of the computer systems on which the supplier proposes to initially place the company's transaction processing. If the company judges the system to be too small, there is a risk of system down time while the supplier goes through system conversions to upgrade to large hardware and software, which may interfere with company operations. If there appears to be a danger that the supplier's systems are too small, the company should probably pick a different supplier who can start the company on a larger system. Therefore, outsourcing a company's transaction processing to the large computer systems of a supplier is a reasonable way to avoid problems with system upgradeability.

In summary, system upgradeability is a serious issue for an explosive growth company. If systems constantly require replacement, a company will make inordinate expenditures of time and money to install better systems. The problem can be partially alleviated by using hardware based on the Intel standard, as well as by only using application software that runs on the Windows NT operating system. Another approach is to spend millions up front on an enterprise software package that will handle all transactions no matter what the volume. A cheaper alternative is to outsource transaction processing to a supplier and thereby entirely avoid the upgrade expense.

CONTROLS

The computer services function requires special attention to certain controls in order to keep a tight watch over costs, keep systems from interrupting operations, and to ensure that upgrades and implementations are completed on schedule. These controls are useful irrespective of there being an explosive growth situation, but they are absolutely mandatory for an explosive growth company. This section explains each of the controls.

The computer services function is usually a very expensive area for a company, so tight cost controls are needed. Several of the most important are noted as follows:

- *Review capital budget.* New computer hardware and software can be extraordinarily expensive, so the capital budget should be reviewed regularly, and every item questioned, to ensure that the company is expending the minimum possible amount to provide adequate computing capacity to the company.
- *Review lease options.* Because most explosive growth companies are chronically short on cash, it is useful to constantly review the option for leasing computer capital items rather than purchasing them. This control should be a mandatory review prior to purchasing any capital item.
- *Review outsourcing contracts and unit costs.* If a company elects to outsource some of its computer functions (as was recommended in the Outsourcing section), the unit cost per transaction being charged by the supplier should be

regularly compared to the prices noted in the original outsourcing contract. Outsourcing deals have a habit of incurring spiraling costs when company personnel ask suppliers to take on a few additional tasks without first inquiring about the associated costs, so this control is a good one for spotting those cost increases.

- *Compare budgeted to actual costs.* Comparing actual costs to the budget may not work for an explosive growth company, because growth rates may require expenditures that quickly outstrip the budget. However, the computer services manager should not take this as an excuse for ignoring the budget. It is still possible to review trends in costs to see if they are reasonable and to review the underlying detail of costs to see if any are inappropriate or unauthorized.

One of the underlying principles for the computer services department is that it should not interrupt ongoing operations. This means that the computer systems should not fail during business hours. The best control to keep such a failure from occurring is a frequent audit, preferably conducted by the company's internal audit team, of the company's backup systems. The audit should review the following items that are related to avoiding interruptions to operations:

- Is there a person who is responsible for creating daily backups of information?
- Is there a procedure for storing backup information off site? Is it followed?
- Is there an adequate secondary source of power to keep systems from failing in the event of a failure in the primary source of power?
- Is there a disaster recovery plan? If so, is it regularly reviewed and tested?
- Is there fire and flood protection for computer systems at all locations?

If the audit team finds any exceptions as a result of its review, it should note them in a report and present it to the computer services manager as well as the company's audit committee. There should then be regularly scheduled follow-up reviews by the audit team to ensure that its recommendations were followed.

A crucial control is the collection of complaints about the computer services function. The information can be stored in a database that is made available to as many people as possible. Making one person responsible for the resolution of recurring problems that are highlighted by the database allows management to keep control over any problems that occur in this area. Another way to ensure that complaints are resolved is to tie the computer service manager's compensation to the rapid resolution of complaints, which can be independently verified by the company's internal audit team. A complaints database provides management with a tight focus on computer service problems as noted by users.

A final control is the continuing review of scheduled system implementations and upgrades. Delay or failure of the implementation of a key system can seriously impact a company's operations, and hence its growth rate. A careful, regularly scheduled review of implementation and upgrade schedules may not eliminate these problems, but they can at least reduce their frequency. If a knowledgeable outside consultant is included in these reviews, the number of potential problems may be reduced, because the consultant can point out problems that may not be apparent to the computer services staff. A key control is the advance review of plans for system upgrades and implementations.

In short, an explosive growth company requires particular attention to those controls that can keep costs down, avoid system downtime, and ensure timely system implementations.

MANAGEMENT

A few extra management skills are necessary for someone managing the computer services function of an explosive growth company. One is the ability to oversee the services provided by any suppliers to whom work has been outsourced. It is a common misconception that, once a task has been outsourced, a company can assume the work will be done correctly without any oversight. In reality, it is in the interests of the supplier to charge extra for all additional work requested, while also doing the minimum amount of work to fulfill the requirements of the basic contract. This results in the smallest amount of definable results at the highest cost. The best way to avoid this situation is to continually compare supplier work to what is specified in the contract and to determine which additional tasks will be completed by the supplier for extra fees. Thus, supplier management skills are necessary to ensure that suppliers complete their assigned work at the contract price.

Another required management skill is the willingness to delegate authority to the computer services managers at any company subsidiaries. As noted in the Data Warehousing section of this chapter, it is not a good use of company resources to consolidate the computer systems of the subsidiaries of an explosive growth company, so many computer services staffs may manage their own systems. If the manager of the corporate computer services function is uncomfortable in the role of merely supporting all of these varied staffs, there may be trouble in getting resources to them, and the manager may push for consolidated systems, even though it is not a good use of company cash or time. Thus, the willingness to delegate authority to outlying computer services staffs is key for the manager of this function.

The computer services manager should also have some experience with software selections, or should be able to call on consultants or staff personnel who have this skill. Packaged software should take the place of most custom programming in an explosive growth company, so having the skill and experience to identify company software requirements and to use this information to pick from a variety of software packages is mandatory for a computer services manager. If this skill is not present, a company may find itself saddled with a package that is poorly supported by the supplier, is incapable of handling the company's ever-increasing transaction volumes, or which does not meet the company's most critical feature requirements. Because buying the wrong software package could seriously hinder company operations, having some experience in selections is a key management skill.

The computer services manager must also be concerned with not interrupting company operations, which was one of the key principles outlined in the second section of this chapter. This means that the manager should focus on frequent backups of information, storing of backups in multiple secure locations, and disaster recovery plans to rapidly bring up computer systems in a secondary location if there is a disaster that destroys the primary computer services location. The manager can delegate this task to a staff person, but should still have sufficient experience in this area to know when computer backup systems are being properly handled.

In short, the key skills required for a computer services manager in an explosive growth company are to oversee the activities of suppliers who have taken on some of the function's services, as well as the services provided by outlying computer services functions at subsidiaries. Also, the manager must have experience with software selections and backup systems. This does not imply that these are the only skills needed for a computer services manager, but rather that these skills are necessary as well as the usual set of management skills required for this position in a company that is not experiencing rapid growth.

MEASUREMENTS AND REPORTS

If an explosive growth company is using packaged software, there should be a relatively small number of software bugs, and the cost of running the system should be clearly defined, with very few personnel needed to support it. If this is the case, management will be primarily concerned with performance measurements that predict when the computer service function will not be able to provide sufficient service to other parts of the company to support its existing (or increased) rate of explosive growth. Those measurements attempt to predict the time when a company will run out of computer storage, computer licenses, and adequate response time. They are as follows:

- *Predicted time to fill computer storage.* The computer services manager can calculate the amount of time left before all hard drive storage is filled, which should give ample time to plan for a conversion to a larger storage device. To calculate it, determine the amount of space available on the storage media, which is easily obtained by querying the operating system, and plot the amount of available space on a trend line to see at what point in the future additional storage will be needed. This is very important, because a maxed out storage device keeps a company's computer systems from operating, which violates one of the key principles for an explosive growth company, by allowing systems to stop ongoing operations. One problem to be aware of with this measurement is that there may be sudden increases in the amount of storage space used, which are usually caused by the addition of new application programs and related databases to the storage media. However, a continual review of all planned software additions, which should include the amount of storage space required for each one, is sufficient for giving a reasonably accurate picture of when the computer storage will be filled.

- *Predicted time to obtain additional user licenses.* If a company is using packaged software, it may have only purchased licenses for a specific number of users. If so, additional users will not be able to access the software, which violates the key principle of not interfering with ongoing company operations. To guard against this problem, the computer system administrator should periodically review the maximum number of users logged into the software to see if the company is bumping up against its maximum number of user licenses. If plotted on a trend line, it is possible to predict when the company must purchase additional licenses. However, because this purchase is highly dependent on the number of employees who may require access to the software, it is sometimes better to keep track of hiring plans for the functional areas that will use the software, and obtain additional software users licenses based on increases in these numbers.
- *Predicted time to exceed maximum allowable response time.* The most important predictive measure of all is to determine when computer systems will slow down, due to overuse, to the point where response times are unacceptable for the continuing operation of the business. The point when system performance drops is exceptionally difficult to measure. One highly qualitative approach is to simply wait for users to complain and then upgrade the hardware and software to improve response times. However, this approach is not proactive. Also, an explosive growth company may find itself hamstrung when it opens new lines of business, thereby nearly stopping the computer systems overnight. A better approach is to conduct a continuing audit of the response time for a representative set of queries, reports, and transactions during the peak usage period. This audit will reveal a set of response times that management can then compare against a set of standard maximum response times. When plotted on a trend line, especially when additional users are factored in for upcoming increases in staffing, it is possible to roughly estimate the date when the computer system response time will require improvement.
- *Percent of system downtime during business hours.* Because a major principle for an explosive growth company is to not let the computer service function stop operations, it seems reasonable to measure the percentage of time that systems are not operational. This measurement typically applies to

the central accounting, production, and materials management software, and is measured either by collecting downtime information from the system log on the computer operating system, or by manually tracking down time (which can be highly inaccurate).

Only a few reports for computer services are especially useful in an explosive growth company. One is the Gantt chart or an equivalent format. This report is used to determine milestones for completing system installation projects. It is mandatory to use when a crucial factor is the shortest possible time period in which to roll out new systems, which is one of the operating principles for an explosive growth company. Without it, there is a much greater chance that, due to having less information about how a project is progressing, the system installation will take longer than anticipated.

The other primary report is the programming status report. An example of one is shown in Exhibit 12.2. This report is necessary for prioritizing and tracking any programming projects. Despite many comments earlier in this chapter about the need to use packaged software, there will still be programming projects of many kinds. For example, even with packaged software, programming is still needed for new reports, interfaces, or inputs. Also, some managers insist on modifying software packages, rather than waiting for package upgrades that may contain the desired modifications. Thus, there will always be programming changes, so a status report is needed to prioritize and track them.

Most programming status reports contain the same fields, although the format may vary somewhat from the one shown in Exhibit 12.2. The first column lists the programming priority, which is usually assigned by the Executive Committee. The next two columns, the estimated completion date and the estimated total cost, give the reader some idea of the time and cost commitment needed for the programming project. The next column lists the name of the person requesting the project, which gives the reader a trace on where the project originated. The date of the request is sometimes used by the Executive Committee on the (false) grounds that a project should be given a high priority if it has been in queue for a long time. The final column gives a very brief description of the project. The details of the programming status report are listed here because the report is fundamental for the proper functioning of the computer services function.

SUMMARY

The computer services function must provide sufficient information to management for it to run the business, so an executive information system is mandatory, although a complete data warehouse may be too expensive and time-consuming to build. Also, computer services should not act as a hindrance to the rapid growth of the company, so it is easier to install packaged software that has already been tested than to take a chance on creating entirely new software from scratch. Also,

Exhibit 12.2 Programming Status Report

Priority	*Estimated Completion Date*	*Estimated Total Cost*	*Requested By*	*Date of Request*	*Description*
1	10/09/xx	$31,000	Amy H.	01/01/xx	Create interface between A/P software and purchasing to verify that purchase orders were issued for supplier invoices
2	10/15/xx	$100	Ralph B.	03/17/xx	Add unit of measure to inventory location report
3	10/20/xx	$4,500	Steve Q.	05/19/xx	Create cycle counting report based on random number generator
4	10/28/xx	$	Doris K.	07/28/xx	Create expedite report comparing bills of material to quantities in inventory, resulting in quantities to order and the name of primary supplier
5	11/13/xx	$	Harold H.	10/12/xx	Create open jobs report that lists last date on which labor was charged to a job and the total cost charged to each job
6	11/29/xx	$	David G.	11/25/xx	Alter the new customer input form to require a valid nine-digit zip code
7	12/04/xx	$2,500	Ron H.	09/21/xx	Create A/R aging report that lists accounts receivable in 10-day buckets

because packaged software comes with its own documentation, there is much less need for documentation work on the software. In addition, management can outsource a variety of computer services tasks to suppliers, who can keep the company technologically up-to-date while also reducing the amount of management attention that must be devoted to the function. Finally, it is more useful for the function to create and maintain a variety of corporate intranets for the rapid dissemination of information than to spend its time converting the systems of all locations and subsidiaries to a common software standard. In short, paying close attention to the correct tasks within the computer services function will support management in growing the company as rapidly as possible.

Chapter 13

Customer Service

INTRODUCTION

The customer service function is one of the most important functions for a company experiencing explosive growth. Even if a company's sales are being driven by an outstanding product, poor service will keep repeat customers from coming back. In addition, customers who have a gripe are usually very vocal in communicating their dissatisfaction to other potential customers, which may influence their decision to buy products or services from the company. The result is that a company may experience an initial surge in sales for a variety of reasons, but sales are tempered over time simply because customers are not willing to put up with bad service. Not paying attention to customer service will not significantly hurt sales in the short term, but it will bring about a serious loss of sales over the long term.

The foundation of the customer service function is the customer complaints database, which the company uses to manage and measure the service function. The layout of this database as well as a variety of procedures that are built around it are described in this chapter. In addition, the need for proper recruiting, new employee training, and how it relates to high-quality customer service is discussed. Finally, the need for customer service is described in several key functional areas—order entry, sales, inbound and outbound call centers, and warranties. These and other key customer service issues are shown in Exhibit 13.1. Several customer service problems and solutions, as well as monitoring methods, are noted for each of these functional areas.

By describing the complaints database and how it is integrated into the customer service function, as well as the need for proper recruiting and training, this chapter gives the reader a basic understanding of how to achieve high-quality customer service in an explosive growth company.

MONITORING

The single most important means of monitoring a company's customer service is the complaints database. It is a collection of information submitted by customers and employees concerning all possible company shortcomings that irritate cus-

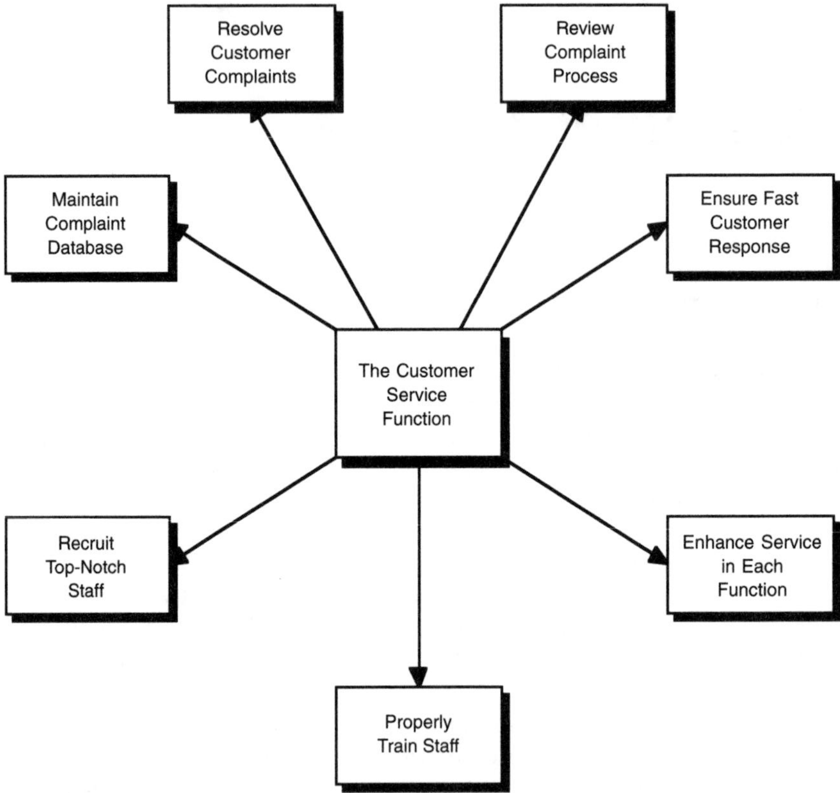

Exhibit 13.1 Explosive Growth Tasks for the Customer Service Function

tomers. When properly used by management to track down and correct problems, it can resolve the bulk of a company's customer service issues.

A complaints database includes information about the complaints made by customers and what was done to fix those problems. The exact format of the database can vary by company or industry, but should be similar to the one shown in Exhibit 13.2. It notes the date on which a complaint was made, so that management can create statistics that show how long it takes for the company to take action. It should also contain some kind of identification code that puts the complaint into a general category, such as product quality, late shipment, or rude service. This code is useful for summarizing the complaint information, so that all complaints related to one problem area can be extracted from the database for review at one time. The database should also include the name, address, and phone number of the person making the complaint, because the company should contact this person at least once to discuss the problem. In addition, there should be a text area in which someone can enter how the problem was resolved. Finally, there should be a dates section that lists the date when the customer was contacted for

Exhibit 13.2 The Layout of a Customer Service Database

Start Date	*Cate-gory*	*Complaint*	*Resolution*	*Customer*	*2nd Call Date*	*Final Call Date*	*End Date*
12/01	2	Screw pops out of bottom of unit.	Engineering change order #2101-A issued, plus product recall.	Neil Smith 303-291-0032	12/02	12/18	12/18
12/03	1	Salesperson pushy and rude.	Discussion with salesperson, plus extra training.	Nellie Jones 508-402-1130	12/04	12/05	12/05
12/07	4	Hourly rate too high.	Compared costs to competing companies in area, and reduced rate by $2 per hour.	Norman Beckes 978-461-0091	12/09	12/17	12/17
12/09	3	Took three months to have warranty work completed.	Supplier lost the order. Changed procedure to include phone call after warranty form is faxed.	Nan Oberon 602-528-9832	12/11	12/11	12/12

Categories:
1. Rude service
2. Poor product quality
3. Late service
4. High price

follow-up information, contacted again to be told of how the problem was resolved, and a completion date that notes when the complaint record was closed (which is frequently the same date as the one when the customer was last called). All of this information is needed in order to properly manage the identification and resolution of a customer service problem.

Once the layout of the complaints database is decided upon, it is also important to determine the hardware on which it will run. Because the company is either in or expects to be in an explosive growth situation, it is important that the hardware be capable of handling a rapidly expanding volume of customer complaints, which means that management must alter its expectations from a small database that is maintained on a personal computer to a robust and ever-expanding database that must be maintained on a powerful computer. This computer should be linked to as many employees as possible, so that solutions to problems can be gathered from the largest possible cross-section of the staff. Therefore, the computer on which the database is stored should be a file server, with communications connections not only to the company's local area network (LAN), but also to the company's LANs located at other company facilities, possibly throughout the world.

In addition to hardware, it is important to determine the appropriate database package to use. Some complaints databases are available as generic packages, which give the typical company most of the functionality that they require. For a company that is rapidly expanding, it is generally better to go with a prewritten package, because it has already been debugged, which avoids any delays required to fix problems that would otherwise appear in a custom-made package. Also, because a rapidly growing company is under severe time constraints, it is better to quickly purchase a complaints software package from a supplier, rather than taking the time to custom-program a similar package, which involves such steps as determining programming requirements, going over input and output screens, programming, and debugging the resulting software. Also, software packages usually only operate on a few hardware platforms (with the notable exception of Oracle software), so it is better to select the software before buying computer hardware. In short, it is better to purchase software for a complaints database than to create it from scratch, and it is necessary to do so prior to purchasing a computer hardware platform.

Once the hardware and software have been selected for the complaints database, it is necessary to develop and install as many means as possible for customers to enter complaints into it. If the method for complaining is difficult to access or too structured, customers will not complain, and the company will therefore not know what it is doing wrong. To avoid this problem, there are a variety of ways to collect information from customers. One is the telephone. Customers should be presented with a phone number to call, which can be located on the product they buy, brochures they receive, or even the trucks they see hauling the company's products. They call this number to lodge a complaint, and an employee transcribes the information into the database. Another approach is to leave complaint forms in all locations (typically at sales counters) where customers can easily find them; they should be designed as cards that can be mailed, including preprinted postage. When received at a central processing location, a clerk can enter the information on the card into the complaints database. Yet another approach is to allow customers to send complaints by electronic mail to an e-mail address that can be listed in the same locations as the company's complaints phone number. This approach has the advantage of allowing an automated interface to the complaints database, which avoids the need for a data entry person. However, most complaints databases are so structured that some rekeying is required even for complaints sent by e-mail. These approaches are shown in Exhibit 13.3. Giving

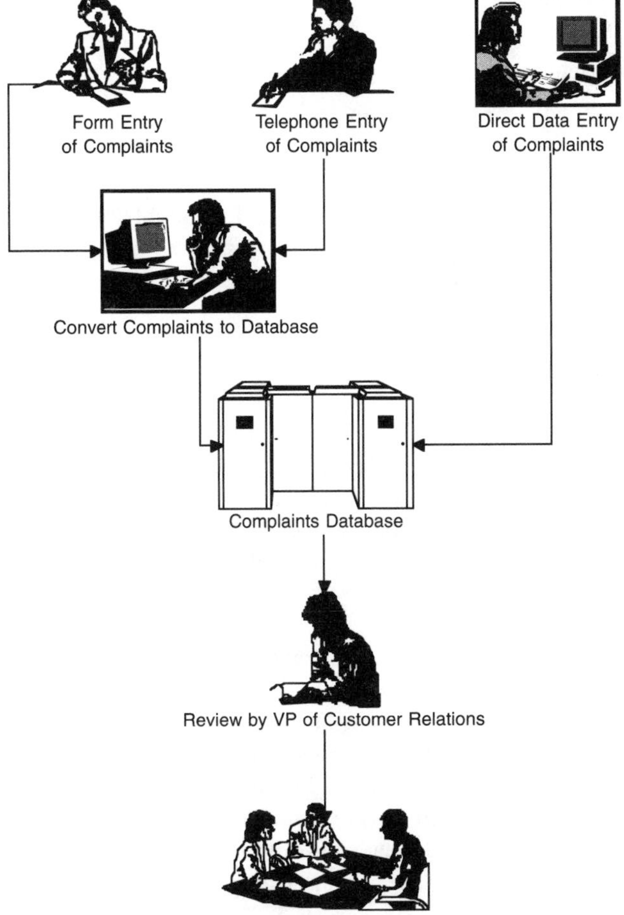

Exhibit 13.3 The Complaints Database

customers as many channels of communication as possible is critical to accumulating all possible complaints.

What kinds of information can a company mine from a completed complaints database? It can reveal problems in a wide range of areas, which allows it to improve operations by tracking down the reasons for each problem and eliminating it. Some of the problems uncovered by complaints are as follows:

- Long delivery times
- Bad product design
- Incorrect billings
- Late billings
- Bad phone manners
- Pushy sales personnel
- Trouble getting replacement parts
- Slow warranty or servicing work
- Inadequate instruction materials

The foregoing list does not begin to cover all of the problems revealed by a complaints database, but it shows the value of having the database, because it can spotlight such a diverse range of problem areas.

MANAGEMENT

The customer service process flow is built around the complaints database described in the preceding section. Accordingly, the process flow begins with putting accurate information into the database, and then using the database as an information source for solving company problems. This section notes each step in the process flow, which is also noted graphically in Exhibit 13.4. The 10 steps are as follows:

1. *Log in customer complaint.* A customer's complaint may arrive through a variety of sources—a form, phone call, or e-mail message. Whatever the method of transmission, the complaint must be translated into the complaints database format without losing the gist of the communication. The complaints database has a specific set of fields in which information must be entered, so the data entry clerks who receive complaint information must be trained in where to enter the appropriate complaint information.
2. *Call customer to clarify complaint.* The initial customer complaint almost never contains enough information for the customer service staff to adequately define the problem. It is dangerous to attempt to correct a problem based on

inadequate information, so the company should make every effort to contact customers as soon as possible after they have lodged a complaint. Not only does this give the company a chance to collect additional information, but it also makes the customer feel better, because the company took the time to listen to the customer's complaint.

3. *Modify complaint based on call.* The customer service staff can modify the complaint information in the database based on its follow-up contact with the customer.

4. *Route to head of customer relations.* The head of the customer relations function should review all new customer complaints as soon as complete information has been obtained on each one. This person can then allocate resources to resolving them. It is also useful for this person to occasionally review the list of complaints for which complete information has not been obtained, in order to get some idea of the number of hanging complaints, and the number of days that these complaints have gone unresolved. Action may be necessary if the number of incomplete complaints rises to an excessive level that delays responses to customers.

5. *Route to functions for resolution.* A complaint is not always directly solved by customer service. It is much more frequently a problem that can only be resolved by personnel in another functional area. The manager of customer service is responsible for handing over these issues and determining, in association with the managers of the affected functions, the timeline needed to solve the problem.

6. *Track daily to resolve problem.* The customer service staff should maintain project tracking information about each complaint that the company is currently working on fixing. At a minimum, there should be a list that notes the number of days that have elapsed since a customer complaint was received. The staff can then sort this list to show those items that have not been solved in the longest period of time, and work on fixing them first.

7. *Finalize problem resolution.* Once a functional area informs the customer service staff that a problem has been resolved, there should be a meeting to discuss the problem and to verify that it has indeed been resolved. It is possible, as a result of this meeting, that the problem was not properly understood, and has not actually been fixed, so it is important to have this meeting. Do not just take someone's word that the issue causing the complaint has been resolved.

8. *Call customer to report on problem.* Contact the customer to point out that the problem has been fixed. It is worthwhile to encourage the customer to report any other problems; a customer who is willing to take the time to lodge a complaint is a valuable resource and should be considered an important feedback tool regarding the quality of the company's operations.

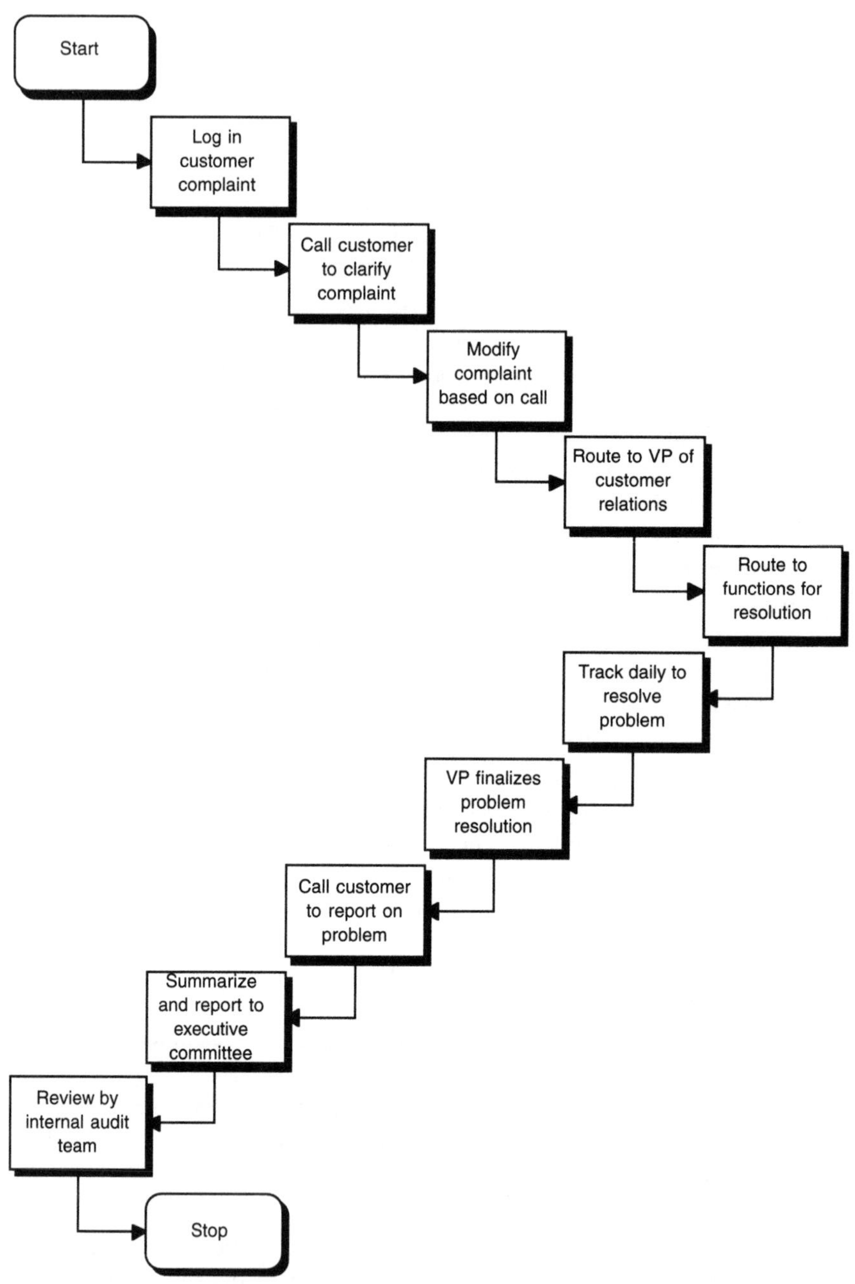

Exhibit 13.4 The Process Flow for Handling Customer Complaints

9. *Summarize and report to executive committee.* Summarize all complaint activity for each month, how the complaints were resolved, and report this information to the company's executive committee. The committee will be particularly interested in the general areas in which problems are recurring, so the report should include a summary listing that notes the quantity of complaints received by problem area.
10. *Review by internal audit team.* Review the process used by customer service to resolve complaints, and verify the accuracy of the information it has in the complaints database. This task should be regularly scheduled for the company's internal audit function. It is a valuable tool for ensuring that the company's customer service function is operating properly. The results of this review should be reported to both the executive committee and (more usually) the board of directors.

The customer service process flow requires accurate complaint information from the customer before it can begin, and then it requires the help of other functional areas to resolve complaints. This cooperation requires a great deal of tact by the customer service manager, since other functional areas do not want to be saddled with complaint problems. Giving this manager a large amount of power (frequently at the vice president level) is necessary to ensure that other areas fully cooperate in the resolution of complaint problems.

MEASUREMENTS AND REPORTS

Once the process flow for the customer service function appears to be operational, it is important to measure its key operating characteristics to ensure that its performance meets company standards. This section describes those measurements and how they may be calculated. In addition, the function's overall performance must be evaluated by the company's internal audit staff. This section describes the more common audit steps to use for the customer service function. Using both performance measurements and periodic internal audit reviews are sufficient for senior management to form a picture of the customer service function's ability to resolve customer complaints.

Not that many measurements give management a reasonably accurate view of the level of customer service. In an explosive growth situation, it is less important to focus on the cost of the service and more important to ensure that customers are happy, so only a few of the measurements presented here are related to the cost of customer service—instead most are used to track the service levels provided to customers. Each of the following measurements are briefly described, along with notes on how to derive the measurements. They are as follows:

- *Number of rings before answering the phone.* A tracking system used by an increasing number of companies is the number of times the phone rings before being answered. This is directly related to customer service, because customers do not like to be left on hold for long periods. This information is provided either by the phone company or in-house tracking software. The measurement is calculated by adding the total number of calls and the total number of rings, as noted on the call report, and dividing the total number of calls into the total number of rings. This measurement can be misleading, because the average number of rings for the entire day may be quite low while the number of rings during peak calling periods is still extremely high. Those companies who are the most devoted to customer service have responded to this problem by also tracking the number of rings during peak periods, and adding staffing during those periods to avoid long customer waits.

- *Time to respond to complaints.* A customer is happier just receiving a call-back from a company to discuss a problem, even if it does not result in a final resolution of the problem. To track the time required to contact customers, go to the complaints database and subtract the field that shows the initial date of the customer's complaint from the date on which the customer was first contacted. The difference is the time to respond to complaints. Obviously, this calculation requires that the two date fields be present in the database, and that they are consistently filled in by the customer service staff.
- *Time to resolve complaints.* It is critical for the company to track the time needed to resolve complaints, because this function is the most important of the customer service functions. It is rather hard to measure, because it should be the average time interval needed to resolve all complaints, but some complaints are not resolved for very long time periods, resulting in an incomplete measurement while waiting for these last few problems to be fixed. The solution is to run the calculation on a somewhat smaller percentage of the total number of complaints, which bypasses the few remaining open complaints. Thus, the measurement is to subtract the initial customer complaint date in the database from the completion date to arrive at the time to resolve complaints, and to average this number for all complaints in the database except a predetermined (and very small) percentage of uncompleted complaints, such as two percent of the total.
- *Cost of customer service as a percentage of sales.* Management may want some way to measure the relative size of the cost of the customer service function. Comparing it to the company's sales is one way to do this. However, this measure is subject to considerable variation, because sales may fluctuate from period to period. For a company undergoing explosive sales growth, this measure will probably show a customer service cost that is constantly shrinking in proportion to sales, because the function cannot hire staff fast enough to keep up with sales. Also, senior management may compare this measurement to those of other companies in a benchmark study. However, the cost of customer service is one of the few measurements that should not be used to match an industry benchmark, because the cost can vary wildly

depending on the level of service that each company wants to provide to its customers. The cost of customer service also varies with the quality of a company's products and processes, because a company that performs well in these areas needs to expend less in service costs—there are simply fewer complaints to address. Comparing the cost of sales to a benchmark can be very misleading and should only be used to compare costs in a very general way, if at all. To calculate the measurement, compile the cost of the function from the relevant general ledger accounts for a specified time period, and divide those costs by the total sales dollars for that period.

- *Cost per complaint*. The cost per complaint is a useful measure of the customer service function's average cost to resolve a complaint. To calculate it, summarize the function's total cost for the period being measured (easily obtained from the general ledger), and divide this amount by the total number of complaints currently outstanding as well as resolved during the period. This measure is not reliable for short time periods involving few complaints, because the measure may include a disproportionate number of complaints that are still open and still accruing costs. Calculating the measurement with a large number of open complaints yields a cost per complaint that is too low, because the open complaints collect additional expenses before they are completed. However, over a longer time period, such as a quarter or year, there will be enough closed complaints in the measure to provide a reasonably accurate cost.
- *Outbound customer service calls as a percent of the customer base*. If a company elects to reach out to its customers for comments through a regular outbound calling function, it should measure what percentage of customers are being called, in order to determine if this effort is reaching the same proportion of customers each month. This answer is easily ascertained by keeping a tracking log that lists the number of customers contacted each month, and dividing it by the company's total number of customers, which can be obtained from a customer list. For a company in an explosive growth situation, it is easy for the proportion of calls to customers to drop below target levels, because the customer base is expanding so quickly. In this situation, adding a stream of new staff to the customer service function is the only way to maintain a constant proportion of outbound service calls to customers.

The results of the foregoing measurements do not have to be kept secret. Instead, management should list them on an erasable white board in the customer service area, so that the staff can see how they are doing. The layout of such a white board is shown in Exhibit 13.5, where the measurement is listed down the left side, the goal for each one is listed down the right side, and the measurements for the last three months are noted in the middle.

Some of these measurements should be reported to the customer service staff

Exhibit 13.5 White Board Layout for Reporting Customer Service Measurements

Measurement	*January*	*February*	*March*	***Goal***
Number of rings before answering phone	4.4	4.2	3.4	**2.0**
Time to respond to complaints	1.7 days	1.5 days	1.6 days	**1.0 day**
Time to resolve complaints	6.4 days	6.0 days	5.9 days	**4.0 days**
Cost as percent of sales	2.0%	1.9%	1.7%	**1.0%**
Cost per complaint	$279	$283	$259	**$150**
Outbound service calls as percent of customer base	2.1%	2.3%	2.2%	**4.0%**

alongside goals, so that they will know how well they are doing in comparison to expectations. Examples of such goals are as follows:

- One day to respond to all initial customer complaints.
- One week to fix 80 percent of all customer complaints.
- One month to fix 95 percent of all customer complaints.

Note the split of goals for fixing customer complaints. The problems that are the root cause of complaints are usually easily fixed for most complaints, so there should be a goal that addresses the quick fixes. However, others are much more difficult to resolve and require much more time. An additional goal should address these items, while still allowing room for the very small number of extremely difficult problems that cannot be fixed within any reasonable period of time.

Once the complaints database is operational, a manager is made responsible for correcting the problems it uncovers, and if it appears that the operation is running smoothly, it is time to begin scheduling periodic reviews of the entire system by the company's internal audit function. The internal audit team should review any performance measurement on which the customer service manager is judged, such as the average time to correct problems uncovered by complaints. Because the manager is responsible for measurements on which that person may be receiving changes in compensation, it is important to develop an unbiased opinion of the accuracy of those measures. The audit team can do this. Another objective of an internal audit is simply to find out if the process is working properly. If not, the customer service manager can use the audit team's report to make needed corrections, which ultimately helps the customer by ensuring that complaints are being dealt with in a timely manner. Thus, the objectives of an internal audit review of the customer service function, and especially of the information in the database on which the function is grounded, are to review the accuracy of performance measurements, as well as the efficiency and effectiveness of the entire process.

An audit program for the customer service function should verify that customer service performance measurements are being correctly calculated and should determine that customer problems are actually being dealt with. For example, an audit step for verifying the accuracy of the time required to respond to a customer complaint would be as follows:

- *Verify accuracy of time required to contact customer following receipt of complaint.*
  1. Take a sample of 10 customer complaints from the complaints database. For each one, subtract the date in the database for when a customer was contacted from the date on which the customer's complaint was received. Compare the resulting number of days to the calculated amounts used to derive the average number of days to contact customers. Note any variances.
  2. Compare the dates on documents received from customers to the receipt dates noted in the database. Note any variances.
  3. Compare the dates in the database on which customers were contacted to the dates on which calls were actually made, which may be collected from call logs or conversations with the staff who made the calls. Note any variances.

The foregoing audit steps are useful for determining the accuracy of the customer complaints database, and in particular put the manager of that function on notice that the function's performance is of great concern to management and will be closely monitored.

Of equal importance to measurement accuracy is for the audit team to review the customer service department's ability to solve problems pointed out by customer complaints. A sample audit step for this is as follows:

- *Verify that problems reported as solved have actually been dealt with.*
  1. For a sample of 10 complaints in the customer complaint database, document the investigation process conducted by the customer service personnel in resolving each complaint. This action requires interviewing the person to whom each complaint was assigned, obtaining a list of specific action steps resulting from each complaint, and auditing those action items to ensure that each item has been acted upon.
  2. Conduct a follow-up audit at a later date to verify that the action steps identified in the previous audit are still being followed to ensure that the causes of the relevant customer complaints have been eliminated.

A detailed review of the specific steps taken to eliminate customer complaints is critical for ensuring that flaws in company processes are permanently eliminated.

Some measurements are available that can give management some idea of the cost and level of service being provided to customers, although the service measurements do not give a complete picture of the situation. Internal audits can be used to track the efficiency and effectiveness of the customer service function. Using measurements and internal audits is a good way to verify customer service levels.

RECRUITMENT AND TRAINING

Among the most important linchpins of customer service is a quality staff. Without them, it is impossible to maintain even adequate customer service, and above-average service is clearly out of the question. How does a company acquire these people, and how does it mold them to provide the desired level of service? This section discusses these issues.

The traditional ways to acquire new employees are through newspaper advertisements and search firms. However, when a company needs to hire possibly hundreds or even thousands of employees per month, these two avenues are not sufficient for attracting enough qualified personnel. As is discussed in Chapter 17, the company must develop a series of alternative hiring channels. These may include job fairs, job postings on the World Wide Web, bonuses to current employees if they recommend people who are later hired, or even the unique approach of the network hardware giant, Cisco Systems, which is to purchase advertising space at local cinemas. Some Silicon Valley companies have even resorted to purchasing billboard space next to the facilities of their competitors, offering jobs to the employees of competitors. A mix of all or some of these approaches will bring in the largest number of potential recruits.

What mix of recruiting methods works best? A good approach is a combination of low-cost "shotgun" advertisements and more expensive "rifle" searches. A shotgun approach is a general advertisement in regional newspapers that will only be seen by those people who are actively looking for a new job. A rifle approach is frequently very expensive, and is carefully targeted at bringing in a specific kind of person who may not be looking for a new job at all. Examples of this approach are paying a search firm to find someone, or combing scientific journals to see who has published on a specific topic that matches an open job position, and then contacting that person. Both broad-based and tightly focused searches are needed to locate qualified employee candidates.

It is also important to search throughout the national, if not international, labor markets, rather than just locally. The best potential employees may be located a very long way away from the company. Of course, hiring employees who live far from any company facility brings high additional costs, such as flying the person in for an interview and paying moving costs to bring the person to the nearest company facility. In an explosive growth situation where money is extremely tight, it is common for a company to only recruit with the cheapest methods, and only locally, and later to branch out into the more expensive recruiting methods as well as to search further afield, once the local talent pool dries up. Thus, a company caught in an explosive growth mode will find that its new employee search costs grow nearly logarithmically as the job of searching for new employees becomes more and more difficult. This is a very difficult proposition for those companies who rely on highly trained employees in a narrow field of technology, and less of a problem for companies such as inbound call centers, who can set up a regional call center and easily attract large numbers of untrained local people at a single job fair to staff the center. In short, searches for qualified employees may require looking all over the planet, which can be very expensive, and is usually only resorted to after the local labor market has been picked clean of candidates.

Besides the high cost of finding candidates, there is the additional cost of paying extra for the right ones. A company in an explosive growth situation must keep its customers happy in order to keep growing, or they will take their sales elsewhere. Keeping customers happy requires good customer service by employees, which is much easier to achieve if the employees are above average. However, a good employee requires higher pay. How much higher must the pay be in order to attract the right individual? The following cost-benefit analysis is based on paying an employee a rate that falls into the 75th percentile for a job category, rather than the usual mid-point pay rate; a rate that should attract nearly all highly qualified prospective employees. There is no way to derive the amount of increased pay needed to reach an average 75th percentile, since there are hundreds of job categories, so we will assume for the example that the 75th percentile requires a generous pay boost of 25 percent over the median rate.

Cost per customer service employee:

Median pay rate per year	$25,000
25% pay boost	6,250
Total pay for high-end employee	**$31,250**

Savings by using high-end employee:

Customer Sales Volume Retained	*Gross Margin on Sales (%)*	*Dollar Margin Retained*
$200,000	30	$70,000
175,000	30	52,500
150,000	30	45,000
125,000	30	37,500
100,000	**30**	**30,000**
75,000	30	22,500
50,000	30	15,000

Under the foregoing assumptions, a quality customer service person must keep a company from losing $100,000 in sales volume in order to pay for a very high increase in pay. Clearly, the margin, pay rate, and customer retention level vary drastically by industry, but it is worthwhile for a manager to make a calculation similar to the previous one when considering the need to hire above-average employees at above-average rates.

When determining how many recruits are needed to fill the customer service ranks, a company should consider that the number devoted to solving customer problems may not have to increase at the same rate of growth that the company's sales growth track would indicate, because a company will have a flood of problems to deal with at the beginning of its growth spurt, when problems with products, procedures, and quality will require a large number of personnel to frantically find solutions. However, once these problems have been resolved (assuming that they *are* resolved!), the company will require proportionally fewer service personnel to deal with complaints as the company increases in size. This factor should be considered by the human resources staff when coming up with expected staffing levels for its recruiting efforts.

Even if a company can bring in a flood of candidates, the managers of an explosive growth company will not be able to interview them all without seriously impairing the amount of time they have available for other tasks. To mitigate this problem, the human resources function must perform an in-depth screening of each candidate, so that managers are only presented with a limited number of highly qualified people to interview. This prescreening does not involve an in-depth review of a candidate's technical abilities, because the human resources interviewer probably does not have sufficient skill to decide if the interviewee actually has enough technical knowledge to succeed in the position. Instead, the prescreening should focus on baseline criteria, such as a college education for certain jobs, or perhaps a specific type of person that a company has had success with in the past. For example, a well-known rental car company looks for college graduates from the bottom half of their classes, since these are willing to work for less money. The recruiters can also probe for indicators of poor work performance, such as unexplained departures from jobs and short tenures on previous jobs. The human resources group can also access one of several national databases that list any convictions of potential employees. By the time a candidate is referred to a manager for a "real" job interview, the human resources function should have already determined that the candidate meets the company's minimum employment standards, thereby keeping the interviewing manager from having to ascertain this information.

Having acquired new staff, a company must find a way to mold them into the type of person who will help sustain the company's explosive growth pattern. Unfortunately, what most companies do who are in an explosive growth pattern is to hire personnel and "dump them into the trenches," where they are immediately buried with work. This gives them no opportunity to understand the company's mission, ethics, strategy, or even the simplest procedures, such as how to deal with a customer complaint. The solution is adequate training. This section only deals with training for customer service issues (see Chapter 17 for commentary on additional training).

There are three levels of customer service training. The first level covers direct contact with the customer. The second level delves into the most basic procedural issues surrounding customer service issues that can be solved directly by the contact person. The final level addresses the problem of what to do with customer complaints that are too complex to be handled directly and must be handed off to other people in the company for resolution. The discussion of each training level is as follows:

- *Training for direct contact with the customer.* At the most elementary level, new customer service employees must know what manners are expected by the company when dealing directly with customers. This may include the exact language to be used when taking an order or selling through an outbound call center. If so, the training should include practicing with a scripted dialogue. The training should also include a series of role playing exercises for soothing angry customers, with an emphasis on getting sufficient information from them regarding the problem so that the company can resolve it.
- *Training for procedural issues.* Once the employee has determined from the customer the nature of the problem, the employee may be able to handle it on the spot. If so, the training should include procedures for resolving these more simple problems, such as altering a customer order, taking back a product, exchanging a product, or issuing a credit. The training should include role playing for each of these situations. This training is the only type in which learning the procedures is more important than role playing, because learning them is of great benefit to the customer, who wants to have complaints handled immediately and efficiently, which requires a solid knowledge of the procedures.
- *Training for complex problems.* The last training element covers the most difficult customer complaints, those that the customer service person cannot immediately resolve. Employees need training in identifying these types of problems, obtaining additional information from customers, passing them along to other functional areas for resolution, and contacting the customer later on when the problem has been solved. This training requires a heavy emphasis on role playing over procedures, because the types of problems encountered may vary so dramatically that no procedures can handle every variation.

The simplified customer service training curriculum shown in Exhibit 13.6 covers the basics of dealing with a customer, the most elementary procedures for dealing with basic customer requests, and how to hand off a more complex customer problem to someone else who is better able to solve it. The most important

Exhibit 13.6 Sample Customer Service Training Curriculum

Category		*Topic*	*Time Needed*
Part One: *How to deal with a customer.*			
	1.	Interpersonal skills	8 hours
	2.	When to call a supervisor	4 hours
	3.	Role playing	8 hours
Part Two: *Problems you can fix.*			
	1.	Give sales credit	2 hours
	2.	Receive an order	2 hours
	3.	Return goods	2 hours
	4.	Accept complaint form	1 hour
	5.	Role playing	3 hours
Part Three: *Problems others must fix.*			
	1.	Examine the problem	2 hours
	2.	Present the problem	2 hours
	3.	Track the problem	2 hours
	4.	Dealing with difficult people	4 hours
	5.	Role playing	6 hours

item is the training time required, which is listed in the far right column. According to this example, even the most basic customer service training requires six days! A manager in an explosive growth company may think that even this limited amount of training simply is not possible when the company is in desperate need of new employees *right now*, and cannot wait for the training to be completed.

However, what is the price of not training a new employee in the fundamentals of customer service? When a new employee is thrust into a new customer service position at a company with no training and is left to fend for himself, there will be several problems with customers. One is that there is a good chance of irritating a customer who is not dealt with correctly. Another problem is that the employee does not follow the procedures necessary to process customer complaints and resolve their problems, resulting in even more customer unhappiness. Also, an untrained employee has almost no chance of properly resolving a really difficult problem that must be handed off to another function for resolution, resulting in *really* annoyed customers. In addition, the new employees will probably continue to make mistakes involving customers, since the only way they can learn to handle customers in some other way is through formal training or by being chastised for guessing and doing it the wrong way, which eventually leads them to the correct approach after they have tried a number of other methods and failed. To make matters worse, the new employees will become so frustrated with trying to do their jobs without guidelines that they will be far more likely to quit than someone who has been properly trained, which means that even more untrained recruits will replace the ones who were starting to learn their jobs. Thus, the ramifications of not training employees in customer service are severe—poor customer relations and high employee turnover. Spending even a few days in customer service instruction seems like a minor inconvenience in the face of the consequences of not doing so.

One problem in an explosive growth company is that procedures to address a variety of problems that arise change constantly as the company deals with new markets, products, and computer systems. There is considerable confusion while everyone learns the new procedures, which can interrupt the quality of service given to customers. To avoid, or at least reduce, this problem, management should consider making only the most minimal changes to procedures in any areas that deal with customers, and then only with the heaviest possible training to introduce the changes. This allows the company to present a well-trained front to the customer, who does not want to experience reduced service levels because the company has dramatically changed its procedures without sufficient training of its staff.

Once a company decides to offer formal classes in customer service, it faces the decision of keeping it in-house or moving it to a supplier. In an explosive growth situation, it may be difficult to find enough trainers and training facilities to meet the training needs of hundreds or thousands of new employees. Also, the company must be mindful of the possibility of slow or vanishing growth in the future, which may leave it with a large training staff and no new employees to train. The best approach is to keep enough personnel in-house to create the underlying material for customer service training classes, which is a relatively small number of people. The trainers and facilities may belong to a supplier, so that the company can quickly scale back its training resources with few (if any) layoffs when the explosive growth period eventually comes to an end. Thus, the creation of materials for new training classes should be the primary training function kept in-house, while the bulk of customer service training personnel can be outsourced.

This section covered the myriad of recruiting and training issues that an explosive growth company faces in the customer service area. It is clear that customer service will suffer, and sales along with it, if the company does not pay close attention to its hiring and screening process, as well as insist on detailed upfront training for those employees who will be in direct contact with customers.

SERVICE BY FUNCTION: ORDER ENTRY

Customers must place an order. When they do so, the experience should be as painless as possible. The customer does not expect this to be an exceptionally pleasant experience, just one that is handled as efficiently as possible. Accordingly, the emphasis should be on following a script that rapidly guides the customer through the order entry process.

The script is a standard one that we are all familiar with, and has five points as follows:

1. Has the customer ordered from the company before? If so, the order entry person can call up the customer's record in the computer, and avoid the next block of questions relating to the customer's address, phone number, and even method of payment.
2. If this is a new customer, then what is the customer's name, address, and phone number?
3. What would the customer like to order, and how many?
4. What is the method of payment?
5. Reiterate the order to spot mistakes.

The foregoing script, with modest variations, is good for ordering most types of goods. A company can develop its own script that varies from this, but it runs the risk of irritating customers if the script is too long.

In an explosive growth situation, a company may have trouble keeping enough people available to take orders. If orders are coming in by phone, a good solution is to outsource the order entry function to an inbound call center. These suppliers have long since perfected the multitude of script variations to use, and can quickly create a call center that will take all inbound customer orders on behalf of the company, and even enter the orders directly into the company's order entry database. This outsourcing also reduces a company's managerial headaches in hiring large numbers of order entry personnel, and eliminates the need to staff a nonstrategic company function that is still critical to maintaining customer relations. Outsourcing the order entry function for inbound calls is an effective approach for maintaining a professional demeanor when accepting orders, while avoiding any daily management of the function.

The order entry process is one of the easiest functions to control if most orders arrive over the phone. The company (or its supplier, if the function has been outsourced) can simply monitor a selection of inbound calls to see how well the script works and also to find any staff problems that require additional training to correct. If orders are taken in person, the best approach is for a manager to be present occasionally to monitor the way orders are taken. It is also possible to compare the customer complaints database to the order entry database to see if there is a high correlation between orders taken by specific employees or for specific products or options that are causing continuing complaints. If so, management can avoid future complaints by altering the order entry process or retraining employees. Thus, typical controls over the order entry function include call monitoring or monitoring in person, as well as comparisons of orders to customer complaints.

SERVICE BY FUNCTION: WARRANTIES

Several customer contacts are required when a company correctly operates a warranty function, but this requires streamlining for an explosive growth company.

A properly functioning warranty function contacts the customer three times after the warranty claim has initially been filed. The first contact is to tell the customer when the company estimates that the warranty work will be completed. This contact frequently happens at the same time the customer brings in the product for repair work. The second contact is to tell the customer that the product has been fixed or replaced, and is available for pickup. The final contact is a follow-up call to verify that the customer is satisfied with the service received. This series of contacts is necessary to ensure that the customer is happy with the warranty service received.

The problem for a company in an explosive growth situation is that it cannot afford to make so many contacts with the customer. It is probably inundated with warranty claims, with an avalanche of additional ones pouring in at all times. Faced with this work load, the people working in this area may try to skimp by not calling the customer at all. Instead, employees can wait for customers to call them to see if claims have been completed, while any postwarranty contacts are ignored. This approach is exceptionally poor customer service. A better approach is to replace the phone calls used for most customer contacts with a mailing. These can be very generic when telling the customer that warranty work is completed, because it is strictly a notice of completion. The warranty staff can stick a mailing label on the back of a post card that is pre-printed with a work completion notice, and send it to the customer. The postwarranty call can be similarly handled by mailing out a generic questionnaire to the customer, based on a mailing list of all customers picking up their warranty work in the last few days. As for the initial contact with the customer in which the company gives the customer an estimated completion date, this should always be given at the time when the warranty work is left with the company. The estimate is easy to make simply by giving an estimate that is always well beyond the probable estimated time of completion—this gives the company so much extra time that is is very difficult *not* to meet the due date. This technique is used by a leading mail-order computer company, which estimates every shipment several days late, and then always ships sooner, resulting in more satisfied customers. Thus, the traditional number of customer warranty contacts can still be made when a company is in the throes of explosive growth—only the type of contact changes.

SERVICE BY FUNCTION: INBOUND AND OUTBOUND CALLS

The inbound and outbound call center can provide quality customer service very easily because the entire staff of the function is located in a fixed area where management can review all activities, and because all contacts with customers are on the telephone, which can be monitored by quality review teams to ensure that there are no problems with customer contacts. In addition, a good call center manager puts new employees through extensive training, which should include role playing, before the employee is ever put in contact with a customer. All of these reasons mean that a properly managed call center should be a cause for few customer complaints.

A way to ensure even better customer service through a call center is to outsource the function to one of the larger suppliers in this field. They are expert at recruiting, training, and monitoring staff and have been doing so for years. Realistically, because of their experience in this area, they can probably provide a higher degree of customer service than a company that operates its own call center but has not had much experience.

SERVICE BY FUNCTION: SALES

The most personal and direct form of customer contact is the direct sales pitch made by a company salesperson who goes to the customer. It is very difficult to maintain a high level of customer service through this form of contact, because it is difficult to monitor, but there are a few approaches that an explosive growth company can follow, depending on the type of sales force used.

If a company uses independent agents to sell its products and services to customers, it is extremely difficult for the company to ensure a high level of customer service, because the sales agents work for themselves or someone else and have no obligation to use the company's sales methods. A company can insist that every sales agent attend a training class sponsored by the company, but they may not follow its guidelines. In this sales scenario, the company can only check with customers being contacted by the sales agents to see if they are receiving proper customer service from the agents. This contact can be by mail, but responses to mail surveys are notoriously low. A better approach, no matter how labor intensive, is to personally call a selection of customers to ask them about the service they are receiving. If a problem arises, the company can then target a larger proportion of a specific sales agent's territory to see if the problem is rampant. The ultimate solution may then be to terminate the sales agreement with the agent. Direct customer contact is the best way to verify the customer service of independent sales agents.

The direct calling approach is not possible if a sales agent is a distributor who keeps its customer list away from the company. In this case, the company has no way to tell who customers are, and therefore cannot contact any of them to inquire about service. One solution here is to passively wait for complaints from customers, which are rare. Another approach is to avoid giving out sales territories to distributors as much as possible. However, awarding distributorships is a classic way for an explosive growth company to rapidly increase its sales, so a company may be forced to go with distributors. If so, the only remaining approach is to use the references of a potential distributor to see how it already treats its customers before awarding a distributorship. Controlling customer service through independent distributorships is very difficult, and it is best handled by being careful about who is given a distributorship in the first place.

Controls over internal sales staff are the easiest to implement and maintain, but the company still suffers from the inability to directly control every contact with customers. After all, the salespeople are going to the customer, so there is no way to directly oversee the level of service being administered. The best way to mitigate this problem is a combination of advance sales training and initial two-person sales calls. The two-person calls allow the new sales recruit to see how a sales call should be conducted, and also allows the company to keep an eye on new sales employees for their first few sales calls before they switch to making sales calls by themselves. However, a company in an explosive growth situation may not have enough sales personnel available to accompany a new recruit on a sales call, so this option is used by very few companies. In addition, a company can still rely on customer surveys to see how their sales personnel are doing, as well as waiting passively for customers to call them with complaints. A combination of all these techniques is necessary to provide some assurance that a company's own sales force is providing adequate service to its customers.

Customer service by the sales function is increasingly difficult to impose and maintain as a company moves from using its own sales staff to outside sales personnel and on to independently owned distributorships. Control options include salesperson training and accompanied sales calls as well as customer surveys. However, since sales calls are made away from company premises, this remains a difficult function in which to assure quality customer service.

SUMMARY

Poor customer service can quickly derail an explosive sales track by driving away customers. To prevent this, a company must create a database of customer complaints and then develop procedures for the collection, review, measurement, and resolution of those complaints. In addition, active recruiting, screening, and training of employees is necessary to ensure that a company has the right types of well-trained people working in every function that has direct contact with the customer. Finally, there are a variety of ways to maintain control over customer service in the key functions that the customer sees—order entry, warranties, call centers, and sales. If a company does not implement the complete customer service package described in this chapter, its service levels will falter, resulting in growth that is less than explosive.

Chapter 14

Distribution

INTRODUCTION

Many companies, unfortunately, give minimal attention to distribution. They simply build warehouses as needed, deliver goods to customers by whatever transportation method is immediately at hand, and then spend the remainder of their attention on other issues. An explosive growth company cannot make the mistake of ignoring the distribution function, because it can absorb a startling amount of cash, the fuel that this kind of company needs to spark its growth.

This chapter does not attempt to describe the multitude of distribution issues faced by any company, only those that are crucial to the operations of an explosive growth company. These are shown in Exhibit 14.1. The chapter begins with a short discussion of the key underlying principle that drives the direction of the entire chapter, and then describes the key tasks to focus on, as well as those distribution tasks that are of lesser importance in a high-growth environment. The chapter concludes with a review of several measurements, reports, and control points that can be used to manage the distribution function. By following the recommendations in this chapter, a company can distribute products to its customers with a minimum of expense, while keeping its limited supply of cash available for other purposes.

UNDERLYING PRINCIPLE

There is only one underlying principle needed for the distribution function, that of minimizing working capital and capital costs, because distribution can tie up an enormous amount of working capital due to having excess inventory, multiple warehouse facilities, and a trucking fleet. An explosive growth company has very little excess cash, so it must work hard to avoid putting cash into the distribution function. Therefore, every topic in this chapter is based on the principle of minimizing working capital and capital costs.

SELL THROUGH DISTRIBUTORS

The best way to avoid investing in a warehouse distribution system is to bring together a group of distributors who take on the burden of buying and storing

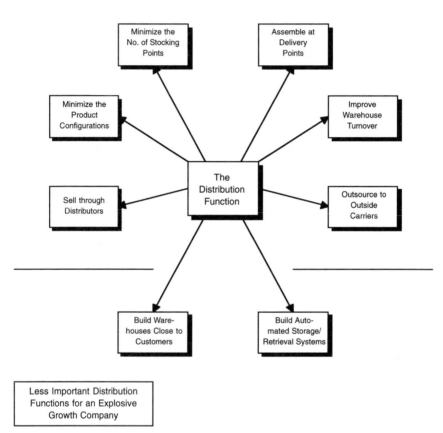

Exhibit 14.1 Explosive Growth Tasks for the Distribution Function

inventory. Sounds simple? Perhaps. This section describes the pluses and minuses of the approach.

By using distributors, a company can avoid a considerable investment in warehouse facilities and inventories, because the distributor takes on this responsibility. This option is especially worthwhile if the company is small, with a limited product line, because the cost of distributing and selling its products may exceed all revenues. In this situation, it is a good business decision to sell through a distributor who has the distribution and marketing muscle to help the company grow its sales.

However, there are several concerns to be aware of when using distributors. They are as follows:

- *The company may have to take back inventory.* Part of the distributor agreement usually allows distributors to return inventory for a restocking fee, either at any time or only when the distributor agreement is terminated. Returns can be a severe blow to a company's profits if the goods are too old to be sold again to other distributors. This risk can be capped by formalizing a specific time limit on all returned goods.
- *The distributor sells competing products.* A distributor probably sells competing products alongside the company's products; it is difficult for a company to force a distributor not to do this, unless the company's product is so valuable that it can threaten to terminate the distributor agreement as a penalty for selling competing products.
- *The distributor sells the highest-margin products.* Distributors put the bulk of their sales efforts behind those products that yield the largest profit margins, so a company may be under pressure to offer exceptionally low prices to distributors in order to be assured of sales.
- *The distributors must be managed.* If there are many distributors, a company should hire one or more managers whose task is to coordinate relations with the distributors, track distributor agreements, and resolve any disputes with them. This expense must be included in any cost-benefit analysis of a distributor network.
- *The service level may be low.* A company has no direct control over the quality of service given to customers by distributors; if service is poor, customers may refuse to buy a company's products.
- *The transition to a new distributor harms sales.* If a distributor is not fulfilling a company's sales or service expectations, it takes some time to terminate the distribution agreement, switch the territory to a new distributor, and wait for the new distributor to build up sales. Sales in that territory during the transition period will be minimal, which can have a serious impact on the rate of revenue growth.

The foregoing discussion outlines the risks of using a distributor network. Nonetheless, for a small or cash-strapped company that cannot afford to set up its own distribution network, it is still an excellent choice—just be aware of the problems, and try to mitigate them.

MINIMIZE PRODUCT CONFIGURATIONS

A company needs to stock a smaller number of inventory items if there are fewer product configurations, which allows it to reduce the amount of working capital invested in inventory. This section describes the advantages and disadvantages of minimizing the number of product configurations.

The following example illustrates the problem with having many product options. A manufacturer of bicycles offers a single model of bicycle in just one size, because it is adjustable to any height. However, it offers two choices of seat, handlebars, frame color, pedal clip, and tire. How many variations on the bicycle must the manufacturer keep in stock to cover all possible variations that might be ordered by a customer? The answer is to add up the number of variations (five) and calculate the factorial for that amount, which is (1 × 2 × 3 × 4 × 5), resulting in 120 possible variations. Thank goodness there was no sixth option, because that would have raised the number of stocking variations to 720! Clearly, reducing the number of product configurations has a major impact on the amount of inventory that a company must keep on hand.

In addition to reducing inventory, there are a number of other reasons why it is useful for a growing company to avoid multiple product configurations. They are as follows:

- *Needs less engineering time.* The engineering staff must create each of the product variations, which requires a considerable amount of time.
- *Needs fewer replacement parts.* The warehouse can avoid stocking large numbers of replacement parts if there are fewer parts to replace.
- *Needs less customer service training.* The customer service staff can be overwhelmed by the volume of product variations, making it difficult to repair products or advise customers about how to use them.
- *Needs less production training.* The production staff can have a difficult time figuring out how to install a multitude of product variations, which can also lead to a higher rate of faulty products, because they may not have been installed correctly to begin with.

Having pointed out the many flaws in the strategy of offering many product configurations, it is now time to point out a situation where it can also work. The example is the early rivalry between Ford and General Motors. Ford opted for a single product with no options, the famous black Model T automobile. General Motors opted to fill all possible product niches by offering a wide variety of cars in all shapes, sizes, and colors. General Motors won the market share battle and dominated Ford for the next half-century. Thus, in a situation where it is possible to gain significant market share by addressing many market niches, having many product options can be a reasonable strategy.

How can one reconcile these two irreconcilable strategies? The best approach is the one pioneered by Dell Computer, where it builds computers at the last possible moment from a standard set of parts to create a custom configuration for every computer. This strategy is covered later in this chapter, in the Assembly at Delivery Point section. However, the Dell strategy is a difficult one to implement, so a reasonable half-way strategy for a growing company is to follow the path of minimal options while it is growing rapidly, thereby avoiding cash flow problems and streamlining several processes, and then multiplying the number of options when growth slows down, in order to sell to more market niches, which allows the company to bolster its sales growth.

In short, an explosive growth company should avoid a large number of product configurations, not only because it requires a large amount of inventory to support, but also because it requires large amounts of extra work and employee training in the engineering, customer service, and production functions. This issue is also addressed in Chapter 15.

MINIMIZE THE NUMBER OF STOCKING POINTS

If a growing company wants to minimize its working capital and capital investment in its distribution system, the single best way to do this is to reduce the number of locations where it keeps finished goods inventory, for several reasons. One is that multiple warehouses require multiple buildings, staffs, materials handling equipment, storage racks, and computer systems, far more than would be the case if a company had a single large facility. Another reason is that, when a company has multiple inventory locations, it is easy for inventory to be idle in one location but to be out of stock in another, which leads to poor inventory turnover while customers are unhappy because they cannot purchase goods from the company when they need it. Also, if a company introduces a new product, it must spend time and money analyzing the market served by each warehouse to determine the amount of stock to deliver to each one. This process is not only expensive, but also frequently incorrect, resulting in, as previously noted, excess inventory in some locations and shortages in others. Finally, because there are pockets of unused inventory throughout the warehouse system, it is common for a company to have obsolete inventory that must be cleared out from time to time at considerable expense. For all of these reasons, a company will find that it is very expensive to maintain multiple warehouses.

In these days of reliable overnight delivery services, it is not only feasible but it makes economic sense to reduce the number of warehouses to the absolute minimum and rely on a speedy delivery service to bring products to customers. A good example of this is NetGrocer, which competes with local grocery stores by shipping dry goods from a single distribution point located in Dallas, Texas. Customers order goods through the Internet, which are picked up at the warehouse and sent via FedEx, which charges a surprisingly low rate for this service, to customers anywhere in the country within three days from the time of shipment.

Unfortunately, many companies are switching to the just-in-time (JIT) delivery concept, which works best if suppliers have warehouses as close to the company as possible. If a company has a customer who insists on a nearby warehouse and who will not accept overnight deliveries from a distant location, it may still be possible to mitigate the warehouse investment by creating a very small local storage facility that is only stocked with the parts used by that customer. Some customers even allow their suppliers to build small warehousing facilities inside their production plants, operated by customer employees, which allows suppliers to avoid the expense of a warehouse while still providing customers with the inventories that they think they need. Therefore, although JIT deliveries can run against the concept of warehouse centralization, there are alternatives to discuss with customers that may lead to a solution agreeable to both parties.

Finally, if a company cannot reduce the number of its warehouses for any reason, it may still be possible to increase inventory turnover and reduce obsolescence by installing software that links together the inventory databases of all the warehouses. This software reveals the location of all finished goods throughout the company, allowing employees to quickly track down products and have them shipped to customers from any location. Not only does this system reduce the amount of stagnant inventory in the system, but it also makes customers happier, because there will be more inventory available to them. This approach is used by the Lexus division of the Toyota Motor Company, which uses it to find the exact automobile, anywhere in the country, that matches a customer's specifications, and then ships it to that customer. However, this system is not perfect, because it is expensive to maintain; it requires a large database, supported by a central computer, and is linked by leased phone lines. Also, it is highly dependent on the accuracy of the inventory information in each warehouse. Thus, if a company must have multiple warehouses, it can link them by computer so that they can swap inventory, which improves inventory turnover and reduces the need for a large working capital investment.

ASSEMBLE AT DELIVERY POINTS

As pointed out in the Minimize Product Configurations section, a company must invest in a large amount of inventory if it has many product configurations—a minimum of one inventory item for every product variation. It is therefore reasonable that an explosive growth company that wants to conserve cash can do so by limiting the number of product configurations that it offers. However, is there a way to offer many configurations while still keeping inventory low? Yes, there is.

The way to avoid mounds of inventory while still offering the customer a wide range of product configurations is to assemble the product at the last possible moment. This concept has been perfected by Dell Computer, which can convert a customer order into a finished product and ship it to the customer in just a few days. This method allows Dell to avoid assembling a vast array of products that must be held in stock, awaiting the day when a customer orders the exact configuration it happens to have available. Instead, Dell keeps on hand just enough component parts for a very limited amount of production, and orders new parts from suppliers based on the immediate needs of customers. By waiting to assemble anything until a customer order arrives, Dell avoids massive inventories, sales forecasting problems, and inventory obsolescence. If a company can perfect this production method, which is not easy, it can still offer a reasonable amount of product variability to customers while avoiding a large investment in inventory.

Some companies are taking the Dell production model a step further by conducting final product assembly at a number of distribution points. This idea is good, because companies can stock a minimal number of parts at each distribution point, thereby vastly reducing the amount of inventory that must be kept on hand at each location. However, it is best if a company perfects this assembly method in one location before expanding it to all of its distribution points. There are several good reasons for doing so:

- *Needs extra management.* If there are many assembly points, many more managers and technical staff are needed to oversee the assembly. Without these people, there is a much greater chance that products will be assembled incorrectly, leading to customer complaints, many product returns, and fewer future sales.
- *Needs a sophisticated materials management system.* It is one thing to route parts to a single assembly point, and quite another to ship parts to a many of them. Having many assembly points requires a very advanced materials management system, as well as a highly experienced staff to run it.
- *Needs an order routing system.* There must be a system in place that routes customer orders to the nearest distribution point to the customer, so that the customer receives the finished product as soon as possible. Although not a difficult system to implement, it must be closely tied to the materials management system so that parts are routed to the assembly point along with the order.
- *Needs an investment in assembly equipment.* Although a final assembly point is designed to be a fairly simple operation, it still requires some equipment to ensure that assembly is done as efficiently as possible. If there are many assembly points, this can involve a moderately large investment.
- *Needs staff training.* The staff at each assembly point must be trained in how to assemble the final product. Depending on the complexity of the product, this training can take some time and involve considerable expense.

Given the number of reasons why it is difficult to set up and run multiple assembly points, why should an explosive growth company bother with this approach? There are three reasons. The first is that the company may be in an industry where sales are largely dependent on the ability of the company to deliver customer orders as rapidly as possible, which is easiest if assembly is close to the customer. The second reason is that the company may sell a product that is so bulky that it cannot ship it from a single assembly point without either significantly cutting into its profits or charging a price to the customer that raises the product's price well above that of its competitors. Finally, to a customer, assembling to order is slower than building to stock (which allows a company to immediately remove a product from stock and deliver it to the customer); to reduce the overall time needed to ship to the customer, it is useful to assemble near the customer, which reduces the delivery time. In any of these cases, assembling at multiple locations not only allows a company to compete on price as well as delivery time, but to do so without investing in a large amount of inventory.

IMPROVE WAREHOUSE TURNOVER

Much of the discussion in this chapter has focused on centralizing warehouses and keeping the number of product configurations to a minimum. These are the best ways to reduce a company's investment in the distribution area, but what if none of these options are available? Although it may not be possible to cut into a company's capital investment, another option is to work on improving the turnover of inventory through those warehouses, which decreases the amount of working capital needed.

As noted in the Minimize the Number of Stocking Points section of this chapter, a company can install a central database that contains the location and quantity of inventory in all of its warehouses, allowing it to ship products from any location and keeping the number of stale inventory items to a minimum. However, this system does not work well unless every warehouse has perfect record accuracy. For example, if a warehouse shows a quantity of 20 of a product when there are actually two units on hand, the company will promise shipments to customers of up to 20 units from that location, which not only requires an expediting scramble to fill the order, but also results in a dissatisfied customer, because it does not receive the promised product on time. Thus, for a centralized inventory tracking system to correctly assist in improving inventory turnover, every warehouse linked to it must first have excellent inventory record accuracy.

Good warehouse management includes a continual review of old inventory, which must be cleared out of stock and liquidated as promptly as possible. When done properly, this process is heavily assisted by automation. For example, a company can run a report for each warehouse that lists all inventory for which there have been minimal sales for a specific time period (as shown in Exhibit 14.3). A knowledgeable person can review this report for errors, and then authorize the removal and sale of everything on the report to a reseller at a discounted price. When done in this manner, clearing out old inventory is an easy task that frees up much-needed space for the storage of fresher merchandise, thereby saving a company the capital expense of building additional warehouse space. In contrast, a company that does not have good management of its old inventory lets it sit idle until just prior to the annual audit, when a large multidepartment team personally reviews all inventory to decide on what should be eliminated. Not only does this approach waste the time of many people, but it also may be too late to keep perishable, fad, or technologically outdated products from being liquidated within a time frame that allows the company to realize a reasonable amount of revenue; by waiting too long, a company may be forced to liquidate products at pennies on the dollar. In short, a continual review of inventory, assisted by some automation, allows a company to liquidate outdated inventory rapidly enough to realize a moderate return, while also clearing out extra storage space for new incoming products.

Another way to improve inventory turnover is to use cross docking. This approach splits up an incoming delivery at the receiving dock, and moves the component parts directly to waiting trucks for outbound shipments without the inventory ever spending any time sitting in a storage bin. Not only does this approach reduce the amount of inventory in stock, but it also saves storage space and eliminates the labor that would otherwise be needed to store it and then retrieve it from stock. However, the approach requires a great deal of coordination between inbound and outbound trucks, as well as an information system that tells the receiving staff where to send an inbound delivery as soon as it is received. This option can be difficult to implement. Cross docking greatly increases the speed of inventory flows through a warehouse, thereby increasing inventory turnover and reducing a company's working capital investment in inventory.

OUTSOURCE TO OUTSIDE CARRIERS

Some companies invest in their own fleets of trucks. This is a sensible direction for those companies, such as Wal-Mart, that have such vast delivery needs that they can justifiably prove that it is cheaper to maintain their own fleet than to use the services of a contract carrier. As long as shipments are so widespread and continuous that a high rate of utilization is possible, it makes economic sense for a company to purchase its own fleet of trucks. However, there are many reasons to avoid owning a delivery fleet, which are noted as follows:

- *Driver cost.* A truck requires one driver for local hauls and sometimes two for overnight, long-haul driving. These drivers are usually a mix of fixed and variable costs, because they may receive a fixed amount of base pay, plus additional compensation for (sometimes considerable) overtime, or a rate per mile driven.
- *Fuel cost.* A full-size, fully loaded truck may use up as much as a gallon of fuel every four miles, with multitrailer rigs using even more fuel. This expense is considerable for long-haul transport, and will go up as fuel prices gradually climb, either due to supply restrictions or to added federal and state taxes.

- *High acquisition cost.* The only underlying principle for this chapter is to avoid high capital costs, and a trucking fleet requires a large capital expenditure. Even if a company leases the trucks and trailers instead of purchasing them, there is still a significant cash outlay.
- *Insurance cost.* The company must insure not only its trucks and trailers, but also the cargo being carried. The rate charged varies based on the company's past safety record.
- *Maintenance cost.* Trailers require little maintenance, but the tractors that pull them require considerable overhaul work at regular intervals.
- *Replacement cost.* A fleet gradually wears down to the point where outright replacement is a cheaper option that continuing with expensive maintenance. This cost is offset somewhat by the residual value of the equipment that is being sold off.
- *Utilization issues.* A truck fleet is profitable if it can continuously haul products around the clock, and less so if it cannot. This utilization includes not only having a full load on the way to the destination, but also on the way back. If a company finds that its fleet is not being sufficiently utilized, it is squandering cash on too many trucks.

The foregoing points make it clear that owning a fleet is a bad choice for an explosive growth company, but what is the alternative? The cheap approach is to outsource the delivery function to an outside carrier. This is any delivery service, such as Yellow Freight, UPS, or FedEx, that pick ups and delivers parcels. There are also many local delivery operations that handle same-day deliveries within a small radius of the company. All of these options make it possible to avoid any investment in a fleet.

However, there are a few problems with outsourcing delivery. One is that, on a per-unit basis, deliveries are clearly more expensive. When this issue comes up, management should conduct a complete cost comparison on deliveries. This comparison will almost certainly show that an outside carrier's charge to deliver a parcel is far less than a company's cost to do so when all overhead costs are added in, such as the cost of the truck, maintenance, insurance, gasoline, and the driver's pay. The other problem is that the company has less control over its delivery schedule, because it must now deliver in accordance with the capabilities of the carriers who move its products. There are two contrary solutions to this issue, either of which can work, depending on the circumstances. One option is to spread the company's business across many carriers, thereby allowing it to find *someone* who can deliver products to specific destinations at the needed times. The alternative is to do the opposite and concentrate all delivery work with just one supplier; this makes the volume of business so important to the carrier that it will change its schedules to accommodate the company. The second option is only viable if there is a sufficient quantity of shipments available to sway the behavior of the carrier. If not, then a company should use the first option. Thus, carrier freight charges are not more expensive than those of an in-house fleet, although a company may have some difficulty in meeting customer delivery expectations when working with outside carriers.

TASKS TO AVOID

The list of activities for an explosive growth company to avoid, as noted in Exhibit 14.1, is quite short: Do not build extra warehouses and do not install an automated storage and retrieval system. These items are discussed in this section.

As noted exhaustively in this chapter, the creation of additional warehouses consumes a startling amount of working capital. For example, if a regional company wishes to expand to national distribution, it may decide to add 11 warehouses to service each of the 11 new sales regions. If one warehouse requires $5 million to maintain a fully stocked range of inventory (not to mention operating costs!), then the company has just used up $55 million to go from one warehouse to 12. Before using up so much working capital, a company should work through all possible alternatives, such as having distributors store the inventory at their expense, operating from fewer warehouses, or (best of all) using overnight delivery service or cheaper forms of transport from a single warehouse. If the company cited in the previous example were to find an alternative to multiple warehouses, it would have the option of shifting the saved $55 million to such other areas as product development, marketing, paying down debt, or building more efficient production facilities, all of which contribute to better financial and operating performance for an explosive growth company.

Some customers require a company to build a warehouse next to the customer, so that the company's parts are so close to the customer's production facilities that the company can more easily deliver parts within the scheduled time frame. This is a great deal for the customer, but is subject to some analysis before the company should agree to expend funds to build and stock another warehouse. As just noted, an extra warehouse is a considerable burden on working capital, so the following items should be considered by management before agreeing to build one:

- *Will the company receive more business?* If the company is willing to go to the expense of creating a warehouse to exclusively service one customer, will it receive extra orders for its pains? If not, and the customer does not have access to a different supplier who is willing to make the commitment to build a warehouse, then the company should see if the customer is willing to foot part of the bill for the warehouse. If not, then the company is taking on a great deal of extra financial risk with no prospect of added gain to offset the risk.
- *Will the company lose business?* To follow up the previous point, if the customer is not willing to increase purchases from the company, will it eliminate

purchases if the company does not build a warehouse as requested? If so, the company must decide if the resulting revenue loss will so severely cut into sales that it has no alternative but to comply with the customer's wishes. This problem is common when a single customer makes up a very large proportion of a company's sales.

- *Is there a legal agreement?* If the company decides to go ahead and build a warehouse to help service the customer, it must then consider the risk of having no recourse if the customer suddenly decides to purchase parts from someone else, thereby destroying the company's investment in the warehouse facility. If the customer is not willing to enter into any kind of legal agreement that mitigates the company's risk, management should carefully review the situation to see if it really wants to proceed with the new warehouse project.
- *What is the customer's viability?* Even if there is an ironclad agreement for the customer to purchase parts exclusively from the company at a good price and in adequate volumes, there may still be a significant risk that the company or the product line will not be in business long enough for the company to recoup its investment. To mitigate this risk, a company must not only look at the credit worthiness of the company, but also make an educated guess regarding the viability of the product line for which the company is supplying parts. Even if the customer is a strong one, the product line may be weak and subject to being terminated. If either problem is evident, company management must decide if the risk of termination exceeds the return from additional potential sales.
- *What is the impact on profits on sales to the customer?* If a company is forced to construct, fill, and staff a warehouse next to a customer, then profits on sales to that customer will certainly decline, since there is much more overhead to charge against profits earned from that customer. If there is only a minimal expected profit, then the warehouse project should not proceed. An illustration of the calculation to use for determining profits by customer is shown in Exhibit 14.2 in the next section.

In short, there are a number of considerations to ponder before going ahead with the construction of a warehouse for the specific use of one customer. Generally, it is not a good idea to do so unless the customer is financially strong, has a good product line, formally agrees to do more business with the company if the warehouse is installed, and sales to the customer comprise an important percentage of the company's business.

The Improve Warehouse Turnover section discussed ways to improve inventory turnover within warehouses. That discussion did not include the use of automated storage and retrieval systems (AS/RS), for one very good reason—they cost too much. An AS/RS can cost millions of dollars to install in a large warehouse, because it includes a complex interlocked set of conveyors, bar code scanners, computers, and (in some cases) robots that can automatically put inventory into open bins and extract inventory for use. Although it reduces the amount of manpower needed to run a warehouse, speeds the flow of materials in and out of the warehouse, and results in perfect inventory accuracy, the following points go against it:

- *Expense.* An AS/RS is very expensive. This is an up-front cost, unless a leasing deal can be finalized, so an explosive growth company will spend a considerable amount of cash for the system. Also, the time needed to pay back the installation is very long, if it is ever paid back at all. Since the only underlying principle of this chapter is to avoid working capital and capital expenditures, it is clear that an AS/RS violates the rule.
- *Fixed cost.* By purchasing an AS/RS, a company has greatly increased its fixed costs, which means that the company has a higher break even point, so that more sales are required before the company can earn a profit. This position is not good if a company already has a high break even point or if there is a risk of a sudden decline in sales, either of which could lead to sustained losses.
- *Maintenance.* Anything with moving parts breaks down, so a maintenance staff is needed to ensure that an AS/RS is always functioning properly. Therefore, this means that the savings gained from eliminating some of the warehouse staff is illusory, because they must be replaced by more expensive maintenance personnel. Also, the AS/RS must be stopped at some point for routine maintenance, which makes the warehouse nonfunctional during the downtime.

Thus, an AS/RS is usually not a good use of cash. If a company decides that it must have one, it should at least confine it to one centralized warehouse, rather than spending additional cash for multiple installations. Another option is to outsource the warehousing function to another company that already has an AS/RS installed, so that they incur the expense instead of the company.

MEASUREMENTS AND REPORTS

This section presents many measurements and reports that are useful for monitoring a company's performance in the distribution area. Because the primary focus of this chapter is on reducing working capital and capital costs, the measurements and reports tend to focus on that objective. They are as follows:

- *Amount and percent of damaged goods.* This measurement is useful for determining the ability of a company's distribution system to deliver goods to customers without damage. If the measurement indicates a significant amount of damage, management must inquire further to see if the problem is caused by the warehouse, the carrier, or the (lack of) packaging materials. To calculate it, have the receiving staff tally the total amount of damaged goods returned from customers for each reporting period, and divide this amount by the total revenue for the same period. The problem with this measurement is that it may be skewed if a customer returns goods that were damaged prior to the current reporting period. However, in most cases, customer receiving departments inspect goods on arrival and immediately send them back if they are visibly damaged.

- *Amount of capital invested in distribution.* This measurement is useful for a company that is looking for sources of cash. To calculate it, summarize the raw materials listed on the general ledger and the total amount of fixed asset investments in warehouses, racks, materials handling equipment, and trucks. The result should be adjusted by the amount of depreciation already taken to give the user a better idea of the resale value of the equipment (although resale value may not directly correlate to the depreciation-adjusted value of the fixed assets).
- *Cost of transport per order.* This measurement is used when deciding between keeping an in-house fleet for deliveries or outsourcing to an independent carrier. To calculate it, summarize all in-house fleet costs, including insurance, the payroll of the distribution staff and drivers, maintenance costs, utilities, taxes, fuel, and the interest cost of the funds used to purchase the fleet and other fixed assets. Then divide this amount by the total number of orders shipped with the fleet during the reporting period.
- *Cost of warehousing per order.* This measurement is used when deciding between an investment in warehouse facilities or purchasing the service from an independent warehouse. To calculate it, summarize all warehouse costs, which should include the salaries of all personnel who work in it, all utilities, insurance, interest costs on the cash used to purchase all fixed assets, and miscellaneous operating costs. Then divide this amount by the total number of orders shipped from the warehouse during the reporting period.
- *Distribution cycle time.* This measurement is useful for determining the average interval that a company takes to deliver a product to a customer from the time an order was received. To calculate it, subtract the date of order receipt from the date on which the last line item of the order was shipped. This should be done for all shipments; however, if the level of automation is not sufficient to do so, then a sample of orders can be used. The measurement can be thrown off if a few orders are not closed for a long period of time; this discrepancy can be mitigated by providing a supplementary report that lists all orders for which the distribution cycle time is unusually long; management can use it to find and correct distribution problems.
- *Inventory accuracy.* This measurement is important for those companies concentrating on improving inventory turnover within their warehouses. It is

difficult to find and ship products if the accuracy of product locations and quantities is minimal, so this measure must be used to determine if there is a problem, and its extent. To calculate it, compare a sample of the inventory in the warehouse to a printout of the inventory database that lists quantities, descriptions, and locations. If any of these data elements do not match, it is an error. Divide the total number of correct items by the total number sampled to derive the inventory accuracy.

- *Inventory turnover.* This measurement is useful for determining the degree to which inventory is sitting in each of a company's warehouses. It should be calculated separately for each warehouse in case there are significant differences between them. To calculate it, divide the total amount of inventory shipped from a warehouse during a reporting period by the average amount of inventory in the warehouse (which is the sum of the beginning and ending inventories, divided by two). This measurement can be skewed if there is an unusual fluctuation in the average inventory number used in the denominator.
- *Number of potential product configurations.* This measure is a good indicator of the potential number of products that must be kept in stock to satisfy all possible customer orders. To calculate it, add up all possible options for a product and calculate the factorial of that amount. Then repeat this calculation for all company products. The grand total of these calculations is the number of potential product configurations.
- *Percentage of sales through distributors.* This measurement is useful if a company is comparing the cost of its direct distribution to customers versus the cost of distributing through its network of distributors. To calculate it, summarize all sales to distributors, which is usually achieved by collecting all invoices with distributor sales codes and dividing it by the total amount of sales for the period. This measurement can be skewed if distributor sales are seasonal or come in large chunks, so it is best to use a long time period, such as a full year, when calculating this measurement.

Thus, there are several measurements that track the condition, amount, and cost of inventory and related assets, whereas others note the cost of delivery and warehousing.

Several reports are useful as supplements to the foregoing measurements, because they provide additional information and can be used to note the key problems hinted at in the primary measurements.

A key report that should be used for all larger customers is an analysis of the company's profitability by customer, including a number of distribution costs that can have a profound impact on profitability. It is important to add such costs as warehousing, distribution, and packaging to the usual gross margin on sales to a customer, because these added costs can determine the difference between a customer that is profitable and one that is not. Profitability can vary considerably if customers demand special treatment. An explosive growth company that is trying to grow by using internally generated cash cannot afford to have unprofitable customers, so this report is mandatory. A sample of this report is shown in Exhibit 14.2.

In the example in Exhibit 14.2, it is evident that the logistical cost required to serve Hardy, Inc., is much too high to be worthwhile; the relationship should either be terminated or modified by discussing the situation with customer management. The other two customers only cost the company a minimal additional amount for logistical expenses and still produce good margins.

Another report, which is also shown in Chapter 19, tracks obsolete inventory. This report is extremely important for those companies that have little space available in their warehouses, and must either clear out old stock or invest in additional warehouse space to make room for new stock. Because adding warehouse space is a capital expense that a growing company tries to avoid, the only alternative is to reduce existing stocks. The report shown in Exhibit 14.3 lists the key information that a company needs to determine not only if a product is obsolete, but also where to find it, so that it can be removed.

A company should know where its capital expenditures are invested throughout the distribution system. The assets should be clustered by location, so that management can determine the amount of cash it can potentially realize by selling off a warehouse site. Exhibit 14.4 shows categories of fixed assets, sorted by location.

The final report, Exhibit 14.5, lists all transactions for which the time required to deliver the product to the customer was longer than a preset limit. This report is sorted by the length of the delivery periods in descending order, so that the worst problems are listed at the top. The report then lists key information about

Exhibit 14.2 Total Cost by Customer

Description	*Earnest Co.*	*Hardy Inc.*	*Inuit Corp.*
Revenue	$4,500,000	$700,000	$14,300,000
Product cost	3,150,000	490,000	10,010,000
Gross margin	1,350,000	210,000	4,290,000
Gross margin percentage	30%	30%	30%
Warehousing cost	47,000	82,000	120,000
Repackaging cost	0	32,000	45,000
Transportation cost	104,000	91,000	210,000
Total logistical cost	151,000	205,000	375,000
Adjusted gross margin	1,199,000	5,000	3,915
Adjusted gross margin percentage	27%	1%	27%

Exhibit 14.3 The Old Inventory Report

Product No.	*Description*	*Quantity on Hand*	*Extended Cost ($)*	*Last Date Used*	*Location Code*
ABM-42	20" Red bicycle	3	600	07/04/88	A-00-B
ABM-43	22" Blue bicycle	5	1,108	02/19/89	A-04-C
ABM-45	22" Brown bicycle	16	3,250	09/07/93	B-08-D
ABM-50	24" Red bicycle	12	2,880	10/09/83	E-07-E
ABM-52	25" Ochre bicycle	4	812	05/11/93	E-09-F
ABM-55	26" Blue bicycle	2	516	03/27/97	B-04-A
ABM-58	27" Red bicycle	9	1,742	12/12/92	B-05-B

Exhibit 14.4 Fixed Assets by Warehouse Location

Asset Description	*Memphis*	*Denver*	*Seattle*
Facility	$1,250,000	$1,575,000	$2,150,000
Land	450,000	275,000	1,000,000
Racks	82,000	87,000	95,000
Conveyors	45,000	92,000	41,000
Forklifts	45,000	60,000	75,000
Depreciation to date	–182,000	–12,000	–418,000
Total	1,690,000	2,077,000	2,943,000

Exhibit 14.5 Long Distribution Cycle Times

Days to Deliver	*Delivery Date*	*Customer Code*	*P.O. Number*	*Job Number*	*Invoice Number*
128	12/08/xx	ACME	AC789	M0401	74023
69	12/07/xx	WENDELL	00442	M0422	74059
65	12/07/xx	BURTON	BU-2288	M0434	74001
62	11/30/xx	DAVIS	AA00041	M0439	74028
58	12/09/xx	SOUTHERN	123486	M0521	74039
54	12/05/xx	APPLECO	822241	M0528	74112
51	11/28/xx	WINBROS	00409	M0533	74069

each customer order that allows management to rapidly find the order and determine the cause of the problem. The report serves primarily as an index for looking for more information elsewhere, so it is full of reference information, such as the customer code, customer purchase order number, job number, and invoice number.

CONTROLS

The primary control points that the management of an explosive growth company must use are trend line comparisons that reveal where a company is absorbing increasing amounts of cash, and that note where expenses are changing over time and where distribution operations are changing in efficiency. By monitoring these controls and taking appropriate action where necessary, a management team can be assured of the minimal investment in the distribution function while still running a cost-effective operation that delivers good service to customers.

More than for other functional areas, the distribution function requires a great deal of maintenance activity, not necessarily to improve performance, but to ensure that it does not drop below a level that dissatisfies customers. This means that the best control points for the distribution function are a large number of trend lines that show any variations in the function's performance over time, with any unfavorable trends requiring immediate management action to correct. The trend line analysis can also include an extra line for a targeted performance level, so that management can see if performance is gradually trending in the desired direction. A typical trend line should have a duration of at least three months if measurements are taken weekly, or a full year if measurements are taken only monthly; this duration provides enough data points to give users sufficient information to establish a good trend line. Also, the trend line should be on a rolling basis, so that there is always a complete set of data points on the graph, rather than just a few to one side. The more important trend lines to track are as follows:

- *Trend line of assembly volume by location.* If a company elects to conduct final assembly of products at multiple distribution points, thereby reducing or eliminating the amount of finished goods inventory it must stock, it is very useful to know how much assembly work is being done at each distribution point. If the volume is too low, an assembly operation can be shut down and its assembly work shifted to a different assembly location.
- *Trend line of average shipment cost.* A rise in the cost of a company's shipments to customers can have a serious impact on profitability. However, the trend line can be misleading if it does not factor in the amount that customers are paying toward the freight cost. It can also be misleading if shipments are skewed to locations for which freight costs are extremely high, such as international destinations.

- *Trend line of distribution expense as a percent of sales.* It is misleading for an explosive growth company to review the distribution cost in dollars, because this figure is bound to increase in lockstep with increasing sales. Instead, it is useful to create a trend line that shows the distribution cost as a percentage of sales, which more accurately reflects any cost overruns on a proportional basis.
- *Trend line of inventory turnover by warehouse.* If a company has more than one warehouse, it should track inventory turnover at each warehouse to see if there are any locations where inventory is not moving. If so, these warehouses may be targets for elimination, which allows management to reduce its need for cash by liquidating inventory while selling off warehouse space.
- *Trend line of maximum product configurations.* Management must be aware of sudden increases in the number of possible product configurations, because this number may have an impact on the amount of a company's finished goods inventories. This measurement should be grouped by product families, because some products may require many options while others only have a single model; clustering all product families together might hide a dangerous increase in the number of configurations of a single product family.
- *Trend line of shipment volume by warehouse.* A previous trend line showed differences in inventory turnover between warehouses. A different approach is to strictly focus on the volume of shipments going out of a warehouse, which can be measured either in dollar volume or as the number of order line items shipped. In either case, a comparison of warehouses may reveal that some have minimal shipment volume, thereby giving management a reason to consolidate warehouses into a higher-volume location.

A control point that does not involve a trend line is the measurement, noted in the previous section, for listing the amount of damaged inventory. This control does not require a trend line, for even one instance of damage may be an indication of larger problems to come, such as a persistent packaging problem that will shortly result in a flood of customer returns. In this area, even one damage problem should be assumed to be the beginning of a trend and must be dealt with at once. If not, damaged goods may become a major problem very quickly, resulting in customer dissatisfaction and lost sales—something an explosive growth company does not want.

A listing of transactions with long distribution cycle times, as shown in Exhibit 14.5, is a very useful control point, for management can use it to track down specific instances where problems have occurred in the distribution process. Because the report excludes any item for which there was no distribution problem, it provides a tight focus of management attention on the key distribution problems. By addressing these issues early and investigating and correcting the underlying problems, management can avoid continuing problems with late deliveries, which improves customer satisfaction.

The controls over the distribution function of an explosive growth company must center on a trend analysis of a number of key factors, including inventory turnover, customer delivery cost, and warehouse performance. Coupled with this trend analysis should be a continuing review of reports that list damaged inventory as well as problems with long distribution periods. Only by implementing these controls can management have sufficient assurance that the distribution function is using the minimum amount of cash to deliver goods to customers in a timely manner.

SUMMARY

This chapter covered the key factors that a company must consider in order to keep the distribution function from tying up a large amount of a company's cash. It is important to reduce capital expenditures by avoiding purchasing a fleet or warehouses, while also reducing the working capital investment in inventory by selling through distributors, minimizing the number of product configurations, reducing the number of warehouses, assembling to final specifications at the shipping point, and improving inventory turnover through each warehouse. It is also possible to keep capital expenditures down by not taking several actions, such as building multiple warehouses near customers and building automated storage and retrieval systems. When all or a mix of these suggestions are implemented, a company can extract cash from its distribution function and use it to support its explosive rate of growth.

Chapter 15

Engineering

INTRODUCTION

It is a rare company of any kind, much less an explosive growth one, that maintains an engineering function that is both efficient and effective. Both of these characteristics are necessary in an explosive growth situation where a company depends on a constant flow of good products from the engineering staff to feed new sales, but cannot afford to support a large engineering staff for cash flow reasons. This chapter describes how to do it. The key elements of a good engineering function are shown in Exhibit 15.1, which also shows several tasks that should be avoided, because they tend to lengthen the design time and require additional resources. Each of the subsequent sections expands on the points noted in Exhibit 15.1. The chapter also includes a brief discussion of the key principles that underlie the need for each task, and it concludes with a review of the measurements, reports, and controls needed to manage the engineering function. By reading this chapter, you will gain an understanding of the key tasks to complete to ensure that the engineering function properly supports a company's growth.

UNDERLYING PRINCIPLES

An engineering staff can concentrate on many tasks, some of which are more important to an explosive growth company than others. The underlying principles discussed in this section focus attention on only those tasks that are critically important in a high-growth situation. The key principles are as follows:

- *Compress design time.* A company must issue new products to the marketplace as rapidly as possible in order to take advantage of short windows of opportunity and to grow sales by offering a complete product family that is constantly being renewed to reflect technological changes. This situation is only possible if a company is constantly focused on compressing its design time in order to not only make the best use of the engineering staff's time, but also to deliver product designs on schedule.
- *Compress materials management time.* A company's materials management system cannot operate without an accurate bill of materials created well in advance of the first procurement of parts for a product. This bill must be created

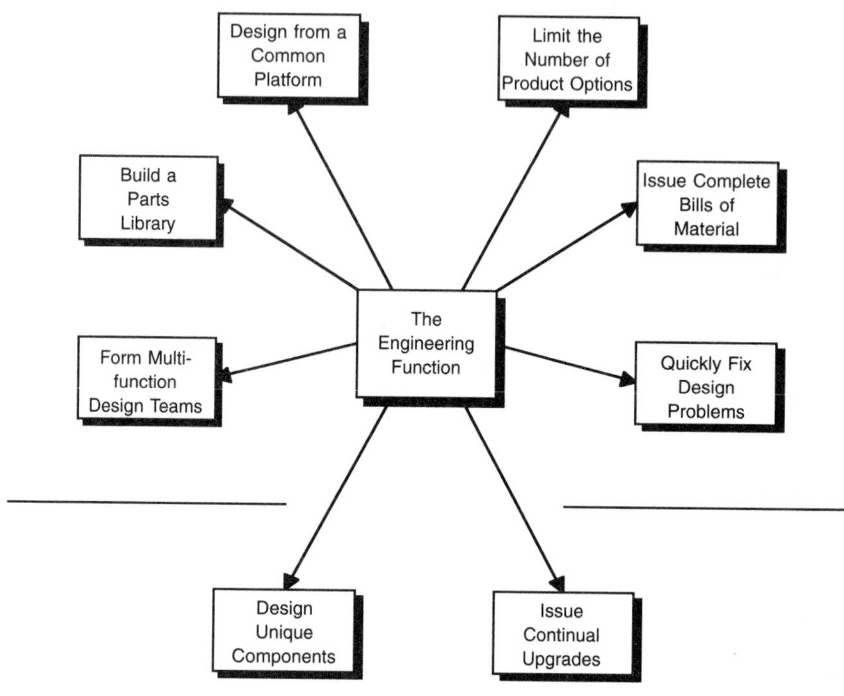

Exhibit 15.1 Explosive Growth Tasks for the Engineering Function

by the engineering staff, which has the most knowledge regarding the exact composition of each product.

- *Immediately address design flaws.* An explosive growth company will find that its sales will plummet if there are design flaws in its products that are not immediately corrected by the production staff. Fixing significant flaws in existing products should be considered more important than creating new products, because the flaws may result in the company not being in financial condition to launch any new products, no matter how well designed they may be.

The principles that the engineering function of an explosive growth company must follow are to process time compression and to immediately fix flaws in released products. Only by doing so can the engineering staff make a meaningful contribution to company growth.

FORM MULTIFUNCTION DESIGN TEAMS

A typical company designs products sequentially. That is, a product concept goes through a series of steps that eventually result in a finished product. Each step involves a different group of people, each of whom complete their work before passing along the project to the next group in line. This is grossly inefficient in terms of both time and money, because each succeeding group will find something wrong with the information it is given that requires rework by a previous group. Thus, it can take years, with many iterations of the design cycle, before a completed product reaches the market. This approach is impossible for an explosive growth company, because it is under constant pressure to release a constant stream of new products in order to bolster its revenue flow. What can be done to improve the situation?

One of the underlying principles for the engineering function is the compression of design time, which results in a faster release of new products. The best way to compress the design time is to switch from a sequential design method to a multifunction design team, whereby everyone is involved in every step of the design process. This approach has the considerable advantage of bringing up problems much sooner than is the case under a sequential design approach. For example, the purchasing staff may know that tooling for the product will not be available for a time period that extends past the market window; by making this known to the design team as soon as possible, it can design a product that requires a different kind of tooling that is more readily available. Under a sequential approach, the purchasing staff would not have known what type of tooling was needed until after the engineering staff had completed its design work and passed the drawings along to the purchasing personnel. Thus, scrapping the sequential approach in favor of design teams compresses the design time.

Who should be assigned to a design team? It depends on the tasks that the team must address, which are usually the following:

- Research the design
- Create initial product design
- Create prototype and test the design
- Revise the design
- Finalize and document the design
- Purchase or build production tooling
- Test and correct the production process
- Produce in bulk

Given the foregoing tasks, it is evident that the design team should include design engineers and marketing personnel for the early phases of the project, when product specifications must be assembled; industrial engineers, buyers, and production managers for the later sections, when the production process must be created to produce the product and purchase equipment for the assembly process. In addition, a cost accountant should be a part of the team, so that there is a continually updated product cost and expected gross margin available, which the team can use to design a product to meet the company's margin target. By assembling this group, a company can have all impacted parties involved in the design process from the start, which avoids the problems that would otherwise arise late in the design process and require reiterations of the design cycle.

There are two problems with using design teams, and they have caused difficulty for many companies that have attempted to switch over to this design methodology. One issue is that the members of the design team come from many different departments—engineering, accounting, marketing, materials management, and production. Therefore, there may be different agendas operating on the team (i.e., interdepartmental politics) that will keep the team from functioning as effectively as possible. The second problem is that, due to the diverse backgrounds of the people on the design team, it requires an exceptionally skilled manager to run it. The two problems are interrelated, because the team manager may have difficulty managing people who report to supervisors in other departments. These problems are not easily solved. Their solution depends on the support of the team concept by senior management, as well as the presence of very strong managers to run the teams. Without both of these elements, the design team concept has a much lower chance of succeeding.

Offsetting these problems are several benefits that make it quite worthwhile to overcome the problems. They are as follows:

- *Reduce conflict within the company.* Although it may seem that putting representatives of multiple departments on one committee is a recipe for a world war, it is actually better to make them work together as a team than to segregate them, as is the case for sequential design flows. By working together, or at least attempting to do so, representatives of different functions can better see the point of view of other functions, resulting in less conflict in the long run. A more harmonious staff can also have a favorable impact on staff turnover, because fewer people will become frustrated with interfunctional conflict and leave.
- *Reduce inventory and capital asset expenditures.* A company can spend considerable money on advance purchases of inventory and production tooling for a new product design. If the product goes through additional design iterations that negate the need for these purchases, then the company has just wastefully invested a large amount of money. This problem is entirely avoided if the design team approach results in no additional design iterations.
- *Reduce the total amount of design work.* By using design teams to reduce the

number of design iterations, a company can greatly reduce the number of engineering hours needed to complete a product design. A company can use this savings to cut back on the size of the engineering staff, but a better approach for an explosive growth company is to use the extra engineering capacity to create additional products that can fuel its rate of growth.

- *Shorten the time to market.* One of the most important benefits of using design teams is that a company can rapidly design a product and get it on the market in a short enough time span to address the changing tastes of consumers. For example, the latest version of the Ford Windstar minivan did not include a driver-side rear door, which consumers wanted. Ford must now go through a multiyear redesign of the vehicle before it can introduce one with that key feature. In the meantime, Chrysler's competing product that has the extra door is eating up market share and earning Chrysler a large profit. Would the situation be different if Ford had changed its design methodology to focus on a shorter design period? This would have allowed it to recognize the design problem and rush a new minivan version to market.

BUILD A PARTS LIBRARY

A properly functioning engineering staff stores the design of a new part in a parts library, and reuses the design whenever possible. This means that the staff only has to create all of the backup information for a part just one time; the only effort in the future is to use indexing to find the part in the library. This activity follows the principle of compressing design time, because the engineering staff is not wasting any time on redesigning parts.

An example of using a parts library is a car built by any of the major car companies. It will have a different exterior to differentiate it from another model, but many of the component parts are shared between models. For example, the instrument package is frequently the same across an entire line of cars, while there is also no need to provide different versions of power window controls. There are even greater similarities in the engine compartment, because car buyers do not look for differences in this area.

Why go to such lengths to build a parts library and reuse part designs? Here are some reasons:

- *Consolidate purchases to reduce per-unit part costs.* If a company uses a few parts to build all of its products, it must buy more of each part. It can use this purchasing volume to negotiate volume discounts with suppliers, thereby reducing the materials portion of the cost of goods sold.
- *Easier to train production personnel.* The production staff is much easier to train in building new products if it is already familiar with the parts being included in new designs. The more "old" parts that are used in new designs, the easier it is for production personnel to create new products, which also

leads to a reduction in product failures that would normally be caused by employee unfamiliarity with new parts.

- *Easier to train service people.* If the service personnel who repair products are familiar with the parts that form the innards of each product, it is much easier not only to repair the product, but to do so on the first try. If many new parts are included in a new model, the service staff may require a number of repair visits to fix the model, which does not help to increase customer satisfaction or increase the rate of customer retention for follow-on purchases.
- *Reduce the confusion caused by too many parts.* When a company deals with a large number of parts, it creates inefficiencies in many areas. For example, the item master (i.e., the list of all parts used) becomes so long that it is difficult to find the correct part on the list. Also, the purchasing staff is more likely to be confused about which part to buy if a company is using a multitude of variations on a single part. Furthermore, the materials management staff has more trouble pulling the correct part from stock, thereby causing inefficiencies in the production area. These problems are reduced as the number of parts declines.
- *Save design time.* There is much less design work to complete if an engineer can simply pull a part design from a library of standard parts instead of creating a complete set of parts specifications from scratch. The only time needed when using a library is the search to find the correct part, but this is insignificant compared to creating a new part design.
- *Smaller working capital investment in inventory.* If a company consistently uses its parts library, then it uses a smaller number of parts, which means that there is less need for a wide range of parts to be kept in inventory, either as safety stock, remainders, or service parts. This represents a clear reduction in the amount of a company's working capital investment in inventory.

The foregoing points make it evident that the engineering staff of an explosive growth company should actively pursue the use of a parts library to improve its overall design speed, thereby allowing the company to produce new products more rapidly.

DESIGN FROM A COMMON PLATFORM

A company can also compress design time by designing many products using a common platform. For example, car manufacturers use a common platform for many of their automobiles. This means that such features as the chassis width, frame, brake assemblies, and suspension systems are identical for a number of vehicles, with only the cab (the part that customers notice) being significantly different. This approach is not the same as designing with a parts library, for that approach assumes that identical parts are scattered throughout a product design;

using a common platform means that a sizable subassembly of the product is shared with other products.

Designing from a common platform yields a number of advantages. One is that a company can create a number of products with far less engineering labor, because a large portion of the design work was completed when the platform was originally created and does not need to be redesigned. Since less design time is needed, this also enhances a company's ability to rapidly create new products, which is very useful when market windows open and close with extreme rapidity. It is also much easier to switch the production line over to a new product if the underlying platform is always the same. To use the automobile example again, a car manufacturer can easily switch to a new model year of the same car if the platform is always the same, whereas a change to the platform that, for example, alters the chassis width by a few inches requires a complete retooling of the production line so that all of the assembly equipment is properly repositioned. To take the example further, if a company finds that one car is not selling well but another car that uses the same platform is doing better, it is a comparatively easy matter to increase capacity for the popular car by switching over the facility to produce that model. Thus, using a small number of platforms allows a company to easily switch its production capacity to produce more of the most popular products. There are a number of advantages to using a common design platform.

In addition to the foregoing advantages, there are more that were noted in the previous section, Build a Parts Library. They are noted again here as bullet points; please refer to the previous section for a more complete explanation of each item.

- Consolidate purchases to reduce per-unit part costs
- Easier to train production personnel
- Easier to train service people
- Reduce the confusion caused by too many parts
- Save design time
- Smaller working capital investment in inventory

In opposition to the many benefits associated with using a common design platform, there is only one problem: A company can become so wedded to a singularly successful platform that it keeps it, and all products whose designs are based on it, far longer than is wise. When a company keeps a design platform in the face of rapid technological innovation, it may find that its entire product line rapidly becomes obsolete, because all of it is based on obsolete technology. A good example of this problem is General Motors, which has stayed with the same engine designs for a number of years, while its Japanese competitors have continued to sink money into designs of increasingly sophisticated fuel injection engines. Although it has taken a number of years for this practice to become a competitive disadvantage, General Motors now finds itself in the position of having to play catch-up or lose sales to its more sophisticated customers who appreciate a smooth-running power plant. Thus, excessive dependence on an old design platform can harm a company's competitive position if technological advances bypass the platform.

LIMIT THE NUMBER OF PRODUCT OPTIONS

Some companies offer their customers a large number of product options on the grounds that they can gain more sales by appealing to every possible market niche. This strategy is not necessarily a good one for an explosive growth company, especially one that is in a weak financial position. This section discusses the reasons in favor of and against having multiple product options.

The underlying principle that this section addresses is compressing the amount of design time needed to create a product. When there are many product options, it takes a long time to incorporate the designs into the product design package, which lengthens the overall design period needed before the product is released. In addition, because there are more parts for all of the options, it takes longer for the materials management staff to procure them, and longer to train the production staff in the intricacies of creating products with multiple options. Thus, it is best to keep the number of product options to a minimum in order to keep the design period to a minimum.

In addition to the design compression principle, there is a principle from Chapter 19, Materials Management, to consider—that of reducing a company's working capital investment in inventory. When there are more product options, there is more inventory, because the extra parts used in the optional features must be kept in stock, not only to produce new products, but also as service parts in case options break in the field and must be quickly replaced. Thus, the number of options also impacts the amount of inventory.

In addition to the foregoing problems with having too many product options, there are a number of advantages to avoiding options that were noted in the previous section. They are shown again here as bullet points; please refer to the previous section for a more complete explanation of each item.

- Consolidate purchases to reduce per-unit part costs
- Easier to train production personnel
- Easier to train service people
- Reduce the confusion caused by too many parts

Despite all of the problems with adding product options, it is quite possible to make a case in favor of doing so. This situation occurs when the product niche that is served by adding an option is so large that it vastly outweighs the cost of creating and servicing the option. This route may be especially enticing if the company's revenue growth rate is starting to decline, and management is looking for a way to accelerate growth. Creating options is also worth reviewing when the work alternative for the engineering staff is to create new products for which the level of projected sales is not high. In this case, management should create a list of all possible engineering projects, sorted in descending order by projected sales volume, and put the bulk of its effort into the projects at the top of the list. An example of this list is shown in Exhibit 15.2. If the selected projects happen to include designing options for existing products, then that is still a good allocation of engineering resources. Thus, it is still logical to spend time designing product options, as long as they have a large return in projected revenues.

Exhibit 15.2 also notes a second criteria for picking a project besides projected sales volume—the estimated time needed by the engineering staff to complete the project. Note that for project 54-403, only 50 hours of engineering time are needed to complete it, with an estimated return of $375,000. Given the high return for a minimal time expenditure, this project may take precedence over other project designs that have a higher estimated revenue number. Another way to review the priority list is by estimated gross margin, rather than by estimated revenues. This gives management a better idea of the total return on its engineering investment.

There is also a large distinction between designing options that are built into the original product and creating options that are sold separately from the product, and which are attached to the product by the customer. An example of the first instance is when Boeing Corp. offers an option of a different kind of leather seat that it can install in the business class section of a jet. An example of the second instance is when Motorola sells a walkie-talkie, for which a customer can separately purchase a microphone. In the first case, the primary product must be designed differently to accommodate the seats, whereas in the second case, the product is unchanged. Thus, it is quite acceptable for an engineering staff to design options that are sold separately from the primary product.

A word of caution regarding having the engineering staff cut back on the number of options: It frequently is not the responsibility of the engineering group to authorize new options—the marketing function has this responsibility. If so, engineering management must be very forward in describing to senior management the problems with designing too many product options. This issue is addressed further in Chapter 20.

Exhibit 15.2 Engineering Priority List

Project No.	*Project Description*	*Estimated Revenues ($)*	*Estimated Hours Needed*
54-101	Reading lamp	2,500,000	2,400
54-007	Desk lamp	1,450,000	1,000
54-018	Workbench lamp	825,000	500
54-201	Option—hood for reading lamp	400,000	200
54-403	Option—hood for desk lamp	375,000	50
54-882	Option—hood for workbench lamp	325,000	125
54-741	Option—brass lamp base	200,000	200

In short, it is a good idea for the engineering staff of an explosive growth company to limit the amount of its time allocated to creating multiple options for its products, because this causes problems in a number of areas throughout the company. This restriction does not apply to those options for which significant sales growth is projected or for options sold separately from the basic product and that do not require modification of the underlying product.

ISSUE COMPLETE BILLS OF MATERIAL

It is quite common for an engineering staff to neglect the creation of a bill of materials (BOM) to go along with a new product design. It is the engineering view that the BOM is a lesser matter, and a less prestigious one, that occupies a priority well below that of designing new products. What these engineers are missing is that the BOM is the primary input to the materials management function from the engineering function, because it is used to purchase parts. For an explosive growth company, the BOM is critical, because having an accurate one allows a company to purchase the exact parts needed in an orderly manner, without any extra purchases for the wrong part, or last-minute freight charges to bring in missing parts. In short, the BOM saves a growing company a very large amount of cash while compressing the time needed by the materials management staff to supply the production function with parts.

A simple example illustrates the amount of money a company can lose if it does not have an accurate BOM. Assume that a company builds a lawn mower that costs $200 for the components. It anticipates that it will sell 50,000 of these lawn mowers in the first year of production. The total material cost for the first year, then, is $10,000,000. It negotiates a blanket purchase order with a supplier to produce a 20-inch blade, costing $10 each, to cut grass, and sole sources the first years' production to this supplier. Unfortunately, the negotiations were conducted on the assumption that the blade was the same one used on all of the company's other lawn mowers, and there was no finalized BOM to inform the purchasing staff that the specifications had changed. In reality, the hole bored in the blade was too large, because the new 4.5 horsepower engine for this design had a different size shaft. Since the supplier had already completed a long production run for all 50,000 blades when the error was discovered, and because the supplier was fully justified in doing so under the terms of the blanket purchase order, the company was forced to pay the supplier the full-year cost of the blades, which was $500,000 (50,000 units × $10 per blade). If the engineering staff had spent a modest amount of time creating the BOM, this error never would have happened. At an average salary of $60,000, the error would have paid for more than eight additional engineers for a full year, which would be vastly more than enough to create a BOM for the lawn mower. Thus, not creating a BOM can wreak havoc downstream from the engineering function.

A BOM allows a company to avoid considerable waste in a variety of areas.

One is the reduction in time needed by the materials management staff to procure parts; this time compression is one of the underlying principles noted at the beginning of this chapter. By avoiding the wasted time that occurs when a buyer must cancel an order when part specifications change, the number of buyers can be reduced or switched to more productive tasks. A company can also eliminate a variety of overnight freight charges and expediting fees when it has a good knowledge of parts requirements, because there should be no unwanted last-minute surprises when the production staff finds that it has suddenly run out of a key part. Also, because the wrong parts are no longer ordered, the company does not have to incur restocking fees for returning unwanted parts to suppliers, nor does it have to worry about taking obsolete inventory charges for parts that were incorrectly ordered and which now languish in the warehouse. In addition, the company can avoid interest costs on the debt needed to fund the purchase of excess inventory that the company has incorrectly ordered. An accurate BOM is also a key component of a material requirements planning system, which is described in detail in Chapter 19. All of these problems are greatly reduced or vanish when the engineering staff creates an accurate BOM.

Thus, the engineering staff must make it a high priority to create a BOM whenever it completes the design of a new product, since a multitude of benefits occur downstream from the engineering function when this is done.

QUICKLY FIX DESIGN PROBLEMS

A key issue for an explosive growth company is to immediately fix any design problems in existing products that could impair continued revenue growth. Without a quick fix to a major design flaw, a company will find that its growth rate can stall overnight. This section discusses the implications of not fixing major problems and of telling the difference between a major flaw and a minor one.

The business literature is chock full of stories about companies that did not fix design flaws as soon as they could have, resulting in disastrous declines in sales as customers flocked to competing products. For example, the famous test of the Suzuki Samurai car by *Consumer Reports* that documented the car's instability virtually wiped out sales of the formerly popular vehicle. By comparison, a small car built by Mercedes that was about to enter production was found (by automotive journalists) to have a similar problem. However, Mercedes immediately fixed the problem, resulting in minimal bad press. Not fixing a major problem, then, can obliterate a product.

One of the biggest problems for a company is to decide if a problem with its product is a major one that requires an immediate fix, or if it is a minor one that can be safely ignored until the introduction at a later date of the product's successor. This is a major issue because, as noted in the next section, Tasks to Avoid, the engineering staff does not want to make too many changes to existing products, because this causes a great deal of inefficiency throughout the organization. There are several ways to make this determination. They are as follows:

- *Use a review board.* A group of people can determine the need for a product fix, although there are several variations on the composition of the committee. One approach is to rely on a single expert, usually the senior engineer who designed the product, to make a determination. Another variation is to just use the product manager, who can tell from a marketing perspective if the problem will interfere with sales of the product. It may also be useful to include an engineer on the committee who specializes in the safety of each product; because a company may be subject to considerable litigation if a product design flaw causes injury to a customer, this is good position to include the safety engineer on the committee. The best approach is to make the senior design engineer, product manager, and safety engineer responsible for the final design decision. It is also useful to include a cost accountant in the process who can compile the cost of each proposed engineering change, which may have an impact on the decision to proceed.
- *Ask the customer.* The company can input all customer complaints regarding a product to a complaints database, which the engineering function can then use to determine how customers feel about a particular design problem. This is a very good method for determining what problems should be fixed, because customers may be highly irritated about a problem that the engineering staff considers to be a very minor issue. In this case, whatever the customer wants determines what must be fixed.

Thus, either an inside opinion by an experienced committee or reference to a customer complaints database is a good way to determine which problems can be fixed and which can be safely ignored.

No matter which approach is used, there should be a person who is responsible for the day-to-day tracking of product problems, so that a new problem can be spotted and corrected as soon as possible. This person should have the authority to immediately call a meeting of the review committee if a problem arises that appears to be so serious that the issue cannot wait. Having this person in place gives a company the ability to rapidly respond to any product design issue.

Some companies prefer to reduce the cost of a design change by waiting until their stocks of all component parts for the old design have been used up before starting production of the new and improved product. This policy may be a mistake. If a company is using up old parts that may be faulty, either it does not care if the faulty parts are sold to customers (which brings up some customer service issues) or else the design change is so minor that it does not matter which version of the product the customer receives. If the company does not care if the customer receives a faulty product, the company deserves to go out of business, and hopefully will eventually do so. If the product change is so minor that the customer will not care which version of the product he or she receives, then one must wonder why the change is being implemented at all. Only in cases where the existing parts are clearly flawed should the company throw them out in favor of revised parts; in any case, where the company decides to retain its existing parts until they are used up is a clear sign that the product change probably should not be made at all.

TASKS TO AVOID

There are two tasks that an engineering staff must avoid. One is designing a large proportion of unique components for every one of its products, and the other is issuing continual product upgrades. This section discusses why these tasks interfere with the rapid introduction of new products and thereby hinder explosive growth.

There are several problems with designing numerous unique components. The main one is the impact on the available resources in the engineering function; designing new parts rather than using existing designs that are readily available in the parts library takes up considerable time, thereby cutting into the function's capacity for designing new products. Another problem is that it greatly expands the size of the parts library, resulting in a massive array of part designs, many of which are almost identical. Because there are so many parts in the library, it becomes increasingly difficult for an engineer to quickly find a part to use in a new design, thereby wasting additional time. It also results in more inventory items to clog the warehouse, because fewer products are sharing components, so a wider range of parts must be kept in stock. In addition, the company must now purchase a small quantity of a large number of parts, which not only reduces the company's ability to negotiate volume discounts on parts, but also requires more time by the purchasing staff to buy the increased number of parts. Finally, it is more difficult to train the production and service employees to assemble or repair a product when the parts are different for every product. For all of these reasons, it is not a good idea to design a large proportion of new parts for every new product.

Issuing continual product upgrades also presents a variety of problems. One is that the company must be careful to use up its inventory of old parts before switching over to new designs; otherwise, the company may find itself with huge inventory that it cannot use. In addition, the company must maintain a small amount of inventory for all old parts that are no longer used, because they may be needed to service existing products that customers have returned for repairs; this can add up to quite a large amount of inventory. Also, the user manual for a product must be scrapped, rewritten, and reprinted every time an upgrade occurs. This revision not only requires a company to incur the expense of throwing out all the old product manuals, but also of issuing new ones. Finally, the production and service staffs must be retrained in how to assemble and service the modified product. Clearly, there are many reasons to keep the number of product upgrades to a minimum.

Despite the number of reasons for not modifying a product, it is still sometimes necessary to do so. The most obvious reason is when the product has a flaw that may impact the safety of customers or which is so irritating to customers that it is driving down sales; this type of upgrade must be made as soon as the problem is discovered. The other case is when the company can clearly show that it will save sizable sums of money by altering the product. In most other cases, such as when there are minor design flaws to correct, it is frequently better to concentrate on incorporating the changes into the company's next version of the product rather than to spend a large amount of engineering time on the current version. This focuses the company on creating new products that will bolster future sales, rather than on making changes to the current version that may have no impact on sales at all. Thus, a company should upgrade its existing products, but only when the upgrade fixes a serious problem or results in a significant cost savings.

MEASUREMENTS AND REPORTS

Many measurements and reports that target several key areas are available for tracking the engineering function. For example, the ability of an engineering team to reuse existing parts on new products is measured by tracking the number of products per design platform and the percentage of new parts used and old parts reused. The effectiveness of the design process is measured by looking at the percentage of designs completed on schedule, the number of design revisions after release to production, and the number of iterations of the design cycle. Thus, it is apparent that the following measurements can be culled down to a subset that should adequately meet the measurement criteria of most engineering functions. Each measurement includes a description of how it can be calculated, as well as a brief description of its use, and any reasons why it may generate inaccurate results, if applicable. The measurements are as follows:

- *Average number of distinct products per design platform.* A company that can create a multitude of designs from one basic product can save considerable design work while still issuing many new products. Consequently, a good measure of this type of efficiency is to determine the number of distinct products based on a common underlying product design. This measure should be taken separately for each design platform, so that management can see which platforms are not being fully utilized, which may lead to the elimination of an underutilized platform.
- *Bill of material accuracy.* If the engineering staff cannot provide an accurate BOM to the materials management staff well before a product is scheduled for production, it will be very difficult for the company to efficiently bring in the correct parts at the right time and in the correct quantities to ensure that production will begin as scheduled. To calculate it, select a sampling of BOMs and review them for errors. Count each incorrect part quantity, missing part, and part that is listed but not required as an error. Summarize all correct line items and divide by the total number of line items (including the line items that should have been added to each bill, but were absent) to determine the BOM accuracy.
- *Number of engineering change notices issued for each product.* An engineering team has not done a good job of creating a new product if it must subsequently release a flurry of engineering change notices to correct design flaws. To calculate this measurement, add up the number of engineering change

notices that were issued for each product. This information should be obtainable from the engineering librarian, who is responsible for tracking this information. The measure can be misleading if it covers a long time period, because a product may have many changes over a multiyear life cycle. A more refined measure is to track it for only the first few quarters subsequent to product release, which is more revealing of the number of changes due to design flaws, rather than ongoing enhancements.

- *Number of iterations of the design cycle.* If a company uses design teams to create new products, then it goes through one iteration to create a new product. If it does not use this approach, there may be many iterations, while a design is bounced back and forth between different functional areas before a completed product is available. If a company uses the second course, it should measure the number of iterations of the design cycle for each product, because this is an excellent indicator of the time needed to design a product and the underlying reason why design times exceed the budget. To calculate it, audit the engineering correspondence file for each product to determine from memos the number of iterations that have been completed. This measurement is inexact, because a good case can be made that only portions of a design must go through multiple iterations before a product design is complete.
- *Number of product options per product family.* Too many product options requires an excessive amount of engineering design time, as well as many further difficulties in the materials management area (see Chapter 19 for details). To calculate this measurement, add up the total number of options available for each product. This information is usually available through the order entry system or from sales literature. This measurement does not include supplements to a product that are not an integral part of it, because they do not involve design modifications to the underlying product.
- *Percentage of existing parts reused.* A design team that can build a new product by using a high proportion of already designed parts can save a large amount of design time. To calculate this measurement, determine the number of parts in the new product that were already used in existing products. For companies with a materials requirements planning system, this information is available on the Where Used report. Then divide the number of reused parts by the total number of different parts required to build the product.
- *Percentage of new parts used.* This percentage is the reverse of the preceding measurement, and is calculated by adding the number of new parts included in a product, and dividing the sum by the total number of different parts required to build the product. The number of new parts can sometimes be determined by adding the number of new parts drawings accompanying the product design package, although there may not be a drawing for every new part.
- *Percentage of product designs completed on schedule.* A company's ability to create complete product designs by the scheduled date is a good indicator

of its ability to have products on the market in time to take advantage of openings in the market. To calculate it, go to the scheduling file for the project and determine the original date on which it was scheduled for completion. Then add up all projects completed by their scheduled dates and divide by the total number of projects reviewed. This measurement can be severely skewed if major product features are added after the original schedule was imposed; in these cases, the baseline target may require modification to include the impact of the extra requirements, although adding too many features can also be a sign of poor project management.

Although the previous measurements give management a good overall view of the performance of the engineering function, they do not give any detail that tells management where to look for underlying problems. The following reports fill this gap by giving more detailed information. The reports fall into two categories: Either they are the complete list of transactions that roll up into one of the previous measurements, or they are exception lists that show only those transactions that have fallen outside what the company considers to be a normal range of results. The first of these reports is shown as Exhibit 15.3, and is a list of the complaints received from customers through the complaints database. This list is selected for only engineering-related complaints, and is reviewed by engineering management to see if there are any complaints that may indicate the presence of a problem with a product design that requires immediate action. The report begins with an identification code assigned to each complaint, which is used to sort complaints into various categories. The next field lists the complaint, and the following fields list the name and phone number (if available) of the person lodging the complaint, in case management needs to contact the person again to follow up on an issue. The report finishes with the date on which the complaint was lodged, which is useful for determining the time required to resolve it. See Chapter 13 for more complete information about the complaints database.

The next report shows all of the parts in the company's item master report that are not used in any of a company's products. The item master is the master list of all parts that the company uses. This report, shown in Exhibit 15.4, is very useful when cleaning out the item master, which should be done monthly. This cleaning process is very helpful, because it reduces the level of confusion for engineers who are searching it, looking for the parts they want to include in new product designs. The report is a simple one, and only contains the part number, description, cost of the units on hand, and the last dates on which it was purchased and used. This information is sufficient for the engineering staff to decide if the part should be deleted.

Another report, shown in Exhibit 15.5, lists the cost of an engineering change notice. This is an excellent feedback mechanism for the engineering staff, because it can use this information as a learning tool to making estimates of what future product changes will cost, which may lead to a decision not to undertake some changes. The report includes the cost of any inventory that will no longer be usable

Exhibit 15.3 List of Engineering Complaints from Customers

Sort Code	*Complaint Description*	*Customer Name*	*Phone Number*	*Complaint Date*
EN-data	Inaccurate instrument readings	Paul Able	508-292-4073	07/13/xx
EN-data	Inaccurate instrument readings	David Strunter	617-202-1133	03/13/xx
EN-mtl	Barometer gauge broken	Mabel Gaines	212-940-1200	02/12/xx
EN-mtl	Barometer gauge broken	Bertha Nowles	202-555-4321	11/01/xx
EN-mtl	Barometer gauge broken	P.J. Summons	970-493-7832	12/22/xx
EN-pkg	No parts list in product manual	Sam Friesen	303-442-5300	05/17/xx
EN-pkg	No parts list in product manual	Al Dunn	719-534-4300	07/14/xx

as a result of the change, extra tooling and tool installation costs, additional training for the production and servicing staffs so that they know how to handle the altered product, and the estimated cost of retrofits to products that customers may bring in. The report also includes the cost to purchase extra parts that have been modified, so that the company has spare parts in stock for repair or warranty work. Finally, the report includes the cost of old product manuals that must be scrapped, the cost to design new ones that incorporate the design changes, and the cost to print them. Taken together, this report forms a comprehensive view of the cost of an engineering change.

The engineering manager should closely review the time needed by the engineering staff to complete changes to design flaws. There tends to be a rush on the completion of these changes, because there may be safety or customer satisfaction issues that must be dealt with at once. Accordingly, a complete listing of the time needed to complete each change is a good starting point for a complete analysis by the manager of why some changes take longer than others. The report,

Exhibit 15.4 Item Master Unused Parts List

Part Number	*Description*	*Cost on Hand ($)*	*Last Purchase Date*	*Last Usage Date*
BZ-0412	4" wind gauge	2,345	07/13/92	03/13/89
BZ-0397	Anemometer, full height	213	03/13/89	11/01/91
BZ-0442	Wind sock, yellow	884	02/12/97	12/22/92
BZ-0512	Gauge housing, brown	4,504	11/01/91	05/17/88
BZ-9904	1/4" chrome hex screw	8,002	12/22/92	07/13/92
BZ-9990	Barometer, 8" brass casing	12	05/17/88	07/14/89
BZ-9993	Wind vane, 3 foot	11	07/14/89	02/12/97

Exhibit 15.5 The Cost of an Engineering Change Notice

Description of Cost	*Cost ($)*
Cost of obsolete inventory	14,500
Tooling purchases and installation	48,000
Assembly and service personnel retraining	12,000
Retrofit cost for existing products	5,000
Spare parts restocking	3,200
Old product manuals to be destroyed	4,000
Redesign of product manual	8,000
Printing of new product manuals	12,000
Total	106,700

as shown in Exhibit 15.6, breaks down the time element into several components, so that management can tell where the time delay occurred in the redesign process.

The engineering manager must have information about the budget versus actual costs and time for each project, so that there is some evidence that a job may be running over its budget. This gives the manager time to intervene to see if there is some way to bring the project back on track. A very summarized version of this report is shown as Exhibit 15.7, which has one line item for each engineering project. A variation on this report is to show multiple line items, one for each phase of a project. However, it is only easier to track costs by line item if a company uses a sequential design process instead of design teams, because costs are more easily segregated. If a company uses design teams, as is recommended in this chapter, then costs are not so easily segregated, resulting in a lump sum cost for the entire project.

Two additional reports that are not shown here are the Gantt chart and the

Exhibit 15.6 Cycle Time to Complete Design Fixes

Project No.	*Days to Identify Problem*	*Days to Design Solution*	*Days to Implement Production Change*
EN-1401	2	18	12
EN-2402	3	82	5
EN-3101	18	2	17
EN-3845	142	3	28
EN-4004	32	1	8
EN-5398	81	5	61
EN-7290	4	2	2

Exhibit 15.7 Budget versus Actual Cost and Time Tracking by Project

Project No.	*Actual Cost ($)*	*Budget Cost ($)*	*Cost Variance ($)*	*Actual Hours*	*Budget Hours*	*Percent Variance*
EN-1401	42,800	40,000	2,800	571	525	9%
EN-2402	100,412	100,000	412	1,300	1,250	4%
EN-3101	52,801	55,000	–2,199	650	600	8%
EN-3845	12,442	15,000	–2,558	150	225	–33%
EN-4004	89,543	90,000	–457	1,100	1,200	–8%
EN-5398	1,209	1,000	209	10	10	0%
EN-7290	12,389	15,000	–2,611	125	100	25%

revenue trend line. A Gantt chart is useful for each current engineering project, because it shows the time needed to complete each task and the key milestone dates along the way. This chart is an excellent control tool for engineering managers who need to know about the progress of the design teams that report to them. The revenue trend line is also a useful control tool, because it tells management when the sales of an existing product are beginning to decline, which is a good time to have a succeeding product ready to replace the old product and generate additional sales.

CONTROLS

This section discusses the controls needed to manage the engineering function in an explosive growth company. Engineering is an extremely important area for a growing company, because it must have a steady stream of new product designs to feed its growth. One way to control the function is to simply have a staff person compile all of the measurements and reports noted in the previous section and give it to the manager, who skims through it when time is available. Given the size of the heap provided by the staff person, it is a reasonable bet that the manager will not be able to consistently review all of the information and follow up on it. This is also a poor way to feed information to the individual design teams. What can be done to improve the situation?

There are four steps to complete before a company has adequate control over the engineering function, and they are founded on the notion that the design teams are quite capable of managing their own activities, given enough information to let them know when they are deviating from expectations. The control steps are as follows:

1. *Create a measurement summary for each design project.* Since there are so many measurements and reports to choose from, why not consolidate them

all into a single-page report for each project? This form makes it easy for someone to glance at the summary and immediately know the status of a project. The types of information shown on the report vary by type of project. A sample that applies to many design efforts is shown in Exhibit 15.8. The report shows two sets of information: several measures that give everyone a good idea of the percentage of completion of the project (which is needed because of the notorious inaccuracy of any single percentage-of-completion measurement) and a set of measures that describes the efficiency of the engineering staff (e.g., the ability to use existing parts and drawings). In Exhibit 15.8, Project GHI is clearly having difficulty in completing its work within the estimated budget, and the primary reason appears to be that it is using an inordinately high percentage of unique parts, rather than mining the company's parts library for standard parts. This may be a case of a unique product that was severely under budgeted, but it is also quite likely that this project needs stronger management to force the team to use standard parts.

2. *Distribute it to all design teams every day.* The design teams are composed of professionals who not only *should* take responsibility for team results, but *must* do so, because top management cannot be expected to closely manage every design team in a high-growth situation where there are many teams and not enough senior managers. Accordingly, a measurement summary, such as the one shown in Exhibit 15.8, should be sent to every design team every day, so that they know exactly how their project is progressing. However, if the information is too difficult to collect daily, it may be better to distribute a lesser amount of information every day, either by memo, e-mail, or by posting it on a white board, while sending out the full measurement summary somewhat less frequently.
3. *Distribute it to engineering management less frequently.* Higher-level managers can receive the same summary reports as the teams, but perhaps only on a weekly or biweekly schedule. For all but the shortest projects, this gives management sufficient information to see problems arising and to correct them before too much time has gone by, while avoiding burying them with too much information.

Exhibit 15.8 Engineering Project Measurement Summary

Description	*Project ABC*	*Project DEF*	*Project GHI*
Target completion date	04/17/xx	07/18/xx	11/19/xx
Percentage of drawings signed off	92%	85%	79%
Percentage of total budget used	95%	91%	101%
Percentage of hours budget used	88%	99%	95%
Percentage of unique parts	12%	31%	59%
Percentage of drawings added	2%	8%	52%

4. *Schedule periodic reviews by management with design teams.* Sometimes the information contained on the measurement summary report is not sufficient to determine the true status of a project; perhaps there are personnel issues that are not readily apparent, or maybe there are technical problems, or issues with a supplier. These issues are best communicated face-to-face. Accordingly, there should be a regularly scheduled review meeting covering the activities of every design team. The timing of these reviews depends on the urgency of the project, the history of problems with each team, or even the perceived quality of each team's leadership. Whatever the criterion, the review meeting schedule should be adhered to, so that management does not miss any incipient problems.

Besides tracking current projects, the engineering manager must also be aware of the condition of products that have been released to market, so that he or she can schedule design changes or replacements to bring new products to market to replace aging ones with declining revenues. The report that reveals this information should, however, include a variety of operating statistics as well, so that the manager can see if there are any problems developing with existing products that may require corrective action by the engineering staff. Such a report is shown as Exhibit 15.9. This report summarizes information by product family, because this format consolidates information so that it takes less time to review. The report shows the percentage change in sales for the last quarter. If the percentage drops, it is a signal to improve or replace the product. In addition, it shows a number of internal measures, such as the number of products per design platform and the number of product options; these are useful for seeing if the company may have a chance to increase the number of products per platform or the number of options in order to spur sales. In addition, the report shows the problems the company has had with each product family, such as the number of engineering change notices and their cost, the percentage of unique parts not used anywhere else, the reported accuracy of the BOM, and the total initial design cost. This information is very useful for deciding if a product line is so difficult to maintain that it is best to redesign it from the ground up, or if it has been so trouble-free that the engineering staff should simply make a few modifications and continue to milk sales from the present configuration. All of the information in this report is geared toward determining what to do with a product line going into the future; therefore, it is a good idea to also distribute it to the marketing personnel who manage each product line. The existing product status report is an excellent control over the engineering tasks to be performed on existing products.

The information shown in Exhibit 15.9 reveals that the company has had increasing success in designing new product families, with the best performance coming from product family C. Unfortunately, the first product family (A) is now experiencing declining sales and poor margins. It is evident, based on the large number and high cost of design changes to family A, that it would be best at this point to create a new product family to entirely replace it, because the cost of

Exhibit 15.9 Existing Product Status Report

Description	*Product Family A*	*Product Family B*	*Product Family C*
Sales percent change in last quarter	–15	25	32
Gross margin on sales to date (%)	10	29	32
No. of products per design platform	2	10	8
No. of product options	4	18	5
No. of engineering change notices	28	13	7
Cost of engineering change notices ($)	142,000	23,000	29,000
Percentage of unique parts	58	21	14
Bill of material accuracy (%)	92	98	98
Total initial design cost ($)	508,000	401,000	329,000

continuing to modify it appears to be quite high. Thus, the information presented in the example is a sufficient foundation for making decisions regarding the fate of an entire family of products.

The primary control over the engineering function involves collecting a variety of measurements and reports and summarizing it into status reports that can be used by the design teams and senior engineering management to direct and support the activities of the design teams so that product designs are completed on time. This information can even be grouped into a forward-looking control document that tells management when it is time to revise or replace an existing product.

SUMMARY

This chapter focused on a number of techniques that the engineering function can use to compress the time that it and the materials management function need to complete the tasks of designing new products, procuring parts for them, and fixing design flaws. To do this, the engineering employees must concentrate on using multifunction design teams, building a parts library, designing from a common platform, limiting the number of product options, issuing complete BOMs, and quickly fixing design problems. In addition, it is important to avoid designing a large number of unique components and issuing continual product upgrades, because these waste the time of the engineering and materials management staffs. Only by following all of these steps can a company create enough new products to fuel an explosive rate of sales growth.

Chapter 16

Finance

INTRODUCTION

This chapter discusses the role of the finance function in an explosive growth company. The key topics that the function must address are shown in Exhibit 16.1. This general type of graphic appears in other chapters, but is usually split into a piece that shows necessary functions and another showing tasks that can be safely downplayed without impacting a company's growth rate. In the case of the finance function, however, there are *no* areas that can be minimized, as is noted in Exhibit 16.1. *Every* task is important, for a company that runs out of cash will find its growth coming to a screeching halt.

This chapter begins with a discussion of three underlying principles necessary to understand the following eight sections of this chapter. The chapter then describes the finance function's role in cash forecasting and management, debt and equity placements, and special types of financing, bank relations, and credit policy. The chapter concludes with a discussion of key controls and measurements, as well as personnel issues pertaining to this area.

UNDERLYING PRINCIPLES

This chapter contains a number of sections that describe topics considered crucial for an explosive growth company. Why are they crucial? The following three principles form the underlying reasons for emphasizing the topics listed later in this chapter. Only by doing advance work in lining up new sources of debt and equity and by keeping tight control over credit policies can the finance function contribute to a company's rapid growth.

1. *Always have enough debt lines available to maximize the borrowing base.* An explosive growth company will constantly run out of cash due to its need to fund growth. No matter how well a company forecasts its cash flow in such situations, it will constantly find itself short of cash. One of the best ways to avoid this problem is not to wait for the cash crunch to arrive and then act, but rather to have the largest possible debt lines arranged in advance. This strategy helps to avoid cash problems that can interfere with an explosive growth path.

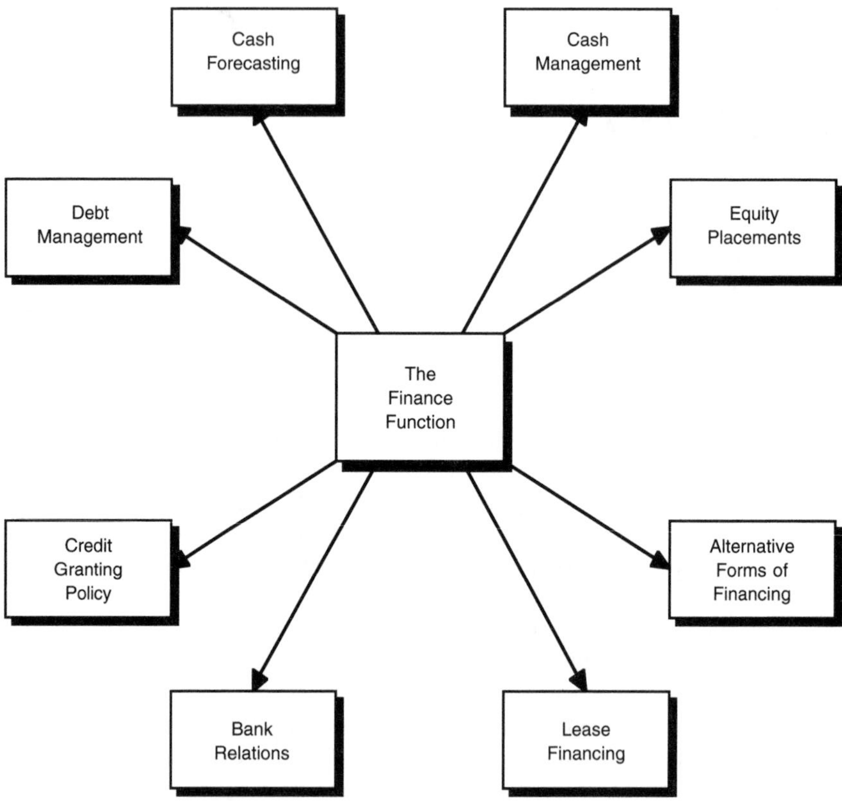

Exhibit 16.1 Explosive Growth Tasks for the Finance Function

2. *Always have a pool of prospective investors available in advance.* When an explosive growth company wants to place equity with investors, it cannot waste valuable time finding them, because the resulting cash shortfall can interfere with growth. It is better to have investors lined up and ready to buy stock, so that there is a minimal time period needed to obtain more equity-based cash.
3. *Minimize working capital requirements.* The best way to avoid new debt or equity is to keep cash requirements at a minimum. The finance function has influence over the amount of working capital through its control of credit policies.

The foregoing principles are used throughout the remainder of this chapter to point out the need for reducing cash requirements wherever possible, while also being prepared enough to have new debt and equity available at all times for sudden cash needs. Only by following these principles can a company adequately fund a high rate of growth.

CASH FORECASTING

The single most important ongoing function in the finance area of an explosive growth company is maintaining the cash forecast, because a company cannot accurately determine when it will need more debt or equity without one, and procuring debt and equity are two of the underlying principles of this chapter.

The cash forecast can be in many formats, one of which is shown in Exhibit 16.2. It typically includes all of the sources of cash, such as added debt, equity, and cash from ongoing operations. The forecast continues with outgoing cash flows, the most important being capital expenditures, payroll, and the material cost of units sold. Thus, subtracting cash outflows from inflows for each period, the cash forecast can give a rough estimate of changes in cash and debt levels in the near term.

Unfortunately, the cash forecast is based on not just one, but many estimates, any one of which can be very incorrect. For example, capital expenditures may not occur anywhere near the estimated time. Accounts receivable may not be collected when expected, which is especially important if the accounts receivable are "lumpy" (i.e., include a small number of very large invoices); if one of the largest invoices is not collected on time, the cash forecast will be incorrect. Also, special payment terms for accounts receivable will alter the timing of cash outflows. Furthermore, if items are bought into inventory and then not used, this unexpectedly adds to cash outflows. In addition, estimated margins on sales may be inaccurate if margins are reduced by unexpected clearance sales, or if margins drop for other reasons. Finally, the sales forecast for upcoming months may be inaccurate. If more than one of these issues arises, the cash forecast will have so many inaccurate elements that it will be wholly unreliable.

There are several approaches to improving the accuracy of the cash forecast. One or a combination of the following methods can be used to improve it:

- *Adjust the forecast regularly.* The most common problem with an inaccurate forecast is that it is set up using accurate assumptions for the time when it was created, but the assumptions are not tested over time. Since the underlying assumptions gradually become more incorrect, so too will the resulting forecast. The best way to avoid this problem is to schedule a regular review of the cash forecast. This review can include a comparison of the cash forecast to actual results, which may result in changes to the cash forecast to include additional factors that caused errors in the earlier forecast.
- *Talk to top management.* The management team may suddenly change direction when a company is in the midst of an explosive growth path in order to stay on that path. These changes may impact cash flow, such as when large capital assets are purchased. If so, regular communication with top management will reveal these changes so that they can be incorporated into the forecast.

Exhibit 16.2 Cash Forecasting Model

	This Month	*Jun-99*	*Jul-99*	*Aug-99*	*Sep-99*
Debt Right Now >>>>>>>>>	4,434				
Cash In: Revenues—New Units	—	1,571	1,640	973	615
Cash In: Revenues—Service	—	175	175	175	175
Cash In: Revenues—Parts	—	150	150	150	150
Cash In: Revenues—Rentals	—	33	33	33	33
Accts Receivable Receipts	269	—	—	—	—
Total Cash In	269	1,929	1,998	1,331	973
Cash Out					
Materials	—	1,037	1,082	642	406
Total Nonmaterial Expenses	—	517	517	517	517
Capital Expenditures	—	85	85	85	85
Less: Depreciation	—	–30	–30	–30	–30
Accounts Payable	528	—	—	—	—
Ttl Payroll (30K/week)	30	—	—	—	—
Total Cash Out	558	1,609	1,654	1,214	978
Net Change in Cash	–289	320	344	117	–5
Ending Debt	4,723	4,403	4,059	3,942	3,947

Backlog Information	*May-99*	*Jun-99*	*Jul-99*	*Aug-99*	*Sep-99*
Total Backlog	1,571	1,640	973	615	447

Assumptions: All payables paid in 30 days
All receivables collected in 30 days

- *Follow procedures.* If a company follows the correct procedures in producing and shipping items according to plan and by promptly billing and collecting cash, the cash forecast will be more accurate. However, if employees sidestep the production plan to produce something else, the cash flows associated with the items that were planned for will not match what is actually sold, resulting in an incorrect cash forecast. Similarly, lack of attention to procedures for billings and periodic collection calls will not bring in cash when it is expected, resulting in a further variance from the cash forecast. Thus, strict attention to a variety of company procedures is necessary if a company wants its performance to match the cash forecast.
- *Use a materials management system.* Many materials management software packages used for material requirements planning include much of the information needed for a good cash forecast, such as a production schedule that can be used to estimate labor and materials expenditures for some months into the future. If available, this information should be integrated into the cash forecast to improve its accuracy.
- *Integrate the cash forecast into the accounting package.* Some accounting packages include a cash forecasting module that combines current accounts receivable and accounts payable, along with the terms of payment for each, to derive a cash forecast. It may also include information from the purchasing software (if any), which gives a longer-term forecast of expenditures. This kind of forecasting is quite accurate in the very short term, but is not accurate beyond one month, because the accounting system does not include any information beyond the current period. However, if the accounting system is linked to a materials management system (see previous bullet point), it can automatically create an excellent cash forecast that is accurate for several months into the future; only planned capital expenditures are not included. Such a forecast can be automatically generated by the software, which saves the finance staff considerable time.

In summary, the cash forecast is necessary for planning the timing of more debt or equity additions to the balance sheet. However, it can be very inaccurate unless constantly monitored. It can also be improved with the input of top management, as well as by consistently following procedures and by integration with a company's accounting and materials management systems.

CASH MANAGEMENT

Cash management is critical for the explosive growth company, for cash is always in short supply and must be carefully managed to ensure that none is wasted. This is part of the underlying principle noted at the beginning of this chapter, that of minimizing working capital requirements. A number of techniques described in this section lead toward that goal.

One approach is to reduce the time needed for incoming checks from customers to clear the bank. The best way to do this is to set up lockboxes throughout the country and instruct customers to send their payments to the lockbox nearest to them. This cuts the time that a check spends in transit, because it will take a short path to the nearest lockbox, where a bank opens the envelope and immediately deposits the check. It is difficult to determine the exact number and positioning of lockboxes, so a company would do well to enlist the services of the cash management consulting group at one of the larger regional banks, who are trained in this work. Thus, using well-positioned lockboxes reduces the time needed to collect cash from customers.

Another way to reduce working capital requirements is to consolidate checking accounts. Companies with multiple locations have a bad habit of opening checking accounts for each location and then spend no time reviewing the amount of cash parked in each account, which can add up to a large amount of unused cash. One way to avoid this problem is to have the fewest possible checking accounts, thereby avoiding the number of places where excess cash can sit. Another approach is to use cash concentration accounts that automatically sweep excess cash from all outlying accounts into a central account at the end of each day, thereby making all cash in the system available for investment by the company. Some way to consolidate the cash in checking accounts is needed to ensure that the cash in the system is being fully utilized.

Even if all of the cash a company has in its accounts is being automatically swept into a single checking account, this does not mean that the company is earning interest on it, because most checking accounts do not earn interest (or only offer a minimal rate). The best way to ensure that cash is earning the highest possible interest rate is to use a zero-balance account, whereby the bank automatically moves only enough cash into the checking account to offset the exact amount of checks being presented for payment, while the remaining cash earns a higher rate of interest in a separate savings account. A zero-balance account maximizes the interest rate being earned on cash.

The principle of minimizing working capital requirements also extends to the treatment of accounts payable. A company can stretch out its payments well beyond terms, but suppliers will rapidly catch on to this tactic and retaliate by raising prices, lowering credit limits, or refusing payment by any means but cash. A better approach, then, is to use controlled disbursement, a sophisticated technique for paying suppliers from banks located so far away that it takes an extra day or two for payments to clear, thereby giving suppliers checks on the expected payment dates, while keeping cash in the company's investment accounts for the same period. Most suppliers equate payment to receipt of a check, and do not notice when the cash actually arrives in their bank accounts, so this is a good way to maintain supplier relations while still withholding cash. Controlled disbursement is an effective technique for reducing working capital requirements.

Beyond maintaining the lowest possible level of working capital, the cash management team also has an obligation to communicate regularly with other people in the accounting and finance functions. The finance personnel must be informed if the cash position is so low that extra debt or equity financing are needed, while the accounting staff must be told to redouble its collection efforts or hold off on paying suppliers for the same reason. Without proper communications, the accounting staff may issue checks that will bounce, which harms supplier relations, so the cash manager must let everyone know when the company's cash position becomes lower than will support ongoing operations.

It is also important for the cash manager to carefully invest cash in those investment vehicles that meet the company's criteria for return, risk, and liquidity. An explosive growth company typically burns through its cash reserves quite rapidly, so the liquidity of its investments must be extremely high in order to allow rapid access to it. For example, investing in an apartment complex would offer poor liquidity, whereas investing in a money market account would allow immediate access to the cash. Unfortunately, high liquidity is commonly associated with low investment returns (as is the case for a money market account), so the cash manager is commonly forced to invest in low-yield investments. In addition, the company cannot run the risk of loss on its investments, because it is critically important to keep cash available to feed the company's growth engine. Since risk is also associated with return, the cash manager must, once again, favor low-yield investments for minimal risk. An explosive growth company cannot have a high investment yield as one of its operating principles, for this ties up cash in investments that are both hard to liquidate and at risk of loss, both of which would harm the company's ability to grow by either tying up or losing cash.

DEBT MANAGEMENT

Several issues described in this section are important for debt management in an explosive growth situation, with the most important point being that the finance manager must be as forward looking as possible in determining when additional debt is needed and in using this information to obtain additional lines of debt as early as possible.

The work of the person in charge of debt management should center around having more debt available than is currently needed. At a minimum, the amount of debt available should at least match the company's borrowing base, which is the amount of assets available as collateral. If possible, the available level of debt that has been formally agreed to by the bank should exceed the current borrowing base, because the borrowing base will probably expand as the company increases in size, thereby allowing the company to borrow more money. Thus, the finance manager should constantly be in negotiations with banks to have debt available that at least matches the amount of borrowing base currently available.

A key part of any debt negotiations with banks should be the percentage of borrowing base that the bank will allow the company to use in its borrowing base calculation each month. An example of a borrowing base report is shown in Exhibit 16.3. It is common for a bank to allow a borrowing base to include no more than 50 percent of the value of all inventories, and 80 percent of the value of any accounts receivable, with the percentage assigned to equipment typically falling somewhere in between, after being adjusted downward for depreciation. Clearly, these percentages cut deeply into the available borrowing base. A major task for the debt manager, then, is to negotiate higher borrowing base percentages from banks, so that the growing company can use it to obtain more debt. It is very possible for an explosive growth company to obtain an unusually high percentage of allowable borrowing base for equipment, for it is usually purchasing large quantities of equipment in order to grow, which means that the equipment the bank might have to repossess is quite new. Because the equipment is likely to be mostly new and therefore easy to resell, the bank will be more comfortable with the idea of allowing a high borrowing base. Also, if the company has a tight credit policy with its customers (see the Credit Granting Policy section later in this chapter), the quality of its accounts receivable borrowing base will be high, because there will be very few bad debts. This situation also may convince the bank to allow a higher percentage for the accounts receivable borrowing base. In short, negotiating higher borrowing base percentages is a key task for the debt manager.

It is also possible for the debt manager to obtain very expensive debt lines that require no borrowing base at all. The interest rates on such loans are exceptionally high, because the lender has no recourse to company assets in the event of default. It is still useful to have such loans available, though unused, because an explosive growth company may have short-term borrowing requirements that force it to obtain cash from any source, no matter how expensive, for a short time. Having an expensive debt line available to meet this need is good management.

Besides having debt lines available, the finance manager must also constantly be aware of the company's cash position. This information should be obtained from the finance function's cash forecast (see the previous section) and the bank every day and carefully tracked, so the debt manager knows exactly how many payments have not cleared the bank every day, how much cash and debt is available, and when the company is likely to tap out its borrowing base. Several of these measurements are noted later in this chapter, in the measurements section. Only by having a good knowledge of the rate at which the company is using up debt can the debt manager predict when available debt will be maximized, which then requires action to either obtain more lines of debt or equity.

Once the finance manager has sufficient debt available and adequate amounts of borrowing base to justify further borrowing, the next issue is which debt lines to draw down first. The usual criterion is to always pick the cheapest debt. The finance manager should maintain a chart (see the Measurements and Reports section) that lists the interest percentage charged on each form of debt and the borrowing capacity available on each one. The manager can then pick the lowest-

Exhibit 16.3 A Sample Borrowing Base Report

ACME WIDGET COMPANY
Working Capital Line of Credit, Loan # 216
Borrowing Base and Compliance Certificate

The undersigned hereby certifies to Bank Two, Puerto Rico, N.A., that the amounts and representations set forth below are true and correct as of November 30, 19xx.

1. Accounts Receivable	$1,939,657
2. Less: Ineligible Receivables	$53,555
3. Eligible Receivables (line 1 minus line 2)	$1,886,102
4. Net Eligible Receivables (line 3 × .80)	$1,508,882
5. Inventory	4,128,370
6. Net Eligible Inventory (line 5 × .80)	$3,302,696
7. Equipment (Net Book Value)	$853,536
8. Net Eligible Equipment (line 7 × .50)	$426,768
9. Total Borrowing Base (lines 4 + 6 + 8)	$5,238,346
10. Less: Line of Credit Outstanding	$2,916,330
11. Net Available Borrowing Capacity Under Lines of Credit (line 9 minus line 10)	$2,322,016

The undersigned further certifies that (a) borrower is in compliance with the covenants contained in the Promissory Note and in the Loan Agreement dated June 3, 19xx, and as thereafter amended or modified, (b) there has been no event of default under the Promissory Note or Loan Agreement which has occurred and no event has occurred with the giving of notice or passing of time would become an event of default, (c) that the foregoing information cited herein is true and correct, and that the collateral reflected herein complies with the conditions, terms, warranties, representations, and covenants set forth in the Promissory Note and Loan Agreement, and (d) the undersigned hereby certifies that the financial statements and supporting information supplied herewith are true and complete in disclosing the Borrower's financial condition as of the date of the statement and there has been no material or adverse changes in the Borrower's financial condition subsequent to the statement date.

cost form of debt. If some debt is cheaper but takes the form of a term loan with a penalty for early repayment, then the repayment penalty should be included in the base level interest percentage, thereby giving the debt a higher cost. However, if there is no immediate prospect of early debt repayment prior to the natural termination date of a loan (a common occurrence for an explosive growth company), then the penalty should not be added to the interest cost when selecting debt lines based on the interest rate. In short, the finance manager is responsible for picking the cheapest forms of debt when acquiring additional debt.

Some banks also require borrowing companies to keep their debt/equity ratios below a set level, which means that the company must add some equity for every dollar of debt, so that the company does not find itself in an excessively leveraged position. If this loan covenant exists, then the finance manager is also responsible for forecasting the time when the debt/equity ratio will exceed the agreed-upon level. The finance manager must inform the chief financial officer of this date, and any changes to it, so that steps can be taken, either through adding equity, altering projected spending, or renegotiating the covenant, so that the maximum debt/equity level is not exceeded.

EQUITY PLACEMENTS

The underlying principle that drives the need for equity in an explosive growth company is to always have a pool of prospective investors available in advance, because the need for cash may arise quite suddenly, not allowing anywhere near enough time for an initial public offering (IPO). In this situation, the better alternative is to issue shares to a few investors, which avoids the many investigations and filing requirements that go with an IPO. However, to have this option available, top company management must be constantly on the lookout for new investors with deep enough pockets to contribute equity to the company on extremely short notice. This search requires constant access to venture capital partners who have the necessary contacts with investors, as well as a variety of other contacts. The basic rule here is that a company can never have enough potential investors, because it is very likely that some will back out at the last moment, or try to drive too hard a deal, wanting to exchange an equity infusion for an inordinately large number of shares. Only by having many investors to choose from at any time can an explosive growth company find ready cash without giving away a large part of company ownership.

Although the previous paragraph points out that an IPO is a considerable burden to go through, it is also the goal of many owners of explosive growth companies, because a company can show superior financial results in the midst of an explosive growth spurt, which is an excellent reason for scheduling an IPO during that time. Once the growth period tails off, as it inevitably will, the company has a lower valuation, because it does not have as much potential for profits.

Thus, there is a strong financial incentive for an explosive growth company to schedule an IPO in the midst of its growth period.

An IPO can seriously impact a company's growth, partially because it is a heavy burden on the accounting and finance staffs and nearly all managers. The IPO process requires a company to spend many hours creating documents to be filed with the government that detail the company's operations in far greater detail than it may use for its own internal operating documents. In addition, management is frequently called upon by the investment bank assisting in the IPO to go on the road to meet financial analysts. This work can go on for months, and keep many people from performing their normal tasks during that period. If a company is growing rapidly during this period, the time taken away from running the business will probably have an impact on sales and profits.

Another reason why an IPO can impact a company's growth is its cost. It requires assistance from investment bankers, accountants, and lawyers to complete an IPO, and all three of these groups charge fees that can safely be called outrageous. The IPO market is a major profit generator for all of the advisors just noted, and they do not stint in finding new ways to charge extra fees for their services. They realize that a company must be willing to pay for experienced advisors during this most important period, and consequently do not stint in tallying their fees. This is not a problem if a company has a successful IPO and sits on a large cash horde, but it is also quite common for an IPO not to succeed for a variety of reasons, such as a downturn in the financial markets or a dip in profits that drastically lowers the company's value. Whatever the reason for stopping the IPO, the bankers, lawyers, and accountants must still be paid, and this cash must now come out of the company's own coffers. This situation can severely impact an explosive growth company's ability to keep on growing, because cash is needed to fund that growth.

Although private placements and IPOs are the most common ways to obtain capital, more imaginative methods are available. For a recent example, PeopleSoft needed cash to fund new software development. It persuaded Norwest Venture Capital to put all of the cash into a new software development entity, with 50/50 ownership between the parent companies. PeopleSoft supplied all of the personnel for the new entity. PeopleSoft had the option to buy out Norwest at a later date, which it did. Thus, PeopleSoft spent no money to create new software, while Norwest Venture Capital got a nice return on its investment. This is an example of the many imaginative ways to receive equity funding.

CREDIT GRANTING POLICY

A traditional finance function is granting credit to customers. It is common for a company to loosen its credit policy, within reason, to increase its sales, although this requires more collection effort and entails more account write-offs. However, when considering one of the underlying principles noted at the beginning of this chapter, that of minimizing working capital requirements in order to conserve cash, it becomes apparent that the credit granting policy may vary for an explosive growth company.

When in the explosive growth mode, a company does not have to go out looking for sales—they are coming to the company, and the company is probably having a hard time keeping up with shipments. In this situation, especially when combined with a likely shortage of cash caused by the rapid growth, the credit policy should not be loosened. On the contrary it should be *tightened,* which may drive away some sales, but this is acceptable if the company cannot keep up with sales. With a loose credit policy, a company's accounts receivable will lengthen, and these extra receivables must be financed by the company. At this point in the growth phase, it is more important to conserve cash. Later on, as the growth phase begins to tail off, the finance staff may want to loosen the policy so that the company can add more sales and keep sales growth moving along. In short, an explosive growth company can afford to keep its credit policy tight until the rate of sales growth begins to slow down.

The one situation in which an explosive growth company cannot afford to keep a tight credit policy is when it wants to sell to all possible customers. This situation arises when the company is trying to take sales away from competitors. If it were to tighten its credit, this would leave room in the marketplace for a competitor to obtain sales from those customers. By locking in those customers with a loose credit policy, a company can make it extremely difficult for competitors to enter the market.

BANK RELATIONS

One of the underlying principles of the finance function is to have extra borrowing capacity available at all times. To do so, it is very helpful to maintain excellent bank relations. There are several keys to bank relations that make bank officers much better disposed toward granting more debt to a company. This section describes those keys, as well as how to obtain good pricing from banks.

The most important issue in bank relations is communications. The chief financial officer (CFO) should be in constant contact with the bank, as opposed to rare calls demanding more money. The best approach is to deliver monthly financial statements to the bank officer who is in charge of the company's account, and then call that person to discuss the financial results. Additional contacts may include quarterly lunches or other social calls. In addition, if the company experiences any financial problems, it is much better to notify the bank officer immediately, rather than to wait a long time while the problem worsens, and then inform the person once the issue has increased to a major problem. Rapid updates of information about problems and how they are being handled gives the bank officer a higher degree of trust in the CFO, which is very important when the CFO comes calling to ask for more debt. Thus, continuing communication is key to obtaining additional debt financing from a bank.

In addition, a bank tries to sell various services, such as lockboxes and zero balance accounts to a company. These are profit generators for the bank, and also tie the company more closely to it, because it is difficult to move these services if the company were to switch to another bank. In the interests of better bank relations, it is reasonable to subscribe to a large number of these services. This does not mean that a company should pay for additional services that it does not need, but it should add services if there is an economic justification for doing so. Buying a broad range of services from a bank helps to improve bank relations.

The CFO should not think that the company will receive the best possible loan terms just because it communicates regularly with its bank and purchases all of its services. An element of competition should be added to the relationship in order to obtain the best terms. To do this, the company should always do a small amount of business with a second bank and be sure to let the primary bank know that this relationship exists. The amount of business given to the second bank should be sufficient to keep the second bank interested in the relationship, without giving the primary bank sufficient cause to complain that it is being constantly played off against the secondary bank to obtain cut-rate deals. Instead, the purpose behind having the secondary bank is to let the primary bank know that the company has an alternate source of funding available in case the pricing it offers becomes excessively high. By having a secondary bank available, a company can usually obtain better terms on covenants, interest rates, service fees, and personal guarantees than would otherwise be the case.

LEASE FINANCING

Leasing is a viable option for those companies that cannot obtain low-cost debt from a lending institution. Leases are more easily obtained, because they are tied to a specific asset that can be reclaimed by the lender in the event of payment default. However, before taking the leasing option, there are several issues to consider.

Lending laws do not require leasing companies to reveal the interest rate being charged, which means that a company can pay a very high interest rate on a lease and never know the rate being charged. This policy is not good for an explosive growth company that needs to keep costs down in order to grow. The best way to avoid this problem is to first determine the base cost of the item being leased, and then use this information to back into the lease rate, based on the total amount of and time interval over which payments are to be made.

The lease rate can be reduced if a company leases many items at once, because the company issuing the lease can cover a large pool of assets with one leasing document, which is cheaper than writing individual leases for each asset in the pool. However, such bulk purchases require some purchasing discipline by the buying company, so that assets are obtained in clusters. Since most explosive growth companies tend to obtain assets in a haphazard manner and without any central control over the process, it can be difficult to obtain bulk leases of this kind.

Although a lease is usually obtained for the full value of the asset being purchased, a company should not think that it is maximizing 100 percent of its borrowing base, because, as the lease is paid down, the percentage of the borrowing base used drops rapidly, until it is less than the amount that a regular lending institution would have allowed for an asset-based loan. Thus, the percentage of borrowing base used is higher for a lease in the short term, but lower in the long run.

In short, there are good deals on leases, but the finance manager should first determine the interest rate offered to see if it is comparable to the rate on regular debt, while also being aware that the borrowing base will not be fully utilized in the long run if leases are used.

ALTERNATIVE FORMS OF FINANCING

This chapter has noted the primary avenues for obtaining cash, debt and lease financing, and new equity. However, many growing companies cannot obtain cash by these means. For those companies, this section provides a brief listing of alternative sources of cash. This section is also a good source of ideas for those companies that have other sources of cash, but that may want to line up alternative forms of financing in case they fall into situations where cash is temporarily unavailable from the usual sources. The extra forms of financing are as follows:

- *Accounts receivable factoring.* Some lenders pay cash for a high percentage of a company's accounts receivable as soon as the company bills its customers, with the provision that the customers must pay the bank, not the company, when each receivable comes due. This form of debt tends to be expensive, partially because of the extra work by the lender to collect accounts receivable. Also, the lender only lends based on a portion of the total accounts receivable being factored, because it assumes that some of the accounts will be bad debts. Because of the high debt cost, it tends to be used on an emergency basis only.
- *Credit card debt.* There are a few cases in the press that describe highly successful startup companies that were funded with nothing more than credit card cash advances. Although this is possible, it is an extremely risky venture, for the interest rate, especially on cash advances, is very high. Also, the amount of cash that can be extracted from one credit card is not large, so a company must obtain a large number of credit cards and obtain advances from

all of them. This can inadvertently turn into a Ponzi scheme that can rapidly bankrupt a company, for management may find itself in the uncomfortable position of having to obtain cash from new credit cards so that it can pay off old credit cards. Also, startup companies frequently cannot obtain credit cards without personal guarantees from company officers. This means that, in the event of default by the corporate shell, company managers may still be liable for repayment of all cash advances. It is clear, then, that using credit cards to obtain cash is a very risky approach.

- *Employee tradeoffs.* A few companies have persuaded their employees to accept large pay cuts in exchange for a share in company profits or a share in company ownership, with the largest recent example being United Airlines. This plan is usually more likely to succeed if the company gives employees some ownership stake, because they can then obtain seats on the board of directors and have a substantial influence over the direction of the company. Pay cuts in exchange for profit sharing is less successful, especially if there is no recent history of profits. If such is the case, this plan is seen by employees as a ploy to cut pay, and will result in the departure of the best employees. Employee tradeoffs should be used only with the greatest care, because a company can quickly lose its best and brightest staff if handled improperly.
- *Preferred stock.* This type of stock is a mix of debt and equity. It requires a fixed interest payment, and precedes debt holders in distributions in the event of a corporate liquidation. It is frequently convertible to either common stock, debt, or both, depending on the accompanying terms. This option can be good for inexpensive debt, because the company can trade off a low interest rate for the option to convert to common stock. Of course, this strategy also runs the risk of having preferred stockholders eventually convert their shares to common stock, which dilutes the ownership interest of the current owners.
- *SBA loans.* The Small Business Administration (SBA) guarantees loans that have been approved by local lending institutions. This makes it somewhat easier to obtain debt, although many lenders apply their normal lending criteria to SBA loan applications, so these loans can still be difficult to obtain. They are also only issued to smaller companies, so this option is not available to larger firms. In addition, the size of such a loan is typically very small. However, for those companies who are able to obtain this type of debt, the interest rates are reasonable.

A variety of additional financing options are available for the explosive growth company that has exhausted all other avenues for obtaining cash. The extra cash sources outlined in this section tend to have additional risks associated with them, so they should only be used after the more traditional avenues for obtaining debt or equity have been eliminated.

MEASUREMENTS AND REPORTS

The finance manager can use several measurements that fall into several categories to better control the finances of an explosive growth company. One is related to the cost of financing, which is typified by the average interest rate measurement. Another category is the working capital investment in accounts receivable, which can be highlighted by the days of receivables measurement as well as the percentage of receivables over a specified cutoff date. A final category is looking forward to see when more debt is needed and when the company's borrowing base will be used up. Measurements in this category are the percentage of borrowing base used and the projected dates to maximize the borrowing base and the debt/equity ratio. A subset of this list is very useful for monitoring the operations of an explosive growth company's finance function. The following measurements each include a brief description, the calculation method, and any problems with calculations or notes on how the results may be skewed. They are as follows:

- *Average interest rate.* A good way to measure the ability of the finance manager to select debt from a variety of debt options is the average interest rate on debt. This measurement is an indicator of the manager's ability to use lower-cost debt prior to accessing more expensive debt lines. It is measured by summarizing the total interest expense for the month, which is easily extracted from the general ledger, and dividing it by the average amount of debt outstanding during the period. However, users should be aware that this measurement can be skewed. For example, a finance manager could commit a company to a debt line with a very low interest rate, but with an outrageously high compensating balance agreement that more than offsets the low interest rate. This problem can be spotted by having the company's internal audit team periodically review the terms of all debt agreements.
- *Days of receivables.* The days of receivables measurement tells management if it has an excessively loose or tight credit policy. If the days outstanding increases, then a looser credit policy has led to a greater investment in accounts receivable, which is not a good trend for most explosive growth companies that are continually short of cash. To calculate it, divide the average accounts receivable by the annual amount of sales on credit, and multiply by 365.
- *Percent of accounts receivable over xx days old.* This measure varies from the days of receivables in that it specifically identifies the amount of accounts receivable that are in danger of never being collected. The exact number of days beyond which accounts receivable are considered to be in danger of becoming bad debts varies widely by industry, so it is left as *xx* days in the title. Clearly, a high percentage indicates that a growing company should put considerable emphasis on collections, so that it can bring in cash that may not otherwise be collected. To calculate this measurement, print an aged

accounts receivable report, then summarize the accounts receivable exceeding the targeted date, and divide this amount by the total of all open accounts receivable.

- *Percent of borrowing base used.* The finance manager must be aware of the amount of borrowing base still available for further borrowings. If there is no borrowing base available, a company could find itself in a major cash bind very quickly, which is especially life threatening if the company is in a fast growth mode that eats up cash. There is no minimum percentage of borrowing base available that is considered dangerous for a growing company, because the scale of growth and the need for large capital expenditures vary the danger zone for every company. Nonetheless, when coupled with a knowledge of projected cash requirements, it is a potent tool for projecting additional financing needs. It is calculated by subtracting the current outstanding debt from the company's borrowing base, which may be a mix of accounts receivable, inventory, and equipment, reduced by some percentage imposed by the lending institution.
- *Projected date to maximize borrowing base.* The finance manager can determine the approximate date when the borrowing base will be maximized by comparing the cash forecast to the remaining amount of available borrowing base. If the resulting date is in the near future, the finance staff must either obtain additional debt that does not require a borrowing base, recommend internal changes (such as halting capital expenditures) to keep the company from exceeding its borrowing base, or arrange for additional equity financing.
- *Projected date to maximize debt/equity ratio.* The finance manager must know when the company will exceed the debt/equity ratio established by any lending institutions that have issued debt to the company, so that action can be taken to avoid breaking this covenant. As was the case with the previous measurement, this date is obtained by examining the cash forecast to see when more debt is required and then dividing the total projected debt by the existing equity base.

The primary report needed by the finance manager is the cash forecast, which was described earlier in this chapter. That report shows the manager when more cash will be needed by the company. This information can then be compared to the listing of outstanding debt, shown in Exhibit 16.4, which itemizes where the required cash can come from. The outstanding debt report is a simple one, listing the total of all debt granted, the amount used, and the amount available, less the borrowing base available. The finance manager can use it to quickly determine the correct source of the cheapest debt for upcoming borrowing needs.

In the example shown in Exhibit 16.4, the first two lines of credit have been tapped out. Line of credit number three still has $50,000 available, but the available borrowing base will not cover that amount of debt, so only $25,000 can be

Exhibit 16.4 Outstanding Debt Report

Description	*Interest Rate (%)*	*Total Debt ($)*	*Debt Used ($)*	*Debt Available ($)*	*Borrowing Base Available ($)*	*Actual Debt Available ($)*
Line of credit #1	8.75	1,000,000	1,000,000	0	0	0
Line of credit #2	9.00	975,000	975,000	0	0	0
Line of credit #3	9.50	850,000	800,000	50,000	25,000	25,000
Line of credit #4	8.25	3,250,000	1,750,000	2,500,000	3,000,000	2,500,000
Line of credit #5	14.10	500,000	0	500,000	N/A	500,000

borrowed. The fourth line of credit has more borrowing base available than the available debt, so not all of the borrowing base can be used; this would be a good place to negotiate a higher level of debt, so that the borrowing base is maximized. Finally, the fifth line of credit has no required borrowing base, which is why the interest rate is so high—the lender is covering its risk of not having collateral by charging a very high interest rate.

CONTROLS

Unlike the accounting function, few controls are needed in the finance area, although they must be performed to ensure that the finance staff provides the proper level of service. These controls center on verifying the accuracy of both the current cash position and the cash forecast, as well as the terms of debt agreements to ensure that management is being informed of the total cost of all debt. Cash controls are not covered in this section; they are noted in Chapter 10.

The finance staff will have a hard time determining the timing of additions to debt and equity if the current amount of cash on hand is incorrect. The best way to correct this problem is to perform a bank reconciliation every month for all major bank accounts. These reconciliations should also be reviewed by the company's audit team from time to time to ensure that they are being correctly completed. A bank reconciliation is the best way to verify that the current cash position is correct.

Even if the amount of cash on hand is accurate, it does not mean that the finance staff is using this as the basis for an accurate cash forecast. On the contrary, the cash forecast could be substantially off because various factors are not being considered in the cash forecasting model, such as capital expenditures or the average number of days during which average accounts receivable remain uncollected. A good control over this problem is to run a monthly comparison of the current amount of debt to the amount that was forecasted one, two, and three months earlier (if not more). If there are significant variances between the predicted debt level and the amount that was actually incurred, the finance staff needs to examine the cash forecasting model to see if it can be made more accurate. An accurate cash forecast allows the finance staff to line up additional debt and equity in a timely manner, so it is very worthwhile to have this control over the forecast.

Finally, the finance manager may be compensated based on his or her ability to obtain debt with very low interest rates. If so, there is a financial incentive for the finance manager to create debt agreements with lenders that have very low interest rates, but which may compensate for the low rates with other costs that are not so readily identifiable. A common example of another cost is a large compensating balance agreement, whereby the company must keep a large amount of cash in an account at the bank, which the bank can then use for other investments. This is an expense to the company, but it does not appear on the company's average interest cost report. The best control over this potential problem is to have the internal audit staff schedule periodic audits of all loan documents to review the terms of each agreement for special conditions that may result in extra costs for the company. Regular audits of loan documents will verify that the company has obtained the best possible terms from lenders.

PERSONNEL ISSUES

There is one personnel issue related to the finance function that causes major problems for many explosive growth companies. The problem is that most of these companies do not initially hire a complete set of accounting and finance professionals, which should include a CFO, controller, and various assistant treasurers and controllers. Instead, they tend to hire what they can afford, which is usually a bookkeeper, and then keep promoting that person as the company expands in size. This situation is a serious mistake for the finance function, because someone who has training as an accountant has no business trying to obtain funding for a company that is in desperate need of new sources of cash. Instead, the chief executive officer should hire the best possible CFO from outside the company, one who has considerable experience in bank and investor relations, and who can point out the millions (or billions) of dollars that he or she has personally obtained for other companies. Do not elevate someone from the accounting side of the business to be the CFO, because it is critical that the CFO of an explosive growth company have a background in obtaining funds, not accounting.

When hiring a CFO into this kind of company, it is possible to ignore some skills that are usually clustered under the CFO function, as long as the person has strong fund-raising skills. One such skill is 401k management. This task can easily be handed off to a subordinate, because it is usually outsourced to a supplier anyway, leaving a company with little to do but process paperwork. Another function that is of lesser importance is risk management, with its subsidiary function of insurance management. Although risk management can be of considerable importance in some industries that are subject to lawsuits, such as manufacturing of consumer goods, it still decidedly takes a back seat to procuring funds, and so it can be safely handed off to a subordinate, as long as there is some management oversight. These tasks are of lesser importance during a growth phase when obtaining cash is paramount, although this priority may change when the growth phase is over, which may require hiring a CFO with a different skill set.

SUMMARY

This chapter discussed the need for advance work in the areas of debt and equity placements, which allows a company to minimize problems with its cash flow while growing at high speed. It is also possible to minimize this risk by keeping a close watch over current and future cash flows as well as through control over the credit granting policy. The chapter concluded with a review of various controls, measurements, reports, and personnel issues that have a bearing on managing the function. The finance function must be well managed and focused on both conserving cash and providing new sources of cash in order for a company to meet its high-growth goals.

Chapter 17

Human Resources

INTRODUCTION

This chapter covers the key tasks that the human resources function must address to perform effectively within an explosive growth company. The human resources priorities change for this kind of company, as indicated in Exhibit 17.1. The most important task is to constantly find new people to bring in to the company—extreme growth requires large quantities of skilled employees. Human resources must also conduct prescreening of job candidates, because company managers, who are already stretched to the limit in meeting the demands of the growing company, do not have time to do so, especially when they are trying to hire a virtual flood of new employees. Following the recruiting function in priority is the need to retain good employees. A company must keep its people interested in working there or else it will lose a valuable knowledge base and also be forced to find even more employees. Retention requires paying attention to the compensation and other requirements of employees.

Other human resources tasks addressed in this chapter are training, to make employees as effective and efficient as possible and to communicate the company's culture to them. Also covered are key management skills for the human resources department to address, and the need for exit interviews, which are one of the best feedback mechanisms for determining how the company can better treat its employees. This chapter covers the main human resources tasks that must be addressed if an explosive growth company is to succeed.

RECRUITING

The key human resources function in an explosive growth company is to find qualified employee candidates as rapidly as possible. This section describes how recruiting normally unfolds for a cash-strapped company that needs thousands of recruits and what methods to use to find the right people.

Recruiting takes precedence over the related task of finding employees within the company who are ripe for promotion, because a company in an explosive growth mode cannot afford to have a person with low experience in a job that requires exceptional experience. In particular, management positions must be filled by

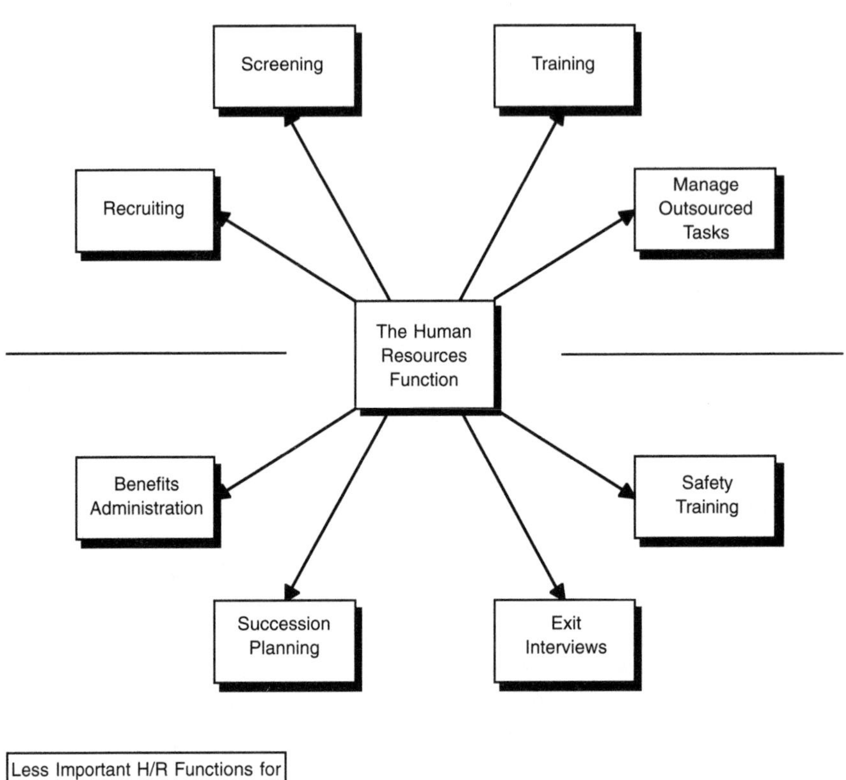

Exhibit 17.1 Explosive Growth Tasks for the Human Resources Function

people who, because of their experience, are the least likely to make mistakes that will impact a company's growth rate.

An overriding issue when deciding how to find new employees is the cost of searching for them. An explosive growth company usually has little cash available, so it must use the cheapest possible recruiting methods. This problem is exacerbated by the volume of people who must be recruited—using an expensive recruiting method to hire 10,000 people can bankrupt a company. The most common approach for keeping costs low is to first recruit in the area closest to the company, because there is no travel cost associated with recruiting. Then the search moves further afield, eventually even moving into other countries. Each jump into new geographical areas, especially foreign ones, further increases the cost of recruiting. However, a company may have no choice if it has exhausted the possibilities near its headquarters. Some companies may even set up subsidiaries in new locations specifically because those areas have a large population of potential candidates. In short, recruiting tends to start locally and expand outward, with attendant higher costs as the search moves further afield.

When the number of locally available recruits has dwindled, the recruiting staff may search in areas where English may be a secondary language. In these cases, other skills for which the company is searching, such as programming skills, may be so important that the company is willing to invest in language training so that the new recruits can understand their programming instructions. A number of companies followed this path when they hired Russian scientists following the collapse of the Soviet Union. This recruiting approach is clearly very expensive, and is usually only adopted after a company has exhausted all other means of attracting new recruits.

There are many ways to find potential employees for an explosive growth company. Some of them are noted in the following list, along with reasons both in favor of and against using each one. One of the key differences between the types of recruiting methods is that some deliver the company's recruiting message to people who fall outside of the target group that the company is trying to attract, such as when billboards are used. This shotgun approach is frequently cheaper, but is not very effective. Other approaches involve precise targeting of the group of potential employees the company wishes to attract—these methods tend to be more expensive. Also, some methods only reach those people who are actively looking for a job, whereas other methods, such as using employee search bonuses or search firms, reach out and contact potential recruits who are not actively looking. Most employee searches require a mix of several search methods to achieve a cost-effective recruiting campaign.

- *Billboards*. This approach was scoffed at until a few years ago, when some Silicon Valley companies erected billboards across from the locations of their competitors. Although this practice is somewhat sharp, it may be a viable option for recruiting positions for which there is fierce competition. Clearly, billboard placement is crucial.
- *Certification societies*. Most professions have some kind of certification (sometimes quite a few) that the most qualified people in those professions can earn. Lists of those who have earned certifications are sometimes available from the certifying societies. The advantage of contacting people on these certification lists is that a company is assured that the people being contacted have a minimum level of expertise. However, this may also mean that the people being contacted are good at taking tests—and nothing more. Still, it

is a good prescreening measure to cut the number of available personnel to a manageable level.

- *College recruiting*. College recruiting is useful for filling entry-level positions and allows a company to quickly meet with and screen large numbers of prospective candidates in a single location, which tends to make college recruiting a cost-effective approach. However, companies are sometimes expected to make the rounds of the same campuses every year, even when they have few positions open, so these extra trips may reduce the cost-effectiveness of the approach. Obviously, college recruiting is a poor way to gain recruits for high-end positions that require large amounts of experience.
- *Employee search bonuses*. An increasingly common recruiting technique is to pay bonuses to current employees if they can find new recruits. This technique is very effective, for people in one profession tend to flock together and to know of those in their fields who have a reputation for excellence. The most successful search bonus programs pay large bonuses—typically in the thousands of dollars—for each person successfully hired. An added advantage is that employees who are about to earn large bonuses tend to be very aggressive in promoting the company to new recruits, resulting in high rates of success with this type of recruit. When compared to the total cost of other types of recruiting, this recruiting approach is not necessarily inordinately expensive. It is heavily used by Milwaukee-based General Electric Medical Systems, which finds that 10 percent of employee referrals result in a hire, as compared to 1 percent for unsolicited resumes.
- *Graduate school recruiting*. Some of the finest potential recruits attend graduate school to hone their skills before entering the job market. Others go back to graduate school to further refine their skills. In either case, a company can find solidly qualified candidates for (sometimes) advanced-level positions, or at least people who are capable of rapid advancement. It is certainly worthwhile to pursue this recruiting approach, although competition for the best candidates can result in very high pay rates.
- *Hire from competitors*. The very best source of potential candidates is competing companies. These contain potential recruits who have the training and experience to step directly into a job for the company with minimal training or other downtime. However, the recruiting staff must be careful not to hire people who have signed noncompetition agreements with their former employers, because these agreements will render them useless and open up the company to litigation by the previous employer. Some companies consider it to be ethically incorrect behavior to actively pursue employees of competing companies. Other firms, especially those in the high-tech sector, engage in this activity with some glee. Company management must decide for itself the extent to which it wants to use this recruiting method.
- *Internet resume brokering*. One of the newest recruiting methods is to request

specific applicant criteria from a job bank that accumulates resumes from potential candidates via the Internet. If the broker finds a resume that fits the criteria requested, it forwards the resume to the requesting company. This service is free to those providing the resumes, because the objective is to accumulate a very large pool of potential candidates. This approach is relatively inexpensive, but only yields resumes from those people who are actively looking for jobs, rather than the larger pool of people who are qualified but must be pulled away from their current positions.

- *Job line*. Many companies maintain a regularly updated voice mailbox on their phone systems that lists all current job openings in the company. Anyone searching for a job can periodically access this listing to see what positions are available. This recruiting tool is inexpensive, but it only accesses those people who are already looking for jobs, and they must contact the company in order to be routed to the job line. Thus, this approach is not capable of accessing a large audience.
- *Movie screen advertising*. Cisco Systems pioneered the approach of listing job advertisements on the movie screens at local cinemas, after it found that its target group of potential employees watched large numbers of movies. This approach is good only if a company anticipates a large target group to attend movies and should be considered only a niche approach to recruiting.
- *Newspaper advertisements*. Newspaper advertising is the most commonly used approach for finding new employees, mainly because it gives relatively inexpensive access to a broad local employment market. However, it does nothing to attract candidates from outside a newspaper's target market. Many growing companies get around this problem by advertising in a wide range of newspapers that cover the major metropolitan areas in the country. The major disadvantage of this approach is that it does not target people who are not currently seeking a job, who may be the best candidates. Also, if there are several newspapers in a metropolitan area, a company may miss part of its target population if it only advertises in a few newspapers.
- *Professional magazine advertisements*. Most professionals subscribe to specialized magazines that carry the most recent information about their disciplines. An excellent way to target this audience is to advertise in the magazines they read. However, even people who subscribe to these magazines do not always review the help wanted advertisements, so a company does not necessarily attract the entire readership of a magazine.
- *Publications*. Some of the best potential recruits are at the leading edge of their professions and like to publish their findings regarding leading-edge improvements in those professional magazines that target their areas of expertise. It is worthwhile to keep track of who has published articles, possibly going back for several years, so that the recruiting staff can call upon its index of authors when recruits are needed in specific areas. Being an author does

not necessarily equate to being a good employee, but at least it indicates that the person being contacted is deeply interested in his or her field of expertise.

- *Search firms.* Professional recruiting companies are in the business of finding good prospective employees fast. They do so partially by conducting their own advertising and mostly by mining their own networks of contacts to find the right candidate. Also, the most reputable search firms do some screening of candidates, which reduces the human resources department's workload in this area. This approach tends to be highly effective, but it is very expensive; a typical search firm will charge a fee that equals one-quarter to one-third of an employee's first-year compensation. This approach is used the most frequently as an adjunct to searches for the most important positions, such as for those positions requiring special technical expertise or for high-end managerial positions.
- *Seminars.* Seminars are held throughout the country on a multitude of topics. The speakers at these seminars are considered to be experts in their fields (otherwise they would not be invited to speak), and therefore are potential candidates for employment. The downside of this approach is that these experts are frequently at the top of the pay scales in their areas of expertise and are therefore very expensive to hire. Also, many are independent business people and may have no need or desire to work within a corporate setting.
- *Technical schools.* Technical schools vary somewhat from colleges in that they train only within very specific fields, and usually at technical levels that are lower on the job scale than the jobs for which companies recruit at colleges. However, this situation is changing. Technical specialties are commanding higher pay rates, while recruits from undergraduate-level colleges are not able to justify higher pay rates. Thus, recruiting efforts for technical positions will rely more and more on the technical schools.
- *Web site advertising.* There are two ways to advertise job positions on the World Wide Web. One is simply to list advertisements on the company's own Web site, which has no cost. However, only those people who intentionally access the Web site will see this information, and this excludes most potential job candidates. The second advertising approach avoids part of this problem, because it involves listing jobs on the Web sites of other organizations. This listing costs the company money, with the rate charged usually varying with the number of hits by viewers on each Web site. Lots of hits equate to high advertising fees. The second approach allows a company to advertise precisely where it believes its target audience goes on the Internet. However, this approach is useless for those potential applicants who do not have Internet access.

The foregoing list of recruiting methods may appear to be exhaustive, but new methods are appearing every day as the competition for new employees rises and companies cast about for more imaginative ways to find the right people.

Which methods should a company use? If it needs many recruits in a specific area, it may be worthwhile to interview several typical candidates to see what kind of lifestyle they have. The company can then use this information to set up special kinds of recruiting to advertise where that type of person is likely to read or spend his or her free time. For example, if a company finds that computer programmers spend large amounts of time at bowling alleys, it should advertise in those locations. Knowing the habits of potential employees enables a company to more precisely target its recruiting efforts to find them.

SCREENING

A company that wants to hire a horde of new employees must somehow find a way to interview all possible candidates while still leaving time for managers to do their jobs. In a low-growth company, managers typically do all their own interviewing, but if a manager needs to fill dozens or hundreds of positions, this approach is no longer viable. How, then, to interview potential candidates?

One approach is to let the recruiting method screen out a portion of people applying by avoiding those recruiting methods that attract low-end or otherwise unqualified people. The most obvious recruiting method that requires considerable prescreening is a newspaper advertisement. Instead, several recruiting methods are guaranteed to eliminate the most obviously unacceptable candidates, thereby saving lots of screening time. Examples of these methods are recruiting based on certifications or professional writings—if a person has not achieved this level of expertise, he or she is much less likely to be ideal for a position. Another example is using search firms that prescreen their candidates to weed out anyone who is clearly unacceptable. Thus, the type of recruiting method used has a large impact on the proportion of candidates who must be interviewed.

Even if a company prescreens candidates through its recruiting methods, a flood of candidates must still be interviewed. Managers only have a small amount of time to devote to interviewing, so the human resources department must take on the chore of conducting initial interviews with candidates. The interviewers cannot possibly have the level of technical knowledge to confidently offer jobs to people applying for all possible positions—this practice would lead to a rash of firings after managers realized that the human resources personnel had hired the wrong people. However, the human resources people can focus on minimum standards during an initial interview with the objective of weeding out clearly unacceptable candidates. Their review criteria can cover some of the following areas:

- *Appearance*. A neatly dressed candidate will be accepted, whereas anyone who cannot take the time to dress properly for an interview will have to find employment elsewhere.
- *Aspirations*. There are some positions, especially in the menial labor area, where it is acceptable to not want any further job advancement. However, a

growing company usually wants an aggressive employee with ambitions to move upward in the organization.

- *Minimum technical requirements.* Most positions, especially in the computer services, engineering, and accounting areas, require some degree of technical skill. The interviewer can ascertain the existence of a minimum skill level before accepting a candidate for further interviews.
- *Education.* There may be minimum education requirements for a specific position. For example, a four-year degree may be needed for an engineering position. If so, the interviewer can quickly ascertain the existence of such a degree.
- *Strengths and weaknesses.* An open-ended question regarding what the candidate considers to be his or her strengths and weaknesses can yield some surprising answers. If so, the interviewer can either reject the candidate based on information gained from this line of questioning ("I appealed the money laundering charges!") or at least write down any unusual items for further exploration by the manager who will be interviewing the candidate.
- *Work history.* The interviewer should review the candidate's resume with the candidate, asking why the person left each job. If the potential employee seems to have difficulty staying in a job or cannot provide reasonable answers for leaving previous positions, it is likely that the same problem will crop up again if the person is hired.

Once the interviewer is satisfied that the candidate meets the company's minimum standards, the candidate can be passed along to a manager for final interviews.

It is impossible to keep managers from interviewing *all* candidates. Key positions, especially those requiring special technical knowledge or many years of experience, demand an interview by a manager to be absolutely certain that a potential candidate is right for the job. Examples of such positions are any management post, programming, or any of the more advanced mechanical positions, such as a hydraulic mechanic. Avoiding manager interviews for these positions is a recipe for disaster. However, there are some low-end positions that require minimal training or experience that the human resources staff can safely handle without any interviewing by anyone else. The most common examples of these positions are sales clerks and assembly line operators. Thus, it is possible to avoid wasting management time in interviewing for low-level positions, although crucial positions must involve interviews by management.

An explosive growth company is always in a tight money situation, so it wants to screen candidates at the lowest possible cost. One way to do this is to have people from the human resources department travel to a region to conduct interviews of all candidates in that area, rather than transporting all of the candidates to a company facility. The cost of sending one person to candidates is clearly less than of sending dozens of candidates to the company.

COMPENSATION AND BENEFITS

Once a company has found a candidate that meets the company's needs, what can it offer the individual to work for the company? An explosive growth company is usually cash poor, so signing bonuses and high pay rates are not always viable options. Many companies are resorting to the use of stock options or other noncash perks to attract the best people. For example, a stock option does not directly cost a company any money, and it only earns money for the employee if the company goes public and its stock performs very well, which is an incentive for the employee to work hard to bolster the stock price. Other recruits require different incentives. For example, a pleasant living environment, including on-site day care, jogging paths, free massages, and a workout center are provided by several software programming companies. The overriding point, however, is to be flexible; query each employee to see what hot button will persuade the person to join the company and then provide that hot button in order to hire the employee.

The following list is not complete, because the number of alternative forms of compensation grows every day, but it is representative of the range of noncash compensation items that a company can implement:

- *401k matching.* Many companies match some portion of their employees' savings that are deposited in 401k accounts. A high matching percentage is a good way to attract those employees who are interested in their retirement funds.
- *Child care.* Many parents must pay a large proportion of their pay to day-care centers to watch their children while they work. Having an on-site or nearby child care center is an enormous benefit to these people, and can lock in many employees during the preschool years of their children.
- *Company car.* Employees consider a company car to be a major benefit, because it eliminates their car ownership expenses. Also, a company typically leases a company car, so it is not as large a cash outlay as it may initially seem.
- *Company-financed computer.* A particular favorite with engineers and parents is for the company to guarantee credit on computer loans with local banks, with employees making the principal payments. Although unlikely to retain employees by itself, it causes them to think twice before leaving the company and having to make a balloon payment to end the computer loan.
- *Flex hours.* Many people with families must structure their work hours to meet the needs of their children's school schedules. This option is invaluable for them.
- *Free meals.* This option is frequently watered down into a subsidized lunch, but one company, J.P. Morgan, goes all the way and offers a free lunch to every employee, every business day. Since the cost of all those lunches adds

up, this can be a major benefit to employees, and also saves them the time of preparing lunches at home.

- *Grocery shopping*. For companies who require long working days or extensive travel, employees appreciate free grocery shopping services, thereby giving them more spare time than would otherwise be the case. This does not mean that a company employs a cadre of elite grocery shoppers—instead, it pays the fees of the local grocery delivery service to shop for employees and deliver them to employee houses. This service is increasingly popular and can also be done on-line. A premier provider of this service is Chicago-based Peapod Inc.
- *Laundry service*. A company can arrange to have employee clothes cleaned for them. The company does not necessarily pay for this service, it only makes laundry pickup available at the company location. This service is good if employees travel constantly and have minimal time available to take care of this task during their free time. It is also being offered more frequently, for example, by General Mills, Intel, and Xerox.
- *Massage service*. Many companies have such stressful environments that recruits are not interested in working there unless there is some kind of on-site stress reduction therapy. One inexpensive version is a massage service that comes in during the lunch period to give 15-minute massages to employees. It is inexpensive and very much appreciated, as Eddie Bauer, the outdoor apparel company has found.
- *Medical package*. Nearly all companies provide medical coverage, but the one that provides exceptional medical benefits at little or no cost has a much easier time retaining employees. For example, generous dental coverage that allows the children of employees to get free braces may be a powerful inducement for the parents to stay with the company. Also, in these days where a larger percentage of medical costs are thrust back on the employee, a free medical plan has become a strong reason for employee retention.
- *On-site banking*. Larger companies can persuade local banks to establish bank branches within company locations. This setup saves time for employees because they do not have to travel anywhere for banking services, is of minimal cost to the company because it is simply supplying space for either a banking officer or an ATM, and locks in a large amount of business for the local bank. This option is truely a win–win option and should be explored by any company with enough on-site staff to warrant it.
- *On-site health club*. This option is excellent for companies who put their employees through a great deal of stress, either because of intense or dangerous jobs or (most likely) long work hours. Also, having an on-site health club can reduce a company's health insurance premiums, because participating employees are less likely to be sick.
- *On-site running track*. A running track is an inexpensive alternative to a health

club, because the only thing needed is enough nearby land on which to locate a winding running path. Again, running can reduce employee stress, which leads to lower health insurance costs.

- *Parking valet.* A minor benefit to employees is to have a parking valet take their cars to the employee parking lot for them. This may seem to be a minor convenience, but it has the additional benefit of allowing a company to keep an extremely small parking lot, because valets can jam far more cars into a parking lot. After all, they have all the keys, and can easily park cars several rows deep.
- *Relaxed dress code.* Many companies are now realizing that a relaxed dress code is a major cost savings for employees, because formal dress codes require a major ongoing expenditure, not only for the clothes but also for cleaning. Since many employees do not regularly meet with customers, who may prefer a high-level dress code, this rule can apply to the majority of the employees of most companies.
- *Stock options or pseudo stock.* A company can offer stock options to recruits. These are extremely popular among the employees of high tech companies. The greatest advantage of a stock option is that it requires no cash outlay by the company. The downside is that it will cut into the primary owners' equity stake in the business if the options are exercised. A variation is pseudo stock, where a company grants "fake" stock to an employee. This pseudo stock is assumed to have the same value as the company's real stock, and the employee will be periodically compensated for any increases in the value of the underlying real stock. The downside of pseudo stock is that, although it does not water down the owners' equity stake, it does use up cash when the employee is paid.
- *Telecommuting.* Some companies are allowing employees to work from their homes. This position at home does not have to be full-time, since there is a loss of communication and camaraderie when someone is permanently away from the office, but it is extremely convenient for employees to spend at least some time avoiding the commute to work. This option is available for those people who do not have to be in constant physical contact with customers, although those who must be in contact by telephone can have calls routed to their homes.
- *Vacation time.* A cost-conscious company frequently tries to save money by forcing its employees to accept small amounts of vacation for their first few years with the company. Although it saves money, recruits now place a high value on their vacation time and are more likely to accept an offer from a different company with a better vacation policy. Being niggardly in this area loses recruits.
- *Miscellaneous, less common benefits.* For a smorgasbord of other benefits, Cisco Systems offers early morning calisthenics, Synovus pays employees

$50 to take an annual physical, Fedex offers free rides in the jump seat of its company planes, and L. L. Bean sells its merchandise to employees at a one-third discount. The range of potential benefits is limitless!

Obviously, there are many alternatives to simply granting large salary packages to incoming employees. However, company management must not make the reverse mistake of offering extraordinarily low pay and a huge number of compensation alternatives. Potential recruits will laugh at pay offers that are far below the median pay rate for their skill and experience levels. Instead, the human resources staff must target pay rates that are not too far from the industry median rate—perhaps 10 percent below the industry median. This figure will keep recruits from automatically rejecting job offers. The company must also not make the mistake of offering too many compensation alternatives. If it were to offer every item noted in the previous list, it would be in danger of going bankrupt. Instead, management should poll employees to see what they need and offer only those items. For example, a group of engineers would probably have a strong preference for a relaxed dress code, flex time, and company-financed computers, whereas a group of employees who predominantly have families might prefer on-site child care and an expanded medical package. Only the correct mix of pay levels and compensation alternatives will have a positive impact on both the company's cash flow and the happiness of its employees.

A word of caution when considering alternative forms of compensation is that top managers will still demand (and get!) large salaries and bonuses. A company must have exceptionally qualified personnel in its top positions in order to continue on the explosive growth path, and playing games with compensation will probably not attract the type of person the company must have. It is more appropriate to swap pay for other compensation at lower levels of management and technical skill.

In summary, an explosive growth company has minimal cash with which to compensate its employees, and therefore must look at alternatives to straight cash compensation, such as the options listed in this section. However, management should not grant all of these alternatives to its employees. Instead, it should ask its personnel what they want and tailor the company's compensation package to match those needs. A complete compensation package that matches the majority of employee requirements keeps turnover down, which reduces the human resources function's need to recruit new employees.

TRAINING

Training is a common function for the human resources department to handle. Some companies, such as Andersen Consulting and Motorola, maintain extensive training facilities. While a laudable goal, it is difficult for the human resources staff of an explosive growth company to pour sufficient management time into training while also devoting the bulk of its resources to recruiting. However, there are ways to offer critical training to employees while keeping the human resources management commitment to this function to a minimum. The options are as follows:

- *Offer only basic training.* One approach is to only offer the most minimal level of training to employees. This training can be an introduction to the company, including a review of its organizational structure, history, employee manual, and benefits. There is usually a mandatory safety class in addition to the introduction class. This approach takes little time, because the curriculum rarely requires updating, and teachers require no special skill to teach it. However, a progressive company should pay a great deal of attention to some additional training, because employees can be made far more efficient and effective by receiving training in such areas as quality control, process improvement, and the basic use of computer hardware and software. Without this extra training, the option of providing minimal training is not a good one. Also, a large investment in training typically leads to less employee turnover, so only basic training is not a good option when viewed from that perspective.
- *Outsource the training.* Since the human resources staff is probably overwhelmed with the task of recruiting new employees, it is logical to simply shift the entire training function to a supplier. A training supplier typically has a large set of courses available and trainers who can teach the classes, either at a supplier training facility or by coming to the company location. The advantage is that the company can avoid managing a large part of the training task simply by managing the supplier, and letting the supplier manage the administration of classes and teachers. However, there are usually a number of specialized classes that a company needs that only apply to its operations. These are not available through a supplier, so the company must either create them itself, ignore them, or pay the supplier to create them.
- *Create classes but have others teach them.* If a company has a number of classes that are so specialized that they cannot be obtained through a supplier, it is possible for the human resources staff to create them itself. This involves having a team of trainers create the curriculum and associated training materials for each specialized class, usually with considerable assistance from whatever functional area of the company has the most experience in the area to be covered by the topic of the class. This approach can apply to all classes, including the most basic ones. With this approach, the human resources staff simply supplies the classes. It is up to someone else, either the other functional areas or a teaching supplier, to actually train people. This approach has the advantage of reducing the number of personnel needed by the human resources function, but it requires an expensive staff to create classes that may already exist at a supplier.

- *Monitor training by other departments.* Many companies are in fields where the knowledge base changes so rapidly that many courses offered by the human resources staff are out of date shortly after being created. This problem is compounded if the human resources staff does not have a sufficient level of technical ability to adequately update the classes. A good way to avoid this problem is to shift the training burden to the various functional areas, because the people in those areas have a much better idea of what should be included in the training classes. The role of the human resources staff can then be switched to a monitoring role, verifying that classes are being offered and that employees are taking them. The ability of a functional area to create classes and provide training can even be used as a performance criterion for the manager of the function.
- *Blended approach.* The best approach is to use a blend of all the previous training methods. For the most technical courses that are also subject to rapid change, the burden of creating classes and providing training should be placed on the functional areas in which the training will be used, because these areas are the most qualified to do so. However, this places a burden on functional areas that have other work to do, so the bulk of training classes, those that are not technically specialized or subject to change, should be outsourced to a training supplier who offers these classes to many companies. Outsourcing leaves the human resources staff in a monitoring role, ensuring that classes are being provided and that employees are attending them. This approach also reduces the manpower requirements of providing training to a minimum, which allows an explosive growth company to concentrate its limited manpower in other areas of the company.

The previous discussion noted the need for a training monitoring role for the human resources staff. How would this monitoring work and why is it necessary? Functionally, training monitoring is a simple matter of collecting sign-in sheets from all training classes and inputting them into a database. The output from this database is a list of those employees who have attended classes and the total hours of training they have accumulated. This information is then matched to a list of all employees to see who has not received training. This matching information is extremely useful for determining who needs to obtain a minimum level of training, who is falling behind on receiving continuing professional education hours (of great importance for those with professional certifications), and who needs more training in order to receive a promotion or a raise in pay. When combined with other information, such as management ability and experience, this training database becomes a useful tool for determining which employees are worthy of promotion. This information is of particular concern in an explosive growth situation, where a company can ill afford to promote the wrong person into a position that could seriously impact the company's growth rate. In short, a useful task for the human resources function is to create a database of employee training, which can then be used to spot those in need of training and to highlight those people worthy of promotion.

MANAGEMENT

As noted in many places in this chapter, the primary role of the human resources function in an explosive growth company is to recruit personnel, while also trying to keep turnover as low as possible. A related task is the screening of recruits, and employee training is also a necessary task. How can these tasks be managed as efficiently as possible? A combination of automation, outsourcing, and careful attention to related measurements is the answer.

The human resources function is always understaffed and overworked in an explosive growth company, because it is very difficult to keep up with the demand for finding and training new employees. To reduce the workload, it is necessary to automate as many functions as possible. The most important automation item that impacts one of the key human resources functions is the use of expert systems and scanning equipment to track incoming resumes. For example, a resume arrives at a company and is scanned into the human resources resume database, where the resume image is converted into text. When the company needs to search its resume database for a particular position, key words such as "electrical engineer" are entered; the search software runs through the resume database and prints out only those resumes that include these words. This database saves an enormous amount of time in sorting through incoming resumes to find the ones matching current job openings.

Outsourcing is also a viable option and is most useful in two areas. One is in benefits administration. A necessary function in any company, benefits administration is not critical to success in an explosive growth company, so it is best to shift this work to a supplier. The human resources staff can then monitor the activity in this area from time to time, perhaps through the company's internal audit team, as well as through a database of employee complaints, to verify that the task is being performed at an adequate service level. The more important outsourcing area is in recruiting, which involves using search firms to locate recruits for the company. The key advantage of this approach is that the company can rely on someone else to do all of the search work, which vastly reduces the number of recruiting employees that the company must maintain. A search firm with a global reach through affiliated organizations can search through a much broader area for recruits than can a company's own recruiting staff. However, the cost of this service is extremely high, so there must be a clear advantage to this approach before abandoning all internal efforts to recruit. One way to mitigate the cost of outsourced recruiting is to concentrate the company's recruiting business with just a few search firms, which allows the company to negotiate smaller fees for each person hired. Thus, outsourcing of benefits administration and recruiting are both viable options for the human resources manager who wants to reduce the workload on the function.

The human resources manager can also use a select set of measurements to aid in spotting recruiting and related problems as rapidly as possible. One is continual tracking of overtime as recorded by the payroll system. A continual increase in paid overtime is a telltale indicator of when a functional area needs more staff. Another measurement is the number of people hired through various recruiting techniques and the cost of doing so. This information is useful for determining where the human resources staff should concentrate its recruiting efforts, and which methods are ineffective or too costly and must therefore be discontinued. Finally, a continual review of the reasons for employee turnover, as revealed through exit interviews, is useful for reducing turnover, which in turn reduces the need to recruit and train new people. These measurements, and others that are noted later in the Measurements and Reports section of this chapter, are necessary for the proper management of the human resources function in an explosive growth company.

The key to good management in the human resources area is to recruit top-quality candidates with the minimum effort and cost, which requires the use of some automation, as well as recruiting firms. Also, continual attention to key measurements allows management to take prompt action when recruiting results, costs, overtime, or turnover become excessive. Taking these steps leads to an efficient and effective human resources function that can keep up with the demands of an explosive growth company.

ORGANIZATIONAL PLANNING

A typical human resources function frequently has considerable influence over the organizational structure of a company. However, this is not always the case in an explosive growth company, for several reasons.

Organizational planning tends to be submerged beneath the overriding goal of recruiting new employees as rapidly as possible, which results in most organizational planning shifting back from the human resources staff to the executive committee or even the chief executive officer (CEO) alone. This situation is not necessarily acceptable, because the top management team is not always skilled in designing an organizational structure adequate for maintaining a smoothly functioning organization. The worst case of all is when the CEO coordinates all changes to the organizational structure, because most CEOs have a tendency to keep many managers as direct reports, which means that critical decisions must wait until the CEO has time to address them. Human resources may then be in the awkward position of recruiting for management positions that it knows are unnecessary. The best way out of this situation is continual lobbying of the CEO with advice for the future organizational structure of the company, so that the information is at least available to the CEO, even if it is not used. Thus, an explosive growth company tends to keep responsibility with top management, while the human resources staff is reduced to recruiting and offering advice regarding prospective organizational changes.

If the human resources manager is blocked from the organizational planning process, it is still critical to have access to the structure that other managers have devised, and as early as possible. Because it can take months to fill new positions and because the human resources group is in charge of recruiting, it must know which positions to fill as soon as possible. The required information should be all new positions to be filled, the locations of new facilities, and language, skill, and experience requirements. The human resources staff can use this information to determine how many people must be hired, how many promoted into the new positions, and how many positions must then be filled due to promotions. Then the human resources manager can use this information to develop a hiring plan that includes the number of recruiting staff and methods needed, as well as how much recruiting must be off-loaded to search firms if the department does not have enough recruiting staff available to handle the workload. This plan is the equivalent of the capacity plan used by a production department. This system is used extensively by General Electric Medical Systems, which uses a "multigenerational product plan" to determine the skill sets needed to develop products that may not even begin development for several more years, and then uses this information to develop its hiring plan. In short, planned changes to the organizational structure must still be made available to the human resources staff so that it can create its own plans for bringing in personnel to fill new positions as early as possible.

The recruiting plan may also include information about the replacement of employees who are interfering with the continuing growth of the company. Some employees simply cannot keep up with the level of activity in an explosive growth company and act as a drag on the rapid completion of transactions. It is the responsibility of the management team to locate these people and either shift them from their current positions or terminate their employment. In either case, the human resources staff must be notified immediately if a position is about to become vacant due to poor performance. This is another source of planning information for the recruiting effort that must be integrated into the human resources recruiting plan.

MEASUREMENTS AND REPORTS

Several measurements are useful for tracking the efficiency and effectiveness of the human resources function. Those noted in this section concentrate on a company's ability to attract and retain employees at the lowest possible cost. This same information is also noted in several report formats, which provide somewhat more management information than a simple measurement. In addition, a report is shown that is useful for tracking annual pay reviews and the pay rate increases granted at those times. The pay review and role change report are of great assistance in keeping employee pay within target levels and is useful for reducing employee turnover.

The following measurements cover recruiting costs, recruiting effectiveness, training costs, and turnover. The description of each one includes the calculation method, plus the reasons for using it. They are as follows:

- *Recruiting cost per recruit.* This measurement is very important for determining the cost-effectiveness of a company's recruiting effort, which is the primary human resources function in an explosive growth situation. To calculate it, summarize all recruiting costs, which include the travel cost of both recruiters and candidates, the salaries of recruiters and anyone involved in screening, plus advertising costs. Then divide this total cost by the number of recruits hired during the time period being measured. It is even better to calculate this measurement by recruiting channel, so that management can decide which recruiting methods are the most cost-effective and which should be terminated due to high cost.
- *Recruiting success by method.* This measurement is used to determine which recruiting methods are bringing in the most recruits, which allows a company to not only concentrate its efforts on the most successful recruiting methods, but also to drop those recruiting methods that are not yielding good results. This measurement is calculated by asking all recruits on their job applications how they found out about the company. The answers to this question are then summarized for all recruits who are hired during the measurement period.
- *Training cost per hour.* This measurement is useful for determining the company's blended training cost for all classes offered. When tracked over a time line, it becomes obvious if the training cost is becoming higher. To calculate it, summarize all training costs (as noted in the general ledger) and divide by the total number of training hours offered during the time period to yield the training cost per hour.
- *Overtime by functional area.* The head of a department frequently does not do a good job of anticipating the need for additional staff. The human resources personnel can assist in this task by continually reviewing the total overtime worked by each functional area, preferably after every payroll has been calculated. If it becomes obvious that a function is requiring a continual amount of excessive overtime over several pay periods, more employees probably are required, which the human resources staff can then recruit. This measurement is easily calculated by accumulating the total number of overtime hours by functional area and then dividing this amount by the total labor cost for the area, less any payroll for salaried personnel. The only problem with this measurement is that it is of no use in determining the overtime being worked by salaried personnel, because they are not paid any overtime.
- *Turnover.* This measurement is useful for determining how many people are

leaving the company, and is especially useful when the causes of turnover, as gleaned from exit interviews, are noted alongside the statistic. It can also be compared to industry benchmarks to see if the company has a particularly large problem in this area. To calculate it, summarize the total number of employee departures during the period and divide it by the total number of employees at the beginning of the period. The measurement can be skewed in an explosive growth company, because there are so many new people being hired that the turnover number may appear to be quite small.

One of the primary objectives of the human resources department in an explosive growth company is to reduce turnover, because high turnover means that there are not enough experienced employees for the company to support its high rate of growth. One of the principal tools for achieving this reduction is the simple report shown in Exhibit 17.2. It lists each employee's name, the date when their annual review is due, their current pay rate, and the median pay rate as determined from local surveys of the labor market. This report is used as a reminder to managers to review their employees on time and to make sure that pay rates do not fall too far below the median pay rate. Either factor, missing a review date or paying too low, are primary causes for turnover, so this report is very useful to distribute to company management.

Besides reducing turnover through prompt annual reviews and matching pay rates to local pay levels, it is also important to target the specific reasons why people are leaving the company. This information is usually gleaned through an exit interview and can then be summarized in a report, such as the one in Exhibit 17.3, that shows the amount of employee turnover, sorted in declining order by the reasons given for quitting. This information is invaluable for resolving problems, and it focuses the attention of management on those issues causing the largest turnover. The turnover report can easily have a percentage exceeding 100 percent, because outgoing employees may cite more than one reason for their departures.

Exhibit 17.2 Pay Review Report

Name	*Review Due Date*	*Current Pay Rate ($)*	*Median Pay Rate ($)*
Anderson, Linda	5/12/xx	13.42	15.19
Edwards, James	5/31/xx	17.01	16.78
Guntherson, Olave	7/01/xx	23.23	20.00
Hickory, Hilda	8/03/xx	10.00	10.50
Johnson, Joseph	3/03/xx	15.25	15.00
Onowy, David	4/05/xx	19.10	16.52
Smuthers, Peter	6/07/xx	14.00	14.50

Exhibit 17.3 Turnover Report

Turnover Cause	*Number Citing as Reason*	*Percentage Citing as Reason*
No chance for promotion	28	38%
Low pay	17	23%
Excessive travel	13	18%
Poor medical benefits	9	12%
Minimal vacation time	5	7%
Long working hours	2	2%
Totals	74	100%

A final human resources report that is very useful for an explosive growth company is one that shows the cost and success of each type of recruiting method. This report, such as the one shown in Exhibit 17.4, is used by management to determine where to concentrate its recruiting efforts and limited funds. It is also possible to further refine the report to determine the percentage of recruits who are actually hired subsequent to screening, which gives a company a good idea of the quality of recruits located through each search method. The recruiting costs noted in the recruiting source report will vary by industry, pay rates, and geographical concentration of eligible recruits, and so should be considered only rough approximations of actual costs for most industries. There is a wide range of costs, because some recruiting methods, such as newspaper advertisements, are only targeted at local populations, who do not have to be flown in for interviews. Other methods, such as Web site advertising, are very cheap, but will be accessed by people who are not necessarily in the local area, and so must be brought to the company, which requires additional travel expenses. Search firms are always the

Exhibit 17.4 Success and Cost by Recruiting Source Report

Recruiting Method	*Number Hired*	*Total Cost in Period ($)*	*Cost/Person Hired ($)*
Search firm	1,408	17,600,000	12,500
Newspaper	329	115,150	350
Web site	141	282,000	2,000
Employee bonuses	140	14,000	1,000
College recruiting	78	234,000	3,000
Certification society	52	104,000	2,000
Billboard	9	900	100

most expensive, but can be a highly effective way to bring in qualified recruits. The recruiting method used has a dramatic impact on a company's recruiting costs.

EXIT INTERVIEWS

This section discusses the need for exit interviews, why they are important, and how they should be conducted. This topic is important, for information gleaned from exit interviews can reduce further employee turnover, which cuts the time and cost needed to find replacement employees.

When employees leave a company, they are frequently given a going-away lunch and sent on their way. No one knows why they left, because no one asked. Even if someone did ask, there was no formal way for this information to find its way to a decision maker. The exit interview solves this problem. The human resources department uses a formal set of questions, frequently supplemented based on the circumstances of each departure, to find out why each employee is leaving, what the company can do better to keep other employees from leaving, and to let the employee know (some of the time) that he or she will be welcomed back if the employee wants to be rehired. In short, the exit interview is a valuable tool for a company to find out what it is doing wrong and to bring employees back to the company who would otherwise not think they had that option.

A key objective in conducting an exit interview is to make sure the departing employee understands that rehiring by the company is not only possible but encouraged. An employee may find that a new position with a rival company is not as good as expected and may very well come back to the company. Rehiring these people is a cheap way to recruit, because the cost of interviewing is eliminated. Also, the company already knows the value of returning employees, so there is no risk that the company is hiring a potentially poor employee. Thus, the exit interviewer must realize that a departing employee can always be rehired, and should conduct the exit interview with that point in mind.

The manner in which an exit interview is conducted is critical to its success. The objective of the human resources staff is to glean as much information from the departing employee as possible, so it is important to be as nonthreatening as possible. Therefore, the employee probably should not be interviewed by her supervisor, but by a human resources person, because the supervisor may be the reason why the employee is leaving, so the employee will not only not be responsive during the exit interview, but may not be inclined to even show up for the interview. Also, exit interviews are sometimes looked upon as a painful and distasteful final action before leaving a company, so the person who does the interviewing must make the environment as informal and casual as possible. For example, if the employee does not want to meet on company premises, the interviewer should be accommodating enough to meet wherever the employee wants (within reason). This may be over dinner or drinks at an out-of-the-way location. The key item here is that the company wants to get information from the employee, so it must relax the employee with a casual interviewer and environment to obtain it.

The human resources interviewer should be careful to phrase questions properly during the exit interview to gather the largest amount of information from the departing employee. It is essential not to lead the discussion, but rather to ask open-ended questions that allow the interviewee to lead the discussion in any direction. This approach is necessary to allow the interviewee to point out any problems at all, ones that employees within the company may be unwilling to talk about. For example, employees may feel restricted from talking about sexual harassment by a key manager, whereas a departing employee, who can no longer be fired by that manager, is more than happy to discuss the issue at great length and in some detail. The conversation may even reveal problems in areas that the company was completely unaware of, such as fraud by a fellow employee. This kind of information cannot be elicited by asking questions that can only have a "yes" or "no" answer, so the interviewer should avoid questions such as "Did you like the product you were designing?" Examples of good open-ended questions that may bring forth a torrent of comments are the following:

- Why did you leave?
- What problems can the company fix?
- What did you like about the company?
- How did you feel about your level of compensation?
- How did you feel about the benefits offered?
- How did you feel about the career path offered by the company?

By using open-ended questions, a good interviewer can uncover many issues that the company can remedy, thereby reducing future employee turnover.

It is not sufficient to only gather problems from outgoing employees. This can turn the exit interview into a dumping session, where the interviewee dredges up every possible slight that occurred during the employee's time with the company. Instead, the interviewer should ask the employee about solutions to problems. This turns the discussion into a more positive experience and frequently gives the company good solutions to problems. After all, employees who are so worked up about a problem that they are committed to leaving over it have probably dwelt on the issue long enough to have several solutions in mind that management might not otherwise use. Also, if a company uses these suggestions to improve the situation, the outgoing employee may even be convinced to come back to the company. Thus, asking departing employees for solutions to the very problems they are complaining about can reveal a number of excellent ways to resolve the problems.

SUMMARY

This chapter covered one of the most important areas for an explosive growth company—human resources. The most critical function within human resources is recruiting, for an explosive growth company has an insatiable need for new employees, and it is up to the human resources staff to find the right ones. A number of recruiting methods were described to assist a company in finding the right recruits at the right price. Other topics covered were a variety of cost-effective ways to screen recruits without overloading managers, several alternatives to pay increases that are useful for attracting and retaining employees, and several traditional human resources roles that have somewhat less importance in an explosive growth company—training, organization planning, and performance measurements. The chapter concluded with a discussion of the exit interview, which is a good way to uncover reasons why people are leaving a company. The exit interview ties into the recruiting function, because reduced employee turnover results in less recruiting. In short, the human resources team must drive the recruiting effort that brings in enough new employees to keep a company on its explosive growth track.

Chapter 18

Manufacturing

INTRODUCTION

A poorly conceived or managed manufacturing function can bring a high-flying company down to Earth faster than any other functional area, with the possible exception of the finance function. The reason is that the manufacturing area can not only eat up working capital at an astounding rate, but is also quite capable of producing products that are not only late, but that also do not work. In this case, it is difficult to figure out which will happen first—will the company go out of business because the manufacturing operation absorbed all of its excess cash, or will irate customers with faulty products tank sales through bad word-of-mouth advertising, with the same result? It is important to avoid either of these outcomes, so this chapter is designed to give the reader a clear understanding of the steps to take, as well as those not to take, that will result in a manufacturing operation that uses the minimum of working capital while issuing products in the desired quantities and at the scheduled times.

The chapter begins with a section that lists the three key underlying principles upon which the rest of the chapter is founded; if any modifications to the manufacturing function follow one or more of these principles, then the function will have improved performance. The chapter then lists a number of important tasks, as shown in Exhibit 18.1, that are closely linked to the underlying principles and that result in improved manufacturing performance at a minimal investment. Following these sections is a discussion of several manufacturing activities that are common in many companies, but which would undermine the guiding principles that must be followed by a growing company. The chapter concludes with a discussion of the measurements, reports, and controls that are most appropriate for the modified manufacturing environment. By implementing the key tasks described in this chapter, an explosive growth company can moderate its need for working capital and capital investments in the manufacturing area, yet experience reliable production performance.

UNDERLYING PRINCIPLES

This section describes three principles that must be followed for an explosive growth company to succeed in the manufacturing area. As usual, two of them focus on

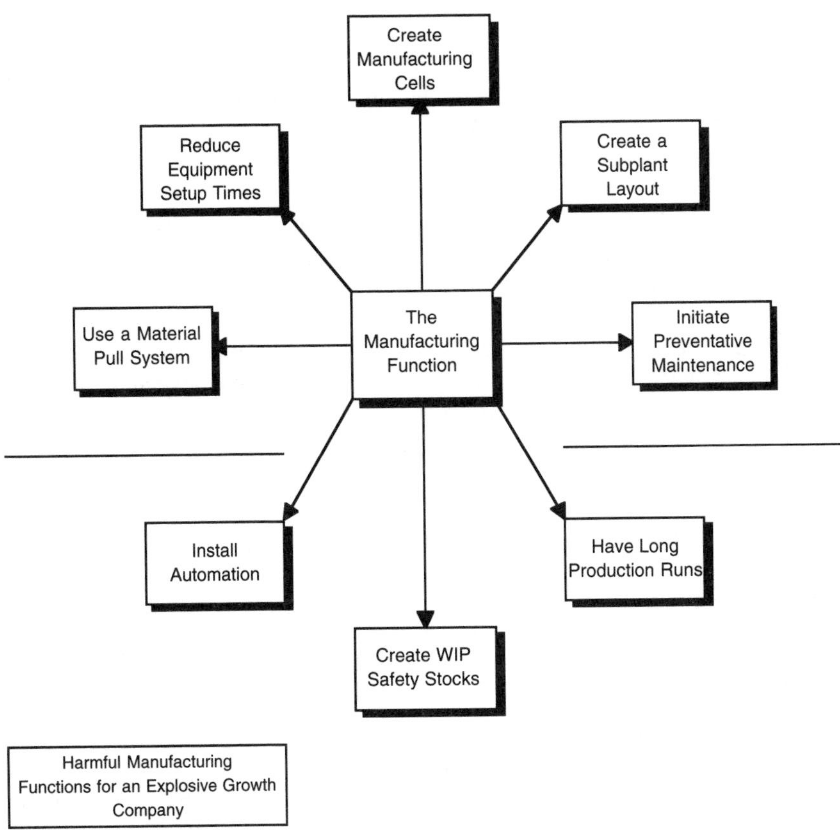

Exhibit 18.1 Explosive Growth Tasks for the Manufacturing Function

the need to reduce a company's cash investment in this area. The final one, avoiding scrap, solves two problems. One is that a company saves money by reducing the amount of materials being thrown away. In addition, however, the techniques used to reduce scrap also yield products that are less likely to break down, which increases customer satisfaction—a key factor for a growing company. The three underlying principles for manufacturing are as follows:

1. *Avoid large capital expenditures.* A company can reduce its cash requirements by avoiding capital expenditures, which can be considerable for manufacturing equipment and facilities. This principle is addressed by several of the following sections, such as creating manufacturing cells and initiating preventive maintenance.

2. *Avoid work-in-process (WIP).* Having less inventory in the production process means that a company can conserve working capital. The just-in-time (JIT) production concept is tailor-made for reducing WIP, and so several of the following sections deal with various JIT techniques, such as a material pull system, reduced equipment setup times, manufacturing cells, and subplant layouts.
3. *Avoid scrap.* If there is less scrap heading for the trash bin, a company can save on material costs. Even more important, however, is that any system for reducing scrap also helps to improve the quality of products sent to customers, which raises customer satisfaction. Scrap reduction is also a key element of a JIT system, so it is covered in many of the following sections, such as a material pull system, reduced equipment setup times, manufacturing cells, and preventive maintenance systems.

This chapter has a heavy focus on many JIT manufacturing techniques, because they support the key underlying principles of avoiding capital expenditures, WIP, and scrap, all of which combine to reduce a growing company's need for cash while delivering a high proportion of quality goods to customers.

USE A MATERIAL PULL SYSTEM

The traditional manufacturing system is a "push" system. A machine operator at the beginning of the production process completes work on a batch of products before forwarding them to the next workstation, where the same process occurs. When the entire process is completed, finished goods are sent to the warehouse and shipped to customers from that location as needed. There are several problems with this approach. One is that, because work is done in batches, there is a great deal of excess WIP inventory in the production process. Also, if a machine operator is making flawed products, it will not be discovered until the operator's entire batch of products is delivered to the next workstation, which may result in scrapping the entire batch. Is there a better way to run the production process to avoid these problems?

The solution is the "pull" system. Under this approach, it is the workstation at the *end* of the production process that starts work. This machine operator receives authorization to produce the exact number of products requested by a customer. The workstation operator then uses up whatever inventory is next to the machine to fulfill the request. If more inventory is needed, the operator requests the exact amount from the previous machine operator in the production sequence. These requests cascade back down through the production system until requests are received by the first machine operators in the sequence to produce just enough for the next machine operators downstream from them. Requests for more parts can be made in a variety of ways. Some are complex, such as electronic notifications, while others are as simple as a request card or a tray that only holds a specific number of parts. The method used is unimportant; the main point is that each workstation only produces the exact amount required for the next workstation in line. The pull system has several advantages, which are as follows:

- *Avoids WIP inventory.* By avoiding the batch processing of products in favor of only having enough product on hand for immediate production needs, a company can avoid a significant amount of WIP inventory investment, which is one of the underlying principles of this chapter. However, this method does not normally mean that there is a complete elimination of WIP inventory, for production processes usually still need some pockets of inventory to guard against problems. Rather, the amount of WIP slowly decreases over time as a company gradually works out the kinks in its pull system, resulting in fewer and fewer parts in the production process over time.
- *Avoids finished goods inventory.* Although the pull system does not necessarily mean that products are only built when they are ordered by customers, this option only to build to customer orders can be included in the pull system. If so, there is no finished goods inventory, which eliminates a company's investment in this area.
- *Avoids scrap.* By avoiding batch processing, flawed parts are much more quickly spotted by the next machine operator in line. For example, if an operator creates just one part, instead of a batch of one hundred, and then hands it on to the next operator, that operator will immediately notice any problems and request a replacement part; this method is a vast improvement over having the next operator detect a problem after a hundred units have already been completed. This method also avoids giving management the temptation to insert flawed parts into products in order to save on scrap costs, because there are no flawed parts to insert. Thus, the pull system fulfills one of the underlying principles of this chapter, that of reducing scrap.

REDUCE EQUIPMENT SETUP TIMES

A typical production facility has many pieces of equipment that require considerable time to switch over to a new setting for the production of different parts. In this type of facility, it takes so long to set up equipment that it makes sense to avoid doing so as much as possible. If a company were to constantly spend hours changing over its equipment, it would never be able to produce anything, for there would be no time left for a production run. Accordingly, most companies have very long production runs of a specific product before switching over the equipment to new settings for a different product. This arrangement is acceptable if a company can immediately sell off everything it produces. However, such is rarely the case. Usually, some of the product is stored in inventory, where it consumes valuable working capital until it is sold. This arrangement also means that the company must invest in a large amount of warehouse space to store the extra inventory. Also, if the inventory is subject to rapid obsolescence, then some portion of the inventory stored in the warehouse may have to be scrapped or sold off at a considerable loss. Finally, it is quite possible for an entire production run to be faulty, because the production equipment may have been set up improperly at the start; if the production run is a long one, a startlingly large amount of inventory must be scrapped. Most companies avoid this problem by carefully testing the first few outputs from a production run for quality; however, it is possible for equipment to gradually become misaligned over the course of a long production run, so product output gradually drifts away from the desired specifications as the production run progresses, resulting in scrapped products. Consequently, long equipment setup times are the root cause of long production runs, which result in several unfavorable side effects. What can be done to improve the situation?

It is necessary to reduce the time needed to change over equipment from producing one product to another. When this time interval is short enough, it becomes cost-effective to rapidly switch over from producing one product to another, which makes it cost-effective to reduce the length of production runs. With shorter runs, a company does not have to store large quantities of completed goods, which not only eliminates the warehousing cost but also the risk of obsolescence. In addition, a short production run means that far fewer parts are scrapped if they are being produced incorrectly. Also, there is less time for production equipment to drift away from its preset specifications, which might otherwise occur over the course of a long production run. These results are in accordance with two of the underlying principles noted at the beginning of this chapter: there is far less chance of incurring a substantial scrap loss, and there is a significantly reduced investment in inventory. Clearly, short equipment setup times solve a number of problems.

Shortened equipment setup times also contribute to a reduction in a company's capital expenditures, which is another underlying principle. The reason is that, when a company uses long setup times, it commits to long production runs of the *same* product; however, if it must produce *several* products at once, then it has to invest in additional equipment and manufacturing space so that it can create the other products on separate production lines. By using short setup times, a company can use the same equipment to produce a variety of products, thereby saving a considerable investment in additional equipment.

There are many approaches to reducing setup times. It is helpful to hire a consultant who specializes in these reductions, because that person's experience can bypass considerable wasted effort by an internal staff that has probably never attempted setup time reductions. Once the consultant has shown a company how to do it, the company can form its own internal team that can work its way through the company, reducing setup times as it goes. The process typically starts with a videotaping session that shows the entire changeover sequence for a piece of equipment. The consultant then goes over this videotape with the equipment operator to spot improvement opportunities. It is quite common to reduce the setup time by 75 percent during this first phase, mostly by examining the tasks that occur while the equipment is not operational, and shifting as many of them as possible to the period outside of this downtime. For example, a machine operator may shut down a machine and *then* go in search of the tools needed to conduct the changeover, rather than doing so in advance. Once these easy hits are completed, the review team looks at such issues as standardizing the bolts used during the changeover, color coding parts for easy assembly, and altering bolts so that they only require one turn to fasten, rather than dozens of turns. The accumulated impact of all these changes can result in a changeover period that drops from hours to seconds. And when the changeover is that short, there is no need for a long production run.

CREATE MANUFACTURING CELLS

It is very useful to use material pull systems and reduce equipment setup times, but there is still a great deal of inefficiency in the production process caused by the distances between machines over which materials must be moved. For example, most companies cluster similar types of equipment in one place; when this happens, a partially finished product must move long distances between clusters of machines before it has gone through every process needed for it to become a finished product. Due to the long distances involved, most companies cluster production into batches so that the materials management staff does not spend all day racing between workstations to deliver one product at a time. The excessive distance between machines, then, results in extra WIP inventory, which goes against one of the underlying principles of this chapter, that of avoiding an investment in WIP. What can be done to avoid so much inventory?

The answer is grouping equipment into manufacturing cells, which solves several other problems, too. A comparison of a manufacturing cell to a traditional manufacturing layout is shown in Exhibit 18.2. A cell layout clusters all of the equipment needed to create a product in one place, usually in a compact U shape. Because the machines are so close, this completely eliminates the time required to move parts between machines, along with any need to cluster parts into batches before moving them to the next machine. Accordingly, the manufacturing cell greatly reduces the amount of a company's investment in WIP inventory.

A multitude of other benefits that demonstrate the superiority of this approach go along with regrouping a company's machines into manufacturing cells. They are as follows:

- *Avoid capital expenditures.* Most companies acquire a few large pieces of highly efficient equipment, but which are also expensive, complex, and difficult to maintain. Since it is not logical to acquire one of these machines for each of a company's many manufacturing cells (because their capacity is too high for a single work cell), a company must get rid of them and instead purchase a large number of much cheaper machines, one for each cell. This

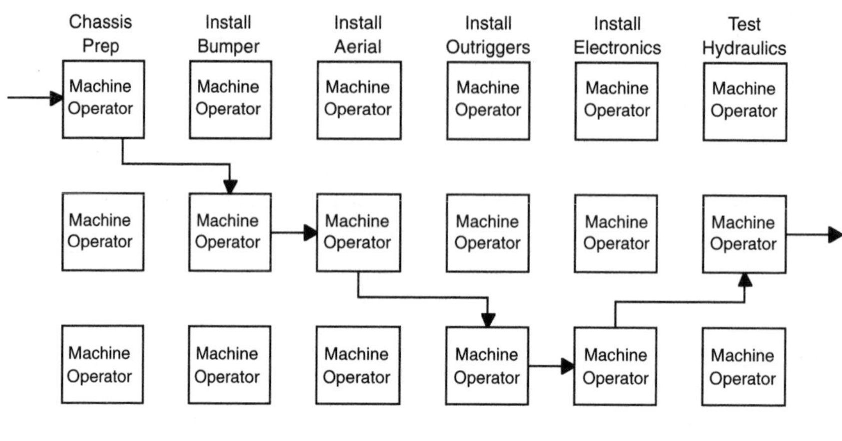

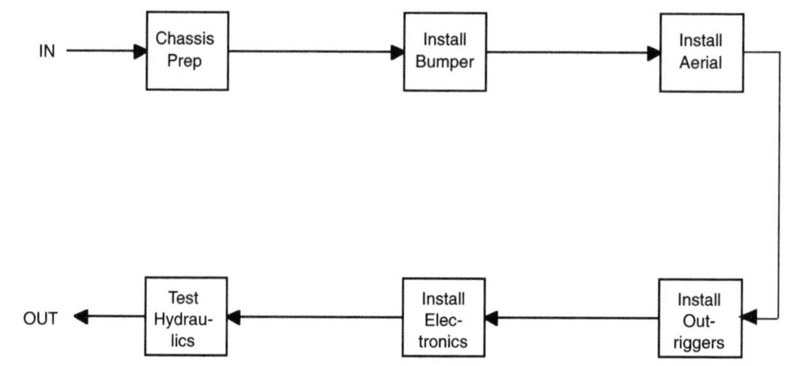

Exhibit 18.2 Work Flow through Traditional and Manufacturing Cell Layouts

tends to result in a net decline in capital expenditures (also a key principle for this chapter), while giving the company new equipment that is smaller and much easier to maintain than the previous equipment.

- *Avoid complex material routings*. In a manufacturing cell, a part inexorably advances through the sequence of machines in a steady and logical order that requires no preplanning by anyone; the part is simply handed off to the next machine in line. This varies from a traditional job shop environment, where batches of materials are moved back and forth across the shop floor to various machines, which requires a great deal of coordination from a production control staff. By switching to manufacturing cells, a large part of this support staff's job goes away, which reduces the amount of overhead needed to create products.

- *Easy equipment layout.* When a company uses many small pieces of equipment, it is much easier to move it about the plant floor. This feature is very useful for altering manufacturing cells with different types of equipment, because they must be changed from time to time as a company's manufacturing needs change. This change is not possible if a company uses large and complex pieces of equipment instead; when this happens, equipment is not movable without great expense, so the manufacturing floor tends to have equipment clustered about the large equipment, which frequently requires extra floor space and is not conducive to the creation of manufacturing cells.
- *Easy equipment repairs.* A manufacturing cell requires smaller machines, which are typically less complex than their larger brethren and, accordingly, are easier to repair. This condition not only makes life easier for the maintenance staff, but also allows the machine operators to complete the easier repairs themselves, if given proper training. By having the operators repair their machines, there is less downtime due to waiting for the maintenance staff to arrive for repair work. Thus, the smaller machines of a manufacturing cell make repairs easier and lead to less equipment downtime.
- *Improved employee morale.* There is nothing more deadening to the mind than the monotonous operation of a single piece of equipment throughout a working day. However, if a machine operator is given control over many machines in a manufacturing cell, not to mention the occasional minor repair job, the day becomes much more enjoyable. Enjoying one's job leads to higher morale, which has the definite added benefit of lower employee turnover. After all, why leave a job like that to work elsewhere on a single piece of equipment once again?
- *No need for materials handling personnel.* Most companies employ a large staff of material handlers who buzz about the shop floor on forklifts, moving batches of parts from machine to machine. These people are not needed when there are manufacturing cells, because parts are handed off directly from one machine to the next. However, they are still needed to move parts between cells, unless the manufacturing area is rearranged into a series of subplants (see the next section).
- *Reduce scrap levels.* Because the machines in the cell are so close together, it is possible for just one employee to operate the entire cell, which means that the person can walk a part through each step in the process and immediately see if there is a problem with each part. If so, there is an immediate adjustment of the malfunctioning piece of equipment, so that scrap problems can always be reduced to just the part that is currently being produced.

CREATE A SUBPLANT LAYOUT

Once a company sets up manufacturing cells, it must see to it that they are linked together, because a single manufacturing cell does not normally complete a product by itself, unless the product is a very simple one. Instead, each cell performs several key tasks and then hands the unfinished product on to another cell that is equipped with a series of different machines to perform different operations on the product. Because the different manufacturing cells are not necessarily grouped next to each other, the manufacturing operation is extremely efficient *within* cells, but not *between* them. For example, if one manufacturing cell is located at one corner of a plant and the cell to which it must send its output is in the opposite corner, it is reasonable to build up batches of completed products at the end of the first cell until there is a sufficient quantity on hand to justify having a materials handling person move the batch to the other end of the facility. Rather than use batches to move products between cells, the shop floor can be rearranged so that those cells needed to complete a product are grouped close together. This configuration is essentially a super-sized manufacturing cell that covers all operations for a product until it is complete, and is called a *subplant*, because it is essentially an entirely closed production process that operates alongside other similar processes that happen to share a production facility. A comparison of a subplant layout to a traditional single plant layout is shown in Exhibit 18.3.

By creating a set of subplants within a production facility, a company realizes a number of benefits, which are as follows:

- *Avoids complex material routings.* When parts can be quickly and efficiently moved between adjacent manufacturing cells, there is less need for a production control staff to monitor and direct the flow of materials. This was the case for a single manufacturing cell, and is more so when all cells are linked together into what is essentially a series of assembly lines. When all cells are linked together, the chief role of the production control staff is reduced to ensuring that the materials needed to begin the process arrive in time and in the correct quantities. The control of materials between cells is no longer an issue, unless there are still parts of the facility that are not directly linked to cells.
- *Avoids investing in WIP inventory.* By reducing the distance between cells, there is less need to accumulate parts into batches before justifying the effort to move them between cells. Thus, there is less need for WIP inventory, which reduces a company's working capital investment; this is one of the key principles for an explosive growth company in this functional area.
- *Reduced need for materials handling personnel.* As was the case for a single manufacturing cell (see the preceding section), grouping related cells close together eliminates the need for a large staff of materials handlers, especially if conveyors of various kinds are used to shift parts between nearby cells. However, it is common for a company to have an extremely large and expensive piece of equipment, such as a paint booth, which cannot be moved into a cell. When this is the case, a materials management staff is still needed to shift products to and from this central equipment.

Single-Factory Layout:

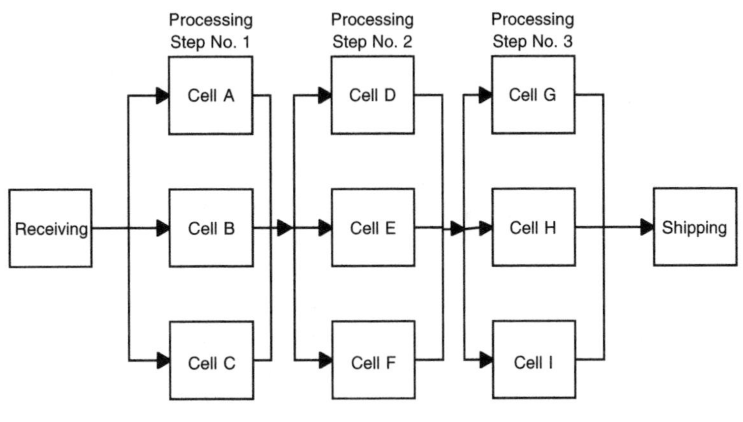

Subplant Layout:

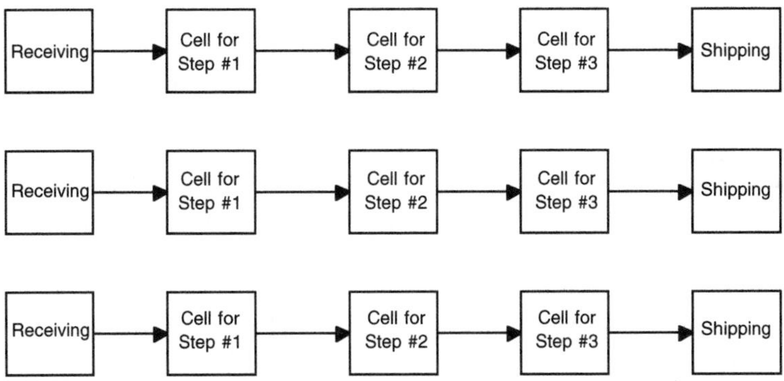

Exhibit 18.3 Work Flow through Single Factory and Subplant Layouts

INITIATE PREVENTIVE MAINTENANCE

Two of the underlying principles noted at the beginning of this chapter were to avoid large capital expenditures and to avoid large scrap expenses. The first is necessary for an explosive growth company, for it must conserve cash for the other demands of a growth situation, rather than pouring it into an array of expensive machines. The second is necessary because scrap can be very expensive and represents a major drain on cash. Both of these principles are addressed when a company initiates a preventive maintenance program for its production equipment.

Any company has a maintenance staff that will fix machines as soon as they break down. This is a reactive form of maintenance whereby repair teams are rushed to machines as soon as something goes wrong and try to bring them on-line again as soon as possible. The problem with this approach is that machines may be out of operation for quite some time while repairs are being completed, which also has an impact on any downstream machines that rely on the output of the inoperable machines as their inputs. To avoid this problem, many companies keep on hand a set of backup machines that are only used when the primary equipment cannot operate; this equipment requires an additional capital investment to obtain. In addition, by simply waiting for problems to occur, a maintenance staff is not taking into account the gradual decline in performance of machines that leads to a breakdown. This decline frequently includes the increasing creation of parts that have significantly departed from specifications, which results in scrap. What is needed, then, is a maintenance program to keep machines running, thereby avoiding the need for backup equipment or early machine replacements, while keeping the specifications of parts coming from those machines within a prescribed set of tolerances, thereby avoiding excessive scrap.

Enter preventive maintenance. This maintenance approach is based on the idea that if equipment is regularly maintained in accordance with a strictly defined maintenance schedule, it will not break down at inopportune moments, thereby avoiding the need for backup equipment or the incidence of excessive scrap. The preventive maintenance schedule evolves as a machine ages and the maintenance staff learns the quirks of each machine. It begins with the maintenance schedule provided by the machine manufacturer, which is then modified based on the company's experience with the equipment. For example, if a machine tends to leak oil, then the maintenance schedule must be accelerated so that oil is added to it more frequently than is called for by the manufacturer. In addition, if the maintenance staff notes that certain parts wear out with uncommon frequency, the maintenance schedule can be modified to include more frequent checks and replacements of those parts. Also, by noting a problem on one machine, the maintenance staff can be warned of the likelihood of the same failure on similar machines; the maintenance schedules are then updated to reflect extra maintenance steps for all similar machines, thereby ensuring that the same problem does not recur elsewhere. This constantly evolving process is required to create usable preventive maintenance schedules.

Once the preventive maintenance schedules are in place, the maintenance staff can schedule maintenance so that it occurs outside of the normal production schedule, such as during a weekend or third shift. This scheduling allows maintenance work to be completed at a more leisurely pace, rather than under the pressure of trying to bring a machine back on line as soon as possible, so that the rate of production is not impacted. By not having this pressure, a full maintenance check can be performed, resulting in better maintenance and fewer equipment problems in the future. Thus, avoiding the rush of conducting repairs during a production run leads to more thorough maintenance.

There are other benefits to shifting maintenance work away from the prime production hours. They are as follows:

- *Avoids unnecessary production labor costs.* If maintenance must be done in the midst of a production run, the production staff must still be paid even though there is no work to do; then, when the equipment is once again functional, the production staff may have to be paid overtime to complete the interrupted production run. These costs disappear when maintenance is shifted away from prime production hours.
- *Avoids excessive demand for maintenance.* When there is no preventive maintenance, equipment failures occur at random, which means that, statistically, some of the failures occur in clusters. When this happens, the maintenance crews will be overwhelmed with work and unable to deal with each maintenance problem as soon as it arises. Since this entails a delay before machines that are further along in the maintenance queue can be repaired, there will be an especially long delay before the production process can be restarted. Consequently, shifting maintenance work away from prime production hours avoids periodic clusters of equipment breakdowns that lead to very long production downtime.

Switching to smaller machines is a common result of using preventive maintenance because, as management tracks the amount of time spent on maintenance by machine, it discovers that the largest and most complicated machines typically require the most maintenance and still break down (due to their complexity), even when the appropriate amount of maintenance has been conducted. Therefore, management concludes that smaller, less complex machines that are easier to maintain are a better choice than large pieces of equipment. In addition, because several less-efficient machines may replace a single, highly efficient machine, a company finds that it can have one or more less-efficient machines down for maintenance while still being partially operational. This would not have been the case if the company only had a single high-speed machine, for any downtime on that would bring down the entire production line that depended on it for parts. Thus, the enhanced maintenance tracking that goes along with preventive maintenance concepts push a company in the direction of using more smaller and simpler machines, rather than a few large and complex machines.

TASKS TO AVOID

Most of this chapter covered those activities that keep a company from spending too much money on the production function. However, most of the activities require wrenching changes if a company already has a manufacturing process in place, especially one that is closely supported by manufacturing management. If so, it may be almost impossible, from a change management perspective, to implement any of the changes. If so, do not despair—it is still possible to at least avoid any future activities that are likely to require large quantities of cash. By doing so, a company can save that cash for more productive purposes that can help the company to grow. What are these forbidden activities, and why should they be avoided?

One action that some companies take in the face of increasing competitive pressure is to install a fully automated factory. Doing so has the advantage of creating a process with minimal WIP inventory, flawless production (when the equipment is tuned properly), and seamless connectivity with the company's production planning system. In addition, it even eliminates the cost of direct labor, because the machines do all of the work. However, there are also several major problems with this approach that greatly outweigh the advantages. They are as follows:

- *Takes too long.* It takes a long time to install and interconnect the complex machinery that goes into a fully automated factory. If a company is doing this installation in response to competitive pressures, then it is to be hoped that the company can still survive under its old production system for several more years, because the benefits of the automated factory will not be realized for quite some time. What company management does not realize (and what the equipment sellers are unwilling to tell them) is that, yes, it is possible to install a series of free-standing machines in a matter of months, but the time required to make products flow smoothly between them takes much longer. In short, system tuning takes longer than equipment installation, so the time required to create an automated factory is a big drawback.
- *Takes too much maintenance.* A company may eliminate its direct labor costs by installing an automated factory, but all it is really doing is substituting direct labor for more overhead, because it must now bring in a large corps of maintenance personnel (who must also be paid more than the direct labor employees, due to their higher skill level) to ensure that the factory equipment is properly tuned so that it produces at the expected levels of efficiency. Depending on the size of the maintenance staff, a company may find that it has not saved any direct labor expense at all.
- *Takes too much management time.* The required investment of time and money in an automated factory is so overwhelming that management must pour a disproportionate amount of its time into ensuring that the equipment is installed on time and within budget, or else the project can bring down the company. However, if production is not the most strategically critical area for the company, then this is a misallocation of valuable management time away from the key areas that are the foundation of the company's growth.
- *Takes too much money.* One of the key principles of this chapter is that a growing company must avoid spending its cash wherever possible, and a primary drain on cash is manufacturing equipment. When a company commits to building a fully automated factory, it needs a vast amount of money,

not only to purchase the equipment, but also to set up all of the automated storage and retrieval systems that link the machines and the warehouse area. In addition, there is a considerable added cost for installation by suppliers and consultants, and the cost of scrapped materials incurred while the system is being tested. In short, the cash demands of an automated factory can wipe out a growing company's cash reserves.

- *Takes too much changeover time.* A fully automated factory requires lots of tinkering before it can reliably and efficiently create products. What happens if a company wants to change to a new product? The company must once again bring in consultants and supplier personnel to modify all of the equipment so that the factory can create a different product. This changeover uses up a startling amount of time. If one considers the entire factory to be a single machine (not an unreasonable assumption when they are all linked together), then the setup time for the entire factory to a new product can be several months. During this changeover period the factory is producing nothing, so the company is not earning any profit on all of the money it invested in the factory. This problem is common in the automotive industry, where changing over an entire assembly line for a new car is considered to be a science that requires volumes of preplanning by large teams of engineers.

The previous bullet points make it clear that installing an automated factory is a highly risky endeavor for any company, much less an explosive growth one, primarily because it requires a very large capital investment and is difficult to rapidly change over to new products.

Another task to avoid is building up WIP safety stocks. This action is common in growing companies that have problems with their production processes, who try to get around them by keeping large stocks of partially completed products on hand to compensate for any equipment downtime. For example, if a key machine breaks down regularly, the production staff runs it as much as possible to build up a store of parts, so that other production activities still have a supply of parts from this machine even if the machine itself is broken. Although the goal is laudatory, because management is simply trying to ensure that products are completed on time, it is also wrong. Here are the reasons for not creating WIP safety stocks:

- *Hides the real problem.* If a company has a problem with malfunctioning equipment, high scrap rates, or bottleneck operations, why hide the problems that are causing the trouble? Adding inventory to WIP hides problems because it creates a buffer between machines. If the buffer goes away, it becomes painfully evident that underlying problems are impeding the clean flow of products through the manufacturing process. To put a stop to building piles of inventory, management should compare the added cost of having extra inventory to the cost of finding and correcting the underlying problems. It is quite likely that the cost of the inventory is much higher than the cost to fix the real problems.

- *Requires an extra investment in inventory.* The last thing a growing company needs is to pour more funds into inventory. This investment can be substantial and is not just the interest cost of the funds needed to purchase the inventory. There is also the storage cost of the materials, the extra materials handling labor required to move it, the cost of extra space on the factory floor to store it, and the cost of obsolescence in case the inventory is never used at all. Furthermore, if management discovers that the inventory will not be used, it will probably hide its mistake by moving the excess inventory to the warehouse, where it will use up valuable storage space instead of scrapping it.
- *Results in additional scrap.* One of the biggest problems with having excess WIP inventory is that machine operators may produce large quantities of a part without realizing that the parts are not within specifications. The problem is usually discovered by the next machine operator who must use the part, but if there are many hours or days worth of parts piled up in front of this operator, it is impossible to discover a flaw until the previous machine operator has produced a formidable pile of inventory. This results in the entire production run from that machine being scrapped. If the company had kept only minimal inventory quantities between machines, the next machine operator downstream from the faulty machine would have discovered the error almost immediately, and informed the previous machine operator that there was a problem, thereby keeping the company from incurring a loss on a large amount of inventory. Thus, large WIP inventories result in high scrap rates.

The above bullet points make it clear that increasing the amount of WIP inventory only soaks up cash while hiding underlying production problems and increasing the potential amount of scrap expense.

A final task to avoid is long production runs. These were the mainstay of American production facilities until the last two decades, because they allowed a company to produce vast quantities of products with highly efficient systems and minimal equipment changeovers that kept unit costs to a minimum. However, it has become increasingly obvious that for any company with more than one product, this approach is much more expensive than is initially apparent. Here are the reasons for avoiding long production runs:

- *Does not allow for rapid changeovers.* If a company is locked into a large production run, it becomes very difficult to respond to immediate customer requests for short production runs of unique products, which results in lost sales.
- *Requires a large inventory investment.* It is fine to have an enormously long production run, but only if there are customers to buy the product. What if a company only sells a portion of the amount it produced? In this case, the inventory goes into the warehouse, where the company must cover its investment until such time as a customer wishes to purchase it.

- *Results in large amounts of obsolete inventory.* If a company manufactures so many parts that many of them are in storage, quite likely the product will eventually be superseded before all of the products can be sold. Of the remainder, management has a choice of losing a modest amount by dumping them on a reseller, or of waiting until even the resellers do not want it, and then writing off the entire amount as being obsolete.
- *Results in large amounts of scrap.* If there is a long production run, it is possible that no one will discover a major flaw in the product until the entire run is complete, resulting in the scrapping of the entire production run.

Thus, long production runs entail a large investment in inventory and run the risk of significant additional expenses for scrap and obsolescence. Short production runs with JIT manufacturing techniques avoid these problems.

MEASUREMENTS AND REPORTS

It is surprising how few measurements and reports are really necessary for an explosive growth company to manage such a large and important function as manufacturing. This chapter covered a number of JIT techniques that are of particular use to a growing company, because they reduce the amount of working capital that must be sunk into this area; a side benefit is that JIT techniques are designed so that problems can be immediately corrected without any record keeping, so little information is available to use in constructing measurement and reports. For example, an assembly worker is trained to fix minor maintenance problems as soon as they arise, in order to avoid equipment downtime; by taking this approach, machines are fixed so fast that it makes little sense to either collect information on this type of equipment downtime (although it is still possible for larger repairs, hence the presence of a measurement for it in this section) or to report on it, because the repair would have been made long before the measurement could possibly have been compiled and sent back to the manufacturing staff for corrective action. Thus, the measurements in this section *do not* cover the control of daily production activities, but rather the tactical changes that can be made to improve the system. For example, accurate bills of material contribute to more efficient assembly time, while the degree of imbalance can be used to alter the configuration of equipment within a cell so that it has a more even flow of production through it. The measurements are as follows:

- *Amount of unscheduled machine downtime.* A company needs to know if its preventive maintenance program is working, and the best way is to see how much unscheduled machine downtime is occurring subsequent to beginning the maintenance program. Ideally, it can be compared to the amount of unscheduled machine downtime just prior to starting the maintenance program, so that there is a good comparison. The amount of downtime should gradually decline as the maintenance staff discovers and focuses on those maintenance features that must be addressed before breakdowns stop. To calculate unscheduled downtime, manually accumulate the number of hours of machine downtime for each factory and list the summary of those hours on a trend line. However, in an environment where machine operators are encouraged to perform their own repairs on equipment, it is quite possible that some of the downtime is not reported, because responsibility for collecting the information is spread across many people, instead of just the maintenance staff that would normally complete the repairs. Accordingly, the measurement can be targeted at only the larger repair jobs that require trained maintenance personnel to correct.

- *Bill of material accuracy.* This measurement is common for many functional areas, because not having an accurate bill has such a large impact on companywide performance. In the case of production, it means that the assembly staff cannot complete production because either there are parts missing or there are extra parts that are confusing the staff. Only perfect bill of material accuracy results in the kitting of exactly the correct number and type of parts, resulting in properly completed products. To calculate it, select a sampling of bills of material and review them for errors. Count each incorrect part quantity, missing part, and part that is listed but not required as an error. Summarize all correct line items and divide by the total number of line items (including the line items that should have been added to each bill, but were absent) to determine the bill of material accuracy.
- *Defective products percentage.* If a company is experiencing a high defective parts rate, there probably are underlying problems with incorrect equipment setups, employee training, or defective incoming parts. Although these problems must be separately investigated and corrected, it is necessary to first track the number of defective products to see if there is a problem. To calculate it, summarize the number of all defective products that are discovered during the production process and add to it the number of defective products returned by customers. Divide this number by the total amount of production during the measurement period. Some companies prefer to alter the measurement somewhat to show the number of defective products per million.
- *Degree of unbalance.* A manufacturing cell is out of balance when there is a bottleneck operation within the cell that is keeping the cell from operating at its full potential rate of output. To calculate it, have the industrial engineering staff determine the difference between the production time on the bottleneck machine and the production times on the other machines in the cell, and then calculate the average difference. This calculation should be made as soon as a cell is set up, so that it can be immediately reconfigured if there is an obvious bottleneck problem.
- *Floor space utilization.* When a company extracts most of its WIP inventory from the production area, as is advocated in this chapter, it clears out a star-

tlingly large amount of floor space. Management can then move equipment closer together, not only to free up floor space, but also to reduce the distances required to move inventory between machines, which further improves the efficiency of the manufacturing operation. To calculate this measurement, determine the square feet of footprint required for each machine in the production facility, and divide this amount by the total square footage of the production area. Some companies also include in the numerator the minimum square footage needed by machine operators, but this number can be highly subjective, and therefore yields a less reliable percentage.

- *Scrap cost.* If there is a large amount of scrap falling out of the production process, it is not only a waste of money, but also a clear indication that the process is not functioning properly. There are several ways to calculate scrap cost. One is to measure the weight of the scrap bins to obtain a very rough approximation of scrap. Another is to have machine operators track the scrap they generated, which usually does not work because the workers do not want to be held accountable for the scrap they created. Another approach is to accumulate all excess materials from the production area and move it through a fixed point for determination of scrap status. This is the best method, because it has the best chance of catching scrap; also, it stands a better chance of determining the cost of each scrapped item, which is more accurate than weighing the scrap bin.
- *Work-in-process material cost.* If there is a large amount of WIP in the manufacturing system, then the company has an excessive working capital investment in this area. This item is difficult to measure, because there is no automated summarization of WIP for the JIT manufacturing system described in this section. Instead, someone must walk through the manufacturing area during a production shutdown (perhaps after hours or on a weekend) and manually determine the quantity and description of parts in the process.
- *Work-in-process turnover.* The previously described WIP material cost is useful for determining the exact dollar value of the working capital tied up in the production process, but this number will rise and fall with changes in production volume, so it is difficult to use as a measure of the efficiency of the manufacturing operation. A better approach is to calculate the turnover of just the inventory in the production process, which, being a proportion, will not fluctuate as the volume of production changes. To calculate it, determine the average cost of WIP materials for a reporting period (by taking the average of the beginning and ending WIP materials costs) and divide this amount by the total cost of goods sold for the same period.

Very few reports are useful for a company that uses JIT manufacturing methods. As noted at the beginning of this section, a JIT system requires few reports because problems are discovered and fixed immediately, rather than waiting for a staff person to measure performance, issue a report, and wait for management to devise a solution. Consequently, few reports are worth mentioning. One is a listing of machines that have suffered serious breakdowns. Minor equipment failures are normally fixed on the spot by the machine operators and thus are not reported anywhere. However, a major failure could mean that the preventive maintenance program is not including a vital maintenance routine, or that some equipment is so heavily used that it is time for complete replacement. The first reason can be fixed by the maintenance staff, but the second reason requires action by senior management to authorize funds for new equipment; for this authorization, it is customary to have a report available that lists a machine's breakdown history, so that the expenditure is justified. Such a report is shown in Exhibit 18.4. The report sorts and subtotals costs by machine, so that management can easily determine the cost and frequency of repairs to a single piece of equipment. This information is vital in determining the timing and amount of equipment replacement expenditures.

CONTROLS

All of the recommendations made earlier in this chapter for enhancing the performance of the materials management function are based on JIT manufacturing techniques. A side effect of most JIT techniques is that they require little central control, because problems are solved immediately on the shop floor. By the time a problem would have found its way onto a control report it would probably already be resolved. Instead, it is best to use the management by wandering around method, which works as it sounds—the manager can best determine the efficiency and effectiveness of the production operation by spending as much time on the production floor as possible, reviewing problems as they arise and watching how they are resolved. This is the key management control in a JIT environment.

However, management by wandering around only shows management how the production staff is responding to short-term problems. It is also necessary to control issues that are longer-term in nature and that underlie the problems with

Exhibit 18.4 Equipment Repair History

Equipment Number	*Equipment Description*	*Repair Date*	*Repair Cost ($)*	*Repair Description*	*Subtotal ($)*
PR-0457	Auto Sorter	04/17/xx	22,814	Replace feed hoppers	
PR-0457	Auto Sorter	04/15/xx	17,032	Replace bagging mechanism	
PR-0457	Auto Sorter	04/12/xx	528	Reset sensors	
PR-0457	Auto Sorter	04/09/xx	14,001	Adjust input feed balance	54,375
PR-1104	Dicer	04/16/xx	3,093	Replace knives	
PR-1104	Dicer	04/14/xx	4,219	Replace input belt feed	
PR-1104	Dicer	04/11/xx	7,904	Replace output wrapper	15,216

which the production staff is confronted each day. Long-term production issues require different controls. One is a continuing review of equipment setup times. The setup times are important, because as they become shorter, the company can cost-justify shorter production runs, which in turn reduces the amount of WIP inventory. Consequently, management should keep close track of the time required to set up all equipment; this measurement can be on a trend line, so that management can focus its attention on those machines for which the company is having difficulty in reducing setup times.

Another area requiring close attention is preventive maintenance. If this is not done properly, the equipment in manufacturing cells will not be operational, resulting in considerable disruption of the production flow. The best control here is to periodically review reported equipment downtime and to follow up with the maintenance staff to verify how it has altered its maintenance schedules to ensure that the same equipment failures will not happen again.

A key control over very long-term production issues is the purchase of equipment. The production manager should be very aware of all requests for equipment. A large new machine cannot be shoehorned into many manufacturing cells, which will disrupt the formation of cells and hence the efficiency of the entire manufacturing process. Thus, management must conduct an exceedingly careful review of the exact kinds of equipment to be purchased, and only authorize the purchase of those that will fit into manufacturing cells.

The final control is to periodically review the efficiency of the entire process, which is most easily done by examining the proportion of WIP inventory and scrap to total production volume. If either of these percentages increases, then the manufacturing manager must dig into the operations in detail to determine what is causing the problem. These are high-level measures, but are good indicators of underlying problems; as such they are excellent controls.

SUMMARY

This chapter covered the primary activities to improve the production area in order to ensure minimal cash requirements and solid production performance, which are both key to rapid corporate growth. These activities included a material pull system, reduced equipment setup times, manufacturing cells, subplant layouts, and preventive maintenance. These core elements of the JIT philosophy of manufacturing result in reduced WIP inventory as well as capital expenditures and minimal scrap. All of these results improve a company's cash flow, which is critical to an explosive growth company.

In addition, the chapter noted the reasons for not making a large commitment to automated equipment, WIP safety stocks, or long production runs, because all of these actions have the reverse result of requiring an investment of additional cash in the production area. Even if a company does not implement any of the recommended activities, at least avoiding these other tasks will keep a company from sinking under a large debt burden to fund the production function.

Chapter 19

Materials Management

INTRODUCTION

When handled properly, materials management allows a company to deliver products to customers on time, without requiring an excessive expenditure to maintain large stocks of inventory. If handled incorrectly, it can soak up all excess cash to fund a huge inventory, while not having the correct parts on hand to ensure that products are built on time. Clearly, the explosive growth company must perform this function correctly if it is to succeed. The most important tasks to manage properly in the materials management area are shown in Exhibit 19.1, along with several tasks that are not only of lesser importance, but which can be harmful if actively pursued.

The chapter begins with a few underlying principles that form the foundation for all of the discussion in this chapter. Each of the tasks noted in Exhibit 19.1 are then addressed in the subsequent sections. In addition, the chapter includes several measurements, reports, and controls that are helpful for managing this function. After perusing this chapter, the reader should have a clear understanding of the key issues to resolve before an explosive growth company can feed materials to its production process with a minimum cash investment.

UNDERLYING PRINCIPLES

The underlying principles that drive the materials management function of an explosive growth company are quite simple and must be rigidly followed if the company is to succeed, because failing at them would result in massive cash expenditures and missing materials that would cripple growth. The two key principles are as follows:

1. *Minimize working capital and capital costs.* When performed incorrectly, the materials management function requires a vast cash outlay, because inventories will swell and warehouses and related storage equipment must then be obtained to house it. This must be avoided if a company is to retain enough excess cash to fund further growth, instead of large warehouses.
2. *Do not interrupt production.* It is hard to grow if a company cannot reliably issue products to customers on time, partially because there is no way to invoice

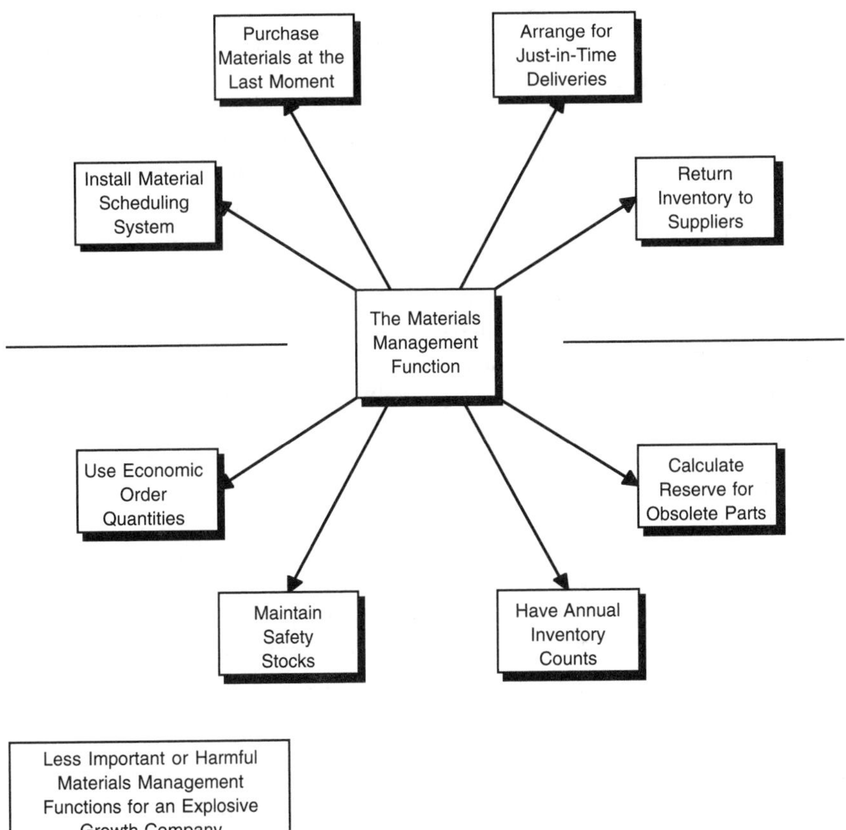

Exhibit 19.1 Explosive Growth Tasks for the Materials Management Function

customers and recognize revenues, and partially because the company will gain a reputation for not being able to deliver products on time, which drives away both current and future customers. Thus, explosive sales growth vanishes if materials do not arrive in time for scheduled production.

The foregoing two underlying principles drive all of the discussion in this chapter, for they are absolutely critical to the proper functioning and continued growth of a company.

INSTALL A MATERIALS SCHEDULING SYSTEM

A good materials scheduling system fulfills both of the key principles; if properly managed, it can schedule a material receipt for the exact moment that it is needed by the production line, which also reduces a company's need for working capital by avoiding a large amount of on-hand inventory. This section describes a typical material scheduling system.

There are three kinds of scheduling systems. One is manufacturing resource planning, which covers both materials and labor scheduling. Another is kanban cards, which are used to pull material through the production process and also from suppliers. Since the first encompasses more than the topic of this chapter and the second is still rarely used in the United States, this section only deals with material requirements planning (MRP). This system takes as inputs the production schedule, which lists all customer orders scheduled to be completed, the bills of material for each of the items listed on the production schedule, and the records of all items in the inventory. It then processes this information by multiplying the products on the production schedule by the bills of material to arrive at the total types and amounts of inventory needed to fulfill the company's production needs, and then subtracts the inventory on hand to determine how much of the material requirements must be purchased. The output from the system is a set of picking lists for pulling parts from inventory, as well as purchase orders to buy any parts that are not in stock. This system is shown graphically in Exhibit 19.2.

Why install such a system? Because it creates an orderly flow of materials to the production process that reduces the amount of inventory in the system, and less inventory means less cash invested. There is a significant cost associated with installing and maintaining such a system, which includes buying computer hardware and software, as well as hiring and training a very experienced staff. However, this cost is more than made up for by a considerable reduction in inventory and a vast improvement in the company's ability to produce on time. In addition, a company can avoid large stockpiles of parts, which reduces the size of the warehouse; this has the added benefit of avoiding inventory obsolescence charges, because less inventory means that less of it may eventually have to be scrapped. These reasons are convincing thousands of companies to switch to MRP systems.

Without an MRP system, a company falls into the expedite mode. When expediting, a company hires a large number of people whose jobs are to shepherd individual production jobs through the system. This approach emphasizes those jobs that are being most skillfully pushed through the production process by the best expediters, which means that all other jobs are shunted to one side to make way for these more critical jobs. Purchasing tends to be on a rush basis, because the jobs to be expedited vary every day, making it hard to predict when materials need to be ready for production. Also, because materials are needed immediately, there are many overnight freight delivery charges, as well as rush charges by suppliers to manufacture the needed parts on short notice. Purchasing managers

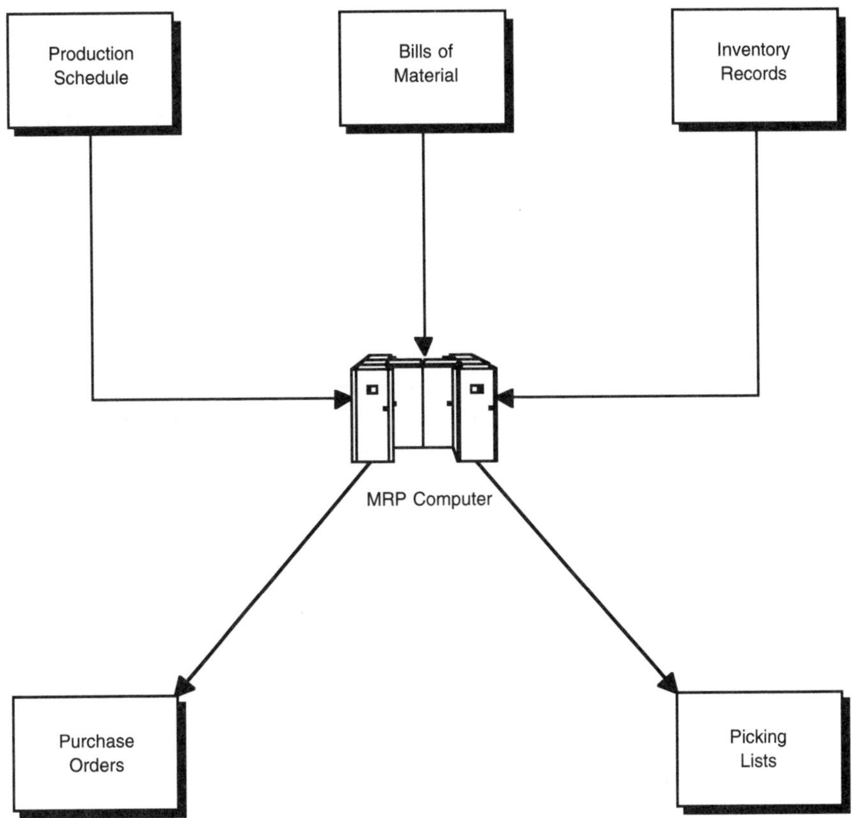

Exhibit 19.2 A Materials Requirements Plannng System

tend to purchase excessive amounts of inventory in this situation, because their performance looks better if they have lots of parts available to support the company's rapidly changing requirements. Also, the investment in work-in-process (WIP) increases because many jobs in the production process have been started but not completed, because expediters have pushed them to one side in favor of more critical jobs. Clearly, this disorderly excuse for a system results in materials not being available in time for production, while increasing a company's investment in working capital that is allocated to inventory.

Although an MRP system has many obvious benefits, few companies are totally successful in implementing it. There are several ways in which a company can trip up while installing such a system, which include the following:

- *Poor bill of material accuracy*. The MRP system will issue an inaccurate set of material requirements if the bills of materials that are used to describe the contents of products are incorrect. Managers frequently believe that accuracy levels of 50 percent or even less are sufficient to run an MRP system, but an accuracy level of at least 98 percent is the realistic level that must be attained before an MRP system will operate properly. This usually requires the addition of extra engineering staff to maintain the bills, which is frequently resisted by management due to the perceived added expense of the new staff.

- *Poor inventory quantity accuracy.* If the inventory quantities on hand are incorrect, then the MRP system will still function incorrectly, even with high-quality bills of material, because the system may assume that parts are already in stock when they do not exist, resulting in no action by the system to purchase parts well in advance of the scheduled need for the parts. The reverse situation is also common, whereby the system orders more parts when they are already in stock, because the inventory records show a quantity that is too low. Additional staff is almost always needed to ensure that inventory accuracy is high, especially when the work is first undertaken. Once again, management tends to resist the addition of employees to this area, because they only see the personnel cost, not the benefits supplied by an accurate MRP system.
- *Poor inventory location accuracy.* Even if inventory quantities are perfect, this is not much good if no one can find any parts. An inventory item with a bad location code is as good as gone, so this is the equivalent of having incorrect quantity information in the inventory database. Managers frequently do not understand the effort required to update the inventory database to include locations and tend not to support the extra staffing needed to do this.
- *Many modifications to the production schedule.* The cardinal sin committed by nearly all companies is to alter the production schedule too near the scheduled production date. When this happens, the purchasing staff must scramble to obtain materials in less than the normal lead time, which usually involves extra freight costs. It also means that other materials that were scheduled to immediately enter the production process upon receipt will now languish on the receiving dock until later, so that the company incurs extra inventory costs. Keeping management (and especially the sales staff) from altering the production schedule is one of the most difficult tasks for the materials management function.

An explosive growth company can install a material requirements planning system in order to greatly reduce its working capital requirements while ensuring that the production process receives needed materials on time. However, it is exceptionally easy for this system to issue incorrect information if management does not commit sufficient resources to ensure that all inputs contain accurate information and does not interfere with the orderly scheduling of production.

PURCHASE MATERIALS AT THE LAST MOMENT

Once an MRP system is in place, it is possible to purchase materials at the last possible moment. If the MRP system works properly, it does not increase the risk of interfering with the production process, while it allows the company to purchase the minimum amount of materials to complete the production schedule, which reduces the company's working capital requirements.

Why would a company want to purchase all of its parts at the last possible moment? Because it does not want to accumulate large stores of extra parts. It is very expensive to keep parts on hand before they are needed, not only because they must be paid for sooner, but also because they require extra storage facilities and are subject to damage while they wait in storage. Also, if a company purchases parts well in advance, the purchasing staff must be burdened not only with the purchase of parts that are needed immediately, but also with those not needed for a long time. Furthermore, parts that are ordered too early may never be needed due to changes in customer orders or alterations to product specifications. For all these reasons, it is a good idea to only purchase parts at the exact moment they are needed, and not a second sooner.

How can a company reliably purchase parts at the last moment? Two methods must work in concert for last minute purchasing to be effective. They are as follows:

1. *Install MRP system.* The material requirements planning system (see the previous section) and all the information that feeds into it must yield accurate information, so that the purchasing staff is fully aware of required purchases.

2. *Send purchase requirements.* All purchasing requirements must be sent to suppliers by the fastest and most reliable means possible, ensuring that there are no lost purchase orders. This usually requires a mix of electronic data interchange (EDI) transactions, faxes, and mail transmissions. It is also possible to open the company's MRP files to suppliers, who can access it to determine the types and quantities of parts to send to the company. There is usually a mix of transmission methods needed, because not all suppliers are similarly equipped to handle the same kinds of transmission methods.

These two steps must be completed before a company can reliably purchase parts from suppliers at the last possible moment, rather than stockpiling parts. The process is never-ending, for a company that successfully implements this process can always tighten its standards, which results in more accurate bill of material, production schedule, and inventory information feeding into the MRP system, resulting in better purchasing requirements being issued to suppliers.

ARRANGE FOR JUST-IN-TIME DELIVERIES

Purchasing materials at the last moment, as described in the previous section, does not necessarily mean that they will *arrive* at the last moment, which is the objective when trying to reduce a company's working capital investment in inventory to the bare minimum. How can a company ensure that the correct quantity of the correct types of parts will actually arrive at the last moment? The following two tasks must be completed:

1. *Certify suppliers*. The company must create a certification process for ensuring that suppliers are capable of delivering parts to the company in the correct quantities and on the dates requested. This certification usually involves a considerable pruning and replacement of the company's supplier list. Good suppliers are attracted to companies that certify their suppliers, because becoming certified frequently means that a supplier is given the additional business of those other suppliers who were not able to meet the certification standards.
2. *Verify that parts are coming*. The MRP system can be used by the purchasing staff to create a call list for checking with suppliers to ensure that requested deliveries will arrive at the company on the requested date. Consistent problems in this area usually result in the retraction of a supplier's certification status and its replacement by another supplier.

Of the foregoing two tasks, the first is mandatory, because a company's purchasing efforts will be useless without competent suppliers who can deliver when asked. The second is very wasteful of the resources of the purchasing staff and, accordingly, is only used for those suppliers with a poor delivery record and for those key parts that absolutely, positively must arrive on time.

While just-in-time (JIT) delivery is an admirable goal, it is also an extremely difficult one to attain. It requires constant and flawless communication with suppliers and perfect deliveries by them. To attain JIT deliveries, a company must be willing to work with suppliers to improve supplier processes, use new methods of communication, swap key information, and trade employees from time to time. The many improvements needed to make it work take years to implement and constant labor to maintain. If a company implements the system properly, it can achieve a delivery system in the same range as that of Toyota, which is so efficient that there is only enough inventory in the company at one time to complete the WIP that is currently under way.

The only problem with JIT purchasing and delivery is that it seems to violate one of the underlying principles noted at the beginning of this chapter, that of not interrupting the production process. However, if this purchasing process works properly, the only task that the materials management staff needs to focus on is bringing in materials for immediate production needs, and if it will really be there when needed. It does not need to focus on what is currently in stock. By switching to JIT purchasing and delivery, there is very little inventory in stock, so the focus shifts from two tasks to one, which focuses the attention of the staff and is therefore more efficient. Consequently, there is no reason why a JIT purchasing and delivery system should be any less effective than a more traditional one.

As was the case for JIT purchasing, JIT delivery is a process that never stops, for the materials management staff can constantly improve the quality, timeliness, and accuracy of supplier deliveries, resulting in an ever-shrinking inventory investment.

RETURN INVENTORY TO SUPPLIERS

One of the key underlying principles for the materials management function is to minimize the need for working capital. Returning inventory to suppliers fulfills this principle admirably, while helping to reduce other problems as well.

Many explosive growth companies are highly leveraged and need to have a very high borrowing base available in order to borrow the largest possible amounts from banks. Therefore, many of these companies are reluctant to take any meaningful action to reduce the size of their inventories. This is a mistake. If a company opts to keep inventories high rather than return some of it to suppliers, it can generally only use a fraction of the inventory as a borrowing base, with 50 percent being a common percentage that the lender allows. However, a supplier typically charges a restocking fee of 15 to 20 percent for the return of unwanted inventory, so a company can receive more cash from the supplier by returning parts than it can from the bank by using the same parts in its borrowing base. In short, it makes more sense for an explosive growth company to return parts to suppliers than to keep them to bolster its borrowing base.

However, the issue is not quite so simple. An explosive growth company may also have a covenant with its lender that requires a minimum reported profit level each period. If so, the company may not be able to return a large block of parts to suppliers at one time, because it may have to record a large restocking expense. In this case, it is best for the company to gradually return parts over several reporting periods in order to avoid any violation of its covenants. However, even this issue is not so simple. Some parts, such as computer parts, drop in value very rapidly, so waiting even a few months to return them could result in much larger restocking fees or an outright rejection of the parts by the supplier. In such cases, it is best to inform the lender that the company must take a one-time expense that will result in a violation of the profitability covenant. If the lender realizes that this is a one-time expense that will not impact ongoing operations, it usually waives the covenant violation. In short, company management must be aware of the expense issues surrounding supplier charges for returned parts, and how this might impact profitability as well as lender relations.

The reasoning behind returning parts does not just involve the realization of extra cash from the sale of the parts. There are also numerous cost savings associated with having a smaller inventory. One is less need for storage space, which may result in subleasing warehouse space to another entity, or selling off warehouse space for cash. Another savings comes from selling off storage racks that are no longer needed for storage, as well as materials handling equipment that no longer has materials to handle. Also, fewer personnel are needed to move, track, and count inventory, so there may be personnel savings. Finally, the cost of insurance needed to cover the inventory is lower if the dollar value of inventory is reduced. In short, reducing the amount of inventory has many benefits that can increase cash flow while reducing expenses.

Although this section builds a strong case in favor of returning parts to suppliers whenever possible, it is important to note the point below which it is no longer cost-effective to return parts. The labor involved in returning parts is considerable. The parts must be identified and then listed on a report (see Exhibit 19.4 in the Measurements and Reports section) that is sent to the supplier. The supplier then reviews the list, determines which ones it wants to take back, and negotiates a return price with the company's purchasing staff. The parts are then pulled from stock, packaged, and shipped to the supplier. Clearly, the labor required to return parts is only justified for larger dollar volumes. The best approach for determining when to stop returning parts is to first determine the potential dollar amount that can be returned to suppliers, and then sort the list by supplier in descending dollar order. Management can then review the list and determine the cutoff point below which it is not worthwhile for the purchasing staff to attempt to return parts. A cost/benefit analysis of returnable parts keeps the materials management staff from becoming bogged down by the work required to return parts for which the company does not receive a significant cash inflow.

What should a company do with those parts for which it is too expensive to return them to suppliers? These are typically small-dollar items, and there are frequently quite a few of them. It is generally not a good idea to keep them on hand to bolster the borrowing base, because they contribute very few dollars to the borrowing base while requiring a fair amount of storage space and labor to keep in stock. It is better in these cases to remove them from stock if the materials management staff is sure that they will not be used. However, if there are cases where suppliers are unwilling to take returns on *expensive* parts, these parts should *not* be thrown out until the company is certain that they will never be used again, because they may form a significant portion of the company's borrowing base.

TASKS TO AVOID

At the beginning of this chapter, Exhibit 19.1 noted several tasks that are critical to the success of the materials management function. It also pointed out several others that were not only of little importance, but which could be harmful in an explosive growth situation if actively pursued. This section discusses the tasks that should be avoided, and why that is the case.

Many materials management staffs still use the old economic order quantity (EOQ) model to purchase parts. This model calculates the amount to reorder based on the lowest combined cost of several factors; the result is almost always a purchase quantity that exceeds the exact quantity actually required for current needs. Since a key principle for this function is to keep working capital costs as low as possible, it is clear that the EOQ model is not suitable in an explosive growth environment. It tends to keep inventory levels higher than would otherwise be the case if a company were using JIT methods to eliminate the inventory entirely. In addition, if a company uses an automatic EOQ formula and then eliminates a part from stock while trying to reduce inventory balances, the system will automatically reorder the part based on the EOQ formula, which puts the unwanted part right back into stock again. The best way around this problem is to be sure to turn off the EOQ feature in the software, or to delete the part record from the database to ensure that nothing is reordered. Finally, the EOQ formula ignores the cost of damage to parts, which inevitably occurs when something is kept in stock for a long enough period of time. For all of these reasons, an explosive growth company should not use EOQs.

Safety stocks are used to ensure that there are no times when a company runs completely out of a part, which would require the company to curtail production and incur rush freight costs to rapidly bring the part back into stock. There is a field in the parts record of most software packages that allows a company to enter a separate safety stock amount for each part. This figure is useful for a limited number of situations, such as for service parts, when the company cannot predict when customers will need additional parts. However, like the EOQ formula noted previously, safety stock violates the principle of keeping working capital requirements at a minimum, because it means that there are more parts in stock than are immediately needed. It also ignores the eventual obsolescence of any parts left in stock. In addition, as was the case for EOQ, if a part's quantity is intentionally reduced to zero, the computer software automatically purchases replacement parts equal to the amount of safety stock entered for that part. To avoid this problem, the safety stock level must be reset to zero or the inventory record must be deleted. Rather than use the safety stock concept at all, it is better to focus on purchasing exactly what is needed and on using drop shipments directly from suppliers to customers, which eliminates the need to keep minimum service part levels on hand.

Annual inventory counts are also wasteful, because it diverts a large amount of labor into a non-value-added activity. To make matters worse, many companies shut down their activities entirely during the physical inventory counting period, which impairs the ability of the company to service customer needs and can slightly reduce the rate of growth, which is critical for an explosive growth company. To make matters worse, the count tends to be inaccurate, because the counters are frequently rushed, and, if they are nonwarehouse personnel, because they do not recognize the parts. Instead of performing year-end physical inventory counts, it is better to focus on using only the more knowledgeable warehouse staff to conduct an ongoing program of cycle counting and investigation of the mistakes uncovered during cycle counting, which results in a much more accurate inventory without requiring a complete shutdown of company operations.

Those companies with large or old inventories must block out time at least once a year to review the inventory in detail to determine the amount of the reserve for obsolete inventory. This requires time by a committee, usually drawn from the warehouse, engineering, purchasing, and accounting staffs, to decide on what parts are now officially obsolete. Clearly, this is a waste of the time of a number of people who would be better off working on more productive activities. It is better to concentrate on shrinking the inventory down to the point where it is so small that there is no need for an obsolete inventory review. If this is not possible, then an alternative may be to alter the materials management software so that it records the last date on which a part was withdrawn from stock, and then use this information to automatically spot those parts that have not been used for a long time, and which are therefore obvious targets for an obsolescence review. This system reduces the time needed by the parts review committee to find obsolete parts. Shrinking the inventory reduces the need to review it for obsolete parts.

MEASUREMENTS AND REPORTS

The materials management function is one of the easiest to track with measurements and reports that give management a very clear picture of its performance. The measurements cover such areas as bill of material accuracy (which is also covered in Chapter 15), inventory accuracy, returnable and obsolete inventory, and the production schedule. These measures are supplemented by reports that list the details of why variances are occurring and where there is room for improvement. The measurements are as follows:

- *Bill of material accuracy.* This measurement is needed to determine if bills of material are sufficiently accurate to provide good data to the MRP system; if not, the MRP system will yield inaccurate results. To calculate it, select a sampling of bills of material and review them for errors. Count each incorrect part quantity, missing part, and part that is listed but not required as an error. Summarize all correct line items and divide by the total number of line items (including the line items that should have been added to each bill, but were absent) to determine the bill of material accuracy.
- *Dollars and percentage of inventory more than xx days old.* This measurement is needed to determine the impact on a company's borrowing base of inventory that must be written off as obsolete. To calculate it, print a report that only lists inventory for which parts have not been released to a job for *xx*

number of days. This requires a field in the inventory database that stores information about inventory being charged out to jobs. If that field is not available, this measurement cannot be calculated. The report should include a grand total amount of inventory selected, which can then be divided by the grand total inventory cost to derive the percentage of inventory more than *xx* days old.

- *Dollars and percentage of returnable parts in inventory.* This measurement is needed so that management can tell if additional effort is needed to return more parts to suppliers. If the measurement shows an unusually large amount of returnable inventory, management should allocate significant resources to clearing out the inventory. To calculate it, find a field in the inventory database that is not being used, and enter a character in that field for every part that can be returned to a supplier. Then run a report that selects only those parts for which the character is listed in the appropriate field, and ensure that the report includes a total inventory cost. The total cost of returnable parts can then be divided by the grand total inventory cost to derive the percentage of inventory that is returnable.
- *Inventory accuracy.* This measure is necessary to see if the inventory is accurate enough to be a reliable contributing component of an MRP system. If the resulting measurement yields an inadequate level of accuracy, then the MRP system will not function correctly. To calculate it, take a significant sample of the total amount of inventory and verify that both the quantity and location for each item sampled is listed correctly on the inventory database; this sample should also include a verification that the items listed in the database are actually in the warehouse. Then divide the total number of correct items by the total amount sampled.
- *Inventory turnover.* This measure indicates the ability of the materials management staff to keep inventories at the lowest possible level, especially when calculated separately for just the raw materials inventory (since the materials management staff is responsible for this portion of the inventory). It is better than measuring the total dollars of inventory on hand, because that number will inevitably rise as a company goes on an explosive growth path and requires extra inventory to maintain a higher level of production. By using a comparison of the inventory dollars to the cost of goods sold to derive a proportion measure, this problem is avoided. To calculate it, determine the average inventory for the period, which is the beginning inventory plus the ending inventory, divided by two, and divide this amount into the annualized cost of goods sold.
- *Production schedule accuracy.* This measurement is needed to verify that the company can produce the correct quantities of products on the dates specified in the production schedule; if not, the materials management staff will have a difficult time procuring materials to match the actual rate of produc-

tion. To calculate it, summarize the number of production jobs that were completed during the scheduling period, and divide this number by the grand total of all jobs scheduled during the production period.

The foregoing measurements give a good overview of the condition of the materials management function, but do not give details regarding why there are problems. For that, there are several report formats to select from that give sufficient additional information to resolve the issues noted by the measurements.

The report that provides extra detail for the old inventory measurement is shown in Exhibit 19.3. This one lists all inventory that has not been used beyond a user-specified date. It lists the part number and description, as well as the quantity on hand, the extended cost, last date used, and the name of the supplier from whom it was purchased. If there is space available, the report can also include the last date on which a part was purchased, which is sometimes more informative than the last usage date, especially when there is no usage date at all. In addition, the report can be sorted in descending extended dollar order to call attention to those parts that represent the largest investment. Other sorting possibilities are to sort by location code, in order to find the parts in location sequence; by oldest usage date, in order to review the oldest items first; or by supplier, so that the parts can be conveniently clustered by supplier for easier return for credit. Since there are so many valid sorting possibilities, it is best if the report contains a sorting feature that allows all of these options. The old inventory report is an excellent way to assist in keeping the number of old parts down to a minimal level.

The report that shows supporting detail for the returnable parts measurement is shown in Exhibit 19.4. This report selects only those parts that are identified as being returnable to a supplier for some kind of reimbursement. It lists each part number, description, quantity, extended cost, and supplier name and phone number. The report is typically sorted and subtotaled by supplier, so that parts can be

Exhibit 19.3 The Old Inventory Report

Part No.	*Description*	*Quantity on Hand*	*Extended Cost ($)*	*Last Date Used*	*Supplier*
A01472	1/4" plate steel	14	72	07/04/88	Armco
A41110	3/8" angle iron	27	104	02/19/89	Armco
C17123	110A bulbs	3	320	09/07/93	Davis Tran.
J00987	Bungee cords	412	412	10/09/83	Buster's
K44321	Chock blocks	300	625	05/11/93	Gameco
L77766	1/4" brake line	22	51	03/27/97	Operta Inc.
P97531	1/4" brake line	5	171	12/12/92	Operta Inc.

Exhibit 19.4 Returnable Parts Report

Part No.	*Description*	*Quantity on Hand*	*Extended Cost ($)*	*Supplier*	*Supplier Phone No.*
43568	Seat, wide	43	103	Gameco	617–333–2222
52888	Valve, release	692	400	Gameco	617–333–2222
30987	Spokes	902	91	Gameco	617–333–2222
21987	Sprocket, steel	80	79	Gameco	617–333–2222
87001	Grips, rubber	27	42	Honton Co.	508–412–0982
75207	Wheel, graphite	43	1,830	Honton Co.	508–412–0982
62004	Wheel, spoked	52	748	Honton Co.	508–412–0982

clustered for easy transmission to suppliers. There should also be a grand total, so that management can readily determine the total amount of potentially returnable parts. This report is an excellent tool for managing the return of parts to suppliers.

A key report is the one shown in Exhibit 19.5, which presents the delivery performance of each supplier by month for a six-month rolling period. This report is useful for determining who cannot consistently deliver products to the company by the requested date. If a supplier cannot improve its performance, the company is justified in dropping the supplier and looking for one with better delivery performance. The report is quite simple, containing the name of each supplier and the average number of days late for deliveries for each of the last 12 months. This information is obtained by creating a report that lists the final receipt date for each purchase order, minus the delivery date; this information is then averaged to arrive at a single summary number for each supplier for each month. The supplier delivery report can also be sent to each supplier for feedback purposes. The report gives management a good tool for picking and retaining the best possible suppliers.

In Exhibit 19.5, it is clear that several companies (Acme Gasket, Charles Dirk, and Franklin Candle) are having difficulty shipping products on time and should be replaced. The Barnes & Struddle Company, however, is gradually improving its delivery performance, and it should be retained to see if it can continue to show improvement. The Doktor Wine Company and Go Fish Card Company are able to ship approximately on time, and should therefore be retained. One company, Engineers Amalgamated, is shipping too soon, probably so that it can be paid earlier; this does the company no good, because the delivery will sit in the warehouse for several extra days until it is needed; to resolve this issue, the company should reject any deliveries that are made too soon. Thus, the simple supplier performance report shown in Exhibit 19.5 shows a great deal of information about the ability of suppliers to deliver on time.

Exhibit 19.5 Supplier Performance Report (Average Number of Days Late)

Supplier Name	*Jan*	*Feb*	*Mar*	*Apr*	*May*	*Jun*
Acme Gasket Co.	42	17	38	32	18	12
Barnes & Struddle	37	34	31	28	25	22
Charles Dirk & Son	5	12	19	26	33	40
Doktor Wine Co.	1	3	2	4	1	0
Engineers Amalgamated	–2	–3	0	–2	–1	–4
Franklin Candle Co.	321	102	48	53	79	81
Go Fish Card Co.	0	0	14	0	2	1

The final report, which shows all cycle counting variances, is included in most computerized accounting systems. To print it, enter all cycle counting changes into the inventory program that updates the inventory database for any inventory counting changes. The system will typically ask if the user wants to print out a list of the entered changes prior to posting; the resulting printout should list all items that were changed, along with the old and new inventory quantities and the extended cost of the change. This report can be used by the materials management staff to track down and correct any procedural problems that may have caused the error, resulting in an inventory that requires less ongoing work to maintain at a high level of accuracy.

CONTROLS

Materials management controls cover three principal areas: bills of materials (which are also addressed in Chapter 15), inventory management, and purchasing. This section discusses the key tasks needed in each of these areas to ensure that an explosive growth company has sufficient control over its materials management function.

It is critical that bills of material accuracy be as perfect as possible, because they are used to purchase the parts for production. Several available controls will spotlight any problems with accuracy. One is to review all parts returned to the warehouse from the production area after a job is finished, which points out any excess parts listed on the bill of materials. Conversely, management can review any extra parts requisitioned from the warehouse, which points out any parts that are missing from the bill of materials. Another control is to have the internal audit staff review the reasons why the company has resorted to the use of overnight freight companies to have parts shipped to the company on short notice; this practice usually points to either a part that is missing from a bill of material, a part that has been damaged and must be replaced, or many parts needed on short notice because a new job was inserted into the production schedule on short notice. Finally, the management team can make available to the production staff a form on which they can note any items that were missing from a production job, were left over, or should be changed, which can be used to update the bill of materials.

It is difficult for management to keep track of the vast array of underlying problems that can cause inventory errors, but there is a simple control point available for spotting the main symptom of inventory errors—the physical inventory adjustment register. Most software packages have this report available, although perhaps under a different name. It lists all adjustments made to the inventory database as a result of cycle counting. Management can use this register to see what quantity changes were made to the database, and then work through each change with the warehouse staff to determine why the changes occurred. This control over the inventory function is the easiest. In addition, the measurement described in the Measurements and Reports section for determining the percentage of inventory that has not yet been returned to suppliers is a key one for management, for it points out the potential amount of cash that can be realized from the return of inventory, which is a major issue for the typical cash-strapped explosive growth company. Similarly, the previously described measurement for obsolete inventory is a good control, especially if management tracks any increases in it; an upward change in the dollar volume of obsolete inventory is a symptom of a problem in one of many areas—either an excessive number of parts were purchased, the bill of materials was changed before using up all of the parts in stock, or the purchasing staff has done a poor job of returning parts to suppliers before they become obsolete. Whatever the underlying reason, an increase in the amount of obsolete inventory is a telling control for the management to review. In short, several good controls are available for the inventory area, although they may simply be indicators of deeper problems that require further investigation by management to resolve.

Purchasing is the most difficult of the materials management functions to maintain control over, because there are so many areas in which problems can develop. A good control over whether suppliers are delivering on time is the supplier performance report, which was shown earlier in Exhibit 19.5. This report spotlights those suppliers who are unable to deliver parts to production by the date noted on the purchase order. However, this report only measures the timeliness of supplier delivery, not its quality. A good control over supplier quality is to have a certification process that requires the supplier to accept visits from company engineers who certify that the supplier's processes result in adequate product quality levels. Another control is to set up incoming quality reviews (which are less desirable, because they require more resources), the results of which can be entered into a report similar in structure to the supplier performance report. This report can be used by management to spot those suppliers who have trouble delivering a consistently acceptable level of quality parts to the company. A more difficult control to create is one that spots problems with buying parts with sufficient lead times to avoid paying rush charges to the supplier or shipper. This report is only possible if there is a computerized materials management system already operating. If so, it must be programmed to issue a report that lists any parts for which purchase orders were not placed with suppliers within the lead times needed to ensure their delivery at the times needed by the production function. Only a materials management system contains and tracks the lead time information needed to run this report, so this system *must* be in place before the report can be created. This control is critical, because management can use it to resolve many late-purchase situations, resulting in large cost reductions related to expediting fees.

SUMMARY

The entire discussion in this chapter was based on the principles of keeping cash requirements to a minimum while ensuring that materials arrive at the production facility on time. Most of the chapter covered the need for a materials management system, JIT purchasing and deliveries, and returning as much existing inventory to suppliers as possible. Also, several materials management tasks have historically been considered core functions that are actually damaging to the cash position of an explosive growth company; the problems with these tasks were also noted. Only by placing the proper focus on the correct materials management tasks can a growing company be assured of minimal cash requirements and a production process that is receiving the correct materials in the correct quantities at the correct times.

Chapter 20

Sales and Marketing

INTRODUCTION

The sales and marketing function seems like one that should not vary much from company to company, or between industries; this premise is true for the most basic tasks, such as devising advertising campaigns, creating sales territories, and tracking the performance of sales by product, territory, and salesperson. However, there are a number of key principles on which this group must focus its attention in an explosive growth situation. These are explained in the next section. Based on those principles, there are six primary tasks that the function must attend to in order to assure a company that the principles will be met, all of which are treated in subsequent sections. There are also some tasks that the function should avoid, because they result in outcomes that vary from the sales and marketing principles; these are noted in a separate section. All of these tasks, both of the beneficial and harmful variety, are shown in Exhibit 20.1. Finally, there is a series of measurements, reports, and controls that help the management of the sales and marketing function gain some knowledge of the performance of this functional area. By reading all parts of this chapter, the reader can gain an understanding of the most crucial tasks that must be completed for the sales and marketing function of an explosive growth company.

UNDERLYING PRINCIPLES

This section covers the principles that form the basis for the recommendations in the remainder of this chapter for key tasks to pursue in the sales and marketing area. They also support several recommendations regarding tasks to avoid, because those tasks do not support the principles. Some of the principles are similar to those covered in other chapters, such as keeping expenses low and conserving cash. However, this area also contains a unique principle, that of having a highly sensitized market awareness; it is especially important in an explosive growth environment. The principles are described in the following list:

- *Add sales with minimal effort.* The job of the sales staff is to gain the largest amount of profitable sales at the lowest possible cost. This is critically important for an explosive growth company that does not have the cash to support

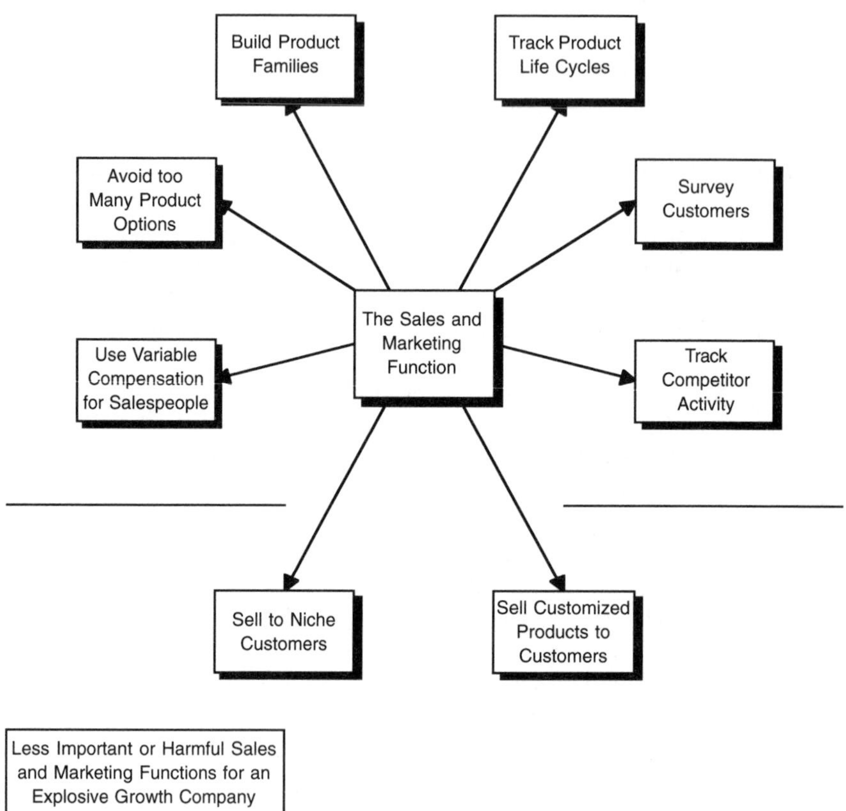

Exhibit 20.1 Explosive Growth Tasks for the Sales and Marketing Function

a major sales campaign targeting small customers or sales with minimal profitability. Thus, the sales staff's emphasis must be on those customers from whom there is a reasonable expectation of large profits with only a moderate expenditure of sales resources in return. If this principle is ignored, a company will either find itself with a ballooning sales expense or sales growth that is too low to keep it on the explosive growth track.

- *Keep break-even low.* A company can make the mistake of creating a sales force with an excessive level of guaranteed base compensation. This compensation adds to a company's fixed costs, which raises its break-even level, resulting in problems if a company experiences sharp drops in revenue. Also, swapping large base pay in favor of a higher commission rate for the sales staff gives the staff a good reason to aggressively pursue new sales, which is just what an explosive growth company needs.

- *Minimize working capital requirements.* This principle is standard for nearly all functional areas. The marketing staff can follow it by working closely with many other functions to ensure that the company is not making an excessive investment in too many product options, because this results in a large amount of finished goods inventory. Also, the marketing staff can work on clustering products together to take advantage of common promotions, which reduces promotional costs considerably.
- *Be aware of the market.* Explosive growth usually occurs in a fast-growing market where customer expectations and new product offerings can change with great rapidity. Because of these changes, a company should closely track all information related to the market, such as changes in the sales of its products, survey or complaint information from customers, and information from a variety of sources that reveals the actions of competitors. Each of these topics is covered in subsequent sections.

USE VARIABLE COMPENSATION FOR SALESPEOPLE

This section discusses the two key reasons why a company should emphasize variable compensation for its sales staff and how to use the variable compensation system to spur sales on particular products.

The first reason is based on the principle of keeping a company's break-even level as low as possible. If a company gives its sales staff a high base salary to supplement commissions, this expense rolls into the company's overall fixed costs, which means that the break-even level increases. For example, if a company increases a salesperson's base pay by $1 and the gross margin percentage on its sales is 25 percent, then the company must add $4 in sales to cover the cost of the increase in the salesperson's base pay. If, alternatively, the company had increased the salesperson's commission by 1 percent of sales, then the cost on the previously mentioned $4 in revenues would have been only 4¢—and would be incurred only if the salesman completed the sale. Thus, it helps a company's cost structure if it avoids large base pay for its sales staff in favor of large commissions on sales.

With all due respect to the finer attributes of salespeople, the primary quality that a recruiter looks for when hiring them is an insatiable need to generate sales in order to earn more commissions. This falls squarely in line with the previous point about swapping higher commission rates for a lower base salary. It also acts to spur on sales to an exceptional degree, which is critical for an explosive growth company, because it lives or dies by its rate of growth. Having pointed out the boundless benefits of a strong commission structure, it is, however, necessary to point out that management should not give all profits to the sales staff by handing out outrageously high commissions. It is quite sufficient to pay commission rates that match or moderately exceed those of the competition, thereby ensuring the retention of the best sales staff. Also, though sales staff retention usually is closely tied to their levels of compensation, it is quite useful to periodically show the company's appreciation for their efforts with contests, trips, awards, and dinners—anything to ensure that the highest-producing staff stays with the company. In short, fairly high commission percentages, when supplemented by other benefits, will drive the sales staff to obtain more sales for the company.

Although a single high commission rate will help to bring in more sales, some variation in commissions can have an even greater impact. For example, a special commission rate on products for which the company has an excessive amount of inventory can be very effective in increasing sales of those items and thereby reducing the company's working capital investment in inventory. Conversely, the company can reduce its commission on those products for which it has a minimal inventory, or for which it cannot obtain components for the immediate future, thereby reducing sales of these items. Such careful variation of commission rates can have a major impact on a company's ability to sell those products of which it has an abundant supply, thereby having a major favorable impact on working capital. However, making frequent changes to commissions places a major burden on the accounting staff's commission calculation system, so it is important to make sure that the commission system is capable of handling rapid commission changes before engaging in this practice; otherwise, there is a strong possibility that the sales staff will be very irritated if they do not receive the commissions they were expecting. It is also important to adequately communicate commission changes to the sales force in a timely manner. Many salespeople travel extensively, so it is difficult to communicate commission changes to them through such traditional means as interoffice memos or formal meetings, especially when the commission changes may only be good for a few days. The best way to disseminate this information is through voice mail or electronic mail, because they can be reviewed from anywhere in the field. Electronic mail is the better of the two forms of communication for this sort of information, because voice mail can inconveniently garble a change in the commission rate. Thus, careful changes in the commission rate can help to reduce inventory levels, if properly supported by continual communication of the commission changes to the entire sales staff.

A final issue is that a growing company does not want to hand out payments to its sales staff before it receives payments from its customers. This would be a cash flow imbalance that could cause financing difficulties if customer payments were to be delayed. Instead, the commission system should require payment of commissions to the sales staff immediately after cash is received from customers. Not only does this approach allow the company to only pay commissions when it has the cash to do so, but also creates a great deal of interest by the sales staff in the prompt collection of accounts receivable; by cutting into the amount of cash invested in accounts receivable, a company can reduce its working capital needs. Therefore, making commission payments contingent on customer payments reduces a company's need for working capital while eliminating a possible source of cash flow imbalance.

It is clear that the proper use of commissions has a major impact on a company's expense structure and working capital, both of which are major issues for an explosive growth company.

AVOID TOO MANY PRODUCT OPTIONS

As was previously noted in Chapters 15 and 19, having too many product options may result in too much inventory. For example, if a product is sold with five options, then the company must keep in stock 120 (which is five factorial, or 1 × 2 × 3 × 4 x 5) variations of the finished product. Keeping every product variation in stock becomes a large burden on working capital, especially if all of the product variations are to be stocked at each of the company's distribution points. Having too many product options goes strongly against the principle of minimizing working capital requirements.

There are several ways to manage this situation. One way is for the company to offer the fewest possible number of product options. This decision is largely up to the marketing staff, which is usually interested in increasing the number of product options in order to increase the number of potential buyers. However, knowing the impact on working capital of too many options, it is important for the marketing manager to only allow the most important options to be offered to customers. It is also crucial for the marketing manager to work closely with the managers of other functional areas in order to understand the impact of many product options on those other functions, especially on the engineering, purchasing, and production areas. Another possibility is to examine the pattern of sales of the various options, and decide to avoid stocking excessive numbers of the products for which selected options are not popular, thereby avoiding large working capital investments. Another option is to use the Dell Computer approach, which is to keep no finished goods inventory at all; instead, Dell uses a very advanced production system to quickly assemble any possible production configuration ordered by a customer. Dell has only a minimal inventory investment. Finally, the marketing staff can work with the controller to find those options that consistently generate the largest sales, and drop all others. This may result in some churning of options, as older ones drop out of favor and new ones are added. This approach also results in some product obsolescence as older options are phased out. There is no clear solution to the large variety of ways to manage product options, except that management must constantly review the issue so that a company does not suddenly find itself with a large variety of finished goods inventory on hand that it cannot dispose of without incurring a loss.

BUILD PRODUCT FAMILIES

An explosive growth company will find it quite convenient to cluster its products into clearly defined families, because, as noted in Chapter 15, it reduces the work of the engineering and purchasing staffs to build products from a common design platform. This principle holds true in the marketing area as well.

Promotions are much easier when many products can be clustered in one promotional campaign. For example, a number of restaurant chains have had difficulty in moving into new geographical areas, because they have only built in one or two locations and then spent considerable money in that area to promote them. A good promotion campaign is very expensive, and in several cases resulted in the withdrawal of some restaurant chains from promising markets. A better approach is to cluster a number of restaurants in one area and then conduct the same promotion campaign; when the promotion cost is spread over the revenues from the extra stores, this marketing approach becomes very cost-effective. This method is successfully used by all of the breakfast cereal companies, which issue coupons for discounts on the purchase of many of their cereals, not just one variety. By clustering many products in one promotion, they reduce the per-unit cost of the promotion. In short, clustering many products under one promotional banner saves a lot of money.

The cost effectiveness of a sales call also goes up when the salesperson can present a number of similar products to the same customer at one time. By increasing the sales per call, the cost per dollar of revenues goes down. This main synergy is one that companies attempt to realize when they buy another company, on the grounds that they can dismiss the sales force of the acquired company and have their own sales staffs handle both company's products. It also fulfills one of the underlying principles of this chapter, that of adding sales with minimal effort. Although this approach is effective, the sales manager must be careful to have the sales staff present to customers a bundle of products that the salesperson is totally familiar with, as well as one that the customer is in a position to purchase. For example, a sales staff may not be adequately trained in sales of new products that have been acquired by purchasing another company, resulting in reduced sales of the new products. Also, a salesperson may sell a computer printer to a department manager, but must go to the Chief Executive Officer (CEO) in order to sell a mainframe computer; accordingly, the clusters of products given to the sales staff should match the people to whom they are selling. Thus, a company can save money by having its sales staff sell clusters of related products, but must be careful to train the sales staff in how to sell *all* of the products, and must be sure to package the products so that they can all be sold to the same person in the customer's organizational hierarchy.

Product families are also useful, even without a sales force. They can be clustered together for sale as a unit, which not only increases company sales, but also forces customers to purchase a block of products from the same company, rather than allowing a mix of sales from several companies. A classic example of this is

Microsoft Office, which is a set of the most commonly used software packages created by Microsoft Corporation. It was introduced with excellent marketing and at a very competitive price. Since none of its competitors had a set of products of comparable quality and did not have the marketing muscle to promote it even if they had, Microsoft rapidly gained market share while pushing several competitors close to extinction. Its main rival, Lotus, was bought by IBM, while a lesser competitor, Borland, was forced into bankruptcy. Such is the potential power of selling similar products as a single package.

From a competitive perspective, it is also very useful to cluster products into families. They can then be packaged into free-standing displays that not only take up a large amount of retail space at a distribution point, but also keep competing products from occupying the same space. For example, Procter & Gamble, the consumer goods powerhouse, is well known for creating a series of closely related products that it can then cluster on store shelves, thereby leaving little room for competing products.

There are several very good reasons for a growing company to cluster its products into product families for sales and marketing purposes. It allows a company to concentrate its promotional dollars on a smaller number of campaigns that cover many products, while also allowing the sales force to sell more related products in a single sales call. Both of these options can save a company a large amount of money. In addition, a company can increase its sales by grouping products together for sale as a single unit. It can also increase sales and block out competitors by filling store displays with large numbers of similar products. For all these reasons, grouping products into product families is a good way to decrease per-unit selling expenses and increase revenues.

TRACK PRODUCT LIFE CYCLES

In a rapidly growing market, it is very common for products to be very hot sellers and then rapidly decline as new hot products enter the market and supplant them. This market variation can cause large and sudden shifts in a company's revenue stream that can bring it to its knees very quickly. This section describes how to track product life cycles so that company management is aware of sudden shifts (especially downward) in a product's life cycle.

The best way to track the life cycle of a product is to closely monitor its revenue. It is an easy matter for most accounting software to compile product revenue into a report format that shows the sales of each product for the last month. This information can then be put on a trend line to show management if sales are changing from month to month. If there are continuing declines in either revenue or the rate of revenue growth, then it may be time for the marketing and engineering staffs to work on enhancements to or replacements of the existing products to jump-start sales. Revenue trending is the best way to track a product life cycle.

However, the revenue trend line is not such an easy indicator of a product's life cycle as would first appear to be the case. One problem is that a growing company is constantly moving into new geographical areas. When this occurs, sales from the new regions may mask sales declines in regions where the product has been selling for some time. To correct for this problem, it is useful to track especially carefully the revenue trend of product sales in the oldest territories; this trend is a good indicator of how sales will later trend in new territories. A common example of this trending is the retailing industry, where the performance measurement most commonly used is changes in same-store sales from the previous year. This measurement tells if there are problems with a company's underlying base of stores that might otherwise be masked by the addition of new stores. The same measurement can be applied to product sales regions instead of stores. In short, the revenue trend line is a better indicator of future product sales if sales from new regions are excluded.

Another problem with the revenue trend line is that it may not include all relevant information. For example, a company may find that it is still selling large quantities of products, but that distributors are now demanding greater discounts in order to carry the product. This demand clearly indicates that the distributors think they have alternative products that they can sell just as easily as the company's products, which will eventually result in lower sales as some distributors drop the company's product in favor of rival products. This development can be spotted by two means. The first is by asking the sales force. It talks to distributors constantly, and is very aware of the inroads made by competing products. A more quantitative approach is to track the average product price on a trend line. As customers are offered greater discounts to take the product, its price will drop. Thus, tracking both the revenue trend line and price trend line gives management a good idea of the stage of a product's life cycle.

A final problem is that, even though a revenue trend line and a price trend line appear to show no weakness, it is quite possible that a company is still losing an increasing proportion of sales to competitors. How is this possible? If the market is expanding rapidly, a company can still show excellent revenue growth and pricing stability while losing market share to a company with a more robust product. For example, Lotus and Novell continued to show excellent sales gains on their software products while Microsoft gradually took larger and larger shares of the markets for their products away from them. This is a difficult item to track, for a company cannot do so by itself. Instead, there is usually an industry trade group that collects sales data from members and uses it to extrapolate an estimated total market size. These numbers can be very inaccurate, but should be sufficient to give management a rough estimate of changes in market share over the long term. The key problem with market share tracking is that the information is usually only collected once a year; in an explosive growth environment where the market changes rapidly, a one-year interval between measurements is too far apart to be of much use to someone trying to determine if a company's products continue to be competitive. Consequently, although it is helpful to track market share information, a company must supplement this information with data collected from other sources, primarily its sales staff, to make an educated guess regarding the company's market share position.

SURVEY CUSTOMERS

Although the accounting staff can certainly provide the marketing staff with a formidable array of information about product revenue and pricing trends, as noted in the previous section, this information can be a month old or more before being disseminated. In a high-growth market, this information may arrive too late to be of use. The marketing staff can avoid this problem by going straight to customers to get their opinions about products, which helps it to fulfill the underlying principle of being aware of the market. There are several ways to obtain information from customers. They are as follows:

- *Customer-initiated comments.* Customers will contact a company about the performance of a product or service if they are sufficiently worked up about it, either positively or negatively. This contact yields valuable commentary on product issues, because customers would not go to the trouble of contacting a company if they did not have a major issue with it. If negative, this type of comment is usually over an item of such importance that the company should take immediate action to correct the problem.
- *On-site discussions with salespeople.* The sales staff collects all sorts of information from customers, because they are constantly meeting with them. This information frequently relates to immediate issues, such as product failures in the last shipment received from the company, or warranty problems that customers are having. Because this information is very fresh, it is of particular use to a company that wants to quickly alter its product to meet customer expectations.
- *Surveys.* A company can mail out survey cards with its products, or have them available at check-out stands or similar locations. This passive approach typically only attracts those customers who are either seriously in favor of or against a company's products. Since a company is also interested in the bulk of customers who are probably only mildly pleased or displeased with the company, it takes extra incentives to get this group to fill out and return the survey. Possible incentives are a small cash payment, a discount on the customer's next purchase, or a coupon for a related product. The field sales staff can also sit down with customers and fill out a survey form with them. It is important to obtain information from these more typical customers, because they may have suggestions that are not critical to a product's success or failure, but which will please customers if added to it.
- *Warranty claims.* If a product fails, a customer wants to have it fixed or replaced. Careful tracking of warranty claims tells a company a great deal about

product flaws. The only problem with this approach is that, if a company works through distributors, it may take a considerable time for the warranty claims to find their way back through the distributors to the company, and by the time the claim information is received, the company may already be working on a new or enhanced product that makes the warranty information worthless.

Once information has been obtained through any of the foregoing methods, it should be entered into a complaints database, which is described in detail in Chapter 13. It sorts complaints by a variety of methods, thereby allowing the marketing staff to quickly search it for problems with specific products. The staff can then use this information to come up with changes to the product to reduce or eliminate customer complaints and hopefully improve sales.

TRACK COMPETITOR ACTIVITY

A company may have the finest product in the world and still have it fail because the company did not track the activity of competitors and take action to prevent losing market share. There are many examples of this problem, all resulting in reduced sales or bankruptcy for the companies that did not watch their competitors and therefore had no way to react to changes to the market brought about by those competitors. For example, Compaq's shift from a provider of high-margin computers to a low-margin, high-volume strategy caught many competitors off guard and secured for it the top market share position in its industry. Also, the shift to personal computers caught Digital Equipment Corporation completely off guard, resulting in its recent acquisition by Compaq. Finally, the advent of the "fat pen" by Mont Blanc resulted in a major revenue decline for the maker of Cross Pens, which stayed with a narrower pen format. Although in different industries, these examples all point to the need for close scrutiny of one's competitors. How should a company do this?

The first step is to create a formal mechanism for collecting the information into a central location, which can be a central database accessible by anyone who can add information to it. For example, an icon on a corporate network can lead an authorized user into a free-form database in which the user can enter any information about a competitor. The person responsible for maintenance of the database can then clean up the data and sort it by any of a number of indexing methods, which allows users to sort the data in a variety of ways.

Once the competitor database is in place, one must then collect the data from a variety of sources to populate it. Some of them are as follows:

- *Ask customers.* If a company bids on a sale to a customer and loses, it is customary for the customer to tell the company who won the bid, and why the competitor won it. This information is useful for determining the product features and pricing options of competitors.

- *Attend trade shows.* The best way to review the newest products being brought out by competitors is to attend the trade shows where they display them. It is usually possible to obtain specification sheets or at least photographs of the competing products, as well as pricing information.
- *Call competitors.* It is possible to simply call up a competitor and ask for information about the company and its products. Although it is usually necessary to pose as a potential customer (about which management may want to discuss some ethical issues), this method remains common for collecting competitive information.
- *Hire a research firm.* A number of good research firms will probe a number of databases on behalf of a client company to uncover information about a targeted competitor. These firms are expensive, but they can generally obtain a large amount of information about a competitor quicker than a company's own staff, since the firm is more experienced in collecting this sort of information.
- *Peruse trade journals.* One of the better sources of information about competitors is the trade journal. These magazines focus on a limited market, therefore they tend to contain more information about specific companies within that market.
- *Purchase competing products.* Most of the automobile companies purchase competing products and rip them apart to see how the competition builds them. This is a practice that is useful in all industries, because it yields information about competing production and engineering methods.
- *Review business magazines.* Business magazines are not as good a source of information about competitors as trade journals, because they cover many markets and consequently contain less information about each one. However, they occasionally contain a spotlight article that gives an in-depth review of a company. They also have annual reviews by industry of the financial results of a number of large, publicly held companies.
- *Review SEC filings.* A publicly held company must file both quarterly (10-Q) and annual (10-K) reports with the Securities and Exchange Commission (SEC), which can be reviewed through the SEC's EDGAR on-line reporting system. It is also possible to obtain an annual report from a publicly held company simply by buying one share of its stock. Any of these reports give in-depth financial information about a company, but have minimal information about new products.
- *Use credit reports.* Such companies as Dun & Bradstreet issue excellent credit reports on most companies in the country, including payment histories, the names and backgrounds of company officers, and selected financial informa-

tion. However, because most of the financial information is provided by the companies being analyzed, it may be substantially incorrect.

A cautionary note regarding all of the foregoing search methods is that a growing company must continually obtain information to expand its current knowledge of competitors; it is not acceptable to have a single data collection campaign once a year to update the competitor database, because this does not tell a company anything if a competitor makes a key strategic move in the interim which the company does not discover until the next annual competitor review. Data collection and analysis in this area must be continuous if a growing company does not want a competitor to abruptly curtail its growth.

Even if a company does an excellent job of obtaining competitor information on a regular basis, it is very easy not to take action on it. Many companies simply collect the data and issue a periodic report to top management, which is shelved after a quick perusal. To avoid this fate, management must link it to a regularly scheduled series of management meetings. The latest information updates should be issued to all meeting participants beforehand, there should be a formal agenda and process for reviewing this data, and the person responsible for running the meeting should be empowered to follow up on any actions needed to counteract the activities of competitors, with full support from the CEO. Only by using this formal review process will a company consistently and promptly take action to bypass competitors' activities with such steps as changing product pricing, discounts, promotions, partnerships, distribution channels, product options, or new product introductions.

TASKS TO AVOID

As noted in Exhibit 20.1, there are two tasks that the manager of the sales and marketing function should avoid. One is selling to niche customers and the other is selling customized products. Although these activities may be perfectly acceptable for a normal company, they are fraught with danger for an explosive growth company. This section explains why.

One of the key sales principles for a growing company is to use great economy of effort when selling, because the funding available for this task is usually minimal. This is difficult to do when selling to niche customers, for several reasons. One is that, if a company occupies only a niche of the total market, then by definition it does not purchase a large amount of product. Consequently, a company must use a significant amount of sales resources in proportion to the amount of revenues received when selling to a niche customer. In addition, niche customers typically require customized solutions that the largest customers in the primary part of the market do not require, such as special pricing or payment terms, different product packaging or delivery schedules, or even alterations to the product. Whatever the alterations may be, they tend to vary by customer within each specialized niche, which once again requires a large amount of sales resources to track. Finally, if a niche customer requires an alteration to a product, then the company may have to store the altered part in inventory as a service part, or may keep several completed products in stock in case of a reorder. In either case, the company's inventory investment rises, which violates a key principle of avoiding any increases in the amount of working capital needed to operate the company. In short, niche customers are a poor target for an explosive growth company because of the extra cost of doing business with them, as compared to the minimal prospect of large sales gains.

The other task to avoid is selling customized products. This requires a great deal of sales work, because each customer order requires different specifications. A highly customized product may require multiple visits by the sales staff and lots of additional communication to verify the product specifications. If customers are located a considerable distance from the sales staff, the sales calls may require such an investment in travel costs alone that the company realizes no profit on sales at all. These factors go against the principle of gaining new revenues with minimal extra sales costs. Also, customized products are more subject to failure, because they are one-of-a-kind and the engineering staff may not have the time or resources to work all flaws out of the product prior to delivery. This situation results in expensive warranty work, for which the sales staff frequently handles the customer complaints, if not the related warranty paperwork. Because of the excessive sales time required for each customer, this sales approach requires a very large sales staff if a company wants to embark on an explosive growth path. In addition, engineering and production require considerable time to design and build a custom product. Thus, selling custom products requires a major investment of time and money, not only by the sales staff, but by several other functions, as well. Only very high margins can justify a growing company's entry into this type of product sales.

MEASUREMENTS AND REPORTS

The measurements and reports listed in this section are those specifically needed for an explosive growth company. There are many more traditional sales reports that a company can use, especially those that slice and dice sales by specific regions, salespeople, and product types. It is assumed that the reader already knows how to generate these. The following measurements and reports are needed to support the topics and principles in the previous sections. For example, the average sales cost per customer measurement supports the principle of adding sales with minimal effort, whereas the product revenue trend line supports the section on tracking product life cycles. For each measurement, there is a description of its uses as well as how to calculate it, and also any shortfalls that may skew the resulting information. The measurements are as follows:

- *Blended commission percentage.* A major factor in determining profitability is the sales percentage a company pays its sales personnel. A high percentage cuts significantly into profits, but may be necessary for rapid market development. To calculate it, divide the total commission expense by total revenues for the period. This calculation may be further subdivided by region, because sometimes companies offer higher commission percentages to salespeople if they develop new areas, which requires additional effort. The problem with this percentage is that commissions may be paid before or after the time period when related revenues are recognized, so the percentage may be off.
- *Market share trend line.* Even if a company is experiencing increasing revenues of its products, it may be losing market share to rivals if the overall market grows faster than the rate of growth of the company's products. If so, it is best to track the trend line of market share for either the entire market or for each product family, if this information is available. To calculate it, divide total company sales for each market by the total sales for all companies in that market. The problem with this calculation is determining the size of the total market. One source is the trade group for each market, which accumulates sales information from its members to come up with a rough estimate of the total. Another option is to call up credit reports on all known competitors and summarize the sales volumes listed in those reports; however, because competitor sales may cover several markets, this estimate can be very innacurate. Thus, market share percentages are not normally very precise.
- *Number of products per product family.* It is easier and cheaper to market and sell a number of similar products, so the more products per family, the better. To calculate it, use marketing brochures or an internal list of products to summarize the number of products clustered in each product family.
- *Number of product options per product family.* Although the sales staff may want the maximum number of product options, it requires much more time by the engineering staff to design all of the options and a large investment to keep all product variations in stock. Accordingly, this measurement tells management how many options are available, which may result in more options to satisfy the sales staff, or fewer to satisfy other functions. To calculate this measurement, add the total number of options available for each product. This information is usually available through the order entry system or from sales literature. The measurement does not include supplements to a product that are not an integral part of it, because they do not involve design modifications to the underlying product.
- *Product revenue trend line.* The marketing and engineering staffs must both be keenly aware of the trend in sales for any product. If there is a marked and continual decline in revenues, or at least in the rate of revenue growth, then it is time to start improving the product or planning to retire it and bring out

a new product that can jump-start sales. To calculate it, simply plot on a trend line the total sales for each month or quarter for each product. If there are many product options, it is best to cluster the sales of all options with the primary product. Also, if the company is rolling out sales sequentially through a number of new territories, it is useful to track the revenue trend line by territory, because a drop in sales in a territory in which the product has been sold for some time will probably be a good indicator of the trend in revenues for new territories.

- *Sales cost per customer as a percentage of gross margin from customer.* A growing company must keep the cost of sales to a minimum, so any customers who consume an inordinate sales expense should be dropped. To calculate it, use salesperson expense reports and time sheets to determine the cost of sales to each customer. Then summarize the total gross margin for each customer for the same time period, and divide the sales cost into the gross margin. Because this report layout is not normally automatic for an accounting system, it may require a periodic manual study to obtain this information. The downside to the measurement is that one must also consider the total gross margin earned from each customer, irrespective of the percentage of sales costs, to see if the customer is still worth retaining, no matter how high the sales cost may be. Also, there is a timing problem, because the sales costs may have been incurred in several reporting periods prior to the sale of any products to the customer; to avoid this problem, the measurement can cover a very long reporting period.

Although the foregoing measurements represent a good start for managing the sales and marketing functions, they do not have any supporting detail that would assist management in correcting any problems uncovered by the measurements. The following reports assist in correcting this problem.

The first report itemizes the base pay of a company's sales staff. This report is important for determining the amount of fixed costs in the sales function that may need to be stripped out if the break-even level is too high to sustain consistent profits. The report also contains each salesperson's total salary and the percentage of each person's pay that is made up by base pay; if this percentage is high, it is an indicator that the salesperson may not be sufficiently motivated by the prospect of commissions to aggressively pursue new sales. The report format is shown in Exhibit 20.2.

Another key report is the trend of product sales by region. Unlike the previously described measurement that only gives an overall trend for product sales, this one splits it by region. It can be shown as a table of numbers, as shown in Exhibit 20.3, or as a graph. The intent of this report is to reveal any sales problems in specific regions. Particularly worrisome is when this occurs in an old, well-developed sales region, for it indicates that there may be future sales problems in newer, less developed regions. In the example in Exhibit 20.3, the oldest territories are at the top of the table, and the newest at the bottom. The oldest territories

Exhibit 20.2 Sales Staff Compensation

Employee Number	*Employee Name*	*Base Pay ($)*	*Total Compensation ($)*	*Base Pay as % of Total*
00427	Donovan, James	35,000	47,000	74
00532	Hardaway, Amy	50,000	52,000	96
00681	Sunny, April	35,000	108,000	32
01002	Davis, George	42,000	71,000	59
01027	Hayes, Alfred	35,000	60,000	58
01053	Jamison, Olivia	35,000	43,000	81
01061	Zurbriggen, John	25,000	37,000	68

show a clear decline in sales for product A, which may extrapolate into a problem for the newer sales regions.

It is also necessary to track the cost of sales expenses for each customer. This information, when sorted to show the most expensive sales efforts, is a key supporting tool in deciding which customers are too expensive to maintain. The report, as shown in Exhibit 20.4, lists the sales expense for the reporting period for each customer, sorted in declining order of sales expenses. However, since this information may simply indicate that the company directs most of its efforts toward sales to its largest customers, it is also necessary to list the gross margin on sales to each customer, and to divide the sales expense by the gross margin. The result gives management a better idea of the need to drop a customer than simply by reviewing total sales costs. In Exhibit 20.4, the customer with the largest sales expense also gives the company its largest gross margin, whereas the customer at

Exhibit 20.3 The Trend of Product Sales by Region

	Product A			
Region	*Quarter 1 ($)*	*Quarter 2 ($)*	*Quarter 3 ($)*	*Quarter 4 ($)*
East	5,431,000	5,204,000	5,003,000	4,837,000
Midwest	4,328,000	4,320,000	4,204,000	4,188,000
Rocky Mountain	3,273,000	3,280,000	3,285,000	3,250,000
Southwest	2,901,000	2,925,000	2,950,000	2,971,000
Pacific	2,007,000	2,017,000	2,211,000	2,314,000
Canada	1,771,000	1,843,000	1,903,000	1,941,000
Mexico	882,000	950,000	1,312,000	1,504,000

Exhibit 20.4 Sales Expense by Customer

Customer Name	*Sales Expense ($)*	*Gross Margin ($)*	*Sales Expense/ Gross Margin (%)*
DieHard Weapons	421,000	3,905,000	11
Howitzer & Sons	379,000	2,007,000	19
Amalgamated Cannons	204,000	891,000	23
Grenades Galore	189,000	742,000	25
Terrific Tanks	174,000	548,000	32
Wonder Weapons	132,000	301,000	44
Miracle Mines	58,000	107,000	54

the bottom of the list requires a large sales expenditure for minimal return, and should be dropped.

Finally, a company should issue a periodic report that lists the results of customer surveys. The report should list each question noted on the survey and the proportion of different types of responses to each one. In addition, a free-form section at the bottom of the report should list any other miscellaneous comments received from the surveys that were not a response to a specific question. This information can also be summarized on a time line, so that management can see if it is performing better or worse over time, according to customers. A survey summary report is a valuable tool for tracking company performance.

CONTROLS

The controls needed over the sales and marketing function do not vary in any situation, whether it be for explosive or declining growth. This section notes the key controls over this area.

Management must be assured that the function is bringing in sales at the lowest possible cost, which means that it should examine the report shown as Exhibit 20.4, which itemizes the sales cost per customer. If there is a customer who is clearly requiring a large sales effort in exchange for a minimal return in sales, then management must drop the customer.

Another major control is to track trends in revenue and market share for all territories and products within those territories. Management uses this information to decide if there is a need for a new salesperson, a new promotional campaign, or product repositioning or replacement. For an expanding company, management tends to most closely review sales in the oldest territories, because information from an established area gives it a good idea of what may happen to sales as time passes in the newer territories, possibly resulting in changes to the product, salesperson training, or the promotional campaign as the geographical expansion progresses.

A key control over short-term problems is a constant review of the complaints database to see how customers feel about the company's products and services. This information should be reviewed every day to see if there are problems requiring immediate attention; these problems can include product flaws, poor behavior by sales personnel, or problems with the order entry system. Whatever the problem may be, this continual scanning of incoming customer complaints is the best way to find and resolve it as quickly as possible. For more information about the complaints database, see Chapter 13.

A company should also maintain a database of all possible information about its competitors. Although this database does not require a daily review, there should be a formal discussion of changes to the competition every month, so that the company can anticipate actions by competitors as soon as possible and act to keep from losing market share to them. In an explosive growth situation, it is quite possible for the competitive situation to change dramatically in less than a month, requiring more frequent reviews of this information.

Finally, it is very important to keep the number of product options from expanding to the point where the company cannot possibly stock every product variation, because this entails large amounts of extra design time by the engineering staff and a large investment in extra inventory. This decision area is not black-and-white, where the number of product options must be cut off beyond a set limit. Instead, the marketing manager must stay in close touch with a number of people in other functional areas to see how the number of product options are affecting them. One key contact is the controller, who can assign a financial analyst to the task of determining which product options are the most popular with customers; if one is not being purchased, it should be discontinued. Another key contact is the engineering manager, who can tell if there is enough time in the engineering schedule to design additional product options likely to return an adequate profit in exchange for the required design time. Yet another contact is the purchasing manager, who can tell if there will be trouble procuring proposed new options. Finally, the production manager can render an opinion regarding the ability of the production staff to assemble new options, because some may be quite difficult to add to the underlying product. All of these contacts are equally suitable for discussions regarding the introduction of entirely new products. In short, a good control is constant discussion with the heads of other functions regarding the suitability of adding new options and products to the company's current mix of products.

SUMMARY

Many of the points made in this chapter can apply to any company, not just one that is experiencing a high rate of growth. However, the areas targeted for special mention are those that *must* be done for explosive growth to continue. These areas include keeping the break-even level as low as possible through salesperson compensation plans, avoiding an excessive inventory investment by avoiding an excessive number of product options, and saving promotional costs by clustering product offerings into related families that can be promoted as units. A company must also do a great deal of tracking: of products, to see when they must be replaced; of customers, to see what problems they are having with the company; and of competitors, to see what reactions the company should take to avoid losing market share to them. Conversely, a growing company cannot afford to invest its sales effort in selling to small niche customers or selling very customized products to anyone, unless there is a significant profit from doing so. If all of these tasks are managed properly, the sales and marketing function can strongly support a company's high rate of revenue growth.

Appendix

Suggested Readings

"America's Fastest-Growing Companies: The Top 100." *Fortune*, September 29, 1997, 86–100.

Barrett, William P. "The Perils of Success." *Forbes*, November 3, 1997, 129–142.

Bragg, Steven M. *Outsourcing*. New York: John Wiley & Sons, 1998.

Browder, Seanna and Andy Reinhardt. "A Fierce Downdraft at Boeing," *Business Week*, January 26, 1998, 34–35.

"Can Oxford Heal Itself?" *Fortune*, December 29, 1997, 238–240.

Courtney, Hugh, Jane Kirkland, and Patrick Viguerie. "Strategy under Uncertainty." *Harvard Business Review*, November-December 1997, 67–79.

Eisenhardt, Kathleen M. and Shona L. Brown. "Time Pacing: Competing in Markets that Won't Stand Still." *Harvard Business Review*, March-April 1998, 59–69.

Freedman, David H. "Food Fighter." *Forbes ASAP*, February 23, 1998, 37–40.

Levering, Robert, and Milton Moskowitz. "The 100 Best Companies to Work for in America." *Fortune*, January 12, 1998, 84–95.

Lieber, Ronald B. "Secrets of the Superstars." *Fortune*, September 29, 1997, 81–82.

Malburg, Chris. "Surviving Explosive Growth." *Journal of Accountancy*, December 1997, 67–72.

Meyer, Christopher. *Relentless Growth.* New York: Free Press,1998.

Stewart, Thomas A. "In Search of Elusive Tech Workers." *Fortune*, February 16, 1998, 171–172.

Zellner, Wendy. "An Old Brakeman Faces His Ultimate Test." *Business Week*, October 6, 1997, 110–111.

Index